# Sex Trafficking

*Sex Trafficking: A Private Law Response* examines existing and potential causes of action against sex traffickers, clients and the state, and argues for fair and effective private law remedies. Combining a theoretical inquiry about the borders of liability in torts and restitution with a political commitment to protecting the interests of victims of sex trafficking, this book offers a comparative doctrinal and socio-legal analysis of private law remedies, their justification, and their effectiveness. Tsachi Keren-Paz innovatively and convincingly makes the argument that all those directly involved in breaching the rights of victims of sex trafficking should compensate them for their losses, and make restitution of the profits made at their expense. *Sex Trafficking: A Private Law Response* will be invaluable to both academics and practitioners concerned with prostitution, modern slavery and trafficking, and those interested in private law theory and practice.

**Tsachi Keren-Paz** is a Senior Lecturer at Keele University Law School.

# Sex Trafficking

## A Private Law Response

Tsachi Keren-Paz

Routledge
Taylor & Francis Group
a GlassHouse Book

First published 2013
by Routledge
2 Park Square, Milton Park, Abingdon, Oxon OX14 4RN

Simultaneously published in the USA and Canada
by Routledge
711 Third Avenue, New York, NY 10017

A GlassHouse Book

*Routledge is an imprint of the Taylor & Francis Group, an informa business*



*British Library Cataloguing in Publication Data*
A catalogue record for this book is available from the British Library

*Library of Congress Cataloging in Publication Data*
A catalog record for this book has been requested

ISBN 978-0-415-58331-2 (hbk)
ISBN 978-0-203-50430-7 (ebk)

Typeset in Garamond
by Keystroke, Station Road, Codsall, Wolverhampton

MIX
Paper from responsible sources
FSC www.fsc.org FSC® C013056

Printed and bound in Great Britain by
TJ International Ltd, Padstow, Cornwall

*To Marie – the shining, lucid, cut diamond*

# Contents

# Acknowledgements

This book builds on research I have conducted for several years on private law remedies to victims of sex trafficking. During that time I was fortunate to have the insights and critiques of many colleagues and practitioners who truly made an invaluable contribution to this book. As will become evident to readers, the claims I make in this book are rather controversial, so the trite disclaimer that the views offered in this book are my own alone could not be truer. I suspect that some of those I am going to thank might shudder at the thought of being associated with part of the claims I defend throughout the book.

For earlier exchanges and conversations about different aspects of the project I would like to thank Abigail Stepnitz, Anita Bernstein, Assaf Likhovski, Craig Rotherham, Duncan Sheehan, Graham Virgo, Harold Luntz, Helen Atkins, James Edelman, James Lee, Jawaid Luqmani, Jenny Steele, Ken Oliphant, Les Green, Nicky Priaulx, Nomi Levenkron, Raggi Kotak, Roy Kreitner, Ruth Fletcher and Steve Hadley. More recent and equally useful input I have received from Andrew Tettenborn, David Enoch, Deborah Renshaw, Doron Teichman, Fiona Cownie, Ilan Benshalom, Israel Gilead, Jane Stapleton, John Glover, John Peysner, John Danaher, Juanita Roche, Kelvin Johnstone, Martin Wasik, Mike Green, Richard Wright, Rob Stevens and Sigalit Zohar.

Several people generously and helpfully commented on earlier drafts of chapters. Lionel Smith and Peter Jaffey commented on chapters 3 and 4. I am especially indebted to Craig Rotherham whose detailed and penetrating comments on these chapters were unparalleled by anything I have seen during my academic career. Ariel Porat, Jane Stapleton, Max Waltman, Nomi Levenkron, Peter Cane and Tony Bradney commented on chapters 6 to 8. Michael Thomson and Nicola Barker have commented on chapter 1, and Marie-Andrée Jacob on chapters 1, 2, 9 and 10.

I was fortunate to present parts of this project in several venues and to receive many valuable comments. These include Law Faculty seminars at the Hebrew University, the universities of Cardiff, Manchester and Keele, and the Haim Striks School of Law; presentations to the Cegla Private Law Forum, Tel

Aviv University and the Oxford Jurisprudence Discussion Group; and conferences at the Oñati International Institute for the Sociology of Law, Colorado University, Westminster University, Warwick University, the University of Girona, the Canadian and American Law and Society Association's annual meeting in Montreal, and the Society of Legal Scholars' annual meetings in Keele and Cambridge.

The research was financially supported by the AHRC Centre for Law, Gender & Sexuality Research Assistance Funding, Keele's Gender, Sexuality & Law Research Assistance Funding, the Society of Legal Scholars Research Activity Fund and Keele's Research Institute for Social Sciences. Kelly Prince and Emma Shacklady provided valuable research assistance to parts of this project.

Chapter 5 is based on two articles published in (2009) 29 *Legal Studies* 438 and (2010) 29 *Law and Philosophy* 307. I thank the publishers of these journals and my co-author of the *Legal Studies* piece for their permission to use these materials.

I owe special thanks to two special women. This book, and my interest in remedies to victims of sex trafficking would not have existed but for Nomi Levenkron who contacted me in 2005 and asked if I would look at a draft article she had written on tort claims against traffickers. Nomi's mastery of the factual background of the trafficking phenomenon in Israel, and more broadly of the policy documents and research on the subject, were invaluable. More crucially perhaps, Nomi's anger, legal imagination and ability to think outside the box have deeply influenced this project. Nomi's partial change of heart that occurred while she was pursuing her own research, in comparison to her views expressed in our co-authored piece, forced me to challenge my own views on this topic. The views offered in this book do not necessarily reflect her current views.

Lastly, words cannot express my gratitude and love to my partner Marie-Andrée Jacob. On the academic side, her insightful and incisive critiques tremendously improved the content, structure and presentation of the manuscript. On the personal side, her love, companionship, humour, patience and advice have made this journey, which has not always been an easy one, easier. In the last year, Marie has provided us with a competing source of interest, which while at least as demanding, has been much more enjoyable. Baby Danielle and her older sister Daphne perhaps postponed the publishing date of this book, but gave in return priceless joy.

Chapter 1

# Introduction

This book grew out of a conundrum: sex trafficking is an indisputable violation of its victims' rights; it also causes significant injuries to its victims and generates big profits for traffickers. And yet, private law claims against traffickers and other potential defendants are rare, and private law's potential as a response to trafficking is neglected in policy discourse, anti-trafficking literature and private law literature. The significant practical hindrances faced by victims who wish to sue defendants are a partial explanation for private law's marginal role as a response to trafficking but could not be the whole story: for a start, with proper legal aid some victims can recover; this has been the experience for instance in Israel. In addition, a private law response to trafficking faces other kinds of objections, which I find unconvincing.

In this book I attempt to demonstrate that private law has an important role as one response to trafficking. I offer an argument to extend the scope of traffickers' liability and to extend the scope of available defendants – beyond traffickers – to clients and the state. The remedies for traffickers' obligations to make restitution of profits and to compensate their victims in torts should be cumulative; the former obligation is based on the appropriation of the value produced by their victims' forced labour, and the latter on forcing victims into prostitution. The state should make restitution to victims of what it confiscated from traffickers as proceeds of crime, since the money belongs to victims, not to traffickers. Clients who had direct contact with victims should be strictly liable to victims in battery and, more controversially, in the proprietary tort of conversion. Clients who purchased commercial sex indiscriminately – where there is the possibility that their consumption contributes to trafficking – should be liable to victims under a theory of negligence, although such liability should be limited in terms of time, geographical scope and amount.

Two facts were crucial to the way the research project has developed. First, I was drawn into the subject while still living and working in Israel, when I was asked by Nomi Levenkron, a prominent Israeli anti-trafficking activist, and at the time the legal adviser of Hotline for Migrant Workers, to comment on a draft paper dealing with a tort response to trafficking. The experience thus far has been of greater awareness in Israel than in the UK and in other common law countries to the role of civil litigation as a protection mechanism, and consequently, more litigation has taken place. In Israel, several claims against sex traffickers have been successful and at least two claims against the state, which are based on a negligence theory, are pending. In the UK, only one successful case exists, which is believed to be the first (and possibly the only so far) in the commonwealth. The US experience with regard to private law litigation (as opposed to statutory-based claims), while not the focus of this study, is also quite limited.

While this book focuses on Israel and the UK, it is not a comparative study. Moreover, the focus is not on a detailed examination of the decided cases (an inquiry I have made elsewhere), but rather on a systematic examination of the main causes of action that should be available to victims, beyond what is currently asked for by victims and awarded by courts. In terms of the experiences of victims, I draw on English, Israeli and international sources. In addition to published sources, I draw also on correspondence with several Israeli and British individuals who have vast first-hand knowledge of the trafficking experience in these countries and on replies to freedom of information requests from relevant bodies. The former include Ms Justine Currell, Head of Human Trafficking and Acquisitive Crime at the Organised and Financial Crime Unit of the UK Home Office; Adv Sigalit Zohar, the Legal Aid Coordinator to Victims of Trafficking; and, most notably, Adv Nomi Levenkron. In terms of private law doctrine, I focus mainly on English law, with limited incursions into other, mostly common law, jurisdictions, and some references to Israeli case law. While Israel is a mixed jurisdiction, its tort law, and to a lesser extent restitution law, have a strong English influence. The normative and theoretical analyses about the proper scope of liability naturally transcend borders, although they are Anglo-American focused.

The second fact relevant to the way the research has been shaped is that my background is in private law theory, not in anti-trafficking regulation, civil procedure, or evidence. Therefore, the main bulk of this book deals with the normative, doctrinal and jurisprudential questions about identifying appropriate defendants and about the proper scope of civil liability. The analysis focuses on bridging the normative question of whether traffickers, clients and the state should be liable to victims, and the doctrinal question, can they be so liable in private law and, if so, how?

## 1.1 Definitional issues

The current international definition of trafficking adopted first in Article 3 of the Palermo Protocol (2000)[1] – the leading modern international instrument

1 Protocol to Prevent, Suppress and Punish Trafficking in Persons, Especially Women and Children, Supplementing the United Nations Convention Against Transnational Organized

on trafficking – and then replicated in Article 4 of the Council of Europe Convention on Action against Trafficking in Human Beings (2005) (the Trafficking Convention)[2] defines trafficking as *acts* (such as recruitment, receipt, transportation) by *means* (such as threats, coercion, deception, abuse of position of vulnerability) for the *purpose of exploitation* (such as sexual exploitation, forced labour, removal of organs or slavery). Improper means are not needed when a minor – less than 18 years old – is trafficked.

For current purposes the following is most significant. Trafficking could also occur domestically; there is no need for a crossing of a border.[3] Turning to the issue of consent, due to the opposing views among drafters about the relationship between prostitution and trafficking, the definition takes a muddled approach by both negativing the role of a victim's consent when improper means are used and not defining what amounts to 'the exploitation of the prostitution of others or other forms of sexual exploitation'.[4] Among the list of improper means several are completely incompatible with consent: 'the threat or use of force or other forms of coercion, of abduction, of fraud, of deception'. The other two means might be compatible with consent but this depends on both a contextual examination and one's ideological stance about the meaning of free consent: 'the abuse of power or of a position of vulnerability' or 'the giving or receiving of payments or benefits to achieve the consent of a person having control over another person'. From a private law perspective, these means potentially vitiate the victim's consent and could be possibly grounded in the doctrines of undue influence and unconscionable conduct.[5] 'Abuse of vulnerability' raises the question about the status of acute economic deprivation which drives women to become commercial sex providers (CSPs)[6] – if no other improper means is used is the woman trafficked? According to the explanatory notes of the Trafficking Convention a positive

Crime, opened for signature 12 December 2000, TIAS No 13127, 2237 UNTS 319 (entered into force 25 December 2003).

2 Council of Europe Convention on Action against Trafficking in Human Beings (Warsaw 2005), CETS 197 ('Trafficking Convention').

3 *Council of Europe Convention Against Trafficking in Human Beings: Explanatory Report* (CETS 197), [80] ('*Explanatory Report*'), and Trafficking Convention, Article 2. For the interpretation that the Protocol's approach is narrower, see A Gallagher, *The International Law of Human Trafficking* (Cambridge: Cambridge University Press, 2010) 114.

4 Cf *Explanatory Report*, id, [88]. For Gallagher's conclusion that the exclusion of consent is unnecessary and her critique of the definition as clumsy, see Gallagher, id, 27–8.

5 *Royal Bank of Scotland v Etridge (No 2)* [2002] 2 AC 773. For exploitation as a ground for restitution, including unconscionable conduct, see G Virgo, *The Principles of the Law of Restitution*, 2nd edn (Oxford: Oxford University Press, 2006) ch 10.

6 I prefer this term to the alternatives of 'prostitute', 'prostituted woman' and 'sex-worker' which are ideologically charged and connote meanings which I do not necessarily want to convey. I use 'CSP' to refer to women who sell sex whether they are forced or not, and 'victims' and 'non-victims' to distinguish between those forced by illicit means to remain in prostitution and those who are not.

answer is possible.[7] This relates also to the definition of exploitation. Would any pimping of a CSP be necessarily exploitative for purposes of the definition? These questions are at the centre of the prostitution debate which is covered in section 1.3 and receive different answers by abolitionists (who call for the abolition of prostitution and are usually associated with radical feminists[8]) and sex-work feminists.[9]

Two other realities further blur the line between valid and invalid consent. First, many CSPs (mainly on the street) are drug addicts who both use drugs as a coping mechanism with their occupation and sell their sexual services in order to support their drug addiction.[10] Whether their consent is free, and should be considered as valid is a matter of debate. Second, many women begin to work as CSPs when they are under age.[11] According to the international definition of trafficking, any action involving the recruitment and receipt of a child CSP implicates trafficking. But due to the social stigma involving prostitution and the relative absence of realistic exit, in what sense is the consent of the CSP who wishes to exit the profession, but feels she is unable to, free?

In the context of private law litigation the following observations about consent are in order. First, having consented to migrate or to work in prostitution should not and does not in itself preclude the claimant from being

7 *Explanatory Report* (n3) 'abusing the economic insecurity or poverty of an adult hoping to better their own and family's lot' listed as a relevant means in [84] but note that [83] relates this to a 'state of hardship in which a human being is impelled to accept being exploited', reverting to the debate of whether prostitution is inherently exploitative.

8 Radical feminism views patriarchy as a system of male domination over women (and other men) which is the defining characteristic of our society. The construction of sexuality and its relationship with men's domination and women's submission is central to the major strands of radical feminism. There are important differences in radical feminist accounts – some view any heterosexual sex as oppressive to women. But for current purposes these differences are irrelevant. For an overview see C Douglas, *Love and Politics: Radical Feminist and Lesbian Theories* (San Francisco, CA: Ism Press, 1990).

9 In fact, non-abolitionist views, which I largely term sex-work feminism, could be split into materialistic views of prostitution as work, and sex radicals' views of prostitution as potential sites of ingenious resistance and cultural subversion, as a therapeutic service, as a distinct sexuality or as an empowering intervention in the production of gender relations. For the former, materialist view, see K Kempadoo and J Doezema (eds), *Global Sex Workers: Rights, Resistance, and Redefinition* (New York, NY: Routledge, 1998); L Kuo, *Prostitution Policy: Revolutionizing Practice through a Gendered Perspective* (New York, NY: New York University Press, 2002) 142; for the latter, see W Chapkis, *Live Sex Acts: Women Performing Erotic Labor* (New York, NY: Routledge, 1997) 29–30; J Nagle (ed), *Whores and Other Feminists* (New York, NY: Routledge, 1997).

10 See e.g. P Alexander, 'Prostitution: a difficult issue for feminists', in F Delacoste and P Alexander (eds), *Sex Work* (London: Virago Press, 1988) 184, 202; C MacKinnon, 'Trafficking, prostitution, and inequality', (2011) 46 *Harv CR-CL L Rev* 271, nn51–2.

11 For a collection of studies, see MacKinnon, id, n21; M Farley, J Bindel and J Golding, *Men Who Buy Sex: Who they Buy and What they Know* (London and San Francisco, CA: Eaves & Prostitution Research and Education, 2009) 14. Whether the findings about age and drug dependency reflect mainly the experience of street CSPs is disputed. Compare the Farley–Weitzer debate (ch6, n53).

defined as trafficked.[12] As long as the claimant is deceived about the conditions of the employment and then lacks control over her working and living conditions and the possibility of exit she is forced into prostitution. This indeed was a typical experience of women trafficked to Israel,[13] and in such cases the claimant is not precluded from suing the trafficker.[14] While border cases exist in which 'force and coercion are at times more subtle or completely lacking – making it difficult to distinguish between freelance prostitution and trafficking, or violations of migration laws and contractual fraud and trafficking'[15] other (and typical) experiences – which are documented throughout this book – exist in which the claimant should clearly be considered as forced into prostitution.

Second, in theory, a claimant might be fully informed about the conditions of her future exploitation, including about her lack of control over her working and living conditions and lack of exit. Such hypothetical enslavement contracts will not be binding and will be considered as void for contravening public order. Third, as mentioned above, whether economic pressures leading a woman to prostitution amount per se to vulnerability, satisfying the trafficking definition is a disputed issue. The definition could be interpreted this way, and is so interpreted by radical feminists who maintain that 'prostitution as actually practised in the world usually does satisfy the elements of trafficking'.[16] This interpretation, however, is disputed. While, as explained below, my definition of coercion is narrower than the one adhered to by radical feminists, the argument made in this book could be expanded to encompass all, or almost all, CSPs. In this sense, the feminist debate about the meaning of consent is largely external to the arguments advanced in this book. Whoever is included in the category of having vitiated consent to become a CSP should be able to sue traffickers, clients and the state, although the extent of the pressure operating on the victim might have some doctrinal ramifications, such as the distinction between void and voidable transactions explored in chapters 3 to 5.

12 *Explanatory Report* (n3) [97]; Civ (Tel-Aviv) 2727/06 *Plonit (YM) v Shivas* (District Court, Israel, 1 December 2011), [17]–[19]. The claim that consent to prostitution should block the victim's claims is sometimes made by defendants. In Civ (Be'er Sheva) 5190/08 *Plonit (OG) v Makeyevski* (District Court, Israel, 13 October 2009), the third defendant's statement of defence (on file with the author) included the submission that *'from the moment in which the claimants asked to work as hostesses in bars, they knowingly waived their dignity, liberty and rights as human beings'*.

13 N Levenkron and Y Dahan, *Women as Commodities: Trafficking in Women in Israel* (Hotline for Migrant Workers, Isha L'Isha – Haifa Feminist Center, Adva Cente, 2003) 33, available at http://vho.org/aaargh/fran/livres5/traficfem.pdf (accessed 9 September 2012).

14 *Shivas* (n12).

15 See A Aronowitz, G Theuermann and E Tyurykanova, *Analysing the Business Model of Trafficking in Human Beings to Better Prevent the Crime* (Vienna: OSCE and UN.GIFT, 2010) 51, who document such border cases.

16 MacKinnon (n10) 300 citing Sigma Huda, *Report of the Special Rapporteur on the Human Rights Aspects of the Victims of Trafficking in Persons, Especially Women and Children*, E/CN.4/2006/62, P 42 (ECOSOC and CHR, 20 February 2006).

Fourth, if those recruited due merely to economic pressures are classified as trafficked, it might still be important to decide whether they are so classified because the victims' consent is not free, or because the CSPs are considered as trafficked notwithstanding their consent. The distinction is important since if consent exists, private law claims to which consent is a defence might fail, notwithstanding the claimant's status as a victim of trafficking. In Sweden, for example, the Supreme Court in a 2001 decision decided that the criminalisation of buying sex does not entitle the CSP to compensation from the convicted client; the CSP's consent was relevant, and the offence was primarily a crime against the public order and not primarily against the CSP as a person. This decision, which was harshly criticised by abolitionists as misinterpreting the spirit of the Swedish Act, led to a legislative amendment under which the court has to consider in any particular case whether compensation should be awarded.[17]

The relationship between arguably paternalistic prohibitions on sexual activity and consent arises in other jurisdictions, such as Canada, Israel, and the UK, and causes much controversy. In *Norberg v Wynrib* which involved a sex for painkillers prescription deal between a physician and a patient, three Justices held that the claimant did not freely consent, so established liability on battery, while three other Justices held that the claimant consented, but imposed liability for breach of either professional or fiduciary duty.[18] In *Abutbul v Kligger*, the claimant sued the defendant who was convicted of statutory rape for having sex with a minor. In a Further Hearing procedure, the majority disallowed the claim in battery, explaining that consent existed and the act of having sex with a minor is prohibited despite the existence of consent.[19] In *R v Brown* which involved only a criminal proceeding, the House of Lords convicted gay men who engaged in consensual sado-masochistic relationships with minors with 'unlawful and malicious wounding' and 'assault occasioning actual bodily harm'.[20] These cases also raise the question of whether the consent of minors to be prostituted (if existing and otherwise free) is not effective so they, like adults forced into prostitution, should be able to file private law claims. Prostituting minors with their consent is clearly trafficking according to the international definition, and is generally accepted to be off-limits by sex-work feminists as well.[21]

17 Nytt Juridiskt Arkiv [NJA] [Scania and Blekinge Ct App] 9 July 2001 527, 532, aff'd, id, 533 [Supreme Court] (Swed); Criminal Code 6:11 (Swed) as amended by An Act Amending the Criminal Code SFS 2011:517; M Waltman, 'Prohibiting sex purchasing and ending trafficking: the Swedish prostitution law', (2011) 33 *Mich J Int'l L* 133, 135, 155–6.

18 (1992) 92 DLR (4th) 449 (Can). The case is discussed further in ch5.

19 FH 5/65; PD 20(1) 561 (Supreme Court, Israel, 1966).

20 [1993] 2 All ER 75.

21 See ch7, section 7.5.

For the purposes of this book, my definition of trafficking focuses on coercion, lack of autonomy and resulting exploitation as the touchstones of sex trafficking.[22] The coercive means operating on the victim deny her the control over her living and working conditions and her exit; consequentially, it results in the economic exploitation of the victim, in that the proceeds of her labour – entirely or most of them – are alienated from her without her free consent.

To the extent that the international definition of trafficking encompasses adult victims who were not forced to remain in prostitution by illicit means, my focus on forced prostitution leaves a potential gap between those recognised as victims of trafficking ('victims') by the international definition and those able to recover in private law. This gap, however, is more apparent than real. First, it has recently been documented that the working definition of trafficking relied on by courts and service providers is limited to instances involving force and coercion.[23] In this sense, my working definition conforms to existing practice. Moreover, Bettio and Nandi's analysis of the International Organization for Migration (IOM) victims' database suggests that only 1 per cent of victims in the sample did not suffer any violation of the relevant rights.[24] This suggests that almost no consenting victims are recorded as victims. Second, as explained in chapter 10, if the formal definition really covers those who subjectively consented to be trafficked, these consenting 'Palermo victims' are unlikely to sue their traffickers or anyone else. Even if they will, a failure to show vitiated consent will fail their claim.

Sex trafficking, therefore, involves forced labour, sexual assault and enslavement. Forced labour is manifested by the fact that the victim is forced to sell her sexual services (and in addition, is misappropriated of the profits produced by her forced labour). Unlike other forms of forced labour, the labour produced itself results in the victim's sexual assault: since the victim does not freely consent to the sexual encounter with the client, each sexual encounter is a battery (a point which is further explained in chapter 5). Other forced labourers might be assaulted in order to force them into the labour but the production of labour itself would usually not involve battery. Enslavement is manifested in the total control extracted by traffickers over victims' living conditions. This includes victims' false imprisonment and 'the exercise of any or all of the powers attaching to the right of ownership over a person and includes the exercise of such power in the course of trafficking in persons, in

22 For a similar definition, see K Bales, *Disposable People* (Berkeley, CA: University of California Press, 1999) 6 (total control, violence, denial of personal freedom, for purpose of economic exploitation).

23 C Hoyle, M Bosworth and M Madden-Dempsey, 'Labelling the victims of sex trafficking: exploring the borderland between rhetoric and reality', (2011) 20 *SLS* 313, 317–18.

24 F Bettio and T Nandi, 'Evidence on women trafficked for sexual exploitation: a rights based analysis', (2010) 29 *Eur J Law Econ* 15, 21–2, 26. Their findings are explored further in ch3.

particular women and children' – the current definition of enslavement in Article 7(2)(c) of Rome's Final Act 1998.[25]

The terms 'enslavement', 'sex slaves' and the like, which I use at times, are contested. Some oppose their use and the conceptualisation of trafficking as modern-day slavery, since these 'accounts tend to deny that trafficking occurs along a continuum of "limited autonomy to complete bondage"'.[26] This partially falls back on the (correct) claim that victims' experiences vary. However, there are some good reasons to keep using the slavery imagery. The experience of many victims, as documented in chapters 3 and 5 is that of chattel slaves with respect to whom the international definition of enslavement cited above (which largely employs the international definition of slavery) applies.

Indeed, in *Rantsev v Cyprus and Russia* the European Court of Human Rights held that

> trafficking in human beings, by its very nature and aim of exploitation, is based on the exercise of powers attaching to the right of ownership. It treats human beings as commodities to be bought and sold and put to forced labour, often for little or no payment.

The Court, however, considered it 'unnecessary to identify whether the treatment about which the applicant complains constitutes "slavery", "servitude" or "forced and compulsory labour"'. Instead, the Court concluded that 'trafficking itself, within the meaning of Article 3(a) of the Palermo Protocol and Article 4(a) of the Anti-Trafficking Convention, falls within the scope of Article 4 of the [EHR] Convention'.[27]

Moreover, the argument against using the slavery terminology – that it denies the continuum of experiences – could be turned against those who make it. After all, throughout history the term 'slave' encompassed very different experiences and some slaves – like some Roman slaves – had usually much more freedom and power than the typical forced CSP has. It might be, then, that those opposing the slavery label err in insisting that the term reflects only the worst case scenarios, rather than those using the term err in applying it to the less severe instances of trafficking.

In any event, to accept the arguments made in this book about the proper scope of liability towards victims and the theoretical basis of such liability, one needs not accept[28] the characterisation of trafficking as slavery, or even as

25 Rome Statute of the International Criminal Court (1998) UN Doc A/CONF 183/10. For documenting victims' experience as property, see ch5, section 5.3.

26 Hoyle *et al.* (n23) 326. Cf R Weitzer, 'The social construction of sex trafficking: ideology and institutionalization of a moral crusade', (2007) 35 *Politics & S'ty* 447, 454.

27 [2010] ECHR 25965/04, [281], [282].

28 A possible exception is the argument that victims should be able to sue clients in conversion since victims were treated as chattels.

forced labour. After all, neither tort nor restitution claims are limited to situations of slavery or forced labour. The lack of free consent, due to measures of physical and psychological coercion, is what forms the basis of victims' claims against traffickers, clients and the state.

## 1.2 Locating private law in the regulatory framework

Trafficking is a complex phenomenon. It is a criminal activity, often a part of organised crime, a profitable business to traffickers, a phenomenon involving largely illegal migration and a severe human rights violation. Unsurprisingly then, the regulatory and theoretical frameworks to analyse the phenomenon often focus on one aspect of it.

The Palermo Protocol, and following it, other international instruments and national frameworks, focus on the three Ps: prosecution of traffickers, protection of victims (which includes compensation) and prevention of trafficking. It has been observed that the Palermo Protocol focuses on criminalisation – only the provisions with respect to prosecution are mandatory, not those with respect to the protection of victims.[29] The Trafficking Convention and the recent 2011 EU Trafficking Directive[30] put more emphasis than the Protocol on victims' protection. However, the extent to which protection of victims is adequate is debated and the Trafficking Convention does not remedy in full the Protocol's weakness that the protection provisions are optional.[31]

Article 39 of the Trafficking Convention states that the convention 'is intended to enhance the protection afforded by [the Protocol] and develop the standards contained therein'. Article 15 imposes duties to ensure access to information, to provide for legal assistance and free legal aid under the conditions provided by internal law, to provide for the right of victims to compensation from perpetrators and to adopt measures as necessary to guarantee compensation, for instance through the establishment of a fund which could be funded by confiscating traffickers' assets. Article 9(5) of the Palermo Protocol, Article 6 of the Trafficking Convention and (with a slight change) Article 18(1) of the EU Directive impose the obligation to 'discourage the demand that fosters all forms of exploitation of persons . . . that leads to trafficking' as one measure of prevention.

Article 12(2) of the Directive, discussed further in chapter 9, imposes an obligation to provide victims with free legal aid, including for the purpose of claiming compensation. Article 17 imposes an obligation to ensure victims

29 Gallagher (n3) 116.

30 Directive 2011/36/EU, 5 April 2011 on Preventing and Combating Trafficking in Human Beings and Protecting its Victims, and Replacing Council Framework Decision 2002/629/JHA.

31 Gallagher (n3) 116.

have access to existing schemes of compensation to victims of violent crimes of intent.

The UK Government was initially inclined to opt out from the Directive but eventually has opted in. More generally, the UK's complex legal, policy and institutional anti-trafficking frameworks were surveyed and evaluated by GRETA – Group of Experts on Action against Trafficking in Human Beings.[32] In accordance with its obligations under the Trafficking Convention (and now also the Directive) the responses revolve around prevention, protection and prosecution, and on identifying victims under the National Referral Mechanism (NRM) framework.[33]

A private law response to sex trafficking could be best viewed as part of victims' protection measures; possibly, but less clearly, it could be understood as a prevention measure to the extent that liability will contribute to deterring traffickers and clients.[34] Currently, a private law response is marginalised at three different levels. First, as mentioned above, the goal of protecting victims took a back seat in the anti-trafficking campaign, at least in terms of the very narrow scope of international obligations imposed on the state and the scope of protection afforded to victims. This is explicable based on both the fact that such protection is expensive and the fact that victims have no political clout. Possibly, victims of sex trafficking are considered as the 'ultimate other' so spending scarce resources on their protection is less likely: they are typically low class women, often migrants, and 'whores'. (At the same time, however, they raise tremendous sympathy, which according to some translates to a moral panic.[35])

At a second level, within the protection framework, issues relating to victims' compensation (as opposed to other measures of protection such as identification, residency permits in countries of destination and access to medical aid and legal employment) again do not take a front seat.[36] At a third

32 GRETA, *Report concerning the implementation of the Council of Europe Convention on Action against Trafficking in Human Beings by the United Kingdom* (Strasbourg: GRETA, 2012).

33 The NRM is a framework to identify potential victims recommended initially by the Organization for Security and Co-operation in Europe (OSCE) and adopted by the UK. The competent authorities (to which suspected victims are referred) are the United Kingdom Human Trafficking Centre (UKHTC) and the UK Border Agency (UKBA). The competent authorities should make a reasonable ground decision within 5 days. If the decision is positive the victim is granted a 45-day reflection period during which the competent authorities should make a conclusive ground decision. Reasonable and conclusive ground decisions are mandated by the Trafficking Convention, Article 10 (n2).

34 The broader questions about the nature of private law and its use either merely to vindicate rights or also in a functional manner are discussed in chapters 9 and 10.

35 See e.g. T Sanders, *Paying for Pleasure: Men who Buy Sex* (Cullompton: Willan, 2007) ch 9; Weitzer (n26).

36 This is evident in the relative coverage of compensation-related issues in works dedicated to trafficking. See e.g. Gallagher (n3) 354–69, 403–4; S Drew, *Human Trafficking – Human Rights Law and Practice* (London: Legal Action Group, 2009) 185–208. In *Human Trafficking:*

level, when the appropriate measures of compensation are analysed or debated, the focus tends to be on compensation orders in the criminal trial in which the trafficker was convicted or on access to state funded victims' compensation schemes.[37] In the academic literature as well, articles dealing with private law remedies to victims are rare.[38] The discussion in these articles is almost exclusively[39] limited to tort claims against traffickers (or statutory-based civil remedies in the US context).

A conspicuous omission in the regulatory framework and the literature is the absence of any discussion of the possibility of a restitutionary claim against the state and tort claims against clients and the near absence of discussion of restitutionary claims against the trafficker.[40] Indeed, these texts do not distinguish between compensation for violation of the victim's liberty and dignity and the restitutionary claim with respect to the trafficker's gain from the victim's forced labour. Similarly, special reports and manuals dedicated to victims' compensation deal only perfunctorily, if at all, with the possibility of civil claims.[41] Neither the Palermo Protocol, the Trafficking Convention nor

*The Government's Strategy* (London: HMG, 2011) 11, there is no mention of victim's compensation in the one-page section dedicated to 'improving the care of victims'.

37 Gallagher, id, 315, 361–4 mentions civil litigation only in passing. Drew, id, covers claims in civil courts in nine pages.

38 See note: 'Remedying the injustices of human trafficking through tort law', (2006) 119 *Harv L Rev* 2574; K Kim and K Hreshchshyn, 'Human trafficking private right of action: civil rights for trafficked persons in the United States', (2004) 16 *Hastings WLJ* 1, 25; S Singh, 'The predator accountability act: empowering women in prostitution to pursue their own justice', (2007) 56 *DePaul LR* 1035, 1049–50; N Levenkron, 'Civil suits of victims of trafficking against the traffickers: and yet, it does move', in G Mundlak and M Ajzenstadt (eds), *Law, Society and Culture: Empowerment* (Tel Aviv: Nevo, 2009) 451 (in Hebrew); T Keren-Paz and N Levenkron, 'Clients' strict liability towards victims of sex-trafficking', (2009) 29 *LS* 438–63; T Keren-Paz, 'Poetic justice: why sex-slaves should be allowed to sue ignorant clients in conversion', (2010) 29 *L & P'hy* 307; 'AT v Dulghieru – compensation for victims of trafficking, but where is the restitution?', (2010) 18 *TLJ* 87; and 'An essay on banalization of slavery, devaluation of sex-workers' labor and deprivation of victims of trafficking', in *Concord Research Institute for Integration of International Law in Israel* (2009) 1, available at http://papers.ssrn.com/sol3/papers.cfm?abstract_id=980075 (accessed 19 December 2012); A O'Driscoll, '"AT v Dulghieru": accounting for the profits of sex trafficking', (2010) 40 *Victoria U Wellington LR* 695.

39 With the exception of my work, id, on claims against clients and on restitution from traffickers and O'Driscoll, id, which dealt with a restitutionary claim. See also T Keren-Paz, 'Moral and legal obligations of the state to victims of sex trafficking: vulnerability and beyond', in S FitzGerald (ed), *Regulating the International Movement of Women: From Protection to Control* (London: Routledge, 2011) 175, which mentions the difficulties in suing the state in torts and restitution, but focuses on moral obligations of the state to victims.

40 See Drew (n36) 203–4.

41 The report of the OSCE/ODIHR, *Compensation for Trafficked and Exploited Persons in the OSCE Region* (Warsaw: OSCE/ODIHR, 2008) dedicates pp 26–32 to civil claims and labour claims (the latter largely cover gain-based claims). There are also references to civil litigation (which with the exception of the UK can be pursued within the criminal

the EU Directive even recognises the right for restitution of proceeds from forced labour.[42] As further developed in chapter 4, the Trafficking Convention's suggestion in Article 15(4) that the state will fund compensation to victims from assets confiscated from traffickers is both non-obligatory and otherwise problematic: it uses victims' money to compensate them for their harm and allows the use of such money to subsidise other anti-trafficking measures. Similarly, the prevention framework is silent on whether measures to discourage demand include civil suits against clients (or indeed, criminalising the purchase of sex[43]). This book responds to this omission by delineating four claims against traffickers, the state and clients.

## 1.3 Diversity of experiences, gaps in knowledge and the prostitution debate

There is no 'one size fits all' description of sex trafficking. While it is accepted that sex trafficking is a gendered phenomenon whose victims are overwhelmingly women,[44] almost all other elements of trafficking reveal considerable variance: the ways victims are recruited, victims' experience in terms of length of exploitation, the extent of the violation of their rights, the number of clients they serve and the venue in which they are forced to sell their services. Victims' experiences depend on different variants such as the country of origin and destination and the nationality of the exploiter.[45] The

procedure) in the specific countries' profiles, but without much analysis of the substantive elements. See also D Werner and K Kim, *Civil Litigation on Behalf of Victims of Human Trafficking*, 3rd edn (Los Angeles, CA: Legal Aid Foundation, 2008) 67–73 (statutory-based claims are covered at 29–67); Anti-Slavery and Eaves, *Rights and Recourse: A Guide to Legal Remedies for Trafficked Persons in the UK* (Anti-Slavery and Eaves, 2009) ch 5, especially 56–8, 66–8.

42 Earlier drafts of the compensation provision in the Palermo Protocol referred to the right to compensation and restitution from offenders. UNODC, *Travaux Préparatoires of the negotiations for the elaboration of the United Nations Convention against Organized Crime and the Protocols thereto* (UNODC, 2006) 365–73; Gallagher (n3) 362.

43 But see GRETA (n32) 43, which views the recent criminalisation in England and Wales of paying for the sexual services of a CSP subjected to force or deception (Sexual Offences Act 2003 (c 42), s 53A, added by Policing and Crime Act 2009 (c 26), s 14) as a discouraging demand measure. Such liability is strict. Section 64 added by s 15 provides the equivalent prohibition to Northern Ireland. The prohibition has been effective since April 2010.

44 86.5 per cent of all victims whose gender was recorded in the *IOM Trafficking Database*, as analysed by Bettio and Nandi (n24) 23, were women. This figure relates to all purposes of exploitation so the percentage among those trafficked for the purpose of sexual exploitation is probably higher.

45 See pp 36 (extent of profits and proceeds involved in sex trafficking); pp 67 (daily number clients); pp 41–3 (varied experience of victims and extent of rights violation); p 175 (health consequences of being trafficked); pp 197–200 (existence of trafficking in all segments of sex markets and move between segments); pp 114, 194–5 (victims' background

incidence of domestic trafficking also varies and in general is rather high in source countries and low in destination countries.[46] There is also no clear correlation between being trafficked across a border and suffering a greater extent of rights' violation. While according to common wisdom a major reason for the vulnerability of victims is their status as illegal immigrants,[47] a recent study found that being trafficked within one's country is associated with higher risk of rights violation and that violations are most severe in countries where the population is least concerned about the phenomenon of human trafficking.[48]

The ways in which traffickers' rings operate also vary significantly. For traffickers, trafficking is a business. The organisation of the business varies in terms of its size and complexity, the modes and intensity of coercive measures to keep victims docile, traffickers' involvement in other illegal activities, and the likelihood of vertically integrating in the business the sale of sexual services – the exploitation end of the chain of trafficking. The way traffickers respond to demand varies, as does the extent to which they supply to different geographical markets and different market segments; naturally, this area in particular is shrouded with uncertainty and suffers from very limited available data.[49] Clients' motivation, awareness of trafficking, taste for buying sex from a victim or non-victim, frequency of purchase, type of services bought, and the venue in which the services are bought vary as well.[50] Lastly, the effects of the manner in which prostitution is regulated on the behaviour of traffickers, clients and CSPs, and its effects on victims' numbers and well being is very hard to assess.[51] Above all, the research on trafficking suffers from limited knowledge due to the illegality of trafficking and the stigma (or, in certain countries illegality) involved in buying and selling sex. Whether it is the economy and sociology of sex trafficking, the

vulnerability); pp 175–82 (estimated number of victims and their proportion among all those in prostitution); pp 189–9 (exploitation of non-victims).

46 See ch7, section 7.1.

47 See e.g. N Mai, *Migrant Workers in the UK Sex Industry – Final Policy-relevant Report*, ESRC final project report (Swindon: ESRC, 2009) 43: 'Immigration legal status is the most important single factor engendering migrants' workers' vulnerability to exploitation in the UK industry'. Cf K Jackson, J Jeffrey and G Adamson, *Setting the Record: The Trafficking of Migrant Women in the England and Wales Off-street Prostitution Sector* (London: Project Acumen, ACPO Migration and Associated Matters, 2010), which did not find any indicator of trafficking among domestic CSPs.

48 Bettio and Nandi (n24) 33–4, 36.

49 Traffickers' business models and supply of victims are covered mainly on pp 197–200, 205–7; sale of victims between traffickers on pp 49–50; objectification of victims on pp 129–30.

50 Awareness is examined on pp 149–52; patterns of demand on pp 161, 200, 209–11; objectification of CSPs on pp 129–30; clients' motivation on pp 184–7.

51 See pp 164–71, 188–9.

psychology of clients, and the history of victims' experiences, we simply do not know enough.

There is an important gap in our knowledge regarding the scope of trafficking. How widespread is the trafficking phenomenon? How many victims are there and what is their proportion among all CSPs? The answers are both contested and politicised. They are contested in terms of both the methodology used to estimate the overall number of victims and the estimated figures themselves, and in terms of the possibility to come up with a plausible estimation at all. To a lesser extent, some also doubt whether those *identified* as victims are indeed victims. Worse still, the figures are politicised along the lines of the debate on how to regulate prostitution, to which I now turn.

Radical feminists oppose prostitution as inherently demeaning to its participants and harmful to all women; prostitution is domination, a way for men to exercise power over women's bodies and minds and is inherently violence against women.[52] Alternatively, the harmful consequences are contingent upon features of the social environment in which prostitution is performed: 'In our society, prostitution represents women as the sexual servants of men'.[53] According to the former essentialist view, free consent to engage in prostitution cannot exist. According to the latter empirical view, free consent is possible but extremely rare.[54] Accordingly, all or almost all prostitution should be equated with sex trafficking. Moreover, an anti-trafficking approach committed to the distinction between free and forced forms of prostitution is potentially dangerous especially since it legitimises what is deemed to be freely chosen prostitution.[55]

Sex-work feminists, while largely aware that prostitution involves rampant exploitation and serious risks to many CSPs, reject an essentialist condemnation of prostitution. Prostitution itself is morally neutral and instances of abuse and exploitation should be targeted in a specific manner. An abolitionist approach is problematic not only because it further curtails the already constrained choice that CSPs have and denies their agency, but also because it further stigmatises prostitution and those practising it, and by this further

52 The main works associated with these views are C Pateman, *The Sexual Contract* (Palo Alto, CA: Stanford University Press, 1988); A Dworkin, 'Prostitution and male supremacy', (1993) 1 *Mich J G & L* 1; C MacKinnon, 'Prostitution and civil rights', (1993) 1 *Mich J G & L* 13; K Barry, *Female Sexual Slavery* (New York, NY: New York University Press, 1979); S Jeffreys, *The Idea of Prostitution* (Melbourne: Spinifex, 1997) 191–3, 265.

53 D Satz, 'Markets in women's sexual labor', (1995) 106 *Ethics* 63, 78.

54 B Sullivan, 'Prostitution and consent: beyond the liberal dichotomy of "free or forced"', in M Cowling and P Reynolds (eds), *Making Sense of Sexual Consent* (Aldershot: Ashgate, 2004) 127–39.

55 D Leidholdt 'Prostitution and trafficking in women: an intimate relationship', in M Farley (ed), *Prostitution, Trafficking and Traumatic Stress* (New York, NY: Haworth Maltreatment & Trauma Press, 2003) 147, 167.

harms them.[56] According to such an approach, anti-trafficking campaigns are problematic for two reasons. First, they could be used to advance an abolitionist view (or are motivated by such indefensible motivation). Second, especially in the context of discouraging demand for the services of victims of sex trafficking, the inability to distinguish between victims and non-victims would mean that, at least arguably, measures to reduce demand for prostitution would harm non-victims. So even if anti-trafficking measures will reduce the number of victims and would not worsen the conditions of remaining victims (and both assumptions are contested by sex-work feminists as will be discussed in chapters 6 and 7), it will come at the expense of non-victims.

The prostitution debate between abolitionists and sex-work feminists is carried over to trafficking and its regulation in the following ways. First, is non-coerced prostitution at all possible? Second, should the definition of trafficking exclude those consenting to their exploitation?[57] Third, how extensive is the trafficking phenomenon? Fourth, how exploitative is the condition of CSPs who are not victims? Fifth, how should prostitution be regulated? Sixth, does criminalisation or legalisation improve or worsen the conditions of victims and non-victims?[58] With respect to the last two issues, both camps are divided in their evaluation of abolitionist regimes such as the Swedish model criminalising the purchase of sex and the regulation or decriminalisation of prostitution in Australia, Germany and the Netherlands. Seventh, are anti-trafficking measures seemingly tailored against the abuse of victims really used (unwittingly or intentionally) to combat prostitution and is the status of victims forced on those who do not view themselves as such by a 'rescue industry'?[59] Alternatively, do sex-work feminist campaigns, by belittling the significance of trafficking, align with conservatives who view trafficking as being mainly a problem of illegal immigration? In a sharp contrast to the critique that anti-trafficking measures force the status of victims on sex-work migrants, the typical litigation scenario in immigration tribunals is of a claimant challenging the state's finding that there are no reasonable or conclusive grounds to classify her as a victim under the NRM framework; anti-trafficking activists and monitoring bodies often criticise the state for failing to recognise real victims as such.[60]

56 T Sanders and R Campbell, 'Why hate men who pay for sex? Exploring the shift to "tackling demand" in the UK', in V Munro and M Della Giusta (eds), *Demanding Sex: Critical Reflections on the Regulation of Prostitution* (Hampshire: Ashgate, 2008) 163, 174–6.

57 For these two questions, see section 1.1.

58 These four questions are discussed mainly in chapters 6 and 7.

59 For such claims, see L Agustin, *Sex at the Margins: Migration, Labour Markets and the Rescue Industry* (London: Zed Books, 2007), and J Phoenix, 'Be helped or else! Economic exploitation, male violence and prostitution policy in the UK', in Munro and Della Giusta (n56).

60 See e.g. M Giammarinaro, *UK Country Report by OSCE Special Representative and Co-ordinator for Combating Trafficking in Human Beings* (Vienna: OSCE, 2011) [9]; L Arocha, *Wrong Kind*

In describing the debate I have focused on the polar views in the feminist debate about prostitution. I have done so for two reasons. First, they are the most pronounced in the policy debate on trafficking and prostitution; indeed, they largely shaped the opposing regulatory responses in several countries including Sweden and the Netherlands.[61] Second, they offer the most sustained critique of my project, as either legitimising prostitution of non-victims, as abolitionists argue, or compromising the interests of non-victims, clients and even victims themselves, as sex-work feminists maintain. As I argue throughout this book, a private law framework withstands these critiques and in fact offers a partial way out from this debate.

I acknowledge, of course, that other participants in the debate are non-feminists (but as a feminist, I discount such views) and that feminist approaches to prostitution cannot be reduced to 'anti-sex' radical feminists and 'liberal' sex-work feminists.[62] In fact, my own position on prostitution can be classified as belonging to what Prabha Kotiswaran terms 'middle ground feminism'. Such approach supports empowering practices to individual CSPs but is against the institution of prostitution itself.[63] From sex-work feminism I take the ontological distinction between forced and non-forced prostitution; and the observations that illicit coercive measures vitiate consent to an extent that dire economic pressures and social construction of sexuality do not, and that some women choose to work in prostitution and do not see themselves as victims. From radical feminism I take the condemnation of prostitution since it is based upon and perpetuates women's subordination in society and since exploitation of CSPs and violence against them is rampant. Whether this in itself is sufficient to criminalise the purchase of sex is debatable, all the more so given the claims, which are hard to verify or refute, that criminalisation worsens the condition of CSPs who are not forced. An important argument I make in this book is a manifestation of this 'middle ground' approach which is attentive to the claims from both ends of the debate: that the problematic nature of prostitution as currently practised is a reason to afford victims some remedies against clients.

*of Victim? One Year On: An Analysis of UK Measures to Protect Trafficked Persons* (London: Anti-Trafficking Monitoring Group, 2010) 8.

61 See e.g. J Halley, P Kotiswaran, H Shamir and C Thomas, 'From the international to the local in feminist legal responses to rape, prostitution/sex work, and sex trafficking: four studies in contemporary governance feminism', (2006) 29 *Harv J L & G* 335, 362 ('Four Studies').

62 For a brief account of materialist, postmodern and postcolonial approaches to prostitution – in addition to the radical/liberal views – see G Simm, 'Negotiating the United Nations trafficking protocol: feminist debates', (2004) 23 *Austl YB Int'l L* 135, 137–42. However, as Simm's discussion demonstrates, the different views can usually be classified as either abolitionist or non-abolitionist, although, as the sources in n63 suggest, the different approaches can be arranged along a continuum.

63 'Four Studies' (n61) 410. Cf C Overall, 'What's wrong with prostitution? Evaluating sex work', (1992) 17 *Signs* 705, 723.

I share with Hila Shamir – who attempts to assess legal reforms beyond prohibitive/permissive visions – the need for both relaxing 'the structuralist assumption of an all-encompassing male domination in which women are nothing more than passive victims', and avoiding 'the romantic . . . individualist assumption of a freely choosing individual in a world of endless market possibilities'. I also share with Shamir the understanding that 'it is not immediately clear that more or better information is actually attainable', that 'facts do not necessitate one position or another, but are produced by these positions' and that 'what might not be widely empirically proven . . . could still influence and enrich policy formation'. Perhaps most importantly, I share with both Kotiswaran and Shamir the understanding that any mode of regulation produces winners and losers, and that the distributive effects of the different modes of regulation on all stakeholders should be taken into account.[64] This also suggests that it is hard to decide which mode of regulation is ultimately superior.

Sex trafficking is a profit-motivated crime; it involves a marked economic exploitation of its victims in terms of the part of the profit that is left (if any) in their hands;[65] such exploitation is based on the alienation (or misappropriation) of the victim's labour; and this type of labour and its exploitation are distinctively gendered. All of this suggests a possible strong affinity between the type of analysis conducted in this book and socialist feminism's insistence that capitalism and patriarchy are mutually dependent.[66] Prostitution might be wrong for being inherently oppressive (the radical feminism view); alternatively, prostitution as generally practised might be condemned based on the exploitation of CSPs' background economic vulnerability, which is to a large extent gendered (a socialist feminism view). But even if one rejects both views, sex trafficking is wrong on both radical and socialist feminist grounds as both a sexuality-based mode of oppressing women, and the site of economic exploitation of their (gendered) labour. It is likewise unacceptable to liberal feminists since (and to the extent that) its victims do not consent to the harming practices to which they are subjected.

Section 1.3 began by highlighting the diversity of victims' experiences and noted the uncertainty about the scope of trafficking. The scope and patterns of trafficking change also over time, not only across jurisdictions; this might be the result of regulatory changes. In Israel, for example, following a 2006 amendment to the anti-trafficking legislation and a law enforcement crackdown on trafficking, the trafficking of women from former USSR countries, which was at its peak between 2000 and 2005, almost ceased

64 'Four Studies', id, 406–11, 414–19.

65 As documented in chapter 3, victims in Israel and England typically receive up to 17 per cent, but often much less and frequently nothing, from the profits they produce.

66 Z. Eisenstein (ed), *Capitalist Patriarchy and the Case for Socialist Feminism* (New York, NY and London: Monthly Review Press, 1979) 22.

completely, but new problems have emerged, such as sexual servitude of African migrants and asylum seekers who are held to ransom in Egypt's Sinai en route to Israel.[67] Recent Israeli civil litigation and pending cases still reflect the peak period of trafficking of East European women to Israel.

The limits of knowledge affect to a different extent the various arguments made in this book. The fault-based claim against clients for their contribution to trafficking by creating indiscriminate demand in the market does depend on contested normative assumptions and on empirical estimations which are almost impossible to verify; these revolve around the proportion of victims among all CSPs, and the prevalence of exploitation and violence in prostitution. Overall, however, a private law framework is relatively immune to this paucity of knowledge, especially since litigation is not only a regulatory tool, but also an instrument to vindicate a victim's rights. Once a victim is identified, the strength of her claim in torts and restitution against the trafficker does not depend on the trafficker's business model or the number of victims and her battery claim against the client does not depend on the motivation of clients. Nor does a victim's restitution claim against the state depend on whether or not the state's response to trafficking is adequate.

## 1.4 The book's organisation

Chapter 2 begins the inquiry by examining the litigation experience thus far in England and Israel. The actual cases are examined against a background of an offered menu of torts and restitution claims against several potential defendants, after clarifying why contract and labour law are ill-suited responses to trafficking. Lastly, the chapter critically evaluates courts' reasoning and holding in tort claims against traffickers, the most commonly litigated cause of action in the menu.

Chapters 3 and 4 focus on gain-based remedies. Chapter 3 examines the potential restitutionary causes of action against traffickers, defends restitution as vindicating the victim's property in the exchange product of her forced labour and explains why restitution and tort damages should accumulate. Chapter 4 argues that the state should make restitution of what it confiscates from traffickers as proceeds of crime to any victim who can trace the money received by the trafficker in return for the sexual services she was forced to provide.

Chapters 5 to 8 turn the focus on tort claims against clients. Chapter 5 advocates the imposition of strict liability on clients who had direct sexual

67 See US State Department Office to Monitor and Combat Trafficking in Persons, *Trafficking in Persons Report June 2012* (Washington, DC: US Department of State, 2012) 194 ('TIP report'); Phone conversation with Adv Sigalit Zohar, Legal Aid Coordinator to Victims of Trafficking (24 April 2012) (conversation notes on file with the author, my translation from Hebrew).

contact with a victim and embeds such liability in the torts of battery and conversion. Chapter 6 argues that clients owe a duty of care to victims with respect to their contribution to trafficking by creating indiscriminate demand. Chapter 7 argues that such contribution is a breach of that duty. Chapter 8 explains the formidable factual and legal causation problems involved in establishing a theory of demand-based contribution to trafficking, argues that these problems could be overcome and delineates the appropriate scope of such liability. Roughly speaking, chapters 3 to 8 are arranged in an ascending order of the extent to which the claims are radical or contested.

Chapter 9 turns from substantive law to issues of procedure and from a doctrinal-normative analysis to brief legal theory and socio-legal inquiries. It examines the practical challenges that victims face in pursuing civil litigation, challenges which arguably undermine the viability of a private law response to trafficking. It argues that these challenges could be partially overcome; it argues further that a private law response is important both since it has a transformative potential and intrinsically since it enables victims to vindicate their rights.

Lastly, chapter 10 concludes that the lessons of the inquiry conducted in this book could benefit both those interested in regulation of trafficking and private lawyers. For the former, a private law response should be valued since it empowers victims and might strike an acceptable compromise between competing feminist views on prostitution. For the latter, the inquiry serves as a springboard for a task which is largely jurisprudential – developing private law's doctrines, challenging its concepts, if not its conceptual framework, and debating competing understandings of the roles of private law.

Chapter 2

# Potential responses, and the experience thus far

The chapter begins by identifying potential defendants who victims can sue and delineating possible causes of actions against them in torts and restitution. It then examines the experience thus far in England and Israel which reveals that only a small fraction of the possible claims has been used, mainly tort claims against traffickers. Lastly, it provides some brief evaluation of courts' holdings and reasoning in these tort claims.

## 2.1 The menu: potential defendants and claims

In theory, all four branches of the law of obligations might be employed by a victim. Trafficking involves both harm to the victim and gain made at her expense. The victim's injuries and violation of rights from being injured are covered by tort claims; the profit made at her expense by the traffickers, by restitution claims; gaps between what was promised to the victim at the country of origin and her actual condition might support a contractual claim; violation of protective labour law provisions might constitute a right for a remedy which is statute-based. Before mapping in more detail the possible claims in torts and restitution against different defendants, we should see why contract and labour law are inappropriate responses.

### *2.1.1 Inadequate private law responses: contract and labour law*

Some victims are recruited in source countries by being promised employment in a job other than CSP, or by being promised conditions which are quite different from those awaiting them as trafficked CSPs.[1] This can give rise, at

1 Y Dahan and N Levenkron 'Trafficking in women in Israel under the auspices of the rule of law', (2004) 24 *Theory & Critique* 9, 22–3; S Stephen-Smith, *Routes In, Routes Out: Quantifying the Gendered Experience of Trafficking to the UK* (London: The Poppy Project, 2008) 12–14; C Galiana, *Trafficking in Women* (Brussels: Directorate General for Research, Division for Social, Legal and Cultural Affairs, European Parliament, 2000) 14–15.

least theoretically, to claims that a contract has been breached. There are several problems with a contractual framework, however. Most crucially, it is conceptually and symbolically inadequate, since free consent does not exist and since the use of a contractual framework normalises the trafficking phenomenon and misses the dehumanisation and objectification of victims. The use of a contractual paradigm which is based on a consensual relationship is ill-equipped to deal with trafficking whose gist is the total enslavement of the victim.

The conceptual deficiency also translates into a practical disadvantage: a claim in contract will yield a lower award than that which the claimant should be able to receive from a tort- or restitution-based claim. The reason is that the profit made at the victims' expense is likely to exceed what is promised to them in the contract. Similarly, the injury suffered by victims far exceeds the amounts promised to them in the contract. Privity of contract further limits the effectiveness of the contractual cause of action. Often, the recruiters are not the pimps 'employing' the victims. As a contractual claim would only be available against the recruiter, the claim is likely to be ineffective.

With respect to traffickers at the site of exploitation, a contractual claim is both analytically unsound and normatively unattractive. It is unsound, since it is often difficult to establish that the local trafficker is a party to the contract which was (arguably) made between the victim and the recruiters. Indeed, often the trafficker would not even know the recruiter. While this difficulty might perhaps be overcome by hugely stretched notions of agency or joint venture, we remain with the normative undesirability of reducing enslavement and torture into a breach of promise. This being said, what was promised in the contract could be a partial yardstick against which the victim's losses could be assessed. However, this amount hardly captures the victim's losses and the profit made at her expense.[2]

The victim's claim might be based on violations of protective labour law provisions. Indeed, manuals covering the remedies available to victims of trafficking commonly include references to claims in labour tribunals, albeit usually not in the sex trafficking context.[3] Usually, a labour relationship is considered as a specific form of a (relational) contractual relationship. However, protective provisions do not depend on the parties' consent. As such, they can be classified from an analytical perspective as the fourth and residuary type of obligation: one imposed by law. Indeed, in some countries, protective labour law provisions – such as a minimum wage and compensation for delays in

2 *AV v Grissman* (n23) is a rare example of awarding victims both a gain-based remedy based on the share of the profits (30 per cent) that was promised to them but not paid, and tort damages for the claimants' false imprisonment.

3 Anti-Slavery and Eaves, 79–95; Werner and Kim, 49–54; OSCE/ODIHR, 27–32 (all three manuals are cited in ch1, n41).

wage payments – apply even in situations in which there is no contractual relationship between the employer and the employee.[4]

The first two difficulties discussed with respect to the contractual claim are relevant here as well, although the first one to a lesser extent. Remedies for violation of minimum wages and other violations of protective labour law provisions are likely to give the victim less than restitution- and tort-based claims. Moreover, using protective labour law provisions is still based on a *paradigm* of consent. This normalises trafficking and renders it to be nothing more than a (regrettably quite prevalent) exploitative relationship between employer and employee. In some countries, forced CSPs would not be able to avail themselves of labour law's protection since prostitution is illegal (as is the case in the US), or since prostitution-related contracts are unenforceable and since, and to the extent that, they are undocumented workers (as is the case in the UK).[5] But while the reasons for blocking the claim are misguided, the result according to which victims' gain-based claims should be litigated in civil courts based on the law of restitution is correct. Section 2.2 and chapter 3 document how the channelling of gain-based claims to the labour courts yielded initially a very problematic decision, which, while rectified on appeal, still has some lingering undesirable effects.

### 2.1.2 Traffickers

Traffickers can be sued in both torts and restitution. Restitution claims against traffickers may be based on vindication of property, unjust enrichment or restitution for wrongs. In the US, a victim of sex (and other forms of) trafficking can bring a statutory civil suit under the Trafficking Victims Protection Reauthorization Act of 2003.[6] More generally, civil claims might also be based on some sort of constitutional torts or breach of statutory duty. Turning to common law torts, forced prostitution typically involves false imprisonment, battery and assault. Typical behaviour along the chain of trafficking can amount to deceit (fraud), negligent misrepresentation and (the statutory tort of) harassment.[7] Other possible torts are negligence, two party intimidation, unlawful means conspiracy and, as argued in chapter 5 (there, with respect to clients), conversion.

Two party intimidation is a threat of an unlawful act intentionally causing the claimant to act in a way causing loss to the claimant;[8] unlawful means

4 This is the position in Israel HCJFH 4601/95 *Sarusi v National Labour Court*, PD 52(4) 817 (1998).

5 Werner and Kim (n3) 56 (US); Anti-Slavery and Eaves (n3) 88 (UK). For my critical discussion of illegality as blocking a claim, see ch3.

6 18 USC § 1595. According to Werner and Kim (n3) 29, by 2008 over 20 civil law suits had been filed under this law.

7 See *AT v Dulghieru* [2009] EWHC 225 (QB), [3].

8 See *Godwin v Uzoigwe* [1993] Fam Law 65 (trafficking for domestic labour purposes).

conspiracy is an agreement to use unlawful means to injure the claimant, as a result of which the claimant suffers damage.[9] The last two torts are rarely used and when they are used, they are often limited to economic loss in the context of unfair business competition. Nonetheless, for two reasons, their use in the context of trafficking is promising and apposite. From the victim's perspective, they better capture the trafficking experience as a whole, rather than as a compartmentalised set of discrete violations performed along the chain of exploitation. From the traffickers' perspective, these torts capture trafficking as an organised, profit-driven and well co-ordinated activity which typically involves several exploiters co-operating together.

### 2.1.3 The state

When the state confiscates from traffickers' money that which the claimant can trace as her own, the state can be liable in restitution, as explored in chapter 4. Matters are far more complicated with respect to tort claims against the state. The state might harm victims by negligently failing to prevent their enslavement or shorten its period, by exacerbating background conditions which cause victims' vulnerability, by actively contributing to the victim being trafficked, or by acting or failing to act in a way which limits or nullifies the victims' chances to recover from the trafficker. The problems, from a victim's perspective, are that police liability for negligent omissions to protect a victim is extremely hard to establish and in practice does not exist in England even when the victim's identity is known;[10] that policy decisions about the level of law enforcement and prosecution strategy are immune from liability; and that claims that the prosecution's negligence eliminated the chances that the victim would recover from the trafficker involve economic loss, the recovery of which is also much restricted.[11]

But consider the following potential test case mentioned in a report published by Eaves' Poppy Project (Poppy).[12] A Lithuanian victim exploited in England and held in a sauna managed to escape and, helped by two female bystanders, ran to the local police station. The police did not understand her as she could not speak English. They escorted her back to the sauna. Apparently no check was made on Interpol, which had her details as a missing person, nor was any attempt made to use an interpreter.[13] Possibly, such

9 *Revenue and Customs Commissioners v Total Network SL* [2008] UKHL 19, [213].

10 *Smith v Chief Constable of Sussex* [2008] UKHL 50. For the more permissive Israeli approach in similar circumstances, see CA 1678/01 *State v Weiss*, PD 58(5) 167 (2004).

11 *Customs and Excise v Barclays Bank Plc* [2006] UKHL 28.

12 The Poppy Project provides high-quality support, advocacy and accommodation to trafficked women and is a major UK anti-trafficking third sector actor. Eaves is a charity providing support and associated services for women who have experienced violence.

13 Stephen-Smith (n1) 19.

behaviour could trigger liability in tort even under the extremely narrow confines of *Smith v Chief Constable of Sussex*, based on the fact that this case arguably involved misfeasance, and not merely nonfeasance. The active creation of risk by the defendant which injured the claimant was manifested by unknowingly handing her over into the traffickers' control. Moreover, *Smith* recognised the existence of a rare exception to the rule of no liability for police nonfeasance – a failure to save the claimant from external risk the defendant did not create.[14] I have documented other potential test cases elsewhere.[15]

### 2.1.4 Clients

Clients harm victims in three principal ways. First, any sexual encounter with the victim infringes her bodily and sexual integrity and impinges upon her autonomy, liberty and dignity. Second, by contributing to the creation of indiscriminate demand for sex services – a willingness to purchase sex acts from a CSP who might be forced – the client contributes to the enslavement of victims. Third, by failing to rescue the victim, the client contributes to the future enslavement of the victim. I do not pursue this avenue in the book. Here, the relevant cause of action is in negligence, but liability, which in any event could be established against only a few clients, is riddled with difficulties. As there is no general duty to rescue, there is a need to find a special relationship between the client and the victim in order to establish duty. Possibly, the fact that the client contributed to the risk of further exploitation of the victim by purchasing (or intending to purchase) sex from her, or the fact that he already violated her right by having sex with her, creates the duty to remove the risk.[16] Next, a negligent failure to rescue should be limited only to circumstances in which the client knew or should have suspected that the claimant was forced. Even then, there is a need to decide what would amount to discharging the duty. Lastly, such a claim also needs to grapple with issues of factual and legal causation. After all, many clients do not rescue the victim and, possibly, from the moment a future negligent client also fails to rescue the claimant, the defendant should no longer be liable.

14 *Smith* (n10) [78], [109], [135].

15 Keren-Paz, 'Moral and legal obligations' (ch1, n39) 180–3. For imposing vicarious liability on the state for the claimant's rape by policemen, see CCT 52/04 *NK v Minister of Safety and Security* (Constitution Court of South Africa, 13 June 2005).

16 Cf *Oke v Weide Transport Ltd & Carra*, 41 DLR 2d 53, 62–3 (Man CA 1963); *Montgomery v National Convoy & Trucking Co*, 195 SE 247 (SC, 1937); *Wright v Lodge* [1993] 4 All ER 299 (HL).

### 2.1.5 Publishers of sex advertisements

Publishers of sex advertisements also contribute to the violation of victims' rights.[17] Whether they should be liable in torts or in restitution is an interesting question which will not be explored in this book. In theory, publishers' liability could be either direct or accessory. When the claim is that the publishing of the ads contributes to the creation of indiscriminate demand which in turn contributes to victims' trafficking, the claim is similar to that canvassed in chapters 6 to 8. Such a claim faces a further difficulty that the contribution is one step removed (and is therefore more remote) than the contribution of each client: the publisher publishes an ad which causes some additional consumption of sex, which leads to some victims being trafficked. On the other hand, in some respects suing publishers is fairer and easier than suing individual clients. It is fairer in terms of loss spreading – liability is not imposed on an individual client who contributed with many others to the creation of demand which led to trafficking. Rather, it is imposed on a corporation, which is a repeat player and able to spread the losses of liability. For these reasons it is easier to identify publishers as defendants, find them liable and recover the awards against them, in comparison to equivalent claims against clients.

Advertising the services of the claimant, including indirectly by advertising the services of the place in which she is exploited, contributes to the violation of her rights by subjecting her to more direct contact than otherwise would be the case. The publisher cannot be liable directly in battery since the contribution is not direct: it is not the publisher who had contact with the claimant's body without her consent. Nevertheless, there are two avenues for liability, despite the fact that establishing either of them is difficult. One way would be to establish accessory liability for the client's battery.[18] The other option would be to establish direct liability under the tort of negligence.

In theory, publishers could also be sued in restitution. Unlike the case against traffickers and the state, the claim is not based on subtraction – no wealth was transferred from the victim to the publisher. But restitution for wrongs might be available, since the acts that violated the victim's rights were those that enriched the publisher. As the discussion in chapter 3 clarifies, not

17 'Met police to crack down on newspapers carrying sex ads', *The Guardian*, 13 October 2010; E Kunze, 'Sex trafficking via the internet: how international agreements address the problem and fail to go far enough', (2010) 10 *J High Tech L* 241.

18 See Dietrich, ch8, n76. In *Dart v Craigslist Inc*, 665 F Supp 2d 961 (ND Ill, 2009) the Federal Court dismissed a suit brought against Craigslist by a Sheriff to enjoin the website owners from posting erotic services and for damages reflecting extended police enforcement against prostitution and human trafficking promulgated by the site. The Court stated that 'intermediaries are not culpable for "aiding and abetting" their customers who misuse their services to commit unlawful acts'. See Kunze, id.

all torts allow the victim to sue for the gain accrued to the defendant from the wrong. These doubts, and the realisation that the value of the loss-based claim is likely to be higher than the value of the gain (what was paid for the ads), make the loss-based avenue more promising in practice.

## 2.2 The litigation thus far

Few of the potential causes of action presented above have resulted in litigation. Most of the claims, and the only ones successful so far, were against traffickers, with an overall focus on tort damages, although the interest in restitution has also been somewhat protected. The first and so far only English 'classic' sex trafficking case is *AT v Dulghieru*[19] in which the High Court awarded £601,000 to four victims of trafficking who were forced into prostitution for periods of 1 and 2 months. Liability was based on unlawful means conspiracy and included exemplary damages of £60,000 which were supposed to undo (with partial success) the unjust enrichment at the victims' expense.[20] In *BJM v Hyre* the claimant was an English male teenager who was forced into prostitution (and subjected to other sexual assaults) for a short period. He was awarded £89,450 in compensation for battery.[21]

In Israel, around 35 victims filed civil claims against traffickers through legal aid, and several others through (mainly pro-bono) lawyers. In about a third of the claims brought with the help of legal aid, settlement was reached for varying amounts (in the range of NIS 10,000–75,000). These settlements are almost always paid. Other claims are either abandoned by claimants for reasons explained in chapter 9, or end with a judgment in favour of the claimant. At times, these claims are not defended, and in these cases, and when the awards are high, claimants face difficulties in satisfying the judgment. Interestingly, of the decided cases, which almost always follow a previous criminal conviction, no cases exist in which the claim was denied.[22] However, it is not uncommon for the awards to be lower than those claimed by the claimants (even in cases of judgment by default) and awards are often decided based on estimation, relying on the facts proven in the previous criminal

19 *Dulghieru* (n7).

20 See my analysis of the decision in *Dulghieru* (ch1, n38).

21 [2010] EWHC 2856 (QB). The award included pecuniary and non-pecuniary elements. Civil and labour claims for trafficking for purposes other than sexual exploitation exist as well. See e.g. *Godwin* (n8) which dealt with trafficking for domestic labour (although the Court did not use the term).

22 Email correspondence with Zohar (ch1, n67), 23 April 2012. More information on legal aid to civil claims exists in the annual reports that the Israeli Ministry of Justice submits to the US State Department for purposes of the annual Trafficking in Persons Report. The Israeli reports, however, are not publicly available and so far I have not been able to obtain a copy of them. A full socio-legal evaluation of private law's potential to protect victims will need to be based on the information contained in the reports.

conviction and without the claimant testifying. It is also common for courts to award a global amount without specifying (especially in cases in which the decision is given by way of settlement) whether it reflects tort damages, a gain-based award or both.

There are at least eight cases in which civil courts awarded compensation to victims, five cases in which labour courts awarded a gain-based remedy and non-pecuniary damages to victims and in one early case the Labour Court did not award a gain-based remedy where the share of the proceeds the trafficker left in the victim's hands exceeded minimum wage, but awarded non-pecuniary damages.[23] Of the eight cases decided by civil (mostly District) courts, one

23 For civil court decisions, see Civ (Tel-Aviv) 2191/02 *Plonit (K) v Jaack*, Tak-Meh 2006 (1) 7885 (2006), [4]–[5] (District Court, 8 March 2006), aff'd in 3806/06 *Jaack v K* (Supreme Court, 26 May 2009) (NIS 300,000 in tort damages of which NIS 50,000 punitive; gain-based claim was deemed to be in the sole jurisdiction of labour courts); Civ (District Court Jerusalem) 7219/05 *AR v Bosulevitch* (6 February 2006) (judgment by way of settlement, both compensation and restitution were pleaded; each claimant was awarded NIS 425,000; in recovery proceedings each claimant eventually agreed to receive NIS 75,000); Civ (Tel-Aviv) 1384/04 *Plonit v Argantir* (20 February 2006) (approved settlement, US$60,000); Civ (Be'er Sheva) 5190/08 *Plonit (OG) v Makeyevski* (unpublished, District Court, 13 October 2009) (approved settlement, NIS 40,000; two other defendants reached settlements with the claimants and paid, one NIS 38,000 to one claimant, the other NIS 50,000 to both; a fourth defendant absconded); Civ (Haifa) 982/06 *SY v Moaiseyv* (District Court, 12 June 2007) (NIS 200,000 based on facts determined in prior conviction and without testimony; had physical or psychiatric disability been proven a much higher award would have been appropriate; an unjust enrichment claim should not be ruled out); Civ (Tel-Aviv) 2003/08 *Plonit v Lifshin* (25 January 2010) (judgment by default, NIS 1,000,000 in compensatory and punitive damages and NIS 500,000 in restitution); Civ (Haifa) 12680/07 *AV v Grissman* (Magistrates' Court, 5 April 2011) (each of the two claimants was awarded NIS 50,400 reflecting 30 per cent of the proceeds from a period of 4 months, which were promised but not given, and NIS 100,000 for false imprisonment); Civ (Tel-Aviv) 2727/06 *Plonit (YM) v Shivas* (District Court, 1 December 2011) (NIS 600,000 in non-pecuniary damages and NIS 150,000 in punitive).

For labour court decisions, see La (Be'er She'va) 4634/03 *M v Salsrevski*, Tak-Av 2005 (3) 97 (2005), [63]–[70], aff'd LaA 480/05 *Ben-Ami v M* (8 July 2008) (NIS 25,850 in minimum wage and NIS 240,000 as non-pecuniary damages); La (Tel Aviv) 5307/04 *R v Kuchick* (8 January 2007), rvs'd LaA 247/07 *R v Kuchick* (24 September 2009) (NIS 75,000 non-pecuniary damages and around NIS 22,000 in gain-based remedy awarded by the National Labour Court; the latter amount was based on the minimum wage and other protective labour law provisions); La (Be'er Sheva) 1520/05 *Plonit (G) v Normatov* (judgment by default against six defendants, NIS 21,800 awarded as 'unpaid wages'), La (Be'er Sheva) 1528/05 *Plonit (PG) v Normatov (no 2)* (24 August 2009) (after a successful appeal by the Normatov defendant against the judgment by default in La 1520/05, the claimant was awarded NIS 36,333, what was claimed as unpaid salary, the calculation based on the proceeds received by the trafficker minus amounts he left in the claimant's hands. The court based its calculation on the minimal estimation of the daily number of clients served (ten); the claimant testified she served between nine and 18 per day); LaA 628/07 *Tyumkin v Plonit* (27 August 2009) (NIS 50,000 in non-pecuniary damages and NIS 45,000 in restitution based on the Court's estimation, which was half that which the claimant

(*Bosulevitch*) was given by way of settlement, in which both compensation and restitution were pleaded, two others (*Argantir*, *Makeyevski*) were approved settlements, and one (*Lifshin*) was judgment by default, in which the Court awarded both damages and restitution. In the recent decision of *Grissman*, both gain-based remedy and damages for false imprisonment were awarded. In three other cases (*Jaack*, *Moaiseyv*, *Shivas*), only tort damages were awarded. In *Jaack* the Court reasoned that it had no jurisdiction over the claim which was conceived as one for unpaid wages and therefore within the exclusive jurisdiction of the labour courts. In *Shivas*, the most recent private law Israeli judgment in the area of sex trafficking, the Court held that no sufficient evidence was adduced to support the claim and refused to decide about the issue of jurisdiction. Similarly, in *Moaiseyv*, the Court mentioned that an unjust enrichment claim could not be ruled out in principle, but in the absence of the claimant's testimony it only awarded tort damages based on the facts determined in the previous criminal conviction. In both *Shivas* and *Moaiseyv*, the claimants, who were not in Israel at the time of the civil litigation, did not testify and the courts awarded non-pecuniary damages by way of estimation, but no pecuniary damages.[24] A more detailed analysis of some aspects of these decisions is offered in section 2.3; the rather convoluted route of the litigation in labour courts is examined in more detail in chapter 3.[25]

The first decision in civil courts which was not based on settlement, *K v Jaack*,[26] sustained an appeal and cross-appeal in the Supreme Court which in a very short decision acknowledged that part of the District Court reasoning was problematic (in terms of some of the causes of action relied upon by the trial judge) and that the award of damages by way of estimation raises difficulties. However, the Court reasoned, the sum awarded was reasonable and did not justify the Court's interference. Given the incomplete evidentiary foundation in this case (in which the claimant did not testify since she had been previously deported) and the passage of time, the Court did not see fit to have a complete analysis of the panoply of tortious causes of action available to victims, including civil courts' jurisdictions to award gain-based remedies. The Court also expressed support for legislative reform which would better integrate compensation, in one way or another, as part of the criminal

submitted); La 2852/05 (Jerusalem) *Plonit v Almoni* (20 July 2007) (restitution claim denied for lack of evidence, where what was left in the claimant's hands exceeded minimum wage; NIS 50,000 awarded as non-pecuniary loss).

24 The Court in *Shivas* reasoned that the charge sheet did not include details based on which a calculation of profits could be made and rejected the calculation submitted by the claimant's lawyer.

25 See pp 49–50, 65, 72–3, 75–6.

26 The claimant was represented by Adv Nomi Levenkron, who represented several other claimants, including those in *Shivas* and *Lifshin*.

proceeding and mentioned, apparently with approval, a Bill making trafficking a civil wrong which could be compensated by up to NIS 100,000 without proof of damage and allowing the Court convicting the trafficker to award compensation to the victim up to NIS 300,000.[27]

At least two claims against the state are pending in civil courts at the moment. The first is based on atypical (and denied) facts. The claimants are the dependants of a victim who committed suicide a few months after the conviction of her traffickers. The claim is both against the traffickers and against the state. It is alleged that the police used the victim's trafficker as an informant and practically gave him immunity for the trafficking-related offences with which he was implicated. The state denies in its statement of defence such behaviour; it admitted the trafficker was used as an informant but denied that he was given any immunity and insists the informant was warned not to commit any offences.[28]

The second litigation is based on more typical facts and alleges that the state negligently failed to take appropriate action against trafficking which would have prevented or lessened the claimants' health injuries. The two claimants were diagnosed with HIV, Hepatitis C and tuberculosis and the litigation is health-driven and follows a failed petition to the Israeli Supreme Court sitting as the High Court of Justice to oblige the state to finance the required treatments.[29] According to the statement of claim the negligence was manifested in: failing to send Russian-speaking policemen to the raids conducted on the brothels in which the claimants were kept; failing to identify them as victims and free them; failing to close these brothels, but rather carrying out routine checks while maintaining a good relationship with the traffickers; failing to prevent the trafficking of the victims to Israel; and failing to publish appropriate warnings in the country of origin that would have prevented their trafficking experience.[30] Perhaps surprisingly (for English lawyers, anyway) the claim was not struck out and Judge Gerstel in a pre-trial hearing apparently made comments suggesting that the state is no different from any other litigant and the question is more how much the state should pay than whether liability could be established.[31]

There are no cases known to me in which clients were sued by victims; however, in *Ploni v Migdal*[32] a male claimant injured in a road accident argued that he could have sex only with surrogates and claimed the cost for hiring a surrogate as a pecuniary loss; the Israeli Supreme Court reversed the trial Court's decision awarding an amount reflecting the cost of paying for weekly

27 *Jaack* (n23) [4]–[6].
28 CC (Tel-Aviv) 55775/06 *Plonit v Gaiman* (District Court, Israel) (pending decision).
29 HCJ 5637/07 *Plonit v Minister of Health* (Supreme Court, Israel, 15 August 2010).
30 See http://news.walla.co.il/?w=/10/1851000 (accessed 16 August 2011).
31 N Levenkron, email correspondence with the author, 28 November 2011.
32 CA 11152/04; PD 61(3) 310 (2006).

escort services. The result is partially based on public policy considerations, and the Court's approach, discussed in chapter 7, could be understood as suggesting that given the rampant exploitation of CSPs and widespread trafficking existing in the Israeli prostitution market at the time of judgment, the buying of sex should be discouraged.

## 2.3 Brief evaluation of tort claims against traffickers

Tort claims against traffickers do not raise any special normative and doctrinal difficulties and are uncontroversial from both private law and regulation of trafficking perspectives. They do raise the practical challenges of access to justice, evidence and recovery, but these problems are not unique to such claims and are discussed in chapter 9. I therefore make just a few brief observations on issues relating to tort liability and to remedies.[33]

### *2.3.1 Proof of general and special damages*

Overall, when the awards in *Dulghieru*, *Jaack*, *Lifshin* and *Shivas* are examined, one can discern a tendency to compensate victims for their non-pecuniary loss but not for pecuniary losses and restitution. In *Dulghieru*, three of the four claimants complained of gynaecological problems and pain. In all three cases the courts reasoned that there was no medical evidence showing a causal link between the claimants' experiences and these complaints.[34] In addition, as analysed in chapter 3, the claimants received only between one-third and two-thirds of what they should have been awarded in restitution. A similar tendency is observable from the Israeli Labour Court litigation, especially in early cases. For example, in *Ben Ami* the Regional Labour Court awarded only the minimum wage but about nine times this amount in non-pecuniary damages. Turning back to tort claims, in *Shivas* the claimant (who did not testify) did not receive any specific damages for her physical injury caused during her escape, nor restitution, and in *Moaiseyv* lack of proof of physical or psychiatric disability accounted for the award being on the low side.[35]

To the extent that in the relevant jurisdiction, the size of the award for non-pecuniary (including punitive) damages is unlimited, it might be that judges engage in a mental accounting exercise and award in non-pecuniary damages what they are asked and refuse to award in pecuniary damages and restitution. But while a general judicial reluctance to award special damages without proof

33 I analyse the tort aspects of *Dulghieru* in (n20) and those of *K v Jaack* in 'Banalization' (ch1, n38).

34 *Dulghieru* (n7) [16], [22], [26].

35 *Moaiseyv* (n23).

is easy to understand, it is harder to justify in circumstances in which it is the trafficker, rather than the victim, who is ultimately to be held responsible for the victim's inability to adduce sufficient evidence, because, for example, she has been deported or repatriated.

Moreover, at the expressive level, given the general evidence (and simple common sense) about the vast health consequences of being trafficked and the significant amounts that are made at the victim's expense, a practice denying victims special damages and restitution is highly questionable. If indeed courts award non-pecuniary damages in lieu of restitution, this practice reveals sympathy to plaintiffs as victims, but not as CSPs. Victims can get compensation for the injury suffered, but they cannot profit from the sale of their sexual services, even though the victims did not sell these services voluntarily. The desirability of this expressive message could be doubted, although it somewhat depends on one's position in the feminist debate on prostitution.

Of the five tort decisions in which an opinion was given, two involved judgment by default and in two other cases the claimants were represented by a lawyer whose expertise was trafficking, not private law. Consequently, some aspects in the decisions are either unclear or problematic. For example, in *Jaack*, liability was not established on battery, but rather on false imprisonment and on violating the claimant's dignity and autonomy according to the Basic Law: Human Dignity and Liberty – 1992[36] and on *Daaka* damages for mere interference with autonomy.[37] But it is far from clear that a constitutional tort for violating the Basic Law provisions exists and the reliance on *Daaka* is doubly mistaken. First, the award there – the equivalent of the solatium raised as an option and rejected by Lord Hoffmann in *Chester v Afshar*[38] – was explicitly held to be a new head of damages (under the tort of negligence) rather than an independent tort.[39] Second, this solatium is meant to afford compensation in circumstances in which there is no consequential loss from the breach of the duty to provide information allowing the patient to make an informed decision, therefore the injury to autonomy (and hence the compensation) is relatively low. Such solatium is the wrong basis for comparison when the injury to autonomy is manifested by the claimant's sexual enslavement.

The Court's laudable willingness in *Jaack* – replicated in *Moaiseyv* and *Shivas* – to award compensation without specific proof of damage is marred by an analytical blur: the Court vacillated between the view that the mere violation of the victim's right requires an award of damages even if no damage

36 SH 1391.

37 CA 2781/93 *Daaka v Carmel Hospital*, PD 53(4) 526 (1999).

38 [2004] UKHL 41, [34].

39 *Daaka* (n37), Justice Or [27]. This, along with the holding that injury to autonomy is not a constitutional tort, was confirmed in CA 1303/09 *Kadosh v Bikur Holim Hospital* (Supreme Court, 5 March 2012).

can be proven (or was done) and the view that the Court can make an estimation of the victim's damage, based on the facts admitted by the defendant in the criminal process. The distinction between these two alternatives is important – the former is less clearly compatible with corrective justice and with the view that the purpose of damages is compensatory – and the Court's indecisiveness follows the Supreme Court's lack of clarity on similar matters.[40]

Compensation for mere violation of the right might (but does not have to) disregard factors such as length of enslavement, number of clients 'served' and other data. If, on the other hand, courts would prefer to stick to the more traditional damage-based compensation, still, in the absence of specific proof, courts can and should make estimations, which might be based on known parameters (such as length of the enslavement period). In the absence of such parameters, the courts should base compensation on figures relating to the average victim, when this rule could (but does not have to) be qualified by allowing the trafficker to try and show that the damage inflicted by him was in fact lower. The desirable solution is that compensation would be given for a mere violation of the right, and *in addition*, for proved or assumed average damage.[41]

A further confusion is apparent from *Shivas*, in which the claimant also suffered physical injury as a result of jumping from a porch in order to escape and, as could be recalled, at the time of trial was already living in her country of origin, did not come to testify but gave an affidavit regarding her injury. While the Court explicitly discussed under pecuniary damage only the claim for restitution it held that in the absence of testimony no pecuniary damage was to be awarded, but accepted that a non-pecuniary award was warranted.

However, it did not make a distinction between compensation under battery, which is actionable per se, so that the violation of autonomy and dignity involved in sexual battery can itself ground a substantive award of damages, and a non-pecuniary award in cases of personal injury, mainly for pain and suffering.[42]

40 See e.g. 1081/00 *Avnaal v State*, PD 59(5) 193 (2005); T Keren-Paz, 'Compensating injury to autonomy: normative evaluation, recent developments and future tendencies', (2007) 22 *Colman LR* 187, 190–217 (Hebrew).

41 However, this view which I advocated (id, 198–200) in the context of the *Daaka* ruling was recently rejected by the Supreme Court in that context in CA 10085/08 *Tnuva v Rabi's Estate* (4 December 2011).

42 *Shivas* (n23). At [8], the Court relied on both a false imprisonment case and a personal injury case (in which the claimant lost consciousness permanently) without distinguishing between the two. Moreover, at [9] the Court suggested, in a badly phrased sentence, that it is *un*reasonable to award compensation without proof of damage when constitutional rights are infringed, such as in cases of battery and false imprisonment. However, the following analysis and the authorities cited by the Court clearly *support* compensation for violation of a constitutional right without proof of damage. Lastly, at [10] the Court

### *2.3.2 False imprisonment*

Few issues exist as to false imprisonment and its compensation. First, to establish false imprisonment the restriction of liberty needs to be complete.[43] There could be some doubts whether this is so at the lower end of the coercion spectrum. By and large, establishing that false imprisonment has occurred has not been an issue in the decided cases. In *Deressa v Gobena,* for example, a US Court held that false imprisonment can occur when the victim is threatened, even though the victim of trafficking for domestic labour was left alone with a key when the defendants were abroad.[44] Recently, however, the Court of Appeal in *R v Vinh van Dao* dealt with an appeal against a conviction for cultivating cannabis by alleged victims of trafficking, and held that the claim for the defence of duress was not supported by the facts. The Court relied as one indication on the existence of a key left in the premises in which the appellants were held, despite the fact the appellants denied knowledge of its existence.[45]

Second, courts in England and Israel seem to accept the idea of diminishing marginal disutility from losing one's liberty. In particular, Israeli courts did not follow a submission by counsel that the award should be based on multiplying the daily award in cases of short false imprisonment in other contexts with the length of the claimant's imprisonment.[46]

Third, and this applies more generally to all items of non-pecuniary losses, we should examine whether the awards are consistent across different cases of sex trafficking, and in comparison to other cases. While I do not want to suggest that inconsistency or bias exist, the status of victims of trafficking as often foreign and as CSPs (and therefore 'unrapable') requires a careful examination of the size of the damages awarded to them.[47] In particular, the awards in *Jaack* of NIS 300,000 (in 2006) for 5 months of enslavement and in

mentioned that given the lack of evidence, the claimant will receive less than she might have otherwise received.

43 *Robinson v Balmain New Ferry Co* [1910] AC 295.

44 No 05 Civ 1334, 2006 US Dist LEXIS 8659 (USDC for the Eastern District of Virginia, Alexandria Division) 14–15.

45 [2012] EWCA Crim 1717, [29]. In *obiter* ([33]) the Court expressed a provisional view that 'we would have been strongly disinclined to accept that a threat of false imprisonment suffices for the defence of duress, without an accompanying threat of death or serious injury'. But false imprisonment alone is a ground for establishing duress for purposes of restitution. See ch3.

46 *Shivas* (n23) [16], [19].

47 Compare the awards to Israeli citizens falsely imprisoned by the authorities discussed in Levenkron (ch1, n38) at n106, which range between NIS 10,000 and NIS 20,000 per day, with awards to illegal immigrants falsely imprisoned by the authorities who routinely receive NIS 1,000 per day. See CC (Tel-Aviv) 68061/03 *Marinka v State* (2004); CC (Tel-Aviv) 15395/04 *Akuasa v State* (2005); CC (Tel-Aviv) 25213/04 *Baren v State* (2005); cf CC (Tel-Aviv) 72598/04 *Pitag v State* (2006) (NIS 2,500 per day).

*Shivas* of NIS 750,000 (in 2011) for 2 months of enslavement seem unduly low.[48] In *Shivas*, the claimant's experience included, among other things, being raped by one defendant, being subject to a threat to wrap her with a rug and then beat her and having suffered a physical injury resulting from a jump from a porch while attempting to escape. The claimant in *Shivas* knew she was going to work in prostitution but changed her mind on arrival. One can only wonder whether this consideration wrongfully led to the award being on the low side. Lastly, the Court in *AT* held that the trafficker was not responsible for the period in which one victim was detained by the authorities as an illegal immigrant. As explained in chapter 3, this is a mistake.

### 2.3.3 Punitive damages

Sex trafficking cases are obvious candidates for awarding punitive damages. The profit motive, the intentional infringement of rights, the importance of the rights violated and the extent and duration of violation are all pointing in the same direction. The only argument against awarding them is the prohibition on double punishment for the same offence. In all, or almost all cases so far, the civil claim followed a previous conviction. The question of whether a previous conviction should and does prevent the award of punitive damages receives different answers in different jurisdictions. In both England and Israel, courts awarded punitive damages after conviction, although, in England, the purpose of the award was to reverse the defendants' unjust enrichment at the expense of the claimants. This goal is remedial and as such the award of exemplary damages cannot be considered as double punishment.[49]

### 2.3.4 Joint and several liability?

Israeli courts tend to impose several liability on traffickers. In the first Israeli decision by the Labour Court in *Salsrevski*, which involved a series of sales of the claimant from one trafficker to another, the liability to compensate the claimant for her non-pecuniary losses and to pay her a minimum wage was several, but no explicit analysis of this point was provided. The apportionment was calculated according to the length of time the victim was exploited by each trafficker.[50] In the most recent Israeli decision, the District Court in *Shivas* explicitly rejected the claimant's submission that liability should be joint and several, based on the reasoning that the extent of violation of rights by each defendant was different – for example, one of the defendants raped the victim.[51]

48 For a critique of the award in *Shivas* by the Legal Aid Coordinator to Victims of Trafficking, see Yuval Yoaz, 'Jurisdiction', *Globes*, 2 January 2012, 11.

49 Compare *Dulghieru* (n20) 91, 100–2.

50 *Salsrevski* (n23) [135].

51 *Shivas* (n23) [14].

Arguably, traffickers' liability should be joint and several, at least as regards tort damages. In torts, joint and several liability of all traffickers can be supported based on one of three bases: that the injury is conceptually indivisible, that the relative contribution of each tortfeasor is unknown so that the burden shifts to each of them to prove his part, or that the defendants are joint tortfeasors.[52] The analysis should distinguish situations in which the victim is sold from one trafficker to another, as was the case in *Salsrevski*, from those in which the traffickers are part of the same ring, as was the case in *Shivas*. With respect to the former, despite the fact that the following proposition might involve a bit of a stretch, all traffickers who handed the victim from one to another might be considered as joint tortfeasors. Joint tortfeasors include those who co-operate in order to further a common (unlawful) design. Viewing all traffickers along the chain of exploitation as engaging in an illegal joint venture allows us to attribute the actions of one to the other, due to authorisation, ratification, conspiring together and possibly procurement.[53] The fact that all traffickers who 'trade' a victim benefit from this activity, and the affinity and connection between trafficking and organised crime, should lead to a conclusion that even traffickers who do not have privity of contract between them, but who are all links in the chain which trafficked the victim, should be considered as joint tortfeasors.

Alternatively, upstream traffickers – namely, sellers – should be liable jointly and severally with downstream traffickers for the damage caused by the latter based on notions of causality. Had the seller not sold the victim, the damage the buyer caused the victim either would not have occurred, or would have occurred when the victim was under the seller's control. In either case, the seller should be liable for the ensuing harm.

In cases like *Shivas*, in which the defendants co-operated together to exploit the defendant and tame her into submission, it is even clearer that the defendants were joint tortfeasors (a point not discussed at all by the Court). Moreover, in *Shivas*, the claimant eventually jumped from a porch in order to escape and suffered physical injury as a result and the Court acknowledged that the injuries from the jump were the result of the combined actions of all defendants.[54] Therefore, the holding that defendants' liability is several is erroneous also since the injury was indivisible.[55] Such a holding is also arguably inconsistent with the Court's decision to award global damages, rather than separating damages according to the different causes of action.

52 For further discussion, see ch8.

53 *Brooke v Bool* [1928] 2 KB 578; *Restatement (Second) of Torts* (1965), § 876; R Stevens, *Torts and Rights* (Oxford: Oxford University Press, 2007) 245–57 (common law attribution for joint torts).

54 *Shivas* (n23) [15], [18].

55 For the indivisible nature of the injury from trafficking, see ch8, section 8.4.

Chapter 3

# Restitution from traffickers

Sex trafficking is a profitable business. Recently, in *AT v Dulghieru* the High Court accepted the victims' testimony that the daily income made at each victim's expense was between £500 and £1,000. The Dulghieru defendants, who were previously convicted, were issued (unsatisfied) confiscation orders totalling £786,000.[1] Based on figures found in the Israeli Parliamentary Report on human trafficking, it could be calculated that, on average, the daily income made at each victim's expense is around £250.[2] According to the working paper of the International Labour Organization (ILO) on profits from forced labour, each victim in industrialised countries is estimated to generate an annual average turnover of US$96,000, and profit of US$67,000. Based on calculations of average price per sexual act (which is region-sensitive) the annual income from forced sexual labour is estimated at US$33.9 billion.[3] Siddharth Kara estimates that the average annual revenue produced by a victim exploited in Western Europe is US$114,000 and the annual profit is US$78,000 (with the equivalent weighted global averages of US$42,000 and US$29,000); and that less than 2 per cent of revenues are spent on payment to victims in Western European urban centre apartment brothels. The average purchase price of victims in sales between traffickers varies between a maximum of US$5,250 in North America and a minimum of US$660 in South Asia with US$4,800 for Western Europe, US$3,000 for the Middle East and a global average sale price of US$1,895 per victim. Kara further estimates the 2007 global revenues from forced sexual exploitation at US$51.3 billion, global profits at US$35.7 billion, the revenues for 2007 generated from the sale of victims between traffickers – which he terms profits from slave-trading, as

1 *Dulghieru* (ch2, n7) [69], [74].

2 Parliamentary Inquiry Committee, *Trafficking in Persons: Intermediate Report* (Jerusalem: The Knesset, 2002) 6.

3 P Belser, *Forced Labour and Human Trafficking: Estimating the Profits*, ILO working paper 42 (Geneva: ILO, 2005) 14. The study mentions that this is a conservative estimation which is based on the daily average number of clients of all prostitutes (three to four) which is lower than victims' average (five to ten).

distinguished from profits from sexual exploitation of slaves – at US$1 billion, and the corresponding profits at US$600 million.[4]

And yet, of the private law claims brought by victims of trafficking against traffickers,[5] very few resulted in victims being awarded full restitution of the profits made at their expense. Following the recognition by the Israeli National Labour Court in *Ben-Ami v M* that such a right exists, the Regional Labour Court in *Normatov* and *Tyumkin* and the District Court in *Lifshin* did award gross proceeds[6] and the High Court in *Dulghieru* did attempt (unsuccessfully, as explained below) to prevent the defendants' unjust enrichment at the claimants' expense. While I have criticised this failure elsewhere,[7] it should be noted that the possibility of using restitution law in order to claim full restitution of profits was not always fully pleaded in the trial courts in which these claims have been litigated.

Victims' entitlement to restitution of profits raises preliminary objections, a question of taxonomy, and three doctrinal and normative questions. One objection is that public policy militates against restitution, since the profit is made from prostitution and since, sometimes, the claimant is an illegal immigrant. This objection is rejected below. Another objection is based on an anti-commodification sentiment. Since the profit was made by a gross violation of an inalienable right to liberty and sexual autonomy, profits should not be subject to restitution. Otherwise, the argument goes, the law renders a non-alienable right alienable. This objection is rejected in chapter 5, section 5.3. Next is the question of classification. Is the claim based on restitution for wrongs, on unjust enrichment or on vindication of property? The analysis shows that sex trafficking is a manifestation of Birksian alternative analysis, under which the right for restitution could be based on either subtraction or wrong. My major point is that trafficking is an acquisitive wrong involving appropriation of value from the claimant, and not merely a wrong. This means both that the claim is mainly about vindication of property – the novelty of the analysis is in extending the notion of vindication of property to the exchange product of the victim's sexual services – and that enrichment at the expense of the claimant is manifested by interference with the claimant's property (which is not indisputably subtractive).

Within each prong of restitution, there is a need to examine whether the required elements are met. For example, in an unjust enrichment claim, what is the unjust factor? As the discussion below demonstrates, the fact that under English law a promise to pay for sexual services is unenforceable complicates the road for recovery. Another set of questions pertains to the measure of

4 S Kara, *Sex Trafficking: Inside the Business of Modern Slavery* (New York, NY: Columbia University Press, 2009) 19–21, 226, 233. See also n114.

5 See ch2, section 2.2.

6 All cases are cited in ch2, n23.

7 'Banalization'; 'Dulghieru' (both cited in ch1, n38).

recovery and problems of proof. The measure of recovery might change based on the relevant cause of action. In particular, one question which has to be answered is whether the trafficker would be ever allowed to deduct expenses from his obligation to make restitution. But the problem goes deeper than this. Obviously, given the reality of trafficking, victims would face serious problems of proof with respect to the profit made at their expense. How can and should a court respond to this problem? The final question is about election. Should the victim be allowed to accumulate compensation for being trafficked and restitution of profits?

At the outset, it will be worthwhile to reflect on the different ways in which the restitutionary claim by the victim against the trafficker could be conceptualised. Proceeds from sex trafficking are: (a) an exchange product (a 'substitute') of the victim's services or labour forced out of the victim which were either paid directly to the trafficker, or paid to the victim and taken by the trafficker; (b) the benefit derived from an unauthorised use of the victim's body; or (c) a benefit accruing to the trafficker from a third party from committing a wrong (battery) against the victim.[8] At a more theoretical level, the first conceptualisation highlights the nature of trafficking as an instance of modern slavery and forced labour, while the second highlights sex trafficking as a case of objectifying the victim and commodifying her body, a characteristic which is arguably unique to sexual slavery as opposed to other types of forced labour.

The first conceptualisation is straightforward. The client pays for the sexual services the CSP is forced to produce and this amount is taken by the trafficker. Alternatively, the profit is the result of the unauthorised use of the prostituted claimant. The CSP's body is the profit-generating property, and the proceeds of the sexual act stem from the use of that body. This second conceptualisation is supported by the findings discussed in chapter 5 that both traffickers and clients view forced CSPs as property. Lastly, the trafficker, by forcing the victim to have a series of sexual encounters with clients, commits a series of batteries against the claimant. These batteries, alongside the claimant's false imprisonment, produce profit for the trafficker in the form of the money paid by the clients.

Sections 3.1 to 3.3 establish respectively that the victim has a claim in vindication of property, unjust enrichment and restitution for wrongs. They conclude that the victim should be allowed to recover the higher of the actual proceeds made at her expense and the attributed gain from the trafficking activity; and that no deductions for expenses should be allowed. Section 3.4 explains why restitution should accumulate with tort damages.

8 In 'Dulghieru' id 92–3 I have suggested that there are at least seven ways to conceptualise victims' claims. But these could comfortably be reduced to the three mentioned in the text.

## 3.1 Vindication of property

### *3.1.1 Money paid by clients directly to the victim and taken by the trafficker*

Trafficking violates the victim's rights by both forcing her into prostitution and by taking from her the proceeds of the forced prostitution. At times the client pays the victim directly for the (forced) sexual service and the trafficker takes all, or most, of the money from the victim later on. At other times the client pays the trafficker directly for the sexual services.[9] Doubtless, money that was paid directly to the claimant and taken away by the trafficker gives rise to a proprietary claim. First, title in the money passed from the client to the victim; then the title remained with the victim when the money was taken by the trafficker.

#### *3.1.1.1 Title passing from client to victim*

Prostitution itself is legal in the UK and its profits are taxable.[10] Therefore, even if a client's obligation to pay money to a (non-forced) CSP is 'unenforceable as being *contra bonos mores*',[11] once the money was paid the CSP has title to the money.[12] It could be objected that the client paid the money to the CSP as an agent of her pimp so that his intention was that title would pass to the pimp. This is unconvincing for several reasons. For one thing, as a sociological observation, it is rather doubtful that the client intended to pay the pimp. If at all, in the reverse scenario in which the client pays the trafficker (or his agent) directly, it is more likely that the client pays with the intention that the title would pass to the CSP, so that the person receiving the money acts as the CSP's agent. Moreover, an intention to pay the pimp (even in cases which do not amount to trafficking) involves illegality, since pimping, but not prostitution itself, is illegal. Therefore, normatively, it is more appropriate, and more likely, that courts would construe the client's intention to act legally and pass title to the CSP, rather than to act in a manner which contributes to the commission of an offence (regardless of the question of whether clients are criminally responsible as accessories, if they intend to pay a pimp).

In the trafficking context, the client either knows the CSP is trafficked or does not. If he *does not know*, his intention to pay the pimp is based on a mistake which should prevent the trafficker from getting title to the money (this is clearly so when the money is paid directly to the claimant). Almost all clients,

9 While (at least in Israel) both methods exist, the former is more prevalent. See e.g. SCrimC (Be'er She'va) 959/04 *State v Normatov*, Tak-Meh 2006(3) 11134 (2006), [25], [161].

10 *Inland Revenue Commissioners v Aken* [1990] 1 WLR 1374, 1383 (Parker LJ); *Commissioners of Customs and Excise v Polok* [2002] 2 CMLR 4, [14].

11 *Aken*, id.

12 Cf *Lipkin Gorman v Karpnale Ltd* [1991] 2 AC 548 (HL).

if asked, 'this woman is trafficked; would you like to pay her, or her trafficker?' would answer 'the woman'. The research about clients' attitudes towards prostitution and trafficking surveyed in chapter 8 might support such a conclusion. Moreover, as the discussion below demonstrates, if the money paid by clients is the exchange product of services owned by the claimant, the intention to pay a third party mistakenly perceived to be the owner of such services should and does not matter. If the client *knows* that the claimant is trafficked, then an intention to pay the trafficker involves serious illegality and it is hard to see why such intention should be dispositive. The fallacy behind the agency argument is that it assumes that in the absence of agreement between the victim and the trafficker, the default position is that the trafficker is the owner of what is paid as consideration for the services provided, so the claimant should be limited to sue the trafficker for reimbursement reflecting her contribution to the creation of this profit. As I demonstrate below, the claimant owns the value of her labour (and less crucially for current purposes, the trafficker's claim for allowance should obviously be rejected).

#### *3.1.1.2 Title remains with the victim*

The money paid by clients was taken by the trafficker in circumstances where the claimant could not prevent the transfer (powerlessness)[13] or at the very least, where the claimant was under extreme duress, which prevents the transfer of title.[14] When the pressure operating on the claimant was very intense, no legal consequences followed from the victim's apparent consent.[15] In *Lynch v DPP for Northern Ireland* the House of Lords dealt in *obiter* with contractual duress.[16] In general, the effect of duress is to render the contract merely voidable. However, *obiter* in consecutive cases clarifies that extreme cases of duress can render the transaction void.[17] Indeed, in cases in which extreme pressure – such as threats to life or to physical integrity – was applied, the contract was void[18] so that in one case the taking of property under the void

13 Those accepting ignorance as an unjust factor in unjust enrichment claims equally accept powerlessness, since both situations involve misappropriation which the claimant cannot prevent. Those rejecting ignorance as an unjust factor will view both events as yielding vindication of property cause of action. See Virgo (ch1, n5) 131–32.

14 *Friedeberg-Seeley v Klass* (1957) 101 SJ 275; *Duke de Cadaval v Collins* (1836) 111 ER 1006, 1009 (money paid to get rid of pressure created by false imprisonment according to a fraudulent arrest); *Grainger v Hill* (1838) 132 ER 769. Cf *Barton v Amstrong* [1976] AC 104, 120 (PC); *Pao On v Lau Yiu Long* [1980] AC 614, 634–5.

15 Cf D Friedmann, 'The objective principle and mistake and involuntariness in contract and restitution', (2003) 119 *LQR* 74, 82.

16 [1975] AC 653, 680, 695.

17 See *Pao* (n14). Cf A Guest, *Chitty on Contracts*, Vol 1, 27th edn (London: Sweet & Maxwell, 1994) 7-003; however, the scope of *a void transaction* allowed for by Chitty is normatively too narrow and doctrinally not supported by the authorities.

18 *Barton* (n14). Some commentators stress that the point was not argued before the Privy Council and that the result is as compatible with the contract being voidable as with it

contract amounted to trespass to goods.[19] We should not confuse the relationship between a pimp and a non-forced CSP with the relationship between a trafficker and a victim. The former relationship might involve a voluntary agreement between the two about the way in which the profits will be split between them. The gist of trafficking, however, is that the trafficker solely decides how much, if any at all, to leave in the victim's hands, and he usually pockets all the profit. Since the victim does not consent to the money being taken (in whole or in part) by the trafficker, she retains title to the money.

The four claimants in *AT v Dulgheiru* were forced into prostitution by their traffickers who 'took firm control of the claimants by means of coercion'; the victims' 'upset, distress and reluctance was made all too plain, but was cruelly and harshly overridden by the perverted greed of their captors who sought only to use them as instruments for their own profit'. 'None of them saw any of the money they had generated'.[20] This horrid experience is unfortunately typical. According to one UK study, 77 per cent of the victims interviewed

> were adamant that they were "never" free to do as they wished. . . . Few women were free to choose what happened to their bodies, how or when it happened, or by whom. Few were allowed to decide when or what they ate, when they slept, went to the toilet, or rested . . . the abuse and control tactics employed by those perpetrating or participating in their captivity were all-encompassing and affected nearly every aspect of their sleeping and waking moments.[21]

According to another UK report,

> Most of the women who worked in the sex industry were forced to work long shifts seven days a week, many seeing more than twenty clients every day . . . Women were also pressured or forced to perform unsafe sexual activities . . . Often the rationale for this was . . . [to] allow women to pay off their "debts" more quickly. However, for most women, this "debt" did not diminish rapidly, if at all, as women were charged rent for where they lived and worked (sometimes the same place); charged for food they ate; clothing and personal items bought; travel costs and so on. These charges were always disproportionately high compared to real costs.

being void. See e.g. B Haecker, 'Proprietary restitution after impaired consent transfers: a generalised power model', (2009) 68 *Camb LJ* 324, 327.

19 *Friedeberg-Seeley* (n14). Cf *Duke de Cadaval* (n14).

20 *Dulghieru* (n1) [6], [9], [74].

21 C Zimmerman, M Hossain, K Yun, B Roche, L Morison and C Watts, *Stolen Smiles: The Physical and Psychological Health Consequences of Women and Adolescents Trafficked in Europe* (London: London School of Hygiene & Tropical Medicine, 2006) 37, 40, available at http://genderviolence.lshtm.ac.uk/files/Stolen-Smiles-Trafficking-and-Health-2006.pdf (accessed 7 August 2010).

> 77% of the women we have worked with have been beaten, often with objects . . . women disclosed being escorted and having their movements controlled, including being locked in properties; had passport or immigration paperwork removed; told they had to work to pay off "debts"; received verbal abuse and/or threats to themselves; and were threatened with reprisals against their families.[22]

Similar experiences were documented in other studies, in the UK and abroad and in case law.[23]

To be sure, the experiences of victims, the measures of coercion directed at them and the extent to which they feel deprived of choice all vary. For example, a recent analysis of the *IOM Trafficking Database* made by Bettio and Nandi examined the extent of violation of five rights (absence of abuse, freedom to choose services, ability to use condoms, freedom of movement, access to medical care) on a severity scale ranging from negligible to intermediate to severe: 32.5 per cent reported physical/sexual assault and psychological abuse (while 17.5 per cent reported no abuse at all and 50 per cent minor abuse); 89 per cent reported having no choice over sexual services to be performed; 8.5 per cent were never allowed to use condoms (while 53 per cent were always or regularly allowed); 56.5 per cent could not leave the premises at all (while 37 per cent could move only when accompanied); 59% had medical care totally denied (and 24.5 per cent had regular or occasional access). When the right to choose services is left aside, 2 per cent (n = 1,737) reported severe violation of all four remaining rights, 14 per cent of three of them, 38 per cent of two of them, 28 per cent of one of them, 17 per cent no severe violation of any right and 1 per cent no violation at all.[24]

Similar findings about the varied experience of victims exist in other research.[25] But this should not obfuscate the fact that the typical experience of victims – indeed what separates them from other CSPs – is exactly the

22 S Dickson, *When Women are Trafficked: Quantifying the Gendered Experience of Trafficking in the UK* (London: Poppy, 2004) 5–6.

23 Stephen-Smith (ch2, n1) 17–18, 22–3; Levenkron and Dahan (ch1, n13) 26–31; *R v Pacan* [2009] EWCA Crim 2436, [4], [6]; *R v Kizlaite* [2006] EWCA Crim 1492, [7]–[9]; *R v Maka* [2005] EWCA Crim 3365, [3]–[5]; Home Office, *UK Action Plan on Tackling Human Trafficking* (London: Home Office, 2007) 14–15; BS (Haifa) 4891/00 *State v Rabi'ee* (1 January 2001); SCrC (Tel-Aviv) 1210/01 *State v Yosef* (15 January 2003); CrA (Tel-Aviv) 1123/03 *State v Lifshin* (29 January 2004), [2]; *Lifshin*; *Tyumkin; M v Salsrevski*, [6]–[49]; *K v Jaack*, [2]; *Kuchick*, [2] (all cited in ch2, n23).

24 Bettio and Nandi (ch1, n24), 21–2, 26.

25 Hoyle *et al.* (ch1, n23); Jackson *et al.* (ch1, n47); Aronowitz *et al.* (ch1, n15); *UK Action Plan* (n23). Significant variance exists also with respect to the duration of trafficking. Kara (n4) at 221–2 estimates average duration of sexual enslavement ranging between 2.5 and 3.3 years (depending on the region) and mentions that 'in reality, the range in each region varies from a few months to a decade or more'. The reported cases in Israel and England covered in this chapter suggest a much shorter period of a few months.

absence of control over their working conditions, exit and the share of the profits they retain. While the study of Hoyle *et al.* shows that some women were willing to, or chose to, become illegal immigrants, and others knew they would work in prostitution, almost without exception they did not know they would have no control over their working conditions and the possibility of exit.[26] Even if these women 'cannot be dismissed as helpless victims who have no agency' (but likewise 'cannot be seen as authors of their own destiny') the coercion operated against them makes any transfer of value from them to their traffickers void. It would also be a mistake to isolate each measure of pressure and examine whether it is alone sufficient to void the claimant's consent. The combination of threats, physical violence, the creation of emotional dependency, curtailment of movements, tactics of alienation (such as frequent moves between venues to increase disorientation and curtail social networks) and exploitation of vulnerable immigration status would together *typically* render the consent void. But even if one disagrees with this conclusion there are still three things to bear in mind. First, even if what is documented above reflects only the extreme side of victims' experience (rather than the typical experience) the analysis offered here still applies to these individuals. Second, few would dispute that the typical pressures operating on victims would qualify as duress, which makes the transaction voidable and therefore should allow victims to sue traffickers successfully in unjust enrichment (and based on restitution for wrongs). Lastly, as explained in chapter 1, CSPs who do not perceive themselves as victims (even if they are so defined by governmental and international definitions) will not sue.

#### *3.1.1.3 No victim's illegality defence*

Obviously, a trafficker's illegality defence against the victim's restitutionary claim is doomed to fail.[27] Prostitution itself is legal, and the illegality involved in forcing the victim into prostitution, and in any prostitution-related offence is the trafficker's responsibility, not his victim's. The only conceivable ground to bar restitution is based on the alleged claimant's illegal involvement in violating immigration law. But this claim should fail as well. The simplest reason – and the one most pertinent to the proprietary nature of her claim – is that even if the victim were implicated with illegality, she does not rely on it in vindicating her property rights; therefore her claim would not be barred.[28] Similarly, the equitable doctrine of unclean hands would not bar vindication

26 Hoyle *et al.*, id, 320–3.

27 Indeed, Israeli courts rejected this claim in the seminal cases. *Salsrevski* (n23) [103]–[109]; *K* (n23) [11].

28 *Tinsley v Milligan* [1994] 1 AC 340. Virgo (n13) 727 goes further in suggesting that a claimant can rely on an illegal transaction to vindicate property rights as long as the illegality is not particularly serious.

of an equitable proprietary right.[29] But the claim should also fail for reasons which are applicable more broadly to *in personam* restitution claims:

(a) In many trafficking cases the victim does not voluntarily cross borders illegally – namely, either the victim entered legally (or does not enter at all but is trafficked domestically) or she enters without criminal intent to enter illegally, or is forced to enter illegally.[30] For this reason the *Dulghieru* Court erred in its implicit assumption that the defendants were not responsible for the 6-week period one claimant (ML) was detained by the authorities on arrival to England before she escaped (and was immediately recaptured by the defendants' associates); this assumption led to a lower award of damages for non-pecuniary loss.[31] One might have thought that this is explicable on the basis of the principle subsequently affirmed by the House of Lords in *Gray v Thames Trains Ltd*, which prohibits 'sanction shifting' – namely, that the criminal sanction imposed on the claimant in the criminal process would be shifted by means of tort liability to the defendant.[32] Whatever the merits of the reasoning in *Gray* are, sanction shifting should be permitted in this case for two reasons. First, Gray did commit an offence for which he was incarcerated. By contrast, ML's detention was not the result of a criminal conviction. Moreover, had ML's identity as a victim of trafficking been known to the authorities, she should not have been detained.[33] Second, it was the story that the defendants instructed the claimant to tell the authorities that led directly to her arrest. ML was compelled to tell the story and therefore the violation of immigration rules was not her 'own voluntary and deliberate act'.[34] Since the perceived reason to detain ML (her story) was the result of duress, and her real status as a victim of trafficking who is also an illegal immigrant should not trigger detention (and was itself the result of duress), sanction shifting is justified. Moreover, it is obviously wrong to allow a trafficker to raise a defence that relates to illegality that he was instrumental in perpetrating.
(b) The claimant's involvement in violating immigration law is too insignificant or collateral to her restitutionary claim to trigger the *ex turpi*

29 *Tinsley*, id; *Virgo*, id, 725.
30 In *Astley v Reynolds* (1731) 93 ER 939 a restitutionary claim based on compulsion was allowed where the claimant was tainted with illegality.
31 *Dulghieru* (n1) [39].
32 [2009] UKHL 33, [2009] 3 WLR 167. See J Goudkamp, 'The defence of illegality: *Gray v Thames Trains Ltd*', (2009) 17 *TLJ* 205, 208.
33 The Home Office's *Detained Fast Track Processes Guidelines*, available at www.bia.homeoffice.gov.uk/sitecontent/documents/policyandlaw/asylumprocessguidance/detention/guidance/detained_fast_processes?view=Binary (accessed 1 January 2013) ('Home Office Guidelines'), exempts victims of trafficking from immigration-status related detention.
34 *Gray* (n32) [27]–[29].

defence.[35] At the heart of the dispute between the trafficker and his victim are the enslavement and the misappropriation of her money. These have nothing to do with the illegal entry, except that the victim's illegal status increases her vulnerability and the opportunity for exploitation by the trafficker. Moreover, strictly speaking, when the client pays the victim directly, the restitution claim is not even based on forcing the victim into labour (when labour is arguably – and by a big stretch – connected to the claimant's illegal entry to the country for labour purposes). Rather, it is based on taking the victim's money. Even if the trafficker had not forced the claimant into prostitution but had taken the proceeds without her consent, the claimant could have vindicated her property in the money. A contrary conclusion should equally allow the use of the defence against any acquisitive (or indeed any other) wrong committed against illegal immigrants.

(c) The parties are not *in pari delicto*; not even with respect to the violation of immigration law; and obviously not when the overall behaviour of the trafficker and victim are compared.[36] The victim's motivation in entering illegally is often to overcome dire financial need; for this she typically seeks employment which is lawful in itself although she is willing to enter and remain in the country of destination illegally. The trafficker's motivation is to break immigration law in order to commit further serious crimes and to enslave, batter and exploit the claimant.

(d) Barring the victim's claim against the trafficker on grounds of her illegal entry to the country does a disservice to the policy behind the prohibition of illegal entry, since traffickers are more informed than victims (and therefore are more likely to be deterred). If illegal immigrants are denied restitution, employing them becomes more profitable to employers; this is detrimental to domestic low-paid employees whose protection is a major justification for immigration laws.[37] This rationale – which applies to claims by non-forced illegal immigrants – is relevant in the trafficking context as well: not only trafficked women but also other CSPs are worse off because of the trafficking phenomenon (due to race-to-the-bottom market pressures[38]).

35 *Hewison v Meridian Shipping Pte Ltd* [2002] EWCA Civ 1821, [43]. One indication for the correctness of this conclusion is the Home Office Guidelines (n33).

36 *Astley* (n30) (compulsion makes the parties not *in pari delicto*); *Archbolds (Freightage) Ltd v Spanglet Ltd* [1961] QB 374; Virgo (n13) 724 (highlighting the relevance of the relative blameworthiness of the parties), 727.

37 However, if this were the only justification against barring the claim, a still better solution might be to deny restitution and confiscate the money to the state. But this also depends on whether private or public enforcement is more effective.

38 See e.g. B Anderson and J O'Connell Davidson, *Trafficking – A Demand Led Problem?* (Stockholm: Save the Children Sweden, 2002) 31.

### *3.1.2 Money paid directly from the client to the trafficker*

So far it has been suggested that when the money is paid to the victim by the client and taken by the trafficker, the victim can vindicate her property right in the money by a restitutionary claim against the trafficker. Seemingly, a different conclusion is warranted with respect to money paid by the client directly to the trafficker. Since it appears that the claimant has only a personal claim against the client for the interaction between them (the payment for the sexual service and any damages based on battery or alternative torts) and the amount was intercepted by the trafficker, the victim has (if anything, depending on the scope of the interceptive subtraction doctrine) only a personal claim against the trafficker for restitution. However, a different conclusion is warranted.[39] Recall that the proceeds from forced prostitution could be conceptualised as: (a) the substitute for services or labour; or (b) the benefit from unauthorised use (or fruit) of the victim's body. Under either alternative, the non-consensual transfer of the benefit could yield a restitutionary claim that vindicates the claimant's right to her property.

#### *3.1.2.1 Substitute for services*

The best way to conceptualise the proceeds from forced prostitution is as a substitute for the claimant's services or labour. What in fact happens is that the trafficker forces the claimant to produce labour and services, sells them to the client and pockets the consideration. The proceeds, therefore, are the exchange product of something owned by the claimant, and misappropriated by the trafficker. Doubtless, if the trafficker had taken the claimant's car under circumstances of powerlessness or extreme duress and sold it to a third party, the claimant would have been able to trace the proceeds and vindicate her property right. It is submitted that the same is true with respect to services and labour the claimant was forced to produce and to sell to the client. Clearly, there is scant authority in support of this proposition. This is hardly surprising; circumstances in which slave labour gives rise to private law claims are rare. It is time then to develop the appropriate response based on sound policy considerations and first principles.

Seemingly, there are two distinctions between property and services which lead to no end-product that could support a proprietary right with respect to property alienated without the owner's consent while denying such a right

39 An alternative mode of analysis which might lead to the same conclusion reached in the text is based on the assumption that the client intended to pay the claimant and viewed the trafficker as the victim's agent. See pp 39–40. The trafficker's status as arguably a fiduciary (discussed in ch 4) is also relevant.

with respect to services.[40] One is the problem of subjective devaluation. Property received by the defendant augments his assets, the same is not true of services. However, for the trafficker such concern is irrelevant since the amount paid by the client in consideration for the claimant's sexual services does augment the trafficker's assets. The other distinction is that services and labour are usually given voluntarily while there is more scope for property being taken away without the owner's consent. A proprietary base of a claim (and often a proprietary remedy) is more often acknowledged where the asset in question was taken without the owner's consent.[41] In the trafficking context, the victim is first forced to produce value which is then taken away involuntarily by the trafficker. It follows, then, that at least with respect to the trafficker, the victim can trace the proceeds of prostitution as a substitute for the labour the claimant was forced to produce and sell to clients. Similar suggestions to ground restitution in constructive trusts have been made in the context of reparations for slave labour in which the claimants' claim was dismissed on grounds which are irrelevant for current purposes.[42]

The existence of a proprietary base for the purposes of tracing a substitute for the claimant's personal right against a third party is well established in circumstances which do not involve labour, as long as the thing taken (in that context, the value of the chose in action against the third party) was taken without the claimant's consent. In *Lipkin Gorman v Karpnale Ltd*[43] the claimant's firm was merely an unsecured creditor of the bank with respect to the account from which the partner withdrew the money. Nonetheless, the claim to the money drawn, which is the substitute for the personal right against the bank misappropriated by the partner, is based on a property right.[44] Similarly, even if the victim's restitutionary claim against the client

40 Indeed in general, the scope of restitution for services is narrower than for property See e.g. D Friedmann, 'Restitution for wrongs: the measure of recovery', (2001) 79 *Tex LR* 1879, 1906.

41 But a constructive trust is sometimes imposed, in the context of cohabitation, on property acquired, preserved, maintained or improved by the claimant's services, even though these services were rendered voluntarily (but not gratuitously). See e.g. *Peter v Beblow* [1993] 1 SCR 980 (Can).

42 V Verdun, 'If the shoe fits, wear it: an analysis of reparations to African Americans', (1993) 67 *Tul LR* 597, 608; M Armstrong, 'Reparations litigation: what about unjust enrichment?', (2002) 81 *Or LR* 771, 789–91. In *Re African-Am Slave Descendants Litig*, 375 F Supp 2d 721 (ND Ill, 2005) the claimants sought (at 737) 'accounting, disgorgement of profits, . . . a constructive trust, restitution, and compensatory and punitive damages'. The claims were dismissed based *inter alia* on lack of standing, limitation and the political question doctrine.

43 *Lipkin* (n12).

44 See L Smith, *The Law of Tracing* (Oxford: Clarendon Press, 1997) 363–5, who analyses according to similar lines also *Lord Napier and Ettrick v Hunter* [1993] AC 713 (HL); and Virgo (n13) 570. Note, however, that analysing *Lipkin* as having a proprietary base is contested. C Rotherham, *Proprietary Remedies in Context: A Study in the Judicial Redistribution of Property Rights* (Oxford: Hart Publishing, 2002) 98. But even if this view is accepted,

is merely personal, the claim against the trafficker for the exchange product of the stolen labour should be treated as having a proprietary base.

### *3.1.2.2 Unauthorised use of the claimant's body*

An alternative way to conceptualise the proceeds from forced prostitution is as a benefit derived from the unauthorised use of the victim's body. According to such understanding, the trafficker has made a profit by making an unauthorised use of the claimant's property – her body. I defend in chapter 5 the conceptualisation of a victim of sex trafficking as subject and object at the same time and will not repeat the argument here.[45] In essence, since the quintessential experience of sex trafficking is the treatment of victims as chattels, it is only just to give victims the option to sue as if they were chattels and give them the elaborate protection afforded by the common law and equity to the owners of property against interference from third parties. Even if one disputes the appropriateness of such response against clients, who will not necessarily be aware of the victim's objectification by traffickers and do not objectify victims themselves (although many would), surely such a response is appropriate against traffickers who sell and buy victims as a matter of course, who 'sought only to use [victims] as instruments for their own profit'[46] and who subjected the victim 'to an examination which could only be compared to one done to an animal sold in the market'.[47]

As explained in section 3.3, the unauthorised use of one's property can lead to liability based on restitution for wrongs for either fair market value (the user principle) or disgorgement of actual profits derived from the use. But these remedies are usually thought to be personal. For current purposes, however, (and this will become clearer in the context of chapter 4's analysis of restitution claims against the state) the crucial point is not whether the remedy is proprietary but whether the claim is based on property. There are some suggestions in the literature that disgorgement of profits made from the unauthorised use of one's property are based not on restitution for wrongs, but rather on the vindication of property right with respect to benefits derived from the property. An explicit suggestion to this effect is offered by Ross Grantham and Charles Rickett,[48] regarding the disgorgement of profits in the

*Lipkin* still supports a restitutionary claim against a third party who received the benefit and can show no relevant defence. This is relevant for the victim's claim against the state, which is analysed in Chapter 4.

45 In particular, I defend this account against the formalist charge that one cannot own one's body.

46 *Dulghieru* (n1) [9].

47 *Rabi'ee* (n23).

48 R Grantham and C Rickett, 'Disgorgement for unjust enrichment?', (2003) 62 *CLJ* 159, 161.

famous Kentucky cave case of *Edwards v Lee's Administrator*.[49] Similarly, Peter Birks views the cause of action in *Edwards* as based on profit made at the expense of the claimant in the sense of interference with her property (as distinct from subtraction and wrong).[50] His analysis of *Trustee of FC Jones (a firm) v Jones*[51] is also based on the existence of a proprietary right with respect to the fruits of using one's property.[52]

Lionel Smith, too, has suggested that money generated from the unauthorised use of one's property is a traceable product of part of the original interest.[53] Smith distinguishes use value, which is based on alienation of part of the owner's right for consideration, from fruits, where the thing generating them is not itself diminished in any way. Since the owner of the thing generating the fruit has an undeniable proprietary right in the fruits[54] the correct classification of the victim with respect to the proceeds of prostitution is not crucial. A proprietary base is established whether the proceeds are seen as fruits or as use value. Moreover, since the victim's bodily integrity and dominion over her body is diminished by the sexual transaction, the unauthorised use conceptualisation is ultimately more accurate. This is supported by a popular – or at least common sense – understanding of prostitution in which the CSP (despite the colloquial use of the term 'selling her body') allows the client a temporary use of her body. While Daniel Friedmann does not make an explicit reference to the proprietary base of a claim based on unauthorised use, he mentions that unauthorised use could be analogised with unauthorised sale of the claimant's property,[55] in which the claim is clearly based on vindication of property.

### *3.1.3 Proceeds from selling the victim from one trafficker to another*

It is a common practice in the trafficking industry to sell the victim from one trafficker to another, in order to: (a) respond to clients' demand for 'fresh meat'; (b) disconnect women from the supportive ties that they have built up among themselves, thereby increasing their dependence on the traffickers; and (c) keep the victim eternally indebted to the new owner to cover the costs of

49 96 Sw 2d 1028 (1936).

50 P Birks, *Unjust Enrichment*, 2nd edn (Oxford: Oxford University Press, 2005) 84–5.

51 [1997] Ch 159 ('Jones').

52 P Birks, 'At the expense of the claimant: direct and indirect enrichment in English law', in D Johnston and R Zimmerman (eds), *Unjustified Enrichment: Key Issues in Comparative Perspective* (Cambridge: Cambridge University Press, 2001) 493, 510. While Birks (n50) classifies *Edwards* and *Jones* as unjust enrichment cases (at 82–6), for him a proprietary remedy is a possible response to unjust enrichment (at 32–8).

53 Smith (n44) 22.

54 *Tucker v Farm and General Investment Trust Ltd* [1966] 2 QB 421 (CA).

55 Friedmann (n40) 1892.

her purchase.[56] In Israel, one victim of trafficking who sued her traffickers in labour courts claimed the proceeds of such sale, but the case was dismissed without prejudice based on lack of jurisdiction.[57] The victim should have a right to restitution of these proceeds and this too could be viewed as vindication of property. Once the claimant is conceptualised as both subject and object – as the rightful owner of her body, which is the property – the proceeds from the claimant's sale are the substitute for her property taken away and sold without her consent. Since the victim's right not to be enslaved is inalienable, the victim should be allowed to accumulate the amounts paid from her sale from several sellers to buyers. This is an exception to the usual rule (applicable to both conversion and vindication of property by tracing or following), under which the title to the chattel passes to the defendant against the payment of damages.[58] Alternatively, the right for cumulative recovery could be supported on retributive and deterrence grounds of not profiting from one's serious wrongdoing.

## 3.2 Unjust enrichment

The three elements of an unjust enrichment claim are enrichment, at the expense of the claimant, which is unjust. Enrichment, in the form of money received by the trafficker, is easily established in the context of sex trafficking. An unjust factor is equally easily established. 'Unjust' generally refers to the intention behind the transfer being vitiated or qualified. According to the definition used in this book, trafficking involves the coercion of the CSP to remain in prostitution;[59] for this reason duress is necessarily established.[60]

For purposes of establishing the third element, at the expense of the claimant, it does not matter whether the money was paid directly to the victim and then taken away from her, or whether the client paid the trafficker directly. The trafficker coerces the victim both to *produce* the profit by providing sexual

56 Levenkron and Dahan (n23) 24–6, 28; Kara (n4) 19.

57 *Salsrevski* (n23) [137]–[139]. The victim was sold four times for US$6,500, US$3,000, US$4,000 and US$4,000. See [15], [17], [25], [34].

58 *USA v Dollfus Mieg et Cie SA* [1952] AC 582 (HL); *Restatement (Second) of Torts*, § 222A Comment (c) (ch2, n53) (conversion); *Foskett v McKeown* [2001] 1 AC 102 (tracing).

59 See Chapters 1 and 9 which explain away the possibility of consenting victims suing in torts and restitution.

60 For duress as a ground for restitution, see pp 40–1. Since duress is so clearly established in the trafficking context, there is no need to examine in detail whether other unjust factors (such as mistake and total failure of consideration) could be established. Possibly, the mistake about the conditions at the site of exploitation is another independent ground for restitution, especially since this mistake was induced by fraud and misrepresentation, which are classic vitiating factors. *Moses v Macferlan* (1760) 97 ER 676, 681; *Edgington v Fitzmaurice* (1885) 29 ChD 459 (misrepresentation).

services and to *hand over* the profit to him. We saw earlier, that when the client pays the victim directly, and the money is taken by the trafficker, the victim retains title to the money, and therefore her claim is based on vindication of property. But even if one disputes the conclusion that the coercion renders the transfer void, the duress makes it voidable, so it allows the victim to sue in unjust enrichment for restitution.

When the money was paid directly from the client to the trafficker, an unjust enrichment claim could seemingly be based on the trafficker's enrichment, which is unjust, since the benefit was accrued in his hands as a result of extreme duress, and was at the claimant's expense since it is the consideration for the claimant's services. But in order to establish that the enrichment was at the claimant's expense, one needs to surpass the difficulty of interceptive subtraction. Interceptive subtractions involve a defendant (in our case the trafficker) who intercepted an amount owed by the third party debtor to the claimant creditor.[61] Since the claimant (in our case the victim) did not have title to the money, arguably the trafficker's enrichment is not at her expense, but rather at the client's expense, and the claimant can only (if at all) sue the client who paid his debt to the claimant to the wrong person. The relevant questions which need to be examined are: (a) whether factual necessity that, but for the interception, the amount would have been received by the claimant is sufficient to establish that the defendant's enrichment was at the claimant's expense, or rather the third party (the client) needs to have a legal obligation towards the claimant;[62] (b) if the latter, whether the client's obligation to pay for the sexual services is unenforceable on grounds of public policy; and (c) if the obligation is enforceable, whether the receipt of the money by the defendant trafficker discharges the client's debt to the claimant.[63]

If the test for the right for restitution in cases of interceptive subtraction is one of factual necessity, there is no doubt that the enrichment is at the claimant's expense. Even if the client is under no obligation to pay for the sexual service received on grounds of public policy, the payment was in fact made (to the trafficker), so it would have been received by the claimant but for the trafficker intercepting this amount. There is much to be said for adopting a factual necessity as a sufficient condition for recovery.[64] If the third party intended to confer a benefit on the claimant, even though he is under no obligation to do so, why should the defendant be allowed to intercept such benefit when neither the third party nor the claimant intended to enrich the

61 For the reasons given on pp 39–40, the client should be assumed to intend the claimant as the payee, rather than the trafficker.

62 See Virgo (n13) 109–10.

63 Virgo id, 109; L Smith 'Three-party restitution: a critique of Birks's theory of *interceptive* subtraction' (1991) 11 *OJLS* 481, 488.

64 Birks (n50) 76.

defendant? The fact that in most cases the third party would be able to sue the defendant to reverse the transaction is not a sufficient answer. The third party should have priority over the claimant if both sue the defendant for restitution of the benefit intercepted by him (as long as in the relationship between the third party and the claimant the former is at liberty to change his mind and withhold the benefit from the claimant). But this priority does not necessitate a rule depriving the claimant from having a subordinate right to sue the defendant.

If, however, English law indeed adopted the rule that the benefit intercepted needs to stem from a valid obligation owed by the third party to the claimant[65] there is a need to inquire whether the claimant's claim against the client for the value of her sexual services is unenforceable since it is immoral. If the victim's claim against the client is unenforceable, then the trafficker's enrichment in receiving the payment from the client is – legally speaking and however odd this might seem to be – not at the victim's expense. Even if claims by non-forced CSPs would be considered as unenforceable, still a different conclusion is warranted with respect to a claim by a *forced* CSP against a client. Since the victim was forced into prostitution, and, therefore, to the particular transaction, while the client participated in it voluntarily, it is a one party unlawfulness, so the victim (but not the client) can sue to enforce the promise or for the value of her services.[66] The client, on the other hand, is a willing participant to the transaction so the victim could view the obligation to pay as binding on the client while any claim he might have otherwise had against the claimant is barred due to his involvement in the immoral transaction.

On the view (explained in chapter 5) that the extreme duress on the part of the trafficker renders the agreement between the victim and the client void, the client's obligation to pay for the service is not based on contract, which is void due to lack of the victim's consent, but rather on *quantum meruit*: the market value of the services the client received (which in many cases would equal what was promised, a point further explored in section 3.3). But in either view, the willingly participating client cannot be heard in arguing that his obligation to pay is not enforceable based on public policy. Obviously, it is not in the mouth of the trafficker to make such a claim when he is sued by the claimant for restitution.

Nor is a different conclusion warranted with respect to victims who intended to work in prostitution. The push and pull factors operating in this context still justify a conclusion that the victim and the client are not *in pari delicto*. Indeed, chapters 6 to 8 highlight this point by focusing on the contribution clients make to the trafficking of victims by creating demand

65 This is Virgo's conclusion (n13) 110, based on *Official Custodian for Charities v Mackey (No 2)* [1985] 1 WLR 1308, 1314 (Ch).

66 See n36. This unassailable conclusion has lately received a further support by virtue of the criminalisation of buying (but obviously not selling) sex from a forced CSP. See ch1, n43.

for commercial sexual services, which should arguably be considered as negligent. Moreover, once the victim is denied exit and control over the sexual services rendered – recall the finding that 89 per cent of victims had *no* such control – the conclusion that the parties are not *in pari delicto* is inescapable.

More fundamentally, one could seriously doubt the common wisdom according to which the claim by a non-forced CSP against the client is unenforceable based on public policy. Interestingly, there is no *direct* authority for such proposition. The existing dated authorities are either of claims of mistresses involving long-term relationships[67] or ancillary claims arising out of contracts between CSPs and those who provided them with services.[68] More importantly, public policy changes with time; the unenforceability of prostitution-related contracts is a sub-set of Victorian morality condemning extra-marital sexual relationships. Since the broader category underwent a considerable change (so that, for example, cohabitation agreements are not contrary to public policy[69]), it is not out of the question that a modern court would not view a claim of a CSP against a client as unenforceable. Indeed, at least one case dealing with claims arising against the backdrop of prostitution could be interpreted as rejecting the view that prostitution-based claims are unenforceable.[70] Moreover, the recent *Mosley v NGN*[71] decision in which the client's interest in privacy was recognised in the context of a party involving CSPs provides another indirect (and weak) indication that prostitution-related contracts are not necessarily unenforceable any more. If there is no public interest in reporting the purchase of sex, could there be public interest in denying a claim for payment of the service rendered?

One cannot decide whether public policy still requires a conclusion that the claim by a CSP against a client is unenforceable without identifying the policy against the transaction, or the institution of prostitution. Was such a policy based on the general condemnation of extra-marital sexual relationships? If so, given the change of mores on this point surely the CSP's claim should be allowed.[72] Is the policy based (today, presumably, not historically) on the understanding that even CSPs who are not forced are nevertheless exploited?

67 E.g. *Franco v Bolton* (1797) 3 Ves 368.

68 Most notably *Pearce v Brooks* (1866) LR 1; see Guest (n17) 16-060; Edwin Peel, *Treitel on The Law of Contracts*, 13th edn (London: Sweet & Maxwell, 2011) 490–2.

69 E.g. *Tanner v Tanner* [1975] 1 WLR 1346; Guest, id, 808–9.

70 *Polok* (n10) [14] (owners of escort businesses are under obligation to pay VAT; prostitution, as such, is lawful). Cf *Sutton v Hutchinson* [2005] EWCA Civ 1773 (Civ D); *Sutton v Mishcon De Reya and Gawor & Co* [2003] EWHC 3166 (Ch).

71 [2008] EWHC 1777 (QB) (Eady J). Cf the same Judge's reasoning in *CC v AB* [2006] EWHC 3083 (QB), [25]–[28] that there is no consensus in contemporary society about the reprehensible nature of adultery.

72 In the (factually unlikely) scenario in which the client paid in advance and the CSP refuses to provide the service, no doubt specific performance will be denied since the promise is for personal service. Whether restitution of what was paid by the client should be allowed

But then again, if this is the rationale, surely a CSP who provided the service but was not paid should have a claim against the client. Is the policy based on the idea that paying for sexual services is bad in itself? If so, why?[73]

More generally, the traditional common law approach to illegality is unattractive. The no-restitution rule fails to balance adequately between public policy considerations of deterrence and retribution, and the need to do justice between the two parties to the litigation (even though both of them are tainted with illegality). In the context of prostitution, a result according to which a CSP, who provided (even willingly) sexual services and did not receive consideration contrary to expectation or promise, cannot sue the client is manifestly unfair.

Since the victim's claim against the client is enforceable (whatever one concludes about the claim of a non-forced CSP), common wisdom would hinge her unjust enrichment claim against the trafficker on the obligation being discharged by the payment to the trafficker.[74] Under the assumption that the obligation is *not* discharged (since the claimant did not have the intention that the payment to the trafficker would discharge the obligation[75]) conventional wisdom would lead to a conclusion that the claimant cannot sue the trafficker, since she can sue the client and therefore the trafficker is not enriched at her expense.

To those accepting the analysis above that the victim can vindicate her property with respect to the amount paid by clients to traffickers, not much hinges on this conclusion. As the trafficking context demonstrates, however, limiting the claimant's cause of action to situations in which the third party's obligation is discharged is undesirable. Granted, the transaction between the third party and the defendant should not enforce a new debtor on the claimant. In particular, in the trafficking context, a victim who prefers to sue the client for restitution should not be forced to sue only the trafficker, based on the argument that the client discharged his debt to the victim by paying the trafficker. But the opposite is equally true: the victim should not have to bear

depends on whether public policy demands that such a claim be banned due to the CSP's vulnerability.

73 Surely sex-work feminists, socialist feminists and other middle ground feminists will tend to oppose the view that payment for sexual services is so bad that a restitution claim for a service rendered should be denied. But I also wonder whether denying restitution could be supported by radical feminists. See ch1, section 1.3.

74 See n63.

75 Virgo (n13) 109, 223–4. But one can doubt whether in fact such an intention is absent. According to Levenkron, many victims will not want to sue clients in torts since they conceive of them as 'normal men who did what normal men do' and not as victimisers. N Levenkron, email correspondence with the author, 8 November 2011. It is far from clear that such victims view the client who paid for the 'trick' as still owing them the money. Moreover, as a matter of policy it might be desirable for courts to assume that the victim intended to discharge the obligation so she would be able to sue the trafficker.

the risk of finding and suing the clients, while the money the clients paid in return for the claimant's forced services was pocketed by the trafficker. The claimant should be allowed to sue either the third party (client) based on the original obligation, or the defendant (trafficker) based on the interception of the money owed to the claimant. As long as the claimant is not allowed to accumulate the amount, she is not unjustly enriched, and recognising her right to sue the defendant reduces the number of claims and the cost of litigation.[76]

Such a desirable result from a policy perspective is also conceptually sound once the defendant is analogised with a surety and the third party with a debtor. From the creditor's perspective (the victim), the client is still the ultimate debtor. However, at least in cases in which the defendant intentionally intercepted the benefit (as is the case with the trafficker) it is fair to view him as a surety for the third party's obligation. Sureties protect creditors from the risk of the debtor becoming insolvent or disappearing. Obviously, in the trafficking context, the risk the client would not be found is significant and this risk (among others) was created by the trafficker; therefore, it is fair to view the trafficker as surety. More generally, the benefit's interception by the defendant increases the risk that the third party would become insolvent. This, too, justifies holding the defendant as surety.[77]

Interestingly, the third party in interceptive subtraction cases (in our context, the client) can be conceptualised as the surety and the defendant as the debtor, rather than vice versa. At the end of the two law suits necessitated under conventional analysis (the client suing the trafficker for the unjust enrichment and the victim suing the client for the original obligation) it is the defendant trafficker who bears the economic burden of reversing the transaction, while the client merely transfers the amount from the trafficker to the claimant. This is typically the case in surety contracts in which the debtor, if solvent, bears ultimately the financial burden of the obligation while the surety first pays the creditor and then collects the same amount from the debtor. This conceptualisation is supported by the principles governing adjustment among multiple debtors according to which: 'where one party is liable . . . for benefits received while the other is liable based on the basis of fault or risk, the liability of the former is primary while that of the second is secondary'.[78] The trafficker, who actually holds the benefit which ultimately belongs to the claimant should be considered as the debtor, while the client's obligation is merely secondary.

Lionel Smith might oppose the surety analysis by pointing to the fact that the subtraction in unjust enrichment claims is a zero sum game.[79] The

76 This point was acknowledged by Nourse J in *Mackey* (n65) 1315.

77 Cf Smith (n63) 498–502.

78 D Friedmann and N Cohen, 'Adjustment among multiple debtors' in *International Encyclopaedia of Comparative Law*, Vol 10 (Leiden: Brill, 1991) ch 11, 72.

79 Smith (n63) 488.

suggested analysis withstands such critique. Ultimately, the creditor cannot accumulate the benefit made at her expense. There is nothing logically flawed in a conclusion that the trafficker-defendant is enriched at the expense of the victim-claimant by intercepting the benefit owed to her by the client, but that the same enrichment would be at the client's expense if the client eventually satisfied his original obligation to the claimant to pay for the services he received.

## 3.3 Restitution for wrongs

In some cases where the defendant has derived a benefit from committing a wrong against the claimant, restitution of gains is available. However, the wrongs which yield restitution, the measure of recovery and the conceptual and normative justifications for the restitution are all a matter of some dispute. As I will attempt to demonstrate, some of the confusion about the appropriate scope of restitution for wrongs (RFW) stems from the fact that such category conceals three sub-categories. The first sub-category involves cases of subtraction in which the defendant's gain is matched by equivalent loss to the claimant. The second sub-category involves diminution of the claimant's dominion over her property, as is the case where the defendant uses the claimant's property without the claimant's authorisation. These cases raise the question of whether the defendant's gain was transferred from the claimant to the defendant in any meaningful way. The last sub-category involves cases in which the benefit was received from a third party, so it was at the claimant's expense only in the sense that it was accrued due to violating the claimant's interest. Two classic examples are the receipt of a bribe by a fiduciary and the receipt of payment from a third party in consideration for the defendant assaulting the claimant.

To complicate things even further, the above tripartite classification is factually challenged.[80] At times the enrichment is partially by subtraction and partially by receipt from a third party. For example, if the market value of the claimant's car is £2,000 and the defendant sold if for £3,000, only the surplus of £1,000 reflects enrichment from the third party as opposed to subtraction from the claimant.

RFW raises two main questions: which wrongs do and should trigger restitution? And what is and should be the measure of recovery? Since the issues are somewhat related, it will be useful to note at the outset (and the analysis below qualifies this crude statement) that the two main measures of

80 A conceptual challenge might exist as well: gains received by D from third parties might be considered as some sort of exchange product of something D took from C: C's bodily integrity. Consider the payment for attack hypothesis. The defendant took from the claimant her bodily integrity (to which she is entitled) and exchanged it for the third party's money.

recovery are disgorgement of the defendant's actual profits from committing the wrong and the objective (usually lower) market value of the benefit derived by the defendant from using the claimant's property. The latter is usually measured by the reasonable fee that would have been demanded by the claimant for permitting the defendant to interfere with the claimant's entitlement.

English authorities are unclear as to which torts can yield restitution, and a similar lack of consensus appears among academics.[81] It is clear, however, that proprietary torts yield restitution and it is generally accepted that the more important the claimant's protected interest and the more cynical the defendant's breach of that interest, the greater willingness exists to allow RFW and to opt for a higher measure of recovery. In what follows I make two arguments. The first is that, regardless of form, the substance of trafficking is that it is an acquisitive wrong; as such, it presents an uncontroversial case for RFW, even if such restitution should be limited only to acquisitive wrongs. My second uncontroversial claim is that the nature of trafficking, involving both the cynical violation of rights and the violation of an important interest, justifies disgorgement of the entire profit, indeed of all the proceeds, regardless of the nature of trafficking as an acquisitive wrong.

### *3.3.1 Trafficking, interference with property and acquisitive wrongs*

Trafficking is a wrong, the substance of which is interfering with the claimant's property with the purpose and effect of enriching the defendant. Therefore, restitution for wrongs should follow.[82] The wrongs committed against the victim – either the uncontroversial battery and false imprisonment torts or the tort of conversion – result in transfer of value from the claimant to the trafficker. On the user principle of the body-as-property conceptualisation, in which the trafficker makes profit by using the victim's body, it is clear that restitution is due. Indeed, the trafficking scenario could be equated with the unauthorised use of the claimant's chattels and land amounting to trespass to

81 For support for limiting gain-based remedy mainly to proprietary torts, see P Birks, *An Introduction to the Law of Restitution* (Oxford: Clarendon Press, 1985) 328–32. For support for awarding restitution to all torts, see J Edelman, *Gain-based Damages* (Oxford: Hart Publishing, 2002) 81 (award of the objective measure to all torts involving transfer of value); and Virgo (n13) 476. While Virgo does not distinguish between the two measures of recovery, his reasoning, which supports disgorgement, will usually support also the award of market value.

82 Recently, the Court of Appeal's majority in *Devenish Nutrition Ltd v Sanofi-Aventis SA* [2008] EWCA Civ 1086, [75], [156] concluded that gain-based relief in torts was available only for torts that involved breaches of proprietary rights.

goods (or conversion)[83] and trespass to land[84] respectively, for which the award of restitution is well established. In order to award restitution, based on this ground (as opposed to the one explored in section 3.3.2), the courts will have to accept the conceptualisation of the victim as chattel in order to allow her to sue for the user.

The extraction of forced labour and services from victims is done by measures which amount to battery, assault, false imprisonment and possibly two party intimidation and deceit.[85] However, English authorities are unclear on whether these torts can yield restitution.[86] Since, however, in the context of trafficking these torts are committed with both the purpose and effect of transferring value from the claimant to the defendant, by virtue of the unauthorised sale of the victim's sexual services she was forced to produce, they ought, at least in this context, to yield disgorgement. Restitution of the proceeds of the unauthorised sale is the paradigm restitution for wrongs case and has long been effected through an action for money had and received.[87] Not the form, but rather the substance of the right violation should matter. If indeed, as I discuss immediately below, Rotherham is correct that there is an important analytical and normative gain in separating misappropriations from other types of interferences with the claimant's entitlements, so that misappropriations should more easily yield restitution, the wrongs involved in trafficking should clearly be classified as misappropriations even though the relevant torts – battery and false imprisonment – typically involve non-acquisitive interferences.

So far I have argued that trafficking is a form of interference with property and therefore should yield restitution even according to the narrow view which finds support in English case law (at least with respect to awarding market value, as distinct from disgorgement). I now turn to defend a stronger claim still. As can be recalled, trafficking involves both forcing the victim to produce value which would not have existed but for the wrong and the misappropriation of that value. This duality might cause some to doubt whether trafficking is truly subtractive. Nonetheless, I argue that, since trafficking is best understood as the unauthorised sale of the victim's labour, it is subtractive in nature. As such it presents a stronger case for restitution than merely being based on a wrong committed against the claimant.

83 See e.g. *Strand Electric and Engineering Co Ltd v Brisford Entertainment Ltd* [1952] 2 QB 246, 254–5 (Denning LJ).

84 See e.g. *Ministry of Defence v Ashman* [1993] 2 EGLR 102.

85 See ch2, section 2.1. Suing in deceit, however, might involve difficulties similar to those implicated by a contractual claim discussed in ch2, section 2.1.1.

86 See Edelman (n81) 128–36; Virgo (n13) 472–7. Viscount Simon LC in *United Australia Ltd v Barclays Bank Ltd* [1941] AC 1, 12, has specifically mentioned *obiter* assault as a tort which cannot be waived. Account of profits for deceit was rejected in *Halifax BS v Thomas* [1995] EWCA Civ 21. See also nn 82, 88, 95–6, 100.

87 *Oughton v Steppings* (1830) 1 b Ad 241.

For current purposes, I need not make an intervention into the tangential issue which is hotly debated in the case law and literature: whether the user principle – liability for an unauthorised use of the claimant's asset – is subtractive, and if so, in what sense.[88] I do find the concept of diminution from dominion appealing, so that interference with property could be either considered in appropriate cases as a form of subtraction (and this is Edelman's view examined below), or, at least, as a third form of enrichment at the expense of the claimant (Birks's view[89]). On either account the case for restitution is stronger than in cases in which the claim for restitution is based merely on the wrong committed against the claimant (such as the case against publishers of sex advertisements discussed in chapter 2). The following discussion, however, does intervene in a recent debate between James Edelman and Craig Rotherham and is made with an eye towards the claims I make below that restitution should accumulate with tort damages (section 3.4) and that the state should make restitution to victims for what it confiscated from traffickers as proceeds of crime (chapter 4).

On James Edelman's expanding account of RFW, many wrongs could be conceptualised as involving a transfer of value from the claimant to the defendant, at times by subtraction from the owner's dominion, rather than from her wealth. Accordingly, the reversal of such transfer is a matter of right since 'if conduct is deemed a wrong, the law should always be prepared to reverse a transfer of value that is the result of that conduct'.[90] This account has been recently criticised by Craig Rotherham. According to Rotherham, Edelman's account analytically blurs the distinction between non-acquisitive and acquisitive wrongs (and therefore it also proves too much) and is consequently normatively deficient by allowing restitution too broadly while ignoring important distinctions between different entitlements and the defendant's level of fault.[91] I agree with Rotherham that both the nature of the interest violated and the defendant's level of fault are important determinatives in deciding whether to allow restitution and if so, how much. I am also willing to assume with Rotherham that parts of Edelman's account might be hard to defend in that in some examples (such as breaching restrictive covenants) it is hard to see how value was transferred from the claimant to the defendant.

But Rotherham casts his critical net too widely and he over-makes his case. Rotherham characterises the claimant's right to increases in value of

88 For recent accounts of the user principle which also survey different views, see P Jaffey, 'Licence fee damages', (2011) 19 *RLR* 95; C Rotherham 'Wrotham Park damages and accounts of profits: compensation or restitution?', (2008) *LMCLQ* 25; 'The conceptual structure of restitution for wrongs' (2007) 66 *CLJ* 172.

89 Birks, n50, and see the discussion on pp 48–9.

90 Edelman (n81) 81.

91 Rotherham, 'Conceptual structure' (n88).

the exchange product to the asset misappropriated from the claimant as a windfall which 'has nothing to do with the reversal of enrichment by subtraction and everything to do with the disgorgement of the proceeds of the wrongs'.[92] This ignores the fact that this surplus – the difference between the value of the misappropriated asset and the value of the exchange product in the hands of the defendant – is the product (in a 'but-for' sense) of both the claimant's asset and the defendant's contribution (or other factors which are external to the claimant's entitlement). Therefore, even to characterise the surplus *alone* as having *nothing* to do with the reversal of transfer of value is inaccurate. More crucially, the exchange value *in its entirety* reflects *always* a component of subtraction from the claimant and *sometimes* disgorgement of value which was not subtracted from the claimant (if one ignores the previous point that the surplus was partially produced by the original asset). *Typically*, the lion's share of the exchange product's value would consist of the value of the original misappropriated asset subtracted from the claimant. To ignore this reality (if indeed this is Rotherham's point, which I doubt) is to adopt the reasoning of Hersha'le, a famous fictional Jewish folklore character, who ordered two buns in a restaurant and after being served asked to change them for two donuts. After he ate the donuts and was asked to pay he said 'but I gave you two buns in exchange'; when asked to pay for the buns, he then retorted, 'but why, I haven't eaten them'. Since, as explained below, what clients pay the trafficker reflect the market value, no more, no less, of the services the victim was forced to produce and sell, the conclusion that restitution of the profits reverses a transfer of value from the victim to the trafficker is inescapable.

### 3.3.2 Cynical violation of an important interest

Disgorgement deprives the defendant of the profit he actually made from the wrong, regardless of whether such profit was transferred (in whole or in part) from the claimant.[93] As the second most heavy-handed remedy restitution law can offer (the first being disgorgement of proceeds without deducting expenses) it is reserved for circumstances in which deterrence or retribution justify the stripping away of the entire profit. The more egregious or culpable the defendant's behaviour and the more important the claimant's entitlement – entitlement with which the defendant interfered in the profit-making process – the higher the probability that disgorgement will be awarded.[94]

92 Id, 185.

93 Edelman (n81) 72.

94 See in general Rotherham, 'Conceptual structure' (n88) 189–96; H Dagan, *Unjust Enrichment: A Study of Private Law and Public Values* (Cambridge: Cambridge University Press, 1997) 41–4, 82–5.

It is not entirely clear which torts give rise to disgorgement of actual profits.[95] Clearly, cynical interference with the claimant's (real or personal) property yields disgorgement.[96] With the conceptualisation of trafficking as interference with the claimant's right of self-ownership (whether as unauthorised sale of services or unauthorised use of body) disgorgement should be available.

Another way to reach the same conclusion is to acknowledge that disgorgement is not punitive and is less far-reaching than exemplary damages, since it merely offsets an ill gotten gain made by the wrong, rather than reducing for a non-compensatory motive the defendant's wealth below that which he had prior to committing the wrong. Once this is acknowledged, every situation which gives rise to punitive damages should automatically give rise also to the less far-reaching remedy of disgorgement.[97] In England, in which punitive damages against non-governmental defendants are unduly (and exceptionally) restricted to cynical violations of rights which are profit-motivated,[98] disgorgement for sex trafficking should be available, even when the relevant wrong is battery and false imprisonment. Indeed, in the recent decision of *AT v Dulgheiru* the Court awarded exemplary damages against the traffickers *in order* to prevent unjust enrichment and to show the defendants that their misdeeds do not pay.[99]

Lastly, the broadest right for disgorgement would be based on any conscious violation of the victim's right, even if this violation was not profit-motivated. Such a right is supported by the Law Commission and by Edelman, and could be gleaned from Lord Nicholls's critique in *Kuddus v CCLC* of limiting exemplary damages to profit-seeking behaviour. This approach is adopted by

95 Most commentators, including Edelman (n81) 136–48; Virgo (n13) 465–77; C Rotherham, 'Gain-based relief in tort after *Attorney General v Blake*', (2010) 126 *LQR* 102, oppose the limitation of disgorgement to proprietary torts offered in *Devenish* (n82). See also Jaffey (n88). In *Forsyth-Grant v Allen* [2008] EWCA Civ 505, [33], [48], the Court of Appeal's majority leaned towards a conclusion that disgorgement was never available as a remedy in nuisance.

96 See e.g. *Edwards* (n49) (wilful trespass to land); *Jegon v Vivian* (1871) LR 6 Ch App 742 (same; plaintiffs getting the 'whole value of the coal dug'; note, however, that some (e.g. Virgo (n13) 465) view the award given as reflecting a licence fee); *Lightly v Clouston* (1808) 127 ER 774 (a seduction case in which the appropriation of labour by the defendant master is equated with the unauthorised sale of property; the claimant is 'entitled to an equivalent for that labour, which has been bestowed in the service of the Defendant'; what was claimed included 'the profits and receipts of whose work and labour the Plaintiff was, as the master of the said apprentice, by law entitled' *Olwell v Nye & Nissen Co*, 173 P 2d 652 (1946, SCW) (wilful conversion); as Edelman, id, mentions at 141–6 disgorgement was also allowed for deceit, common law fraud, and indirectly through exemplary damages for several other torts including false imprisonment (*Huckle v Money* (1763) 95 ER 769) and assault and battery (*Benson v Fredrick* (1766) 97 ER 1130).

97 Edelman, id, 144.

98 *Rookes v Barnard* [1964] AC 1129, 1225–7.

99 *Dulghieru* (n1) [68], [71], [73].

the *Restatement of Restitution* and is evident in the availability of punitive damages in the commonwealth and the US for cynical violations of rights.[100] It is inconceivable that English courts would refuse to award disgorgement of profits to victims of trafficking; *AT v Dulghieru* (in which restitution was not sought) is a strong indication that this prediction is sound.

Of course, one could think of some limitations to disgorgement. According to one limitation they could be awarded only when the defendant's behaviour was egregious (and not only conscious).[101] Even if such limitation is justified, no doubt traffickers satisfy such requirement. Another limitation would award disgorgement only to violation of important interests. Indeed, Dagan's research revealed that the more important the claimant's entitlement, the stronger the restitutionary remedy given for its infringement. For intentional violation of interests which are constitutive of one's personhood, such as land and copyright, American courts awarded the higher of profits and market value.[102] Needless to say, according to such limitation, the interest in bodily integrity and sexual autonomy should receive the highest possible protection. Clearly, then, trafficking justifies disgorgement.[103]

### 3.3.3 The measure of recovery

#### 3.3.3.1 Objective and subjective value

Several measures of recovery for RFW exist. The main measures available are the market value of the benefit transferred, allowance for the claimant's contribution

100 See Law Commission, *Aggravated, Exemplary and Restitutionary Damages*, Law Com No 247 (London: Stationery Office, 1997) [3]–[51] (deliberate and outrageous disregard of the plaintiff's rights test for restitution); Edelman (n81) 83–6; *Kuddus v Chief Constable of Leicestershire Constabulary* [2001] UKHL 29, [67].

According to the *Restatement (First) Restitution* (1937), §§ 150–159 Introductory Note, the defendant who 'was consciously tortious in acquiring the benefit . . . is . . . deprived of any profit derived from his subsequent dealing with it'. The *Restatement (Third) of Restitution and Unjust Enrichment* (2011), §§ 3, 40 Comment (b), 41 Comment (b), 44, 51(4), 53(3) chooses disgorgement as the measure of recovery for conscious infringement of the claimant's interest and market value for innocent infringement. While the rule in the first *Restatement* could be interpreted as limited to proprietary torts, the rule in the third could not.

The leading comparative cases on punitive damages are *Hill v Church of Scientology* [1995] 2 SCR 1130 (Canada); *Gray v Motor Accident Commission* (1998) 16 CLR 1 (Australia); *State Farm Mutual Auto Insurance Co v Campbell*, 538 US 408 (US).

101 The outrageous conduct test was set by the Law Commission, id. However, this recommendation is a minimum requirement to which courts could add. See also Friedmann (n40) 1888; Virgo (n13) 435.

102 Dagan (n94) 41–4, 82–5.

103 For this reason, I do not discuss here potential extensions to the scope of disgorgement which might be applicable to the trafficking context. These include disgorgement in the absence of conscious wrongdoing in order to protect important interests and institutions, disgorgement for breach of fiduciary duties and disgorgement for crimes.

(while recognising the defendant's entitlement to the profits), proportional profits according to the relative contributions of the parties, profits subject to allowance for the defendant's contribution to the making of the profit, net profits to the claimant and proceeds (without allowing the defendant to deduct expenses). The court might also award the higher award of several options such as the higher of market value and actual profits.[104]

The main factors influencing the choice of the measure of recovery are the degree of the defendant's fault, the type of the claimant's interest infringed by the defendant, the factual and normative significance of the defendant's contribution to the creation of the profit, the type of relationship between the claimant and defendant and the extent of the difficulty involved in calculating the relative contributions of the claimant and defendant in generating the profit.[105]

These factors can also explain why at times the objective measure of recovery, which is usually measured by market value, and actual profits would differ. The difference might be attributed to the defendant's contribution, which might be legitimate or not, or to external factors, such as general market conditions or the special needs of the third party to whom the defendant sold the interest appropriated from the claimant. A related reason for such difference is the occurrence of future events which affect the value appropriated from the claimant; such issue is related to both remoteness and the proprietary nature of the claimant's claim. The difference between the two measures might also reflect the fact that part of the benefit was received from a third party and not subtracted from the claimant.

What is the relationship between market value and disgorgement in the trafficking context? The market value of the victim's forced sexual services would usually equal what clients paid for these services. In the absence of special circumstances there is no reason why the client would pay more or less than the market value for the services. Neither of the reasons mentioned above for a difference between market value and actual profit seems to exist on first reflection. Moreover, the typical characteristic of market value is that the enrichment takes place and should be measured at the moment of the misappropriation of the interest.[106] Each forced encounter between the claimant and a client is the moment at which value is misappropriated from the victim and should be evaluated. Since the payment for each encounter is instantaneous, there is a strong indication that the actual profit reflects the market value of the service.

The following discussion refines this observation by explaining why market value should not and could not be thought to reflect either a licence fee demanded by the victim from the trafficker, or reasonable remuneration for

104 See Friedmann (n40) 1880–3,1898; Dagan (n94) 22.

105 Freidmann id 1887–91.

106 M McInnes, 'Interceptive subtraction, unjust enrichment and wrongs – a reply to Professor Birks', (2003) 62 *CLJ* 697, 702.

her services. Then I examine two potential reasons for market value to be higher than actual profits and the case for awarding this higher measure. Lastly, I argue that neither allowance for the trafficker's contribution nor deductions of expenses should and would be allowed.

### *3.3.3.2 Rejecting the licence fee/*quantum meruit *measures*

The objective measure for restitution is the market value of the benefit accrued to the defendant from interfering with the claimant's entitlement. Clearly, in the trafficking context one could not measure the market value of the benefit conferred to the trafficker as the saving of a licence fee paid by the trafficker to the victim to use her body to make a profit, since this would amount to a licence for enslavement. To be clear, I do not argue that all forms of prostitution are necessarily exploitative so no licence fee is possible with regard to *non-forced* CSPs. Rather, since victims are forced to prostitute themselves, the enrichment at their expense cannot be measured in terms of a licence fee to do so, since that would reflect the market value of the right to force someone into labour (in this case, into prostitution).[107] One result of forcing victims into prostitution is that their working conditions are much harder than those of non-forced CSPs, in the sense that they are not (or at least much less) at liberty to turn down clients and certain practices. This difference in income production capacity is the result of forcing the victims into prostitution and it would be both an immoral and conceptually self-defeating exercise to try to find the market value of a licence to enslave which can produce these benefits.

In a similar manner, since victims of trafficking are forced into prostitution by traffickers, one should not conceive of the benefit misappropriated by the trafficker as the saving of reasonable remuneration for the victim's labour. This conceptualisation is misconceived as it views the trafficker as an employer and the victim as an employee and therefore assumes that the surplus value of the employee's labour belongs to the employer. Accordingly, the trafficker is conceived as the owner of the profit who has to pay the claimant merely the saving of wages. However, in the absence of the victim's consent to being employed by the trafficker, the benefit, which was derived from the victim's labour, belongs to her and if at all the issue should have been whether the trafficker can claim a reasonable remuneration for his contribution to creating this profit or be allowed to deduct expenses (as explained below he surely cannot). As Friedmann explains 'Where properties or labor of A and B contribute to the creation of a mass or an enhanced property, the first issue relates to ownership of the new product'. Only if the new product belongs to one party is there 'the question of whether B is entitled to a claim in restitution for the benefit that A got by virtue of B's contribution, or whether this

107 Cf Rotherham (n95) 115.

contribution should be forfeited'.[108] In the absence of agreement, and given the dominant nature of the victim's contribution to the creation of the profit, the conscious misappropriation by the trafficker, and the illegality involved on his part, the default position should be that the victim owns the profit, rather than the trafficker. The money is paid first and foremost in consideration for the CSP's body, labour and services, not for the entrepreneurial initiatives of traffickers (or for that matter, pimps).

Interestingly, one of the numerous errors made by the Israeli Regional Labour Court in *M v Salsrevski* – the first case known to me in which a victim sought merely gain-based remedies – was that it assumed that the claimant was entitled merely to a *quantum meruit* for her services. Since a market value of the services is impossible to figure, reasoned the Court,[109] the claimant should receive the minimum wage based on the assumption that the market value should be at least the minimum wage. (In addition, the claimant was awarded in non-pecuniary damages – despite the fact that the Court's jurisdiction to award them was not clear – an amount approximating to that which should have been awarded in disgorgement.)[110] But for the reasons explained above, the assumption that the victim's claim is limited to the fair wage is mistaken. As the discussion below demonstrates, not only do retributive considerations demand that all the actual profit should be disgorged to the victim, it is also a mistake to assume, as the Court did, that forced prostitution, or prostitution in general for that matter, does not have a market value, and that the minimum wage reflects the reasonable remuneration owed to the victim.

### *3.3.3.3 Attributed gain: value of non-forced sexual services*

One reason for which the objective value of the benefit extracted from the claimant might exceed actual profits is that the prices charged for sexual services by forced CSPs is lower than the price charged by CSPs who are not forced.[111] Arguably, the objective value of the service should ignore the

108 Friedmann (n40) 1904–5.

109 *Salsrevski* (n23). The Court was silent on whether the alleged impossibility is limited to instances of trafficking or applies to prostitution in general. In either case, the issue is not really one about impossibility to calculate the profit and its division between CSPs and pimps or between victims and traffickers. Rather, it probably reflects courts' reluctance to engage in such an inquiry. This could definitely be understood, and justified, in the context of trafficking, in which full disgorgement of proceeds is potentially available and justified.

110 *Salsrevski*, id, [117], [119], [135]. On appeal (*Ben-Ami* (n6)) this reasoning was disapproved of.

111 J Bindle and H Atkins, *Big Brothel: A Survey of the Off-street Sex Industry in London* (London: Poppy, 2008) 22. This could also be inferred from Kara's findings ((n4) 37, discussed in ch8) that 'for the most part only slave labor can facilitate [the] lower prices' documented as the result of the increased share of victims in the market.

depressed pricing of forced services based on policy and principle alike. The policy behind such a rule is that the trafficker (and the client) should not profit from the fact that the claimant was forced into prostitution; such a rule might also better protect non-forced CSPs by limiting the effect that forced prostitution has on depressing prices. The rule is supported by principle since in the absence of forced prostitution, the client would have paid (if purchasing the service at all) the higher price charged by non-forced CSPs. This approach could face three challenges but I find all of them lacking.

First, forcing the claimant into prostitution depressed the price charged for any sexual act extracted from the claimant but also increased the number of such acts in comparison to that which a non-forced CSP would have offered. Awarding restitution based on the actual number of encounters, but at the price of non-forced encounters, is therefore a 'double whammy'. However, corrective justice restores prior legal *entitlements*, not simply prior *factual positions*. Although the victim 'is factually better off at the end of the story than at the beginning, . . . she is no better off than . . . she was entitled to be at that time'.[112] Obviously, the award of such attributed gain can be supported by punitive purposes, retribution and deterrence.

Second, one could argue that awarding the market value of non-forced sexual services should be avoided based on public policy, since awarding such sums amounts to the legitimisation of prostitution. This argument assumes, contrary to my suggestion above, that a restitutionary (or contractual) claim by a non-forced CSP is still barred as *contra bonos mores*. However, the parties are not *in pari delicto* and it is unclear why the trafficker should not pay the higher amount when it was his own faulty conduct which both forced the victim into prostitution and depressed the price received by the client.

A similar, third objection is that the award of an objective value in general, and in particular an award based on the market value of non-forced prostitution, is problematic from an expressive perspective since it prostitutes the claimant.[113] It should be recalled, though, that this argument is not even prima facie plausible with respect to victims who knew they were going to work in prostitution. In addition, any victim can decide whether the pecuniary gain from receiving restitution measured by the higher objective measure is worth the (alleged) dignitary loss involved in making such a claim. I continue to explore and reject this argument while examining the second factor that enables the market value of the benefit in question to exceed actual profits.

112 K Barker, 'Understanding the unjust enrichment principle in private law: a study of the concept and its reasons', in J Neyers, M McInnes and S Pital (eds), *Understanding Unjust Enrichment* (Oxford: Hart Publishing, 2004) 79, 100–1.

113 Compare n109.

### *3.3.3.4 Attributed gain: number of clients*

The number of clients a victim has to serve and the amount charged from a client are figures that can be, and have been, gathered. According to the IOM's database, the average daily number of clients is six; according to the ILO's database, '5 to 10 customers per day is relatively normal for a victim'; according to Siddharth Kara, the average is between eight and ten sex acts for a victim in most venues in Western Europe and the US. Based on Poppy's 'Routes In' report, the daily average of 53 victims who were able to estimate the number of clients they served is about 13. An earlier Poppy report found that many victims saw more than 20 clients every day. Metropolitan police estimate trafficked women forced into prostitution in London see between 20 and 30 men per day. According to the findings of the Israeli Parliamentary Report, the daily average is between ten and 15 clients, the average amount paid by a client is NIS 120 (about £20), of which the victim retains on average NIS 20 (17 per cent), and the monthly number of days victims have to work is 29.[114]

Accordingly, a finding that a claimant has been enslaved for a certain period can lead to a finding that the trafficker could have made a certain profit at her expense, and this figure could be taken as the objective value of the transfer. In *Inverugie Investments Ltd v Hackett*,[115] the claimant was a lessee of some 30 apartments in a Bahamian hotel complex. The defendants, who were the owners of the hotel, wrongfully ejected the plaintiff and used the apartments as part of the hotel. Despite the fact that the average occupancy of the apartments was about 35 to 40 per cent, the Privy Council calculated the (restitutionary) damages in an amount equal to the rent of all the apartments they wrongfully occupied for the entire period.[116] The cynical defendant could not be heard saying that in fact the profit he made was lower than the objective value of what was transferred from the claimant.[117]

Seemingly, the same conclusion is possible with respect to the number of clients the victim had to serve. If for some reason the London trafficker forced the victim to serve 'only' ten clients a day, while the local average,

114 See p 36; *IOM Counter Trafficking Module Database* (Geneva: IOM, 2010) 21 (on file with the author) ('*IOM Trafficking Database*') (of the 4,182 victims of sexual exploitation who remembered the average daily number of clients (43 per cent) 1,874 reported less than five, 1,895 between five and ten, 271 between 11 and 15, 80 between 15 and 20 and 62 more than 20); Belser (n3) 14; Kara (n4) Appendix B; Stephen-Smith (n23) 17; Dickson (n22) 5; Parliamentary Inquiry Committee (n2) 6.

115 [1995] 1 WLR 713 (PC). For analysis see Friedmann (n40) 1885–7.

116 Note that Friedmann id., views the remedy in *Inverugie* as reflecting attributed gain, which is punitive and different from both actual profits (disgorgement) and an objective measure of recovery (market value).

117 A different result is warranted when the defendant is an innocent wrongdoer. See *Ashman* (n84).

say, is 15,[118] the trafficker could be made liable for the objective measure based on 15 clients per day. According to such an approach, at least against the cynical wrongdoer, the victim has the right to the higher of the market value and actual profit made at her expense. Such a choice is given by English and American courts to claimants in cases of conscious trespass to land (but not innocent trespass for which only market value is afforded), and in cases of conversion (at least if conscious).[119]

Such a solution, however, is problematic for three reasons. First, it gives traffickers an incentive to enslave victims even further. Seemingly, if the trafficker knows that he would have to disgorge profits based on, say, 15 clients per day, even if he insisted that the victim serves 'only' ten, he will make sure that the victim serves at least 15 clients a day. It is doubtful, however, whether traffickers will change their behaviour based on the deterrent effect of rules governing restitution.[120] First, traffickers are not likely to know the exact rules governing restitution (are deductions allowed?). Second, the vast majority of traffickers attempt in any event to maximise the profit they can make at any victim's expense. It is somewhat naïve to believe that an attributed gain rule will cause them to exploit victims more than they would have been willing and able to do otherwise. Moreover, since benefits are immediate and the sanction is delayed in time and uncertain, traffickers will discount the extra risk created by restitution of attributed gain. What is likely to have a deterrent effect (if at all) is the knowledge that profits will be disgorged, rather than variations of the chosen gain-based remedy. Lastly (and in the alternative), to the extent that traffickers are so sensitive to the restitutionary remedy chosen, the incentive to further exploit created by the award of attributed gains should be weighed against the incentive to exit (or not enter) the trafficking industry.

As an aside, the discussion demonstrates that the deterrent effect of the measure of recovery chosen is uncertain. On the one hand, traffickers are repeat players and financially motivated so they are good candidates for deterrence.[121] On the other hand, to the general scepticism about the deterrent effect of law (and private law financial sanctions in particular), one might add the fact that traffickers come from sub-cultures which will not be necessarily well informed about the details of the relevant restitutionary remedy chosen. Affording victims restitutionary remedy against traffickers is nevertheless important for

118 See n114. Based on the findings in *Dulghieru* (n1), it could be calculated that one victim had 20 clients per day on average and I estimate that the averages of the other three victims were 14, 15 and 25.

119 *Tang Man Sit v Capacious Investments Ltd* [1996] AC 514, 525 (PC); *Inverugie* (n115); (unauthorised use of land); *Lightly v Clouston* (1808) 127 ER 774 (seduction case likening seduction to conversion); Edelman (n81) 139–40, 246–7; Friedmann (n40) 1883–4, 1892; Dagan (n94) 73–8 (land), 79–81 (chattels) (both in the US).

120 Cf C Rotherham, 'Deterrence as a justification for awarding accounts of profits', (2012) 32 *OJLS* 537.

121 See Aronowitz *et al.* (n25).

several reasons. First, to the extent that the victim can collect the award against the trafficker, there is an obvious practical benefit in terms of compensating the victim. Second, establishing a right against the trafficker is important for establishing a restitutionary claim against the state. Lastly, acknowledging that victims have a right for disgorgement of proceeds and to attributed gains is important in terms of the expressive message of the law.

The second difficulty with awarding market value when such measure exceeds disgorgement focuses exactly on the law's expressive message. On the symbolic level, ascertaining the market value of a slave's services might be considered as normalising trafficking, and as such offensive or inappropriate. Similarly, it might be considered as prostituting the victim (for example, by charging money for instances of forced sex in which the man who had sex with the claimant has not paid) and as commodifying an interest – in bodily and sexual integrity – which should be inalienable. While the broad version of the commodification argument, opposing restitutionary remedy against trafficking or slavery, should be rejected for reasons explained in chapter 5, it might be that a remedy of disgorgement, which reverses the actual profit made at the claimant's expense, is less expressively problematic. In addition, usually an award of actual profits would be higher, or at least no lower, than market value.

Beyond incentives and the symbolic message, there is a third objection to awarding market value rather than the actual profit gained: such a solution might be considered by some as unfair, since it punishes the trafficker for not exploiting victims further. While, as discussed in chapter 4, the notion of attributed and inflated gain is not foreign to the Proceeds of Crime Act 2002, this particular form of punitive attribution might seem perverse, and there is some doubt whether English courts would be willing to take this route.

The problem with denying the claimant market value is that it denies a potentially more effective remedy to the claimant, who is already marginalised and seriously victimised. Such a solution is also inconsistent with the usual rule in which the victim of a cynical violation of rights is entitled to the higher measure of recovery between disgorgement and market value. In addition, in the unlikely event that courts would not be willing to adopt a flexible approach with respect to the proof of the actual profit made at the claimant's expense (a point discussed below) the entitlement for the market value of the benefit becomes of crucial practical importance.[122] It is submitted, therefore, that claimants should be entitled to the higher measure of recovery between disgorgement and market value/attributed gain. This conclusion is reinforced by the fact that it is the claimant herself who chooses to sue for market value.

122 Nothing stops courts from resorting to average figures in the event of insufficient evidence, or at least placing the burden of proof on the trafficker to prove otherwise. If this is done, attributed gain is no longer supported by the need to overcome evidentiary difficulties.

No court should deny her that remedy, based on paternalistic beliefs about the offensiveness of the award from an expressive perspective.

As can be gleaned from the discussion, market value can be calculated in at least four ways. One way is based on the average profit made at the expense of a similarly situated victim. Both relevant figures (average price per act and number of clients) would be victim-specific (but not claimant-specific). Even here, variations would exist based on the level of concrete information relied upon to establish who is 'similarly situated'. A second calculation is based on the (known or estimated) number of clients served by the claimant but the average price demanded by a non-forced CSP. A third possibility is based on the average number of clients per (similarly situated?) victim, even when this number exceeds the number of clients the claimant was forced to serve, and the average price paid to a non-victim. Options 2 and 3 are based on attributed gain. Lastly, the calculation could be based on the earnings of a non-forced CSP (which will be based on the average price per service and number of clients of non-forced CSPs). There is much to be said that – in accordance with the common approach towards conscious wrongdoers – the claimant should be awarded the higher of market value (including attributed gain) and actual profits. However, some doubts exist as to whether attributing gain based on 'under-exploitation' of the claimant is palatable. More broadly, a judicial reluctance to resort to the market value of prostitution services might direct courts to focus on disgorgement of actual profits, or as we shall see shortly, of proceeds.

### *3.3.3.5 No allowance and deductions*

There is no doubt that the trafficker will not be awarded any allowance for his contribution to the creation of the profit from the forced prostitution. First and foremost, his contribution is illegal.[123] Second, once trafficking is understood to involve either the unauthorised sale of the victim's services or the unauthorised use of her property – her body – the defendant's contribution would be deemed to be too peripheral, so that even an innocent defendant would be liable for the full value of the profit.[124]

The trafficker should not (and in all likelihood would not) be allowed to deduct expenses from revenues so the measure of proceeds would be adopted. The main reason is the reprehensive and illegal nature of his conduct.[125] Even if such an approach is punitive, a punitive approach is appropriate in these circumstances, as the availability of exemplary damages in such cases demonstrates.[126] In contexts involving a value transferred from the claimant,

123 *Reading v Attorney-General* [1951] AC 507 (HL); Friedmann (n40) 1889, 1892.
124 Friedmann id; Edelman (n81) 140.
125 Friedmann id.
126 *Dulghieru* (n1); *K* (n23).

conscious wrongdoing and the infringement of an important interest, such as ownership of land, deduction of expenses is disallowed *even in the absence of criminal illegality*.[127] It is inconceivable that a system not allowing deductions of expenses in cases of bad faith mining of coal will allow the deductions of expenses in cases of human trafficking.

There are also two reasons to doubt whether disallowing deductions is punitive under the circumstances. First, it has been argued that restitution of proceeds from a conscious wrongdoer is consistent with corrective justice since it denies the defendant a protected interest in his own property, a right he denied the claimant.[128] Second, some of these expenses amount to unsolicited benefits which were not freely accepted by the claimant and are not necessarily incontrovertible benefits.[129] For example, a claimant who was duped into leaving her home and is forcefully kept in a flat did not freely accept the benefit of accommodation and, given the fact she had accommodation in her country of origin, the benefit is controvertible. In a similar context in the US, an employer's ability to deduct benefits against employees' claims for the minimum wage, deduction is significantly curtailed. For instance, no deduction is allowed for accommodation if the place is furnished mainly for the purposes of the employer. Moreover, it is not entirely clear as a matter of principle whether incontrovertible benefits, such as food provided to the victim, should be deducted.[130]

Some might rightly mention that the incontrovertible benefits doctrine is relevant for purposes of establishing enrichment as a matter of unjust enrichment while here we are concerned with the appropriate measure of recovery for restitution for wrongs. But the dual and complex nature of trafficking as both wrongful and subtractive justifies a response which cannot be reduced neatly into existing taxonomical demarcations.[131] More specifically, since the gist of the claimant's case is that the profit was misappropriated from

127 *Livingstone v Rawyards Coal Company* (1880) 5 App Cas 25 (HL); *Bulli Coal Mining Co v Osborne* [1899] AC 351 (HL); *Pan Coal Co v Garland Pocahontas Coal Co*, 125 SE 226 (1926); cf *Frank Music Corp v Metro-Goldwyn-Mayer, Inc*, 772 F2d 505 (9th Cir, 1985) (copyright).

128 E Weinrib, 'Restitutionary damages as corrective justice', (2000) 1 *TIL* 1, 25–31. For a critique, see H Dagan, *The Law and Ethics of Restitution* (Cambridge: Cambridge University Press, 2004) 226.

129 For the doctrines of free acceptance and incontrovertible benefits as establishing enrichment for purposes of an unjust enrichment claim, see *McDonald v Coys of Kensington* [2004] 1 WLR 2775 (CA), [26]–[40].

130 See Werner and Kim (ch1, n41) 51–3.

131 Similarly, the rejection of the claim for allowance or deductions which is based on RFW should not prevent the victim's claim against the state which is based on vindication of property (or, according to some, unjust enrichment). In any event, the trafficker's assets which are potentially available to satisfy either a confiscation order or a claim in restitution are likely to reflect net profits, rather than proceeds, since the relevant expenses have already been spent.

her (and not only achieved by way of committing a wrong against her), her ability to subjectively devalue the benefits she received (which form a large part of the trafficker's expenditure) bolsters her claim that deductions should be denied.

### *3.3.3.6 Courts' practice*

While initially in *Salsrevski* the Court opined that deductions should be allowed, on appeal (*Ben-Ami*) the National Labour Court clarified that the claimant is entitled to the full proceeds received from clients for her services.[132] In *Dulghieru*, *Normatov*, *Lifshin* and *Tyumkin*[133] the courts seemed to have attempted to disgorge the proceeds but in all four cases the courts awarded a lower amount than that pleaded by the claimant as reflecting full disgorgement. In all cases the courts did not dwell on the question of calculation, which obviously raises evidentiary difficulties. The three Israeli cases might have reflected the *lowest* possible estimation of the profit made at the claimant's expense. If this is indeed the strategy courts adopted it should be criticised: since it was the trafficker who unlawfully breached the claimant's protected interest, and since his behaviour is also the cause of the evidential uncertainty, all doubts should be resolved against him. Such an approach is used, *inter alia*, specifically in American cases dealing with restitution for wrongs, and in Israeli tort cases.[134]

On a more positive note, the courts' approach regarding quantification reflects a commendable willingness to estimate the proceeds in the absence of accurate and reliable evidence (similar to the willingness of the District Court in *K*[135] to award compensation without specific proof of damage) and if courts continue with this tendency, both judicial time and litigation costs will be saved. On a practical level, courts could rely on findings made in a previous criminal litigation against the trafficker, and at times, on the trafficker's guilty plea to the charge sheet which might include data which will help the civil

132 *Salsrevski* (n23) [117]; *Ben-Ami* (n6) [32].

133 See (n1), (n6).

134 *Restatement Restitution* (n100) § 210 (wrongdoer who mixed his fungible goods with that of the claimant has to prove which portion of the mass belongs to him); cf *Restatement (Third) Restitution* (n100) § 59(2) and Comment (a); see also (in the context of disgorgement) § 51(50(d)); D Dobbs, *The Law of Remedies*, 2nd edn (Eagan, MN: West Pub Co, 1993), § 5.13(2) (recovery of highest value of converted shares in the period between conversion and trial, against a conscious wrongdoer); Dagan (n94) 84 (any doubt in copyright infringement cases as to the computation of costs or in the apportionment of net profits is resolved in favour of the plaintiff); FH 15/88 *Melekh v Kornhoiser*, PD 44(2) 89 (1990, Isr) (defendant must show which part of the overall injury from attacks by different dogs was caused by his dog, failure to do so leads to full liability). See also pp 236.

135 See n23.

court calculate or estimate the profit made at the victim's expense. On a more theoretical level, courts could justify a resort to available figures which are not claimant-specific based on the victim's entitlement to the higher of market value, including attributed gain, and actual profits.

The Court's omission in *Dulghieru* to award full restitution (by way of exemplary damages) is even more surprising since the Court did accept (and hence made a finding) that the estimated daily profit made at each claimant's expense was between £500 and £1,000.[136] When this amount is multiplied by the length of period in which the claimants were sexually enslaved, the overall amount awarded to them is too low. Even according to the lowest estimation of £500 daily profit the four claimants who had been sexually enslaved for a total of 6 months between them should have received around £91,000. They were awarded £60,000. In addition, to reverse the enrichment made at the claimant's expense, the restitutionary award should have been calculated individually. Instead, the Court awarded each claimant the same amount – £15,000 – disregarding the different length of the sexual exploitation of each.

## 3.4 Accumulation of restitution and compensation

Victims should accumulate the compensation for their losses and the profit made at their expense. Election is required where disgorgement and compensation are sought for the same wrongful act.[137] Traffickers violate the rights of victims both (and independently) by forcing them into prostitution and by pocketing the proceeds of the sexual services. Obviously, a (hypothetical) trafficker who forced a woman to work as a CSP would be liable towards her in tort even without taking her money. Similarly, third persons who took from the victim without her consent her profits from forced prostitution would be liable to make restitution to her even if they did not force her into prostitution. There is no good reason to relieve a trafficker who does both from the duty to both compensate the victim for forcing her into prostitution and make restitution for any benefit made at her expense.

Restitution of profits and compensation for assault and false imprisonment protect two distinct interests and therefore should accumulate. This is obviously true when the restitutionary cause of action is based on vindication of property or unjust enrichment. The idea behind election is that when the *same* interest is undermined, the remedy should be either loss- or gain-based, otherwise the claimant would be over-compensated. So if the defendant converts a chattel which the claimant usually hires out, the claimant cannot claim both the use value and the loss from lost hire contracts. But it is well

136 *Dulghieru* (n1) [74].

137 *Tang Man Sit v Capacious Investments Ltd* [1996] AC 514; Edelman (n81) 245–51.

established that loss of use, as consequential damage, accumulates with damages for diminution of the chattel's market value,[138] so the election in the example above should exist with respect to either defendant's gain or claimant's lost hire contracts but either amount should accumulate with compensation for the diminution in the chattel's market value. Similarly, the victim's interest in dignity and physical integrity is different from her interest in not having the value of her forced labour misappropriated.

That conclusion should not change even when the victim's claim is based on RFW. In the scenario which poses the greatest difficulty to accumulation, when the client pays the trafficker directly, the torts of battery and false imprisonment ought to be relied upon for both compensation and restitution. But the form should not obscure the fact that, as just explained, the claimant suffered a setback to two distinct interests by being forced into prostitution and losing its proceeds. The rights protecting both interests should be vindicated by the accumulation of compensation and restitution. A claimant suffering two distinct injuries from the same wrongful act (e.g. where a defendant pushes a claimant who falls and breaks both an arm and a leg) can accumulate compensation for both injuries, despite the fact they both stem from the same act. By the same token, the claimant who suffers both dignitary injury in being forced to provide sex services and pecuniary injury in having the value of such forced services taken by the trafficker should be able to claim both.

There is another way to look at the issue which leads to the same conclusion. Suppose the defendant forces the claimant into prostitution but does not misappropriate the proceeds. In a claim in battery, the court is not likely, and should not, set off the profit produced from the forced prostitution against the injury caused by it. This result is based on the concern for preserving the claimant's autonomy not to be subject to a forced transaction in which one interest (in our case in dignity, autonomy and physical integrity) is traded with another (pecuniary benefit).[139] Otherwise, the court affords the trafficker with a power (in Hohefeld's terminology) to enforce on the claimant such a transaction. Indeed, victims such as the claimants in *AT*, who did not contemplate working as CSPs, could not have made the profit from forced prostitution but for the violation of their rights by the traffickers (for which they claimed loss-based damages). Yet, victims should be (and in that case were, albeit only partially) awarded both compensation and restitution. This result, which is in accord with other instances in which vindicating the victim's rights results in a remedy that puts the victim in a better financial position than they would have been had there been no violation, is justified from a

138 See e.g. *The Fortunity* [1961] 1 WLR 351. The wayleave cases, involving trespass to land, point at the same direction. *Jegon* (n96).

139 Cf *Restatement (Second) of Torts* (n58) § 920, which denies the right to set off benefits accruing to the tort victim from the commission of the tort when the benefit conferred is not of the same kind as the interest infringed.

corrective justice perspective, which (as explained above) restores prior legal *entitlements*, not simply prior *factual positions*. This result is also supported by distributive justice (given the victim's vulnerability), and by retributive justice and deterrence, since otherwise, the trafficker is using the victim's money in order to compensate her for the losses his tortious behaviour caused her.

Arguably, a reason to oppose accumulation might be that by increasing the trafficker's liability, accumulation would leave fewer available assets to other creditors, including other victims. But if the dignitary and misappropriation wrongs are indeed separate, that result is not necessarily problematic. This relates to the debate concerning priorities in bankruptcy, and among victims, on which I touch in chapter 4. In any event, given that victims' claims are scarce, it would be unwise to deny an otherwise sound claim for accumulation, based on concerns about the effect of such a rule on future victims' ability to recover.

The scant English and Israeli authorities are inconclusive, but seem to support accumulation. In *AT*, the award of exemplary damages was purported to prevent the traffickers' unjust enrichment. While the amount awarded (£60,000) to all four claimants failed to capture the full estimated enrichment at their expense – between £90,000 and £180,000 – the fact that this estimated enrichment fell significantly below what was awarded in compensation (around £550,000) indicates that the purpose of the exemplary damages could not have been merely to top up compensatory (and aggravate) damages to the level of the profit made at the claimants' expense. Rather, it was meant to disgorge, as it should, the proceeds in addition to awarding compensatory damages.

In *Salsrevski* the Court awarded the claimant the minimum wage (and compensation for the delayed wages) and non-pecuniary damages, and dismissed without prejudice, for lack of jurisdiction, the claim for tort damages while clarifying that the claimant can sue in torts in civil courts.[140] On the traffickers' appeal (*Ben-Ami*), the National Labour Court clarified that the claimant can recover the higher of minimum wage and disgorgement of proceeds (but since the claimant did not cross-appeal the Regional Court's award was left intact).

The Court's discussion of the accumulation with tort damages was confused: it stated that 'the restitutionary award in Labour Courts does not prevent the claimant from filing a tort suit'. But the following discussion, which mentions the (now discredited in Israel) waiver of tort doctrine, confuses between causes of action and remedies, and hints that the claimant could recover only the higher of the restitution and the tort damages.[141] In *K*, the first Israeli substantive judgment against a trafficker in a civil court (which was decided

140 *Salsrevski* (n23) [136].
141 *Ben-Ami* (n6) [32].

before the *Ben-Ami* decision was given by the National Labour Court) the Court awarded tort damages but mistakenly characterised the restitutionary claim as a claim for unpaid wages, so it dismissed this part without prejudice to be litigated in the Labour Court.[142] Appeal and cross-appeal were both rejected in a short judgment (summarised in chapter 2) and the claimant's cross-appeal about the lack of jurisdiction with regards to a gain-based remedy was not rejected on the merits.[143] Moreover, both at trial and on appeal, the gain-based claim was pleaded as conversion of the money and as a claim for unpaid wages, rather than as a restitutionary claim; therefore one should be cautious about interpreting the decision in *Jaack* as conclusive on both jurisdiction and accumulation.

Recently, in *Shivas* (whose facts and holding are analysed in chapter 2) the Court refused to rule on the correctness of the defendants' claim that the Labour Court has exclusive jurisdiction over the restitutionary claim as claim for unpaid wages.[144] This implicitly suggests that restitution can accumulate with tort damages. In *Lifshin*,[145] the Court gave judgment by default against the first defendant, who did not defend the claim. The Court awarded both tort damages (as non-pecuniary loss and punitive damages together) in the sum of NIS 1,000,000 and restitution of profits in the sum of NIS 500,000.[146] In *Grissman*,[147] the Court awarded each claimant NIS 50,400 in gain-based remedy and NIS 100,000 in non-pecuniary loss.

*Lifshin, Bosulevitch* and *Grissman* are weak indications that restitution and compensation accumulate.[148] But since the first two decisions were not given after full argument on the matter, and the latter is a magistrates' court decision, and since, so far, there has been no victim to my knowledge who has sued in both labour courts and civil courts for both tort damages and restitution, the question of accumulation is currently somewhat unsettled under Israeli law. Given the clarification made in *Ben-Ami* about the available restitutionary cause of action, which according to the short and vague discussion of the National Labour Court is based (correctly) on subtraction from the claimant,[149] it should be hoped that once the issue is presented correctly to the court, accumulation of both compensation and restitution will be awarded.

142 *K* (n23) [11].
143 *Jaack* (ch2, n23) [4]–[6]; ch2, section 2.2.
144 See ch2 (n23) [7].
145 See (n6).
146 The claimant claimed NIS 835,000 in non-pecuniary damages and NIS 1,440,000 in unjust enrichment, based on a calculation of 20 clients per day, NIS 200 per client for the duration of a year. The Court did not explain its reason for deviating from the claimant's calculation in the absence of an alternative calculation argued by the defendant.
147 See ch2 (n23).
148 See also *Moaiseyv* (all cited in ch2, n23).
149 See (n6) [32].

## 3.5 Conclusion

Trafficking is an acquisitive wrong. As such it can support both restitution for wrong and restitution by subtraction. The best way to conceptualise trafficking is as an instance in which the trafficker forces the victim to produce labour (or services) and to sell them to clients, and then pockets the proceeds. The proceeds, then, are the exchange product of an asset owned by the victim and sold without authorisation, so the victim can vindicate her property in the proceeds. Even if one were to dispute that the victim can vindicate her property, the victim can sue the trafficker in unjust enrichment since the duress makes the transfer of money voidable; such transfer remains at the victim's expense even if the payment was made directly to the trafficker. Lastly, since trafficking is a serious acquisitive wrong, the victim would be able to disgorge proceeds based on restitution for wrongs and no deduction of expenses should be allowed.

There is much to be said that the victim can recover the higher of the actual proceeds made at her expense and the attributed gain reflecting the market value of the services she was forced to give. The correct measure, however, cannot be reasonable remuneration for the victim's services. Restitution of profits should accumulate with tort damages since the two awards vindicate two different interests. Otherwise, the trafficker can enforce a transaction on the victim in which she is forced to trade her interest in dignity, autonomy and bodily integrity with a pecuniary benefit which she was forced to produce. A result which allows the trafficker to partially compensate his victim for the injuries he has caused with the victim's money is unfair, does not respect principle and undermines deterrence and retribution.

Chapter 4

# Restitution from the state

Confiscation of profits from trafficking is provided for by international obligations, domestic legislation and executive policy.[1] Article 23(3) of the Trafficking Convention,[2] ratified by the UK, imposes an obligation on member states to adopt such legislative and other measures as may be necessary to enable it to 'confiscate or otherwise deprive the instrumentalities and proceeds of criminal offences established in . . . this Convention, or property the value of which corresponds to such proceeds'. Article 15(4) imposes an obligation 'to guarantee compensation for victims in accordance with the conditions under its internal law, for instance through the establishment of a fund for victim compensation . . . which could be funded by the assets confiscated from traffickers'. Such a fund, for example, was created by the Israeli anti-trafficking legislation.[3] This chapter attempts to show that victims of trafficking have a private law restitutionary claim against the state, with respect to money the state confiscates from traffickers as proceeds of trafficking. Therefore, an attempt by victims to enforce the Trafficking Convention's soft obligation to create mechanisms which would compensate victims is *not* victims' only recourse.[4]

In England the state can reach traffickers' profits by criminal confiscation orders, civil recovery orders with respect to property, civil forfeiture of money, taxation of proceeds of crime and general taxation powers of HM Revenue and Customs. All these avenues, save for the last, are mandated by the Proceeds of Crime Act 2002[5] (POCA). While confiscation orders are made against

1 See EU Trafficking Directive (ch1, n30) Article 7; Sentencing Guidelines Council, *Sexual Offences Act 2003 Definitive Guidelines*, part 6, 105, para 6.9, 130 para 10, available at www.sentencing-guidelines.gov.uk/docs/web_SexualOffencesAct_2003.pdf (accessed 12 March 2013).

2 See ch1 (n2).

3 Penal Law 5737–1977 SH 5737; SH 5766, § 377E (Isr).

4 Providing compensation to victims by using what is in effect victims' money is problematic on several grounds, as discussed in section 4.3 and in ch10, section 10.1.

5 (c 29).

traffickers,[6] it is not clear what sums, if any, have been retrieved from UK traffickers in the ways outlined above.[7]

The normative case for restitution from the state seems compelling and uncontroversial: the benefits extracted from victims are the fruit of slave labour – they result from extreme duress and gross violation of dignity and liberty. While the state attempts to target the trafficker, by confiscating his profits on punitive grounds, the money really belongs to the victim. It is hardly appropriate for the state to piggyback on the trafficker's forced transfer of wealth from the victim to himself and appropriate what is really the victim's money. The structure of the victim's claim against the state is therefore two-tiered: first, the victim has a valid restitutionary claim against the trafficker for any benefit the latter obtained at her expense from forcing her into prostitution; second, any direct benefit the state obtained from confiscating the trafficker's profits gives rise to a restitutionary claim of the victim against the state.

The most promising restitutionary claim against the state is based on vindication of property. I do not examine in this chapter three alternative unorthodox theories which might support the state's liability to victims: swollen assets as an expansion of traditional tracing rules for establishing a vindication of property claim;[8] a personal unjust enrichment claim despite the absence of the victim's title to the money paid by the trafficker to the state (which according to orthodoxy makes the state's enrichment not at the expense of the claimant-victim);[9] and an interceptive subtraction claim against the state. The latter claim is based on the argument that the state received from the trafficker an amount which is owed by the trafficker to the claimant in a personal unjust enrichment/restitution for wrong claim. There is much to be

6 See *Dulghieru* (ch2, n7); 'Brothel owner must pay back £2m', http://news.bbc.co.uk/go/em/fr/-/1/hi/england/west_midlands/8209458.stm (5 January 2010).

7 See OSCE/ODIHR compensation report (ch1, n41) 122–4. The *Serious Organised Crime Agency Annual Report* 2008/09 (London: Home Office, 2009) 32 presents the overall sums of cash forfeiture, civil recovery and confiscation orders from the years 2006 onwards but does not give any indication whether any of these sums reflect proceeds of trafficking. In the years 2006 to 2010, 53 confiscation orders were made in respect of human trafficking with an overall value of just under £8 million. However, this figure comes with the caveat that some of the amounts in other categories like 'money laundering (non-drugs)' may well relate to human trafficking cases but it is not possible to separate out that data. T5604/12, email from Justine Currell, Head of Human Trafficking, Home Office, 19 April 2012. It is unclear, however, whether, and if so, to what extent, these confiscation orders have been satisfied.

8 This theory replaces the transactional link required by the tracing exercise with causal inquiry; if the misappropriated money was put in account A and the payment for the defendant was made from account B, and would not have been made but for the misappropriated money, a claim against the defendant would succeed under a swollen assets theory but would fail under the traditional tracing exercise. See Rotherham (ch3, n44) 80–1, 109–11, 178.

9 The new editors of the authoritative *Goff & Jones, The Law Of Unjust Enrichment*, 8th edn (London: Sweet & Maxwell, 2010) 201–17 ('G&J') defend this unorthodox analysis.

said for adopting these theories; in particular, accepting that value remotely received from the claimant could support an unjust enrichment claim has several potential advantages. First, it relieves the claimant from the need to show transactional links between the money misappropriated from her and the money collected by the state. Victims are likely to face considerable difficulties in showing these links to the extent that some might view the possibility of tracing the money as fanciful. Second, it allows recovery by victims from the state – an undoubted solvent body – of what was confiscated from traffickers, without the need to afford victims with proprietary remedies which some might view as problematic. I return to the problem of priority below.

In order to succeed in a traditional vindication of property claim, the victim needs first to show that she had a property right in the value forcefully transferred from her to the trafficker. This was demonstrated in chapter 3 by conceptualising forced prostitution as a situation in which the trafficker forces, under extreme duress, the victim to produce sexual services and sell them to a third party, the client. The money paid by the client is accordingly the exchange product of the victim's resource, which was taken from her in an involuntary manner.

Second, the claimant ought to be able to identify the original misappropriated value in the hands of the state by an exercise of tracing. Section 4.1 argues that the victim can rely on equitable tracing even though she had legal title (and not merely beneficial interest) in the value misappropriated by the trafficker and even under the assumption that the trafficker is not a fiduciary. Section 4.2 argues that to the extent that English law limits equitable tracing to fiduciary relationships, there is a good reason to hold that such a relationship exists between the trafficker and the victim. Section 4.3 explains that the state is not a bona fide purchaser for value and without notice (BFPV) since it neither provides value, nor could be considered as lacking notice of the victim's right. Therefore, it cannot afford itself the general defence available to third parties against proprietary restitution claims. Section 4.4 rejects the claim that the state should be credited for its collection from traffickers of what is owed to the victim in restitution, which arguably increases the chances of a victim's recovery. Lastly, section 4.5 rejects the claim that the profit made by the victim from forced prostitution is taxable income and as such the state should be able to deduct, from what was collected from the trafficker and is subject to restitution to the victim, any amounts that reflect the tax due from the victim.

Note that a similar argument to that made with respect to the confiscated profits could be made with respect to the trafficker's taxed income from trafficking according to general taxation powers (and as distinct from taxing based on confiscation legislation). I do not defend this view here since it is not clear whether such taxation occurs in practice and since such restitutionary claim raises further doctrinal and normative difficulties. From a doctrinal aspect, fixing the state with knowledge about the victim's claim to the money is more difficult to establish. Restitution of taxes also raises unique policy questions, and at times involves special rules regarding private and public law causes of action. From a normative perspective, there is also a question of line drawing. While in the trafficking context, restitution to victims is undeniably desirable from a distributive perspective, such desirability is more questionable in other contexts in which the state taxed a fraudster. For example, it is not entirely clear that those defrauded by Madoff's Ponzi scheme[10] should have a restitutionary claim against the state for what the state taxed Madoff.

## 4.1 Claimant's legal title and wrongdoer's unconscionability

To vindicate her right to her property, the claimant needs to show that what the defendant received was the claimant's property. In our context there is a need to show that the money taken from the victim by the trafficker (to which she retains title, as explained in chapter 3) is what the state confiscated from the trafficker. This is done by the processes of following and tracing, which despite powerful critiques,[11] are still governed by different rules at common law and in equity. As a preliminary point, the analysis is based on the conclusion of chapter 3 that the victim retains title to the money taken by the trafficker. Paradoxically, it will be easier for a victim to trace the money if the transfer of value from her to the trafficker is only voidable. Once the victim elects to rescind the transfer (although, outside of a contractual context it is not obvious how this can be done), equitable title to the money revests in her retroactively and she would be able to trace its value in the hands of anyone who did not give value in good faith and without notice.[12] For reasons explained below, the state cannot be considered as a bona fide purchaser for value and without notice, so the claimant would be able to claim successfully against the state if she succeeds in the tracing exercise.

The difficulty in the trafficking context lies with the fact that while the victim is deprived of money to which she has undivided legal and beneficial title – under the conclusion that the transfer from the victim to the trafficker is void and not merely voidable – the common law tracing rules are less generous than their equitable parallels, so the victim is not likely to be able to trace the value of the money appropriated by the trafficker. The common

10 See www.ft.com/indepth/madoff-scandal (accessed 12 July 2012).

11 *Foskett v McKeown* [2001] 1 AC 102, 128–9 (per Lord Millett), 113 (per Lord Steyn); P Millet, 'Tracing the proceeds of fraud', (1991) 101 *LQR* 71, 71.

12 *El-Ajou v Dollar Land Holdings plc (no 1)* [1994] 2 All ER 685 (CA); *Shalson v Russo* [2005] Ch 281. Peter Millet, who originated this analysis in *El-Ajou*, has retracted from this view extra judicially 'Restitution and constructive trusts', (1998) 114 *LQR* 399, 417. Other strains in the case law largely expand the availability of proprietary relief beyond rescission. For review, see C Rotherham, 'Policy and proprietary remedies: are we all formalists now?', (2012) *Current L Prob's*, doi: 10.1093/clp/cus003 n.72.

law cannot trace money into a mixed fund,[13] while in all likelihood the victim's money has been mixed in a bank account (or otherwise) with other victims' money, or with the trafficker's own money. The rules of tracing in equity, by contrast, developed to allow tracing into mixed substitutes.[14] This raises the question of whether the more generous rules (from a claimant's perspective) which govern equitable tracing are available to claimants who had full title to, and not merely beneficial interest in, the money from which they were deprived without their consent; and whether equitable tracing depends on showing that the defendant owed fiduciary duty to the claimant.[15]

Despite a lack of conclusive authority, the question is rather academic. It is almost inconceivable that courts would deny a victim of theft the protection of the more generous equitable tracing rules and remedies: 'no one seems willing to accept equity's impotence in this final category in which the proprietary base is purely legal and there is no fiduciary relationship'.[16] It is rightly denounced as absurd that a claimant who has full title in his misappropriated money would have lesser protection than one who has merely beneficial interest.[17] Despite the existence of some views to the contrary,[18] such a conclusion is overwhelmingly supported by judicial dicta, and commentators, although the exact way in which this common-sense and just solution is achieved is hotly debated. It is also telling that it is hard, if not impossible, to find cases in which the claimant whose money was misappropriated when he had full title to it did not get relief in circumstances in which equitable tracing rules would have provided him with adequate protection.[19]

Different solutions have been offered for the problem. One solution is simply to ditch the distinction between common law and equity tracing rules and apply the more generous equity rules to all claimants.[20] A second (related) solution is to view the theft as creating a resulting trust, based on the view

13 *Banque Belge Pour L'Etranger v Hambrouck* [1921] 1 KB 321, 330 (CA).

14 *Re Hallett's Estate* (1880) 13 ChD 696; *Foskett* (n11).

15 As suggested by the Court of Appeal in *Agip (Africa) Ltd v Jackson* [1991] Ch 547, 566.

16 Smith (ch3, n44) 345.

17 *Jones* (ch3, n51) [21] (Millett LJ), [38] (Beldman LJ); cf Smith, id; Virgo (ch1, n5) 610.

18 S Bakerhall Thomas, 'Thieves as trustees: the enduring legacy of *Black v S Freedman & Co Ltd*', (2009) 3 *J Eq* 52, 71; cf W Swadling, 'Ignorance and title', (2008) 28 *OJLS* 627 (no title passes in cases of theft; but Swadling targets the possibility of a personal claim in unjust enrichment, not necessarily the ability to trace. See his discussion at 642); Rimer J in *Shalson* (n12) [110] opposed viewing the thief as trustee, but did not necessarily oppose allowing the application of equitable tracing rules to such situations.

19 See e.g. *Lipkin* (ch3, n12); *Jones* (n17). In *Shalson*, id, the claimant had a right to exercise equitable tracing following rescission of the loan contract, but the tracing exercise was unsuccessful since the account was overdrawn. Moreover, Rimer J specifically opined at [110] that the answer to the stolen money problem is to 'develop those powers so as to meet the special problems raised by stolen money'.

20 See sources in n11; Smith (n16) 345; M Pawlowski, 'Constructive trusts, tracing and the requirement of fiduciary obligation', (2005) 11 *Trusts and Tr'ees* 10.

that a resulting trust is created when there is a transfer of value that is not accompanied by the transferor's intent to confer the benefit upon the transferee.[21] Alternatively, and more narrowly, equity imposes a resulting trust on property bought with value provided by the claimant; value could include stolen money or goods.[22] The latter, narrower version would cover money paid by the client directly to the trafficker as a substitute for the victim's misappropriated services; it would not cover money paid to the victim by the client that was later appropriated by the trafficker.

A third solution would be to view theft as fitting with equity's traditional purview either because theft is a type of fraud, which is one of equity's areas of intervention, *or* because and insofar as the legal remedy is inadequate.[23] A fourth solution would be to view the thief as a constructive trustee. Lord Brown Wilkinson in *Westdeutsche LG v Islington LBC* supported such a solution based on the observation that '[W]hen property is obtained by fraud equity imposes a constructive trust on the fraudulent recipient'.[24] Australian and Canadian courts have adopted such a solution, which is referred to as the theft principle.[25] To address the difficulty of viewing a thief who has no legal title in the money as trustee,[26] it was suggested that titles at common law are relative, and therefore, while the owner has the better title, the thief does acquire a title to the money that makes him a constructive trustee.[27] More broadly, it is well established that a constructive trust would arise (regardless of whether the defendant could be characterised as a fiduciary) where a person obtains property by means of his unconscionable behaviour.[28] This includes the holder of a mistaken payment, from the moment he is conscious of that fact,[29] fraudsters

21 *Air Jamaica Ltd v Charlton* [1999] 1 WLR 1399 (Lord Millett); R Chambers, *Resulting Trusts* (Oxford: Clarendon Press, 1997) 21. For the view that resulting trusts exist merely where the transferor intends to retain beneficial interest, see *Westdeutsche LG v Islington LBC* [1996] AC 669, 708 (Lord Brown Wilkinson). For an overview of the debate, see E O'Dell, 'The resulting trust', in C Rickett and R Grantham (eds), *Structure and Justification in Private Law* (Oxford: Oxford University Press, 2008), ch 19.

22 Chambers, id, 117; Bakerhall Thomas (n18) 62.

23 Smith (n16) 345–6.

24 *Westdeutsche* (n21) 714–15. Cf Smith, id. In *Halifax* (ch3, n86) the lender was refused the beneficial interest accruing to the fraudster as the result of his fraud.

25 *Black v S Freedman & Co Ltd* (1910) 12 CLR 105; J Tarrant, 'Thieves as trustees: in defence of the theft principle', (2009) 3 *J Eq* 170, 170; *Re Kolari* (1981) 36 OR (2d) 473 (Canada); Bakerhall Thomas (n18) 63.

26 This difficulty was noted by Bakerhall Thomas and Swadling (both cited in n18); Virgo (n17) 609–10.

27 Tarrant (n25) 173–8 based on *Costello v CC of Derbyshire* [2001] EWCA Civ 381 [15] and *Islamic Republic of Iran v Barakat Galleries Ltd* [2007] EWCA Civ 1374 [15]; cf Swadling, id, 650–1.

28 Virgo (n17) 608–12.

29 *Westdeutsche*, (n21) 714–15, Lord Brown Wilkinson interpreting the holding in *Chase Manhattan Bank v Israel-British Bank (London) Ltd* [1981] Ch 105.

who obtain property,[30] those who obtain property on the understanding they would give effect to another party's rights and unconsciously refuse to do so[31] and, as explained above, arguably thieves as well.

It is quite apparent, therefore, that courts do not really insist on showing that the person who misappropriated the claimant's money was in fact a fiduciary. Nor should they. Such a requirement is illogical, unjust and undesirable. It is illogical, since as mentioned above, it provides lesser protection to those with stronger rights. It is unjust, because it allows thieves and their transferees to benefit at the expense of the owner, and since it leaves a very serious wrong without an adequate remedy. Moreover, the result does not fit with general rules governing priorities among creditors, which suggest that an involuntary creditor who provided value, did not take any risk of insolvency and is not at fault should have priority.[32] A result that leaves the misappropriated owner without any effective proprietary remedy is unjust also with respect to the claimant vis-à-vis other creditors of the thief.

## 4.2 Traffickers as fiduciaries

I would argue, however, that even if someone were to insist (why?) that equitable tracing should be limited to fiduciaries, the trafficker should be viewed as such. On the broader view, the gist of a fiduciary relationship is the control and power exercised by the fiduciary over the principal's interests.[33] While traditionally the power and control are exercised with respect to the principal's property or financial interests, clearly there is no such limitation.[34] For this reason, physicians and psychologists who sleep with their patients are potentially liable for breach of fiduciary duty.[35] The rationale that having control over the claimant's interests justifies increased duty towards the

30 See e.g. *Stocks v Wilson* [1913] 2 KB 235, 244 (Lush J).

31 *Ashburn Anstalt v Arnold* [1989] Ch 1.

32 But see W Swadling, 'Policy arguments for proprietary restitution', (2008) 28 *LS* 506, who maintains that the question of whether the claimant has title, is antecedent, and should not be confused with the question of priorities in bankruptcy. For a critique of Swadling's account as formalistic and unpersuasive, see Rotherham (n12).

33 This conceptualisation is especially popular among Canadian courts and commentators. See *Follis v Township of Albemarle* [1941] 1 DLR 178, 181–2 (McTague J); *Frame v Smith* (1987) 42 DLR (4th), 81, 98–9 (Wilson J); *LAC Minerals Ltd v International Corona Resources Ltd* (1989) 61 DLR (4th), 14, 63 (Sopinka J); E Weinrib, 'The fiduciary obligation', (1975) 25 *UTLJ* 1; L Sealy, 'The fiduciary relationship', (1962) 20 *CLJ* 69; J Glover, 'The identification of fiduciaries', in P Birks (ed), *Privacy and Loyalty* (Oxford: Oxford University Press, 1997) ch 10, 276–8.

34 See e.g. *Reading v A-G* [1951] AC 507 (HL); *Att Gen v Blake* [1998] Ch 439 (CA); *White v Jones* [1995] 2 AC 207 (acting in relation to the property or affairs of another test by Lord Brown Wilkinson). Contrast with *Sinclair Investment Holding SA v Versailles Trade Finance Ltd* [2005] EWCA Civ 722, [21].

35 See e.g. *Norberg* (ch1, n18) (per JJ McLachlin and L'Heureux-Dubé).

controlled person is relevant to other areas of private law such as undue influence and duty of care towards inmates and pupils.[36] It is also relevant to public law norms such as the quasi-fiduciary duty of public servants, and the criminalising of certain conduct jeopardising the interests of the vulnerable.[37]

The ultimate control that traffickers extract over victims is so extensive as to be unparalleled in all the instances mentioned above. Moreover, the typical characteristics of fiduciary duty – a long-term relationship and opportunities to abuse the power and control undeniably exist. So a fiduciary relationship is clearly established, unless the control that needs to be exercised by the fiduciary ought to be limited to the beneficiary's *financial* affairs. But such limitation is as illogical as prioritising those with mere equitable interest over those with full title with respect to the ability to trace. In fact, even if fiduciary relationships were to be construed so narrowly, it still clearly exists in our context. The trafficker controls (among other things) all the financial affairs of the forced prostitute. He decides how many clients she will see, what services she will provide, how much she (or the trafficker himself) should collect for these services, how much money (if any) the victim will receive and what is done with the money earned. No broader control over a beneficiary's financial interests could in fact exist.

On a narrower view, the gist of fiduciary duty is not only control over the principal (or her financial affairs) but also a trusting relationship. English authorities are replete with entrustment rhetoric. The beneficiary entrusted her affairs to the fiduciary and gave him control over her affairs; and the fiduciary has assumed an undertaking, and therefore the increased duty.[38] One could distinguish between a condition of voluntary entrustment by the principal, voluntary assumption of responsibility by the fiduciary, or a requirement for both. I will proceed on the assumption that both are required, despite the fact that the authorities could be read as suggesting that it is sufficient that reliance by the principal exists, even if such reliance is not voluntary.

36 *Kirkham v CC Greater Manchester* [1990] 2 QB 283; *Bradford Smart v West Sussex CC* [2002] EWCA Civ 7. On the relationship between fiduciary duties and undue influence, see Peel (ch3, n68) 452–3.

37 See e.g. *Blackpool and Fylde Aero Club v Blackpool CC* [1990] 1 WLR 1195, 1201 (fiduciary duty of public authority to ratepayers in managing financial affairs); *Equitable Life Assurance Society v Hyman* [2002] 1 AC 408, [17]; M Conaglen, 'Public-private intersection: comparing fiduciary conflict doctrine and bias', (2008) 1 *Pub L* 58; the Fraud Act 2006 (c 35) (introducing fraud by abuse of position); the Mental Capacity Act 2005 (c 9) (introducing two offences of ill-treatment and wilful neglect of a person who lacks capacity to make relevant decisions).

38 See e.g. *Tate v Williamson* (1866) LR 2 Ch App 55, 61 (relationship involving confidence reposed by one); *Bristol and West Building Society v Mothew* [1998] Ch 1, 18 (Lord Millett) (tripartite test of undertaking, reliance and vulnerability); P Finn, *Fiduciary Obligations* (Sydney: Law Book, 1977) 9 (undertaking test); cf J Shepherd, 'Towards a unified concept of fiduciary relationships', (1981) 97 *LQR* 51 (test of receiving power on condition of duty to utilise it to the best interests of another).

Rhetoric aside, it is doubtful whether the narrower view adequately explains the existence of fiduciary duties that do not necessarily follow voluntary entrustments. From the fiduciary's perspective, the most obvious example of a duty without assumption of responsibility is a fiduciary duty under a constructive trust that arises by operation of law without regard to the parties' intentions.[39] While

> whether the constructive trustee should be regarded as fiduciary is a controversial matter . . . it should be possible for a constructive trustee to be subject to such fiduciary obligation where he or she knew the facts by virtue of which the constructive trust was imposed.[40]

In such circumstances, the constructive trustee might be subject to fiduciary duty despite the fact he did not assume it voluntarily.[41] The position of fraudsters and those who consciously retain money paid under mistake are two cases in point.

Even more common is the recognition of a fiduciary relationship where the principal does not voluntarily repose trust in the fiduciary[42] and in fact might be reluctant to have her affairs controlled by anyone. Bailiffs, who are fiduciaries,[43] might be willing to assume responsibility since they hold this office voluntarily; however the litigant is subject to the bailiff's power without any voluntary entrustment. Patients often choose the physician who cares for them, but it would be odd to suggest that a physician who treats a patient who did not choose him is not subject to fiduciary duty. Wards often do not choose their guardians and many residents of the local authority cannot be considered as choosing to entrust the public official with their interests in any meaningful way. More broadly, in many modern commercial situations giving rise to fiduciary duties the principal cannot control, and often does not even know, the fiduciary's identity (e.g. the individual who buys stock for investment purposes) and there is frequently no meaningful consent to even enter into a fiduciary relationship: employees who are legally or economically compelled to join a pension fund cannot really control the way the money is being invested.

There is also reason to doubt whether the requirement that the principal would voluntarily repose trust in the fiduciary is normatively attractive. While a requirement of assumption of responsibility by the fiduciary as a condition

39 *Air Jamaica* (n21) 1412 (Lord Millett).

40 Virgo (n17) 501. For the relationship between separation of legal and equitable title and the existence of fiduciary duty, see *Hardoon v Belilios* [1901] AC 118 (PC Hong Kong); *Westdeutsche* (n21) 706–7; L Smith, 'Constructive fiduciaries?', in *Privacy and Loyalty* (n33) ch 9, 255–8; Smith (n16) 342–3.

41 Shepherd (n38) 67.

42 Cf *Norberg* (n35) 273 (McLachlin J).

43 See Sealy (n33) 75.

for a fiduciary relationship might be easier to justify, given the far-reaching scope of the duty, at least where the defendant voluntarily took control over the claimant's affairs, it is just to regard him as a fiduciary. Indeed, even James Edelman, who recently defended the thesis that fiduciary duties are duties expressed or implied in relationships involving manifestations of voluntary undertakings stresses that 'voluntary undertakings are assessed by objective manifestations of conduct' to support his conclusion that the duty imposed on custodial parents is a manifestation of voluntary undertaking even for those 'for whom custodial parenthood was not actively chosen'.[44] While one may doubt whether involuntary parenthood reflects an objective manifestation of voluntary undertaking, a trafficker taking control of the victim's affairs is obviously such manifestation.

It is plainly unjust and illogical that a principal whose affairs are controlled by another without her consent be afforded any less protection compared to a principal who voluntarily entrusted a fiduciary with running her affairs and by this took the risk of being mishandled by the fiduciary. If at all, the analogy with rules governing priorities among creditors suggests the involuntary principal should be preferred.[45] When a person entrusts someone else with running her affairs the two inherent risks she voluntarily takes are that the fiduciary would either abuse the trust or be incompetent. No such risks are taken by a person whose property is misappropriated.

In any event, the typical trafficking scenario gives rise to fiduciary duties even under the narrower definition of fiduciary relationships. Typically, as documented in chapter 2, victims are recruited by fraudulent means with respect to either the purpose of the travel or the conditions under which they will be held. Once they entrust the recruiter with their journey and the journey begins, they lose control over their affairs. Recall that fraud was traditionally within equity's purview. On this understanding, trafficking is an extreme case in which the initial fraud is followed by extreme forms of duress which results in significant transfer of value from the victim to the trafficker. Unless one is committed to the view that the voluntary act of entrusting the fiduciary should extend to consent that the fiduciary would control the principal's affairs, fiduciary relationships can be established. But such a view is plainly indefensible: it treats the fraudulent recruiter fiduciary more leniently than the honest recruiter fiduciary. True, typically the fraudulent recruiter is not the trafficker who enslaves the victim and misappropriates her money. But this could and should be solved by viewing the recruiter as the trafficker's agent, or by viewing both as engaging in an illegal joint venture.[46] The Court in *AT*

44 J Edelman, 'When do fiduciary duties arise?', (2010) 126 *LQR* 302, 312.

45 But see Swadling (n32) 517, who observes that priority in bankruptcy does not adhere to this rationale by failing to give priority to involuntary tort creditors.

46 See ch2, section 2.3.4, and Stevens (ch2, n53) 281–3 (equity's attribution for dishonest assistance).

*v Dulghieru* adopted a similar approach by basing the traffickers' liability on conspiracy to traffic the claimants.[47] In conclusion then, fiduciary duty is called for both because the trafficker voluntarily entered into a relationship in which he controls the victim and her affairs and the victim voluntarily reposed trust in the trafficker's associates, and this reliance brought her under the trafficker's control.

## 4.3 No bona fide purchaser for value defence for the state

### *4.3.1 The trafficker's obligation to the state*

The discussion has so far established that the victim has title to the money which the trafficker misappropriated and that she should be allowed to trace the money in the hands of third parties according to the more general equitable tracing rules. The fact that the state, the relevant third party, receives the money by virtue of the relevant legislation, POCA, does not terminate the victim's title.

POCA distinguishes between confiscation orders, which are imposed after conviction, and civil recovery of cash and other forms of property. There are several relevant distinctions between the two avenues. First, the purpose and effect of confiscation orders is not merely remedial, stripping the offender of the unlawful gain, but rather punitive, so the amount subject to confiscation could exceed the actual proceeds of crime.[48] Trafficking for sex purposes and controlling prostitution for gain are criminal lifestyle offences, which allow the court to make several assumptions that facilitate the finding that a recoverable amount exists.[49] Second, the confiscation order is an obligation to pay an amount of money, rather than forfeiture of specific property;[50] therefore the rights of innocent third parties in property held by the criminal are not directly implicated. Clearly then, a restitutionary claim by the victim against the state with respect to the money extracted from her by the trafficker is not blocked or obliterated by the provisions of POCA that govern confiscation orders.

Slightly different conclusions are warranted in the case of civil recovery. POCA creates a distinction between cash and other forms of property;[51] the former could be subject to forfeiture; the latter is subject to a recovery order.

47 *Dulghieru* (n6).

48 *R v Rezvi* [2003] 1 AC 1099, [14]; Smith [2002] 2 Cr App R(S) 33; *Mitchell, Taylor and Talbot on Confiscation and the Proceeds of Crime*, 3rd edn, Vol 2 (London: Sweet & Maxwell, 2002), V.045 ('MTT').

49 POCA (n5), ss 6(4) and (5), 7(1), 10(1) 75(2)(a); Sch 2, paras 4, 8.

50 MTT (n48) V.079.

51 Part 5, chs 2, 3.

Either way, the civil recovery targets the proceeds of crime (termed unlawful behaviour) and is proprietary in nature. It includes provisions relating to following, tracing and mixing of property,[52] and, with respect to property, protects good faith purchasers for value and without notice.[53] For both cash and property, there are provisions protecting the rights of the victim who argues that the cash or property belong to her.[54] The court needs to be satisfied that the applicant was deprived of the cash or property by unlawful conduct, that the cash or property belonged to the applicant and that it was not recoverable property immediately before she was deprived of it. Unsurprisingly, the gist of the victim's vindication of property claim analysed in this and the previous chapter is similar to a claim made under s 301 of POCA, relating to civil forfeiture of cash. Moreover, the analysis does not change much where the vindication of property claim concerns money confiscated under a confiscation order. The victim had title to the money that was not recoverable property immediately before she was deprived of it unlawfully. If the victim can trace the money, the state will need to establish its status as bona fide purchaser for value in order to avoid restitution. As shall be explained, the state cannot establish the defence.

Recall that the confiscation order is an obligation to pay an amount of money, rather than forfeiture of specific property. The analysis should distinguish between the creation of the obligation and its satisfaction. The court order creates the criminal's obligation to pay the state the amount confiscated. That the state might resort to collection practices (such as garnishment) which are involuntary from the debtor's perspective does not change the conclusion that the obligation to abide by the confiscation order is merely that – an obligation.

### *4.3.2 Wrongful calculation and wrongful satisfaction*

In theory, one can distinguish between two possible claims against the state; these claims should be kept separate and are independent of each other. The first type of claim is that the confiscation order was calculated based on property which does not belong to the debtor-trafficker; therefore, the confiscation order should be set aside (based on mistake of fact or some other ground). The second type of claim is that the trafficker's debt was satisfied with money which the victim could trace. Let us assume that the trafficker's recoverable amount was determined to be £100,000, of which £60,000 were derived from the claimant-victim. Claim (1) would be that the recoverable amount for purposes of confiscation should be merely £40,000; so if the order

52 Sections 304–6.
53 Section 308(1).
54 Section 301 (cash); s 281 (property).

was satisfied in full, the state should make restitution to the victim of the extra £60,000 it collected from the trafficker, regardless of whether the victim could trace the £60,000, since this amount was collected based on an underlying confiscation order wrongfully viewing the £60,000 as an amount which could be recovered by the state. Claim (2) would arise if the trafficker paid part of the confiscation order with money traceable to the victim. It is important to see that claim (2) is independent of claim (1). So even if the court would assess the recoverable amount at only £40,000 (excluding the money owned by the victim) but the state will satisfy this amount from money traceable by the claimant, it will still have to make restitution to the claimant, as explained below.

The first type of claim raises interesting and difficult questions and will not be pursued fully here. It could be argued that misappropriated property is not part of the trafficker's property for purposes of calculating the recoverable amount. Section 84(2)(a)–(b) of POCA provides that property is held or obtained by a person if he holds or obtains an interest in it. According to the (disputed) view discussed above that a thief does not get any title in the money or goods stolen, it could be held that stolen property is not part of the criminal's benefit from the crime. Similar analysis could be made based on s 79(3), according to which if a person holds an interest in the defendant's property, the value of the property is the value of the defendant's share. Arguably, stolen property belongs in full to the victim. However, it does not seem that courts and commentators adhere to this approach.[55]

But, in any event, if the trafficker's (arguably excessive) recoverable amount was paid with what is not the victim's money, the victim does not seem to have any claim against the state; she could trace her property which is still in the trafficker's hands. If the victim lost the ability to trace her money in the trafficker's hands then the payment to the state could arguably be recovered only if one of the three unorthodox theories mentioned in the introduction to this chapter could be defended. The following argument, therefore, proceeds on the *assumption* that wrongful calculation does not confer on the victim any cause of action against the state.

Since the state's entitlement to satisfaction of the confiscation order is merely a chose in action, its satisfaction with money which could be traced by the claimant does not in itself terminate the victim's title to the money. This could have been the result had the relevant legislation provided such a specific defence; but it does not. Therefore, the state needs to rely on the general defence available to third parties against proprietary claims.

A bona fide purchase for value is the general defence afforded to third parties against proprietary-based restitutionary claims. Such a defence, however, could not be established where the state confiscates the proceeds of

55 See e.g. *Alagobola* [2004] 2 Cr App R(S) 48; MTT (n48) V.059.

crime. As explained below, there are serious doubts about whether the state gives value in receiving these amounts; but even if it does, it receives the money while it is fixed with notice of the victim's right to the money.

### *4.3.3 No value provided by the state*

The strongest case for viewing the state as giving value is this: the issuing of the confiscation order by the court affords the state with a chose in action against the trafficker. By discharging the trafficker's debt in return for receiving the payment (made with the victim's money) the state provides value.[56] Nevertheless, serious doubts exist whether in our context[57] value is provided.[58] The creation of the trafficker's *underlying obligation* towards the state, which is paid with the claimant's money, was not supported by value received from the state. This is in contrast to cases recognising discharge of debt as value, in which the defendant has provided value in the hands of the debtor prior to the discharge of the debt with the claimant's money. In the typical discharge of debt case, the defence is supported by the accounting for disenrichment rationale which also supports the change of position defence: that of responding to the equities of the interaction and striking a fair balance between the competing parties.[59] Such rationale cannot afford the state with a defence since it clearly did not give value in return for the money confiscated from the trafficker.

This, however, might prove too much. The state never provides value in the relevant sense when it discharges – against payment – any tax-payer of her obligation, imposed by the state, to pay a particular tax. Similarly, the above analysis would exclude tort victims – whose chose in action against the tortfeasor is not typically supported by value provided to the tortfeasor – from

56 See e.g. *Thomson v Clydesdale Bank Ltd* [1893] AC 282, 287–8.

57 I leave aside here the broader doubts of whether the discharge of any debt should be considered as value for purposes of the defence, so that the only defence available to the recipient of the payment is a change of position. For the minority view in American cases rejecting the BFPV defence for discharge of a debt, see A Kull, 'Defenses to restitution: the bona fide creditor', (2001) 81 *Bos ULR* 919, 931.

58 There is also doubt whether 'purchase' is satisfied since the acquisition of the interest is by operation of law as opposed to acquisition through a consensual transfer. See Birks (ch3, n50) 244; Smith (n16) 386. In such cases, of relevance is whether the third party's right does not derive from the transferor (e.g. acquisition by escheat), or does (e.g. forfeiture of estate). In the latter case, which resembles more the confiscation scenario, the superior landlord is bound by the equitable right. See B McFarlane and R Stevens, 'The nature of equitable property', (2010) 4 *J Eq* 1, 6. To the extent that the rationale behind the defence is security of transactions (as opposed to merely accounting for disenrichment), the state should not be afforded with the defence.

59 Cf Kull (n57) 929. Indeed, some view BFPV as the paradigmatic change of position case. Millet (n11) 82. But see n57. Typically, the creditor is not worse off if he is under an obligation to make restitution for discharged debt made with the claimant's money.

relying on the defence in case their chose in action was satisfied with the claimant's traceable money. Whether such result is mandated by the English authorities is unclear; whether such exclusion is justified is debated.[60] Should discharge of any tax debt and tort liability be considered as not satisfying the value requirement?

One possible answer would be that both categories (tax and tort) fail the value test; a second answer would hold that no discharge of tax debt satisfies the value requirement (but a different result might be or is warranted with respect to the discharge of a tort debt); a third answer would maintain that the discharge of both tax debt and tort debt provides value, but not the discharge of the trafficker's obligation to pay the confiscation order due to a distinguishing element. I turn now to defend the latter claim while leaving open the desirability of a solution categorically denying all discharges of tax debt as instances in which value has been provided. I will not try to resolve here the debate about the status of tort creditors. As will be explained immediately below, even if a tort creditor should be considered as providing value by discharging the tortfeasor's debt which was paid with the claimant's money, a different conclusion is warranted with respect to the state, at least in our context.

The real (and narrow) reason, then, that the defence should not be allowed in our context is this: the state's claim against the trafficker is not independent, but is rather parasitic on and therefore subordinate to the victim's claim against the trafficker. In the typical tracing scenario (which often involves the debtor's bankruptcy), the general creditors' rights against the debtor accrue independently from the claimant's right to restitution. Arguably, therefore, it would be unjust to make them the claimant's involuntary insurers against the debtor's misappropriating the claimant's money.[61] In contrast, the trafficker's obligations to the state are not independent from his obligation towards the victim. It is not only that, but for the misappropriation of the victim's money, the trafficker would not have had the money to satisfy the obligation towards the state. This is the case in normal swollen assets situations, for example, where the debtor uses the claimant's money to discharge expenses which he would have discharged in any event from his own money and therefore more money is left to the creditors to be satisfied. Rather, the trafficker's obligation towards the state arises *because*, and is calculated based on the facts giving rise to the trafficker's obligation towards the victim. The confiscation of proceeds

60 In the context of bankruptcy, compare H Dagan, 'Restitution in bankruptcy: why all involuntary creditors should be preferred', (2004) 78 *Am Bank LJ* 247 with Rotherham (n8) 80–1, 109–11, 178, positing that both involuntariness and provision of value are conditions for preference. The latter view is endorsed by *Restatement (Third) of Restitution* (ch3, n100) § 55 and finds support in recent English case law, as documented by Rotherham (n12). Examples include *Papamichael v National Westminster Bank* [2003] EWHC 164 (Comm), [229], and *Sinclair Investments v Versailles* [2011] EWCA Civ 347, [83].

61 Cf Smith (n16) 315.

of crime is based on the breach of duty towards the victim that enriched the trafficker. Such enrichment is the legal *reason* for the *creation* of the obligation to the state.

But once the parasitic nature of the state's claim against the trafficker is understood, its subordinate nature should follow as a matter of principle, logic and policy. The state's interest in punishing the trafficker, or ensuring that he does not profit from his crime, should give way to the victim's interest in preventing the trafficker and the state from being unjustly enriched at her expense. One manifestation of this understanding is that the BFPV defence is unavailable to the state. The argument is *not* based on the premise that the trafficker's obligation to the state does not exist. Were this the case, there would be no value provided by the state in discharging the trafficker's non-existing obligation. Rather, since the creation of the trafficker's obligation to the state is parasitic on the trafficker's obligation to make restitution to the claimant, the former obligation is subordinated to the latter; as such its discharge (unlike the discharge of an independent obligation) does not provide value for purposes of the BFPV defence to the victim's claim against the state.

The conclusion that the state's claim is parasitic or derivative of the victim's claim could face two challenges. First, as mentioned above, the purpose of a confiscation order is punitive, so the amount confiscated might exceed actual proceeds. But since the victim's claim is limited to the profit made at her expense which she can trace, any surplus which reflects a non-parasitic interest is not threatened by recognising the victim's priority. In contrast, the part of the recoverable amount which indeed reflects the profit made at the claimant's expense is parasitic, as explained above. Indeed, the state's (remedial) interest in confiscation of proceeds of crime and in punishing the offender is subordinated to the victim's right to compensation. This principle is well established in confiscation legislation,[62] and legislation dealing with criminal fines. This principle is also partially recognised by POCA in ss 6(6) and 7(3), under which the duty to impose an order becomes a power if the victim has started or intends to start a civil claim, and the court can, but does not have to, decrease the amount to be confiscated below what is otherwise recoverable, in order to preserve the victim's recoverability.

The second challenge posits that the state suffers harm from the criminal activity and accordingly, confiscation of proceeds of crime is an approximate compensation for that harm. If this view is correct, it might belie the characterisation of the state as being unjustly enriched at the victim's expense. But this view is unconvincing for several reasons. To begin with, even if we were to accept that the state is a victim of the criminal activity which ought to be

62 See e.g. Criminal Justice Act 1988 (UK), s 72(7); Forfeiture of Profits from Publications Recounting Crime Law 5765-2005 SH, 1993, § 2(b), § 6 (Isr); NY Exec Law 632-a(3) (McKinney, 2001); Prohibiting Profiting from Recounting Crimes Act, SO 2002, c 2, § 9(3) (Ontario); Israel's Penal Law (n3) § 377E.

compensated for that, a priority to the state is unwarranted. In one view, since victims are involuntary creditors who also gave value, they should be given priority over other involuntary creditors (such as tort victims) which did not. In another view, all involuntary victims should be treated the same. Even if the latter view, which does not reflect existing priorities in bankruptcy law, were to be adopted, the harm to the state, which should be quantified and proven – not an easy task – should be compared to both the harm to victims and victims' claims in restitution, and a pro rata satisfaction of claims should be made.

But both the notions that the state suffers a loss from the criminal activity and that this loss is what justifies confiscation of proceeds of crime are dubious. There is no support in POCA (and equivalent legislation) and the case law interpreting it that its goal is compensatory rather than stripping the offender from unlawful gain or further punishing him. Next, it is not entirely clear in what ways the state as distinct from victims and potential victims is really harmed by the criminal activity. Does the harm lie in the need to have law enforcement activity to fight the crime? (This idea is examined below.) Interestingly, in the context of sex trafficking both source and destination countries reap some indirect and unintended benefits from trafficking which boost their economy and some have even argued that this gives states a disincentive to fight the phenomenon more rigorously.[63] But even if the state is harmed, the loss is essentially unquantifiable and there is no reason to assume that the defendant's gain should reflect the state's loss. In addition, the state's harm, if it exists, is more amorphous than the harm caused to the victim, so the logic of subordination still applies. Moreover, not only does the victim have a concrete vindication of property claim, but she also has a concrete claim for tort damages which ought to exceed the profit made at her expense and should accumulate with restitution. Given the fact that in practice the proceeds of crime would be the only source to satisfy both claims, the approach that these claims could be subordinated to the state's interest in confiscation is highly unpalatable. In the context of sex trafficking, giving priority to victims' claims over the state's is also mandated based on distributive ground, given victims' vulnerability[64] – any other rule would result in a forced transfer of value from a very vulnerable group, through the trafficker, to the state.

### *4.3.4 Notice of the victim's right to the money*

The BFPV defence fails for a more fundamental reason, which is also relevant for the denial of a change of position defence under an unjust enrichment claim. When the state received the money from the trafficker in satisfaction of a confiscation order, or as civil forfeiture of money, it ought to have had

63 Levenkron (ch1, n38) 464.
64 See ch5, section 5.1.2; ch7, section 7.6.

notice[65] of the rights of victims (albeit unidentifiable) with respect to that money. The recoverable amount under POCA's confiscation orders is based on a calculation of the trafficker's benefit from having trafficked the victims. Where the criminal is found to conduct a criminal lifestyle the court is allowed to make certain assumptions under which the property held or disposed of by the defendant within a certain time framework is presumed to reflect the benefit from crime. Despite the fact that this approach does not directly calculate the benefit from the crimes committed, still the presumption's effect is to conclude that the value of the assets subject to confiscation reflects the benefit derived from the criminal lifestyle. Therefore, at least when the relevant offences triggering confiscation or civil recovery are trafficking, or prostitution-related, any amount confiscated from traffickers should at least raise a suspicion that forced CSPs might have title to the money. Our context exemplifies the circumstances – mentioned by Lord Herschell in *Thomson v Clydesdale Bank Ltd* – in which the defence would be inapplicable:

> No doubt if the person receiving the money has reason to believe that the payment is being made in fraud of a third person, and that the person making the payment is handing over in discharge of his debt money which he has no right to hand over, then the person taking such payment would not be entitled to retain the money, upon ordinary principles which I need not dwell upon.[66]

Clearly the same conclusion is warranted with respect to tax assessments made under Part 6 of POCA, since such taxation as well is based on the offender's crime which in the case of trafficking necessarily involves the misappropriation of victims' money.

## 4.4 Costs of collection should not be reimbursed

This section examines a potential partial state defence: arguably, the confiscation of the profits by the state facilitates the claimant's recovery of the amount owed to her by the trafficker in restitution. This could happen either because the state has (at least presumably) greater ability to ensure that the confiscation order is satisfied or because it could act earlier (relative to the claimant) before the money is hidden. If this is true, the claimant stands a better chance of recovering what is owed to her by the trafficker, due to the

65 The claimant's claim is based on equitable tracing rules, so the state's notice ought to be constructive: an objective test to make reasonable inquiries rather than actual, subjective dishonesty. *Nelson v Larholt* [1948] 1 KB 339; *Macmillan Inc v Bishopsgate Investment Trust plc (no 3)* [1995] 1 WLR 978, 1014; Hanbury & Martin, *Modern Equity*, 18th edn (London: Stevens, 2009) 39.

66 See n56; 287–8.

state's activity. Can the state claim reimbursement of these costs in unjust enrichment so that in practice it will be able to deduct these costs from what is due to the victim in her vindication of property claim against the state?

Before examining the chances of such a claim in unjust enrichment it will be useful to note that the Israeli statutory regulation of this matter adopted a very similar approach. Israel's Prohibition of Trafficking in Persons (Legislative Amendments) Law 2006 created a fund[67] in which trafficking-based confiscated property is deposited. Expenditure from the fund is authorised for four purposes: (a) rehabilitation, treatment and protection of victims of an offence; (b) compensation of victims showing a final judgment for compensation and no reasonable possibility to realise all or part of the judgment; (c) prevention of the commission of an offence; and (d) carrying out the functions of law enforcement authorities in enforcing the provisions of this law in respect to an offence. The first purpose should be funded by at least half of the annual amount in the fund. The scheme raises several distributive difficulties discussed elsewhere – it uses victims' money for purposes other than compensating them and involves both a subsidy given by victims to potential victims and other members of society and a subsidy given by victims whose traffickers' assets were confiscated to other victims who can claim compensation from the fund.[68] For our purposes, the important point is that the relevant regulation gives first priority to the payment of a management fee to the fund's administrator.[69] If the following discussion establishes that a right for reimbursement does not exist in unjust enrichment law, the special rule created by the statutory scheme could be criticised for deviating from principle, not being supported by policy and leading to regressive effects according to which vulnerable and poor victims are subject to an exceptional duty to reimburse. As clarified below, the state's unjust enrichment claim with respect to reimbursement of costs should fail for two reasons: first, there are serious doubts whether the victim is enriched from the law enforcement activity; second, since the state acts to further its own interests, and given a proper understanding of the role of the state, there is no ground for restitution, so even if there is enrichment, it is not unjust.

### 4.4.1 Enrichment

There are two problems in concluding that, by confiscating the trafficker's assets and making them available to satisfy a vindication of property claim by the victim against the state, the victim is enriched. One problem is practical and evidentiary. It would be difficult for the state to prove that the confiscation

67 See (n3).

68 Keren-Paz, 'Moral and legal obligations' (ch1, n39) 179–80.

69 Penal Regulation (Managing the Special Fund Handling Confiscated Property and Fines Imposed in Human Trafficking and Enslavement Cases) 2009, KT 6759 (Israel), reg 10.

of profits did indeed increase the chance of recovery in any particular case. After all, the state also faces significant barriers to seizing the proceeds of crime and in cases where it succeeded, it is possible that a victim would have been able to do the same.

The second problem is one of principle. It is not clear that increasing the chances of recovery is enrichment from a legal perspective. The source of doubt is that the victim's chose of action against the trafficker is as valid before as after the state intervention. Moreover, the financial value of such claim, *ignoring issues of satisfaction*, is likewise the same. Arguably, the equivalent of what counts as preservation of tangible property for purposes of a rescuer's unjust enrichment claim (which, as discussed below, is one condition for reimbursement) would be the preservation of the validity of the chose of action, say, filing the suit just before the limitation period elapsed, or – more contested – preservation of the claim's value against the defendant. But recognition of an act leading to increased likelihood that a claim would be satisfied as enrichment widens the definition of enrichment in a potentially excessive way and might create difficult demarcation and remoteness issues. How about a claimant who prevents the defendant's debtor from incurring liability to a third party which would bankrupt the defendant's debtor? Such a claimant increased the chance that the defendant's chose in action against the debtor would be fully satisfied. Should this be considered as enrichment and should the claimant be allowed to sue the defendant in unjust enrichment? And how about the claimant who collects the debt which is due to the defendant from the violent reluctant debtor? Is this enrichment? Should the claimant receive reimbursement (or remuneration) for her services? And is an owner of a stolen car enriched by the police finding the car?

While in a different context *Williams v Roffey Bros & Nicholls (Contractors) Ltd*[70] reflects a judicial tendency to view practical benefit as legal benefit, and by analogy, practical enrichment as legal enrichment, the authorities do not speak in unison. In the closer field of interceptive subtraction, the *Mackey* Court seems to have adopted the rule that the benefit intercepted needs to stem from a valid obligation owed by the third party to the claimant[71] so that the factual necessity that, but for the interception, the amount would have been received by the claimant is *not* sufficient to establish that the defendant's enrichment was at the claimant's expense. This suggests that the legal validity of the obligation is the relevant test for determining whether enrichment has occurred. Accordingly, when the rescuer's activity did not affect the validity of the defendant's chose in action against the debtor, the claim should fail for lack of enrichment. While, as discussed in chapter 3, factual necessity should suffice to establish enrichment in the interceptive subtraction context, it does

70 [1991] 1 QB 1.
71 See ch3 (n65) 1314.

not follow that increasing the chance that the creditor will be able to satisfy its claim against the debtor should count as enrichment, for the reasons explained above.

### *4.4.2 Self-interest conferral of benefits*

The state's claim is based on the provision of an unrequested service which arguably enriched the claimant at the state's expense. The traditional contours for recovery for unrequested services in England (and more generally, at common law) are extremely narrow. The potential ground for restitution is necessity, which operates as an exception to the general rule that officious intervention with the defendant's affairs will preclude restitution from the claimant.[72] While it is clear that English law recognises necessity as a ground for restitution, the scope of the doctrine is unclear and the cases are few.[73]

The best way to analyse the state's action is as a service rendered to preserve the defendant's property. Some of the basic conditions required to allow an unjust enrichment claim seem at first glance to exist: the victim either has property in the money reflecting the profit made at her expense or has a property in the chose of action against the trafficker reflecting the profit made at her expense. The state, by collecting from the trafficker the money owed to the victim, merely preserves the relevant property – the value of the chose in action – rather than improves it.[74] This satisfies the requirement that the service would incontrovertibly benefit the defendant. Moreover, two out of the three remaining conditions required to view the situation as involving necessity seem to exist. The action is reasonable under the circumstances, in both senses that the claimant (the state) is the right actor to take action and that the action is cost-justified with respect to the expected benefit.[75] The action is also justified under the circumstances in both senses that 'there was a possible contingency that serious consequences might have ensued'[76] if action were not taken, and that it conforms with the hypothetical wishes (or best interests) of the defendant while there was (presumably) no practical way to ascertain the actual wishes of the defendant prior to taking action.[77]

72 *Falke v Scottish Imperial Insurance Co* (1886) 34 ChD 234, 248.

73 Virgo (n17) 281.

74 Id, 297.

75 *Re F (Mental Patient: Sterilisation)* [1990] 2 AC 1, 75–6; Virgo (n17) 287–90. Cf Dagan (ch3, n128) 96, 101, contra F Rose, 'Restitution for the rescuer', (1989) 9 *OJLS* 167, 198–9.

76 *The Ella Constance* (1864) 33 LJ Adm 189, 193. For the view that in preservation of property cases this contingency should be probable rather than merely possible see G Jones, *Restitution in Public and Private Law* (London: Sweet & Maxwell, 1992) 145.

77 *Re F* (n75) 75; *The Winson* [1982] AC 939, 961–2; G&J (n9) 494. For current purposes, the distinction between best interests and hypothetical consent does not matter. The former is

Arguably, a delay in confiscation would have allowed the trafficker to dissipate the assets; victims have no reason to oppose confiscation which increases their chances of recovery; and (arguably, although at times this might be contested) there is no practicable way to ascertain the real wishes of the victims with respect to confiscation of profits from their trafficker. A further requirement – that the intervener did not intend to act gratuitously, or that he intended to charge for his services[78] – is described by Goff and Jones as illogical,[79] and its scope might be limited to professionals asking for remuneration, rather than merely for reimbursement of costs. Arguably, such a requirement must present a further hurdle to the state's claim, as discussed below.

The claim is doomed to fail, however, since it was made primarily in order to advance the state's own interest, rather than the defendant's interest. As such, it will be considered as officious and failing the test of necessity.[80] To be clear, the basic common law approach is that an act which protects an interest which is common to the claimant and the defendant, does not entitle the former for contribution from the latter. It is crystal clear that the state confiscates the trafficker's profit first and foremost to advance its own interest in punishing and deterring financially motivated criminal offences[81] and not because of a motivation to afford restitution to victims. Arguably, the same conclusion is warranted with respect to the Israeli fund discussed above. Since the scheme's main purpose is not the compensation of victims, using part of the money to cover the scheme's operational costs (let alone giving such purpose a priority) is incompatible with the test allowing reimbursement for rescuing costs at common law.

A comparative look reveals a less hostile approach to the claims of rescuers.[82] In particular, the common law traditional approach disallowing or restricting restitution of benefits conferred out of common interest is problematic for exacerbating problems of co-operation and encouraging free-riding.[83] However, even those (like me) who accept this critique should recoil from endowing the

largely supported in case law such as *Re F* id and by commentators such as Virgo (n17) 289 and G&J id, 4th edn, 367, 373; the latter is supported by Dagan (n75) 99.

78 *Re Rhodes* (1890) 44 Ch D 94.

79 G&J (n9) 494.

80 *Falke* (n72); Virgo (n17) 284–5, 289–90; G&J (n9) 494.

81 *Rezvi* (n48). Lord Simons in *Winson* (n77) 966 opined that an intervener operating from mixed motives may be able to recover if he acts *primarily* for the defendant's benefit; Lord Diplock suggested id at 962–3 that it is sufficient to show that the defendant derived a benefit from the claimant's act. Virgo (n17) 289–90 and G&J (n9) 4th edn, 374 both posit a predominant self-motive test. See also Rose (n75) at 196–7.

82 J Dawson, 'Negotiorum gestio: the altruistic intermeddler', (1961) 74 *Harv LR* 817; T Krebs, 'Unrequested benefits in German law', in *Understanding Unjust Enrichment* (ch3, n112) 247.

83 See Dagan (n75) 130–6; H Dagan and M Heller, 'The liberal commons', (2001) 110 *Yale LJ* 549, 621.

state with a right to sue victims in unjust enrichment. First, on the efficiency ground, there are no likely problems of co-ordination here; the state's interest in confiscating the proceeds is strong enough, so the state is likely to pursue confiscation even if a claim for reimbursement of collection costs in unjust enrichment is denied. For this reason, restitution is not warranted.[84] Even if we assume that the state makes confiscation enforcement decisions based mainly on economic considerations[85] – not an obvious assumption – still the likelihood that all deserving victims would be able to prove their claims for restitution and will be able to sue is not high. Moreover, even if this were the case, recognising an unjust enrichment claim would do little to improve the state's financial incentive since the amount subject to reimbursement is likely to be small in comparison to the amount due to the victim in restitution.

As an aside, the belief that the state will invest less in confiscation-oriented enforcement if not given reimbursement for costs might seemingly be taken one step further and support a denial of the vindication of property claim against the state on policy grounds: if the state cannot retain the confiscated money, less money would be confiscated to begin with. But such a claim – aside from being incompatible with principle and courts' practice – is also self-defeating as a policy aimed at empowering victims. Victims would still be able to recover more from the state under a rule allowing them to sue the state for restitution, than under a rule denying restitution, notwithstanding the reduction of the overall amount confiscated due to the state's lessened incentive to confiscate, and provided that the state is better positioned, relative to the victim, to get the money from the trafficker. Since, as explained above, the state's interest in confiscation should be subordinated to the victim's interest in restitution, the (unfounded) trade-off of more restitution for less overall confiscation is desirable, or at least acceptable.

A second objection for allowing the state to sue victims has to do with fairness. From a fairness perspective, the justification behind allowing restitution for self-serving conferral of benefits does not support the *state*'s claim for restitution. Even if an anti-free-riding sentiment has general purchase,[86] it is much less convincing when used to demand restitution from

84 Cf Dagan's (n75) suggested criteria in his fifth chapter for allowing restitution for self-interest conferral of unrequested benefits: a problem of co-operation exists, so that 'free-riding may frustrate the possibility of achieving the collective good itself', the defendant cannot devalue the benefit and there is no conflict of interests between the parties.

85 There are some studies suggesting that the extent of investigation of confiscation-yielding offences depends on the rule governing the unit's pay-offs from confiscation. See e.g. E Blumenson and E Nilson, 'Policing for profit: the drug war's hidden economic agenda', (1998) 65 *U Chic LR* 35; K Baicker and M Jacobson, 'Finders keepers: forfeiture laws, policing incentives, and local budgets', (2007) 91 *J Pub Econ* 2113.

86 A powerful critique of an overly zealous anti-free-riding sentiment is offered by W Gordon, 'On owning information: intellectual property and the restitutionary impulse', (1992) 79 *Va LR* 149, 167–8.

citizens for services rendered by the state. This, of course, depends on one's understanding of the proper role of the state. To those believing that a major role of the state is to provide services to its citizens, the fact that the state's actions benefit its citizens is not even a prima facie reason to expect the beneficiaries to pay for the benefit. This is so when the relevant activity is intended to benefit a certain group; this is even more so when (as in our case) the benefit is incidental. When the state confiscates profits of trafficking out of punitive or retributive motives and this has the incidental effect of facilitating the satisfaction of victims' claims against traffickers, victims should not pay for the incidental benefit they receive. Indeed, a contrary view ought to justify restitution whenever the police retrieves stolen goods, or indentifies an attacker, allowing the victim to sue the attacker in battery.

Of course, the fact that an important role of the state is to confer benefits to its citizens should not necessarily preclude it from charging all or some of the recipients of certain benefits. But this relates to a third objection to recognising a right against victims for reimbursement of collection costs: the demands of distributive justice. Victims of trafficking have suffered an egregious violation of their rights and are one of the most disadvantaged groups in society. Moreover, they benefit society and the economy in indirect ways and these benefits were forced out from them. Under these circumstances it is unjust to subject them to a duty to make restitution for incidental benefits received from the state when the state is pursuing its own interest; such wealth transfer is regressive since it finances the state's enforcement activity, which benefits all citizens, with reimbursement (or contribution) from the disadvantaged.

When the self-serving activity also benefited the defendant, the prevention of a free-riding rationale can support at most, and this is the fourth objection, a claim for contribution. Such contribution should be proportional to the (expected) benefit received by each party. Given the fact that the state has a clear and prominent interest in confiscating the proceeds of crime, while the actual benefit to each victim from the confiscation is small and (for reasons explained above) quite doubtful, recognising a right to restitution is also practically undesirable. It might require a considerable judicial time to calculate the relative cost of the enforcement activity and to apportion it to the victims who sue the state for restitution; and the amount which is likely to be deducted from the victim's restitutionary claim against the state is likely to be relatively small. For example, are the relevant costs only those involved in seizing the trafficker's assets or also those involved in investigating where the assets were hidden, or even costs incurred investigating the trafficker's offences leading to his conviction? And how should these costs be allocated between the trafficker's victims, some of whom are not suing the state (or even the trafficker) and others not even identified?

Lastly, all the efficiency, fairness and effectiveness critiques just mentioned are exacerbated by the fact that the rescue being successful is not a condition for reimbursement, provided the rescue attempt was reasonable under the circumstances.[87] Recognising an unjust enrichment claim, then, should allow the state to claim reimbursement of enforcement costs from victims even if the state failed to satisfy the confiscation order (as was the case in *AT v Dulghieru*[88]). Worse still, it could sue even victims who did not sue the state (or the trafficker) for restitution, based on the claim that the attempt to confiscate the profits of crime objectively benefits victims by reasonably attempting to preserve the value of their claim against the traffickers. The undesirability of such a result speaks for itself but it would be difficult to avoid it in a principled way, if a counter unjust enrichment claim is to be allowed against victims who sue the state for restitution.

## 4.5 Income from forced labour should not be taxed

The victim's claim against the trafficker and the state is for restitution of income from forced labour. If this income is taxable, the practical result will be that the amount due to the state in taxation could be reduced, by way of set-off, from the victim's restitutionary claim against the state. Strictly speaking, this is not a private law question: the obligation to pay tax is a matter of statutory interpretation and the victim's vindication of property claim against the state is not affected in the slightest by the possible existence of an obligation to pay tax. Nonetheless, I argue in this section that the income from forced labour is not taxable in the UK and, in general, should not be.

The taxability of profits made by the forced CSP and taken by the trafficker and then confiscated by the state is unclear. Income whose source is trade, profession or vocation is taxable.[89] Prostitution itself is a trade.[90] The difficulty lies with the fact that the potential taxpayer was forced to provide the services for whose value she is taxed, while trade presupposes voluntary transactions. Doctrinally, the voluntariness requirement can be inferred from several badges of trade, albeit inconclusively. HM Revenue and Custom's *Business Income Manual* (BIM) deals with stated intention as a badge of trade. The guidance that 'intention usually has to be inferred from the surrounding circumstances' and that stated intention not to trade could be disregarded where 'the trading intention is implicit from the objective facts and the transaction is unequivocally trading' strongly suggests that real intention

87 *Matheson v Smiley* [1932] 2 DLR 787, although admittedly in a case involving protection of life, rather than property; cf G&J (n9) 495.

88 *Dulghieru* (n6) [69].

89 Income and Corporation Taxes Act 1988 (c 1), Sch D, Case II.

90 *Aken* (ch3, n10).

to trade is necessary in order to establish a trade.[91] Forced prostitution obviously negates a real intention to trade despite the fact that profit was made and is sought in restitution *ex post facto*. Similarly, a profit-seeking motive is another (yet inconclusive) badge of trade[92] that is also missing in the context of forced prostitution. Connection with existing trade is another badge.[93] Obviously, with respect to all victims who were not CSPs prior to their enslavement, the lack of connection with their previous or current trade is another indication that forced prostitution should not be considered as trade. Despite the fact that tax litigation deals overwhelmingly with trade, and that trade, profession or vocation are seemingly alternatives, it is useful to see that forced prostitution could not be considered as either profession or vocation; both terms presuppose voluntariness. By reference to the two alternatives, trade too should be interpreted as requiring voluntariness as a precondition for liability.

The question, of course, is not merely doctrinal or conceptual. At the heart there is a normative question that has to be answered based on policy and justice criteria: should income from forced labour be taxed? There are five reasons to answer in the negative. The strongest reason not to tax proceeds of forced labour is that such practice undermines the inalienability of the right not to be enslaved. While inalienability and anti-commodificaiton sentiments are *not* convincing as a ground to deny the *victim* restitution, they are convincing as a reason to deny anyone but the victim the right to part of the proceeds. The proceeds are the substitute of the victim's inviolable right to freedom and bodily integrity. Taxing these proceeds means that at both practical and symbolic levels the inviolability of the victim's rights is eroded – the trafficker violates the victim's inalienable right to freedom and bodily integrity by forcing her to produce sexual services which he sells to clients; the state gives its imprimatur to the commodification of the victim by cashing in some of the proceeds that were received in return for violating these rights.

Recall that corrective justice restores prior legal entitlements not prior factual positions.[94] The benefits from forced labour are not taxable since, but for the wrong, there would have been no profit to tax. Taxing these profits, therefore, undermines the victim's interest in a remedy that vindicates her right not be forced into prostitution. The same conclusion is also warranted with respect to victims who planned to work as CSPs. The income from non-forced prostitution a victim hoped to make is hypothetical and counter-factual. It was not made and therefore should not be taxed. The income which was

91 *Business Income Manual* (London: HMRC), available at www.hmrc.gov.uk/manuals/bimmanual/index.htm (accessed 20 December 2012), BIM20401.

92 Id, BIM20210, BIM20215.

93 Id, BIM20270.

94 Barker (ch3, n112).

produced resulted from forced labour. Victims who planned to work as CSPs do not forfeit their right not to be forced into prostitution;[95] taxing their profits undermines the vindication of this right.

The non-taxability of proceeds of slave labour should be understood as reflecting society's recognition that the victim's rights should not have been invaded. Suppose a criminal removed a person's kidney without her consent and sold it. Few would seem to dispute that if the victim sues for restitution of the profit made by selling the kidney, it would be inappropriate to tax the victim on the capital gain made by her, even if the profit disgorged exceeded the loss suffered. The fact that trafficking involves the forced sale of services rather than property does not change this conclusion.

The second reason to deny taxation has to do with the distributive justice justifications of income tax. For all but libertarians, income tax is justified despite its redistributive effect, and often redistributive purpose. It is just that those who labour voluntarily, and by this create wealth, will share part of this increment in wealth in return for the benefits the state provides to all residents and out of some solidarity with the needy. But it is unjust that those who were forced to create wealth would have to pool the proceeds of the forced labour as part of the taxable income. To hold otherwise would be to allow other members of society, through the state, to benefit from the enslavement of victims (and in the context of sex trafficking, from victims' rape). That victims of trafficking were denied the most basic protections the state is supposed to provide and that usually they are very needy themselves only makes the taxation of the proceeds even less just.

Third, there is the egalitarian argument. Since victims of trafficking are overwhelmingly very vulnerable to begin with, exempting them from the obligation to pay tax on the proceeds of forced labour is progressive. Fourth, non-taxability of profits of slave labour could be viewed as some form of compensation rendered by the community for the failure to prevent the serious violation of the victims' rights, and as a form of taking some responsibility for the fact that the violations occurred within its borders. It could likewise be understood as an acknowledgment of the fact that the state and the community indirectly benefit from human trafficking and as a rough substitute for restitution of such indirect benefits. Fifth, it has been argued that the direct and indirect benefits accruing to destination states from human trafficking serve as a disincentive to eradicate it.[96] Non-taxability of profits of slave labour decreases this disincentive by decreasing the extent to which human trafficking directly enriches the state.[97] This is just another way to restate the inviolability thesis: a remedy of full disgorgement of profits is important at the practical

95 See pp 4–5.
96 Levenkron (n63).
97 But see the contrary argument (and its critique) about law enforcers' incentives (n85).

and symbolic levels in order to provide full protection to the victims' interests. Taxing the profits of slave labour erodes the protection afforded by a full disgorgement rule.

The non-taxability thesis has a special purchase under the English approach to taxation. The schedular approach, as opposed to the global concept of income, is tied to conceptions of a voluntary and systematic effort by the taxpayer to make income as the basis of liability. Therefore, unexpected and non-recurring receipts are considered as non-taxable windfalls.[98] Obviously, the income from forced labour is neither voluntary nor expected and therefore should not be taxed under the English approach. However, the argument presented above should be accepted also under a global concept of income. It is one thing to tax an income from lottery; it is quite another to tax the income from forced labour. Under the global approach, public policy considerations could and should deny the taxation of certain undeniable accessions of wealth.[99]

Two misconceptions about the argument should be avoided. The argument should be distinguished from Nozick's libertarian argument against taxation based on the view that (almost) any taxation is akin to forced labour.[100] While taxing free labour, *pace* Nozick, does not amount to forcing the payer to labour for someone else's purposes, taxing forced labour indeed makes the state and the beneficiaries of tax accomplices of slavery.

Superficially, the argument supports the general non-taxability of proceeds of acquisitive crimes. If taxing forced labour undermines the inviolability of victims' rights, why is it not that taxing the proceeds of crime in general equally undermines the inviolability of victims' rights? The answer is that the state has a better claim for the money than the criminal (the no profit from crime rationale) but the victim has a better right still than the state. This hierarchy applies to both confiscation and taxation. Value transferred involuntarily from victims should be confiscated (or at least taxed) in order to prevent the criminal from benefiting from the crime. But at least if the victim is identifiable, the state should make restitution to the victim of the benefit it received from the criminal.

## 4.6 Conclusion

Confiscation of traffickers' profits is justified in the relationship between the state and the trafficker, mainly based on the sound policy that no one should be allowed to benefit from his own wrongdoing. But this should not cloud the understanding that the victim has a superior right to the money. What seems

98 J Tiley, *Revenue Law*, 4th edn (Oxford: Hart Publishing, 2000) 131.

99 The test of the American global approach adopted in *CIR v Glenshaw Glass Co* 348 US 426.

100 R Nozick, *Anarchy, State and Utopia* (Oxford: Blackwell's Book Services, 1974) 169–71.

at first sight to be the trafficker's money is in fact the victim's. Failing to recognise this will only result in the state being the trafficker's accomplice by participating in a two-tier forced transfer of value from the victim, through the trafficker, to the state. Luckily, the rules governing vindication of property as properly understood can prevent such an unhappy result. While the argument focused on victims of sex trafficking, its main insights equally apply to all victims of forced labour. These include the existence of a vindication of property right with respect to money paid by clients in exchange for forced labour or the unauthorised use of the claimant's body; a fiduciary duty of the trafficker towards the victim; and the absence of a good faith purchase for value by the state with respect to amounts confiscated, of justification to reimburse the state for increasing the chances of satisfaction and of justification to tax income from forced labour.

Chapter 5

# Clients' liability for direct contact

## Battery and conversion

While hardly anyone disputes that traffickers should be liable to victims in torts, the suggestion that clients who did not have a specific reason to suspect that the CSP from whom they bought sex was forced should also be liable is controversial. The debate between sex-work feminists and abolitionists is conducted against the background of the international anti-trafficking framework which targets demand as one prevention measure.[1] Thus far, this debate has revolved around the *criminalisation* of clients, of which there are two models. The Swedish model, which is discussed in chapter 6, criminalises the purchase of sex from any CSP. Therefore, the client's knowledge or ability to know or suspect that the CSP is forced is irrelevant. Whether this model is mainly motivated by or could be justified with respect to the interests of victims, as opposed to the interests of non-forced CSPs or, possibly, women in general, is debated. The thrust of the argument in chapters 6 to 8 is that the civil equivalent of the Swedish model is justified, although some liability curtailing mechanisms are warranted, and that the justification is precisely because the indiscriminate purchase of sex contributes to trafficking.

The second model, adopted in England under s 53A of the Sexual Offences Act 2003,[2] criminalises making or promising payment for the sexual services of a prostitute who is forced (or deceived), regardless of whether the client was, or ought to have been, aware that the prostitute was forced. The English model, therefore, imposes strict criminal responsibility for purchase of sex from a forced CSP. Despite its narrower scope, the English model raises many of the critiques offered by sex-work feminists.[3] These critiques, which are assessed in chapter 6, are mainly that criminalisation is unfair to clients, that it harms the interests of sex-workers and that it might even harm the interests of victims.

1 See p 9.
2 See ch1 (n43).
3 For an early critique of the draft legislation, see e.g. C Stephens, 'Propose less, listen more', www.guardian.co.uk/commentisfree/2008/nov/19/prostitution-humantrafficking (accessed 12 February 2009).

This chapter offers a defence of the civil equivalent of the English model. I attempt to show that civil strict liability, which is (unlike its criminal counterpart) truly divorced from notions of fault or anti-social behaviour, is justified. One can therefore oppose 'English model criminalisation' and still support the imposition of strict liability for the harm suffered by the victim from the encounter with the client. Section 5.1 defends the imposition of strict liability from a normative perspective, mainly based on fairness and equality. Section 5.2 grounds such liability in battery (non-consensual physical contact), while explaining why no apparent consent by the victim to have sex with the client should be inferred. Section 5.3 offers a more radical argument: that victims should be allowed to sue clients in the tort of conversion (deliberate dealing with a chattel in a manner inconsistent with the owner's dominium) due to the quintessential experience of victims of being treated as chattels. Accordingly, they should be afforded the protection available to owners of property whose dominion over the property has been compromised. Those refusing to accept the argument offered in section 5.3 could still accept the desirability of strict liability, and its availability under the tort of battery.

## 5.1 Policy

By purchasing sex in a market in which part of the supplying CSPs are forced, the client both risks committing sexual battery of any victim from whom he bought sex – this risk materialises randomly whenever the CSP with whom he had contact is forced – and contributes to the trafficking of some victims who are recruited and exploited in order to meet his (and other clients') demand. A client's liability for the former type of harm resulting from the direct sexual encounter with a victim is the focus of the inquiry in this chapter and can be based on one of three grounds: knowledge that the victim is forced (subjective fault), negligence or strict liability. The client might be negligent in not knowing that the victim is forced, or, alternatively, in willing to purchase sexual services despite the inability to rule out the possibility that the CSP is forced.

While most clients could be found to be at fault for taking the risk of battering victims while purchasing sex (for reasons similar to those explained in chapter 7 with respect to finding fault in contributing to the trafficking phenomenon), fault is not required for either defending normatively tort liability for direct contact or establishing liability under battery and conversion. This means that those opposing the view that a client is at fault for creating the risk of battering a forced CSP should accept that strict civil liability is both normatively justified and doctrinally available, even though fault-based civil liability, let alone criminal responsibility, are uncalled for. Those accepting the view that the client is at fault should be content with strict tort liability which could, but does not have to, be supplemented by criminalisation.

While I do not pursue this any further, the policy arguments supporting strict liability for direct contact broadly support also strict liability for contribution to trafficking by creating indiscriminate demand. With respect to the latter, however, in the absence of direct physical contact between the defendant and the claimant, no tort which imposes strict liability is readily available.

Strict liability in our context is justified based on four considerations: fairness (section 5.1.1); egalitarianism (section 5.1.2); the importance of the claimant's interest and the need for consistency across the torts of trespass (section 5.1.3); and several instrumental considerations, including a more efficient level of deterrence (section 5.1.4).

### *5.1.1 Fairness*

One distributive consideration which supports generally strict liability is the idea that those who benefit from a given activity should compensate those suffering from its negative consequences.[4] At times, when the loss is the result of two incompatible activities which each benefits one party, it could be hard to decide which activity should bear the costs of accident. Accordingly, in such cases, liability based on fault might be preferred.[5] In general, however, strict liability could be justified in two different scenarios. The first is when all participants stand, *ex ante*, to benefit to a similar degree from the activity, and are exposed, *ex ante*, to similar risks. The risks, however, materialise *ex post* randomly. Fairness demands that the costs of the activity should be spread among all members of the group benefiting from the activity. Imposing strict liability will achieve this result when the defendant is able to price the cost of liability on those benefiting from the activity leading to the defendant's liability. Such rationale stands, for example, behind enterprise liability,[6] nuisance,[7] vicarious liability,[8] no fault schemes for road

4 G Keating, 'Distributive and corrective justice in the tort law of accidents', (2000) 74 *S Cal L Rev* 193.

5 Id, 217–18.

6 *Escola v Coca-Cola Bottling Co*, 150 P2d, 436, 441 (1944) (Traynor, J, concurring); J Stapleton, *Product Liability* (Cambridge: Cambridge University Press, 1994), ch 8; D Brodie, 'Enterprise liability: justifying vicarious liability', (2007) 27 *OJLS* 493.

7 *Bamford v Turnley* 3 B&S 66 (1862 Exc, Ch) (Bramwell B).

8 P Atiyah, *Vicarious Liability in the Law of Torts* (London: Butterworths, 1967) 17–18; Brodie (n6). Atiyah no longer finds this argument convincing, and other commentators question its ability to justify the expansion of employers' liability: P Atiyah, 'Personal injuries in the twenty-first century: thinking the unthinkable', in P Birks (ed), *Wrongs and Remedies in the Twenty-first Century* (Oxford: Clarendon Press, 1996) 1, 16; C McIvor, 'Re-inventing the doctrine of vicarious liability – again!', (2005) 21 *P'nal Neg* 283; Cf R Stevens, 'Vicarious liability or vicarious action?', (2007) 123 *LQR* 30. However, recent case law in England and other commonwealth jurisdictions clearly endorses fairness as a major justification for vicarious liability: *Lister v Hesley Hall*, [2002] 1 AC 215, 243; *Dubai Aluminium v Salaam* [2003] 2 AC 366, 395; *Bernard v A-G* [2005] IRLR 398, 402; *Majrowski v Guy's & St Thomas's NHS*

accidents,[9] liability of the state for creation of active risks[10] and, outside tort law, in the continental (and to a lesser extent American) tradition, behind contribution rules between co-owners who incur expense with respect to property.[11]

The fact that fairness 'would justify the imposition of strict liability in a wide range of situations in which it is currently not imposed'[12] is not a reason to oppose clients' strict liability for the following reasons. First, as argued below, fairness justifies a major feature of tort liability: strict liability of proprietary torts. Second, in other contexts strict liability might be inappropriate due to the difficulty in allocating the costs to one of two incompatible activities; such a problem does not exist in our context. Third, clients' strict liability – similar to vicarious liability – could be justified due to the combined effect of several policy considerations which might supplement fairness (equality and deterrence) or supplant it (protected interest). Lastly, it might be that indeed other interactions which currently are not governed by a strict liability rule, should; this is hardly a reason not to adopt one step in the right direction.

A second scenario which justifies strict liability to an even greater extent is when those who benefit from an activity are different from those who bear its costs. If even *ex ante*, potential victims do not benefit from the activity, it would be grossly unfair (egalitarian considerations aside) to require them to subsidise the activity which benefits potential defendants. This rationale, which was captured 40 years ago by George Fletcher as the creation of non-reciprocal risk,[13] justifies strict liability in the following instances: (a) the creation of ultra-hazardous risks from the defendant's activity on his land (or the narrower English version of liability under *Rylands v Fletcher*[14] – the requirement for non-natural use is a manifestation of the logic of lack of reciprocity); (b) the American doctrine of incomplete privilege in instances of private necessity; under such doctrine the defendant needs to pay for the cost of his use of the claimant's resource;[15]

*Trust* [2007] 1 AC 224, [9]; *Bazley v Curry* (1999) DLR 174 (4th), 45, 60. See Brodie, id, 496–7.

9 Keating (n4) 215–16.

10 S Kneebone, *Tort Liability of Public Authorities* (North Ryde: LBC Information Services, 1998) 41.

11 See Dagan and Heller (ch4, n83) 611–13; Cf *Restatement (First) Restitution* (ch3, n100) § 105. For the unduly narrow English approach, see *Leigh v Dickeson* [1884–1885] 15 QB 60 (CA).

12 P Cane, *The Anatomy of Tort Law* (Oxford: Hart Publishing, 1997) 46.

13 G Fletcher, 'Fairness and utility in tort theory', (1972) 85 *Harv LR* 537, 544–50.

14 LR 3 HL 330 (1868); *Transco v Stockport Metropolitan BC* [2003] UKHL 61. For the American version, see *Restatement (Second) of Torts* (ch3, n58) § 519.

15 *Vincent v Lake Erie Transportation*, 124 NW 221 (Minn, 1910). The English position seems to absolve the defendant from the duty to compensate, although the interpretation of the case is disputed. See *Romney Marsh v Trinity House Corp* (1870) LR 5 Ex 204; *Cope v Sharpe* [1912] 1 KB 496. See *Clerk & Lindsell on Torts*, 19th edn (London: Sweet & Maxwell, 2006)

and (c) The liability of air carriers for injury on the ground from falling aircraft.[16]

The central doctrinal manifestation of the anti-externalisation rationale is the rule governing a defendant's interference with the claimant's property; with respect to conversion and trespass to land, the defendant acts at his peril.[17] Such liability is not based on the assumption that the defendant stood in a better position than the owner to prevent the accident resulting from the competing claims to the asset.[18] In fact, in many cases the opposite is true. Rather, liability is based on the idea that the defendant is dealing with the asset in order to promote his self-interest. In most cases this risk-taking would benefit him. If in the course of this activity, his dealing with the property is likely to injure the owner, who does not stand to benefit (in any significant way) from the defendant's activity, the former should bear the loss. Note that such a result is not based on the assumption that the defendant is likely to spread the loss better than the owner. It is fair to merely shift the loss (as opposed to having it spread), rather than leave it as it falls, because the defendant, rather than the claimant, stands to benefit from the defendant's activity.

Fairness-based liability does not hinge upon, though it does not exclude liability for, faulty behaviour by the defendant. It is based on the idea that if an activity is really beneficial from an overall social perspective, it would be fair, as a distributional matter, that winners would compensate losers. Translated into the context of trafficking, strict liability is justified under either version of the fairness rationale. Even if it could have been argued plausibly that clients and CSPs all stand *ex ante* to equally benefit from the commercial sex activity, still it would be fair to compensate those who are the victims of the (arguably) unavoidable accident of such activity: women who are forced into prostitution whom clients cannot identify. More realistically, since clients (overwhelmingly men) benefit from purchasing commercial sex, while victims (overwhelmingly women) bear its costs by being subjected to non-consensual sex, it would be most unjust if clients would not compensate victims. Put differently, if indeed purchasing commercial sex is a socially desirable activity, and clients cannot be faulted for purchasing sex from victims since there is no way to sort victims from other CSPs, it is only fair

1140, n91 ('. . . necessity is not favoured by the courts, especially where the defendant acted to protect private . . . interest') ('Clerk & Lindsell'). The current edition (20th edn, 2010, 258–63) does not include this observation. Following references are to the 20th edition.

16 *Restatement (Second) of Torts* (n14) § 520A.

17 *Marfani v Midland Bank* [1968] 1 WLR 956, 970–1 (Lord Diplock). Conversion protects both possession and the immediate right to possess and is found on property while trespass merely protects (and is found on) possession. *Ward v Macauley* (1791) 4 TR 489, 490. This does not affect the conclusion of the analysis. At most (but I do explore this point), one can conclude that a victim of trafficking has a right to immediate possession but not actual possession of herself and therefore she can sue in conversion but not in trespass.

18 Cf M Mautner, 'The eternal triangles of the law: toward a theory of priorities in conflicts involving remote parties', (1991) 90 *Mich LR* 95.

that clients who benefit from the activity should pay its costs, and compensate the victims who bear the significant costs of this activity. These costs are, from a narrower perspective, the result of being subjected to non-consensual direct contact with clients and, from a broader perspective, the result of being trafficked in order to satisfy the demand for commercial sex. Since no one would dispute that the violation of victims' rights and the ensuing injuries are devastating, it would be most unfair to leave the costs where they are, rather than to shift them onto clients, who benefit from the activity which created these costs.

Of course, the fact that the violation of victims' rights is so significant casts doubt on the assumption that the activity as a whole is socially beneficial. Under the alternative assumption, based on data surveyed in chapters 6 and 7, the foreseeable risk to victims could be a good ground to forbid purchase of commercial sex at all, or at least to view each act of purchasing commercial sex as an unreasonable activity. However, even if overall the purchasing of commercial sex is desirable from a social perspective (under the assumptions that it benefits clients and non-victims and that the number of victims is very low), winners should compensate losers.

Whatever the assumption about the number of victims among all CSPs, liability towards victims is justified. If the proportion is high, as suggested in chapter 7, the risk creation is negligent. If it is low, the fairness argument provides a strong basis for compensation, since the alternative is to impose the significant costs of an activity, which overall is beneficial to many, on the few who bear its cost.

Arguably, a fairness argument fails to justify imposing liability on clients, since liability would merely shift losses from one individual (the victim) to another (a client), rather than being spread on all those benefiting from the activity (clients, and arguably – but unconvincingly – non-forced CSPs). Such a result is still justified, since we deal with a category in which winners and losers do not overlap. In this second category of fairness, loss spreading considerations (which partially overlap with fairness considerations in the first category) play a much smaller role. When the activity benefits *ex ante* the defendant and imposes risks *ex ante* on the claimant, the loss should be shifted to the former, even if he does not enjoy any advantage in comparison to the latter in terms of spreading the loss. As explained above, this is the rationale behind imposing strict liability for unauthorised interference with property rights. Less importantly, shifting the loss from victim to client is justified since the client is better situated to prevent the loss from happening by totally avoiding purchasing commercial sex. This seems to fall back on a notion of fault, but should not necessarily be equated with fault.[19]

19 Cf G Calabresi and J Hirschoff, 'Toward a test for strict liability in tort', (1972) 81 *Yale LJ* 1055 (strict liability theory which is based on accident-prevention capacity).

On a deeper level, however, the idea that all clients should share the costs of compensating victims has some normative appeal. Clients as a group submit victims to the risk of non-consensual sex. From the clients' perspective, the materialisation of the risk of violating the victim's right is random. In a more ideal world – in an ideal world, there would be no victims of trafficking, and in the views of many, no prostitution – all clients would share the costs of compensating victims. From the clients' perspective, the problem is that there are no loss-spreading mechanisms such as the purchase of insurance or methods of self-insuring. Theoretically, judges or legislatures can create collective liability of clients, which will be based either on joint and several, or on proportional liability for the creation of the risk. Indeed, the upshot of the analysis offered in chapters 6 to 8 goes in that direction by imposing fault-based liability for a limited amount on clients whose indiscriminate demand contributed to the trafficking of some victims and where such contribution is not too remote. What should be clear from the discussion so far is that, regardless of the merits of liability for contribution to trafficking, a solution which leaves victims to bear the cost of the forced sexual encounter with the client is inferior to a solution which shifts the cost to the client, even if the client found liable cannot spread the cost.

### 5.1.2 Equality

One justification for strict liability could be that it results in progressive redistribution of wealth and entitlements in society. I have previously defended at length the view that tort rules' equality effects should be taken into account by rule makers[20] so I will only briefly summarise the argument here. In the absence of fault, strict liability can be justified based on considerations of distributive justice. Alongside fairness, egalitarianism can serve as a legitimate criterion to justify (at times) strict liability rules. Strict liability will be desirable if typically it will result in progressive redistribution of entitlements from the better-off to the disadvantaged. This view is based on the understanding that legal rules have inevitable distributive results. For those striving to decrease power gaps in society, the fact that the distributive result of a legal rule is progressive serves as an independent justification for adopting such a rule. The idea that the victim's pre-existing vulnerability might increase the defendant's burden to take precautions against the risk that the victim would be injured is not foreign to the common law;[21] this ethic could easily yield a conclusion that strict liability is warranted in order to protect the interest of the vulnerable.[22]

20 T Keren-Paz, *Torts, Egalitarianism and Distributive Justice* (Aldershot: Ashgate, 2007).

21 See ch7, section 7.6.

22 Cf Keren-Paz (n20) 71–2, 175.

Turning to the application of such a framework to the forced-prostitution context, it is easy to see that imposing strict liability on clients would lead to desirable distributive results. First, the result is desirable along the gender axis. Clients are overwhelmingly men, while victims are overwhelmingly women. The result of strict liability is a progressive transfer of wealth, possible enhancement of victims' liberty, autonomy and dignity in society, and at the symbolic level, reinforcement of victims' (and more generally women's) self-worth, and inviolability of rights. Protecting women's rights to bodily integrity and sexual autonomy under a regime of strict liability is not only instrumental at the practical level in protecting these values, but also has intrinsic symbolic value by stressing the importance that society gives to these values and to women's well being.

Similar analysis can be done with respect to the distributive axis of class, and often race and ethnicity. Those who are forced into prostitution are amongst the most disenfranchised in society; they almost always come from (at times extremely) deprived socio-economic backgrounds,[23] and are often (illegal) immigrants, a fact that renders them even more vulnerable. On the other hand, research shows that clients who purchase commercial sex are heterogeneous and come from all ranks of society.[24] This suggests that imposing strict liability will bring about a progressive distributive result, since the receiving side is manifestly disadvantaged while the giving side is heterogeneous.

### *5.1.3 The protected interest and trespass torts*

The most straightforward tort to vindicate the victim's right not to be subject to unwanted sexual contact is the tort of battery. The question is, therefore, whether liability for battery should be strict. In general, the scope of tort liability is the combination of three factors: the claimant's protected interest,

23 According to an analysis of the *IOM Trafficking Database*, 79 per cent of all victims came from poor or very poor family backgrounds. M Di Tommaso, I Shima, S Strøm and F Bettio, 'As bad as it gets: well being deprivation of sexually exploited trafficked women', (2009) 25 *Eur J Pol Econ* 143. Another study based on the IOM dataset found that victim's average monthly salary prior to being trafficked was US$52. M Della Giusta, M Di Tommaso and S Strøm, *Sex Markets: A Denied Industry* (London and New York, NY: Routledge, 2008).

24 See e.g. A Marttila, *Consuming Sex: Finnish Male Clients and Russian and Baltic Prostitution*, paper presented at the 5th European Feminist Research Conference, Lund University, Sweden, 2003, available at http://www.popcenter.org/problems/street_prostitution/PDFs/kennedy_etal_prostitution_2004.pdf (accessed 12 March 2013); M Kennedy, B B Gorzalka and J C Yuille, *Men Who Solicit Prostitutes: A Demographic Profile of Participation in the Vancouver Police Department's Prostitution Offender Program*, prepared for the Vancouver Police Department and the John Howard Society of the Lower Mainland, 2004, available at www.popcenter.org/problems/street_prostitution/PDFs/Kennedy_etal_prostitution_2004.pdf (accessed 12 February 2009); H Ward, C H Mercer, K Wellings, K Fenton, B Erens, A Copas and A M Johnson, 'Who pays for sex? Analysis of the increasing prevalence of female commercial sex contacts among men in Britain', (2005) 81 *Sex Trans Infec* 467.

the type of defendant behaviour and the mode of the defendant's interference with the claimant's interest.[25] With respect to battery, two considerations weigh in favour of imposing strict liability on defendants. First, the defendant's activity (the touching) is intentional. As Robert Stevens recently explained

> [T]hat the law of torts does not require proof of fault where the defendant has acted intentionally, but generally does where the defendant's conduct is unintentional, is justifiable. We are responsible for our conscious choices and their consequences in a way which we are not where actions are unintentional.[26]

As explained in section 5.1.1, this is an aspect of fairness. The defendant (client) is acting to further his own interest (reaching sexual gratification); he should bear the consequences when his conduct resulted in the victim being subject to sexual contact she did not consent to.

While strict liability might also be justified based on Richard Epstein's libertarian theory,[27] I do not pursue this avenue here since I do not share his libertarian premises. Moreover, Epstein's theory, which is causative-based, has been criticised for being indeterminate or leading to too broad liability.[28] This said, Epstein's libertarian reliance on notions of ownership (spelled out in terms of causation) is compatible with the view that greater liability should flow from intentional behaviour and is appropriate with respect to the tort of battery which protects one's self-ownership interest. Moreover, as section 5.3 clarifies, the quintessential experience of victims of trafficking is that they are treated as property; and this justifies strict liability towards them which is grounded in the tort of conversion.

Second, the interest in bodily integrity ought to receive the utmost protection from the legal system. This should be translated doctrinally to strict liability which denies a defence of reasonable mistake. The more important the interest the more it should be (and usually is) protected by the legal system. While this is true in general, it should be especially true in the context of sexual battery.[29] From the victim's perspective, there are few things which undermine one's autonomy, security, dignity and self-worth more than being subject to unwanted sexual contact.

Moreover, battery is a trespass to the person tort. While there are some doubts – discussed below – about whether liability in battery is strict there is no doubt that the common law imposes strict liability for interference

25 See e.g. Cane (n12).

26 Stevens (ch2, n53) 102.

27 See R Epstein, 'A theory of strict liability', (1973) 2 *JLS* 151.

28 See S Perry, 'The impossibility of general strict liability', (1988) 1 *Can J L Jur* 147.

29 Cf E Adjin-Tettey, 'Protecting the dignity and autonomy of women: rethinking the place of constructive consent in the tort of sexual battery', (2006) 39 *UBCLR* 3.

with the owner's right to possession. *Basely v Clarkson*[30] has set the rule that in trespass to land, an honest and reasonable mistake by the defendant with respect to title, the land's border, or a defendant's right to be on the claimant's land is not a defence. Consistency demands that all the manifestations of trespass as an overarching tort relating to persons, chattels and land would afford the same protection: the protection of bodily integrity by battery would be equal to that afforded to property through trespass to land and chattels; all would lead to strict liability. This conclusion is especially compelling if one emphasises the defendant's mode of interference (direct and intentional) as the unifying rationale behind trespass torts which protect both bodily integrity and property. According to such a view, self-ownership of one's body (at least in the limited sense defended below of a right to exclude others from unauthorised interference) is another, indeed the ultimate, form of ownership.

If, on the other hand, one emphasises the importance of the protected interest, surely bodily integrity should receive at least the same (if not more) protection as that given to one's interest in protecting property. On this view, if the common law generally protects property to a greater extent than it protects bodily integrity this is problematic. If a reasonable mistake about title to land or to a wallet leads to liability, while a reasonable mistake about one's consent to a treatment excludes liability, or if a nuisance or *Rylands v Fletcher* claim (in England) allows the owner of land to recover, in the absence of fault, for damage to property, while personal injury is excluded,[31] then there is much to be said that something is wrong with the common law's current set of priorities. It might be that general reform is needed in order to, at least, equate the scope of protection to one's person with the protection to one's possessions, or to reverse the current scheme of priority so to afford broader protection to the interest in one's person. While some doctrinal changes required by adopting this view are likely to be left by the courts to Parliament,[32] as the discussion below reveals, strict liability for battery has considerable support in English courts.

### *5.1.4 Instrumental considerations*

Imposing strict liability on clients is also supported by several instrumental considerations. Strict liability internalises the costs of sex-purchasing activities and by this might bring about a more efficient (i.e. lower) level of consumption. I do not stress this point for two reasons. First, in the context of forced

30 (1681) 3 Lev 37 (CP).

31 See *Hunter v Canary Wharf* [1997] AC 655; *Transco v Stockport Metropolitan BC* [2003] UKHL 61.

32 See e.g. *Transco*, id, [43] (per Lord Hoffmann).

prostitution, when the rights involved are so fundamental, and when distributive considerations are so paramount, the concept of efficiency has less normative appeal. Second, the effects of imposing liability are not clear, for reasons discussed in chapter 6. However, both critiques should not be overstated. 'Inefficient level of sex consumption' simply means that the current level is too high since it ignores the rights' violation of victims and victims' ensuing suffering. While the deterrent effect of strict (or for that matter, fault-based) liability is far from clear; at worst, liability will not reduce sex consumption, and at best it would somewhat reduce it. While it might be that general demand for commercial sex would be reduced rather than the demand for forced prostitution (if clients are unable to tell who is forced), this in itself is not necessarily undesirable, under the assumption that most CSPs are exploited. This is further examined in chapter 7.

In this sense, adopting a strict liability regime has several advantages and one possible disadvantage over a fault-based regime. One advantage is that it is likely to bring higher deterrence since more clients are likely to be sued, and found liable under such a regime, than under a fault-based regime. Needless to say, the result that more victims would be compensated is desirable as well. Another advantage is that the considerable costs involved in proving or disproving fault are saved. This is desirable both from society's perspective and in terms of increased access to justice to vulnerable claimants. Under a strict liability rule all that the claimant has to prove is the fact that she was forced into prostitution and had sex with the client. The second requirement is not easy to meet, but, as explained in chapter 9, it is not insurmountable.

The possible disadvantage in adopting a strict liability regime is diluting at the symbolic level clients' moral responsibility for violating the victim's right, and possibly having less deterrent effect. Arguably, if indeed there is fault in purchasing sex while taking the risk of victimising forced CSPs, strict liability waters down the symbolic aspects of liability, and therefore, a fault-based liability is to be preferred. This argument is unconvincing for the following reasons. First, being sued for purchasing commercial sex in general, and from a forced CSP in particular, is likely to bring about significant negative reputation effects to clients, so both deterrence and the symbolic effect of being found liable are likely to remain significant. Second, the relationships between the symbolic effects of strict liability and negligence regimes are more complicated than appear from the above argument. Strict liability regimes will still stigmatise defendants found liable due to the pooling effect: under well functioning strict liability, all defendants who would have been found liable under a negligence regime would still be liable, and in addition, another group of defendants would be found liable. If members of the community are unable to know whether defendants found liable were negligent or not, they would be likely to stigmatise all defendants found liable, but the stigmatising effect would be lower. Whether this is a good result or not could be debated,[33] and the answer might depend on the context. In our context, the benefits from imposing liability on more clients and providing remedies to more victims clearly outweigh any possible dilution of moral responsibility of clients.

Of course, if one believes that: (a) most clients cannot tell who is forced; (b) cannot be faulted for purchasing sex despite this inability to know; and (c) nevertheless victims deserve compensation for the violation of their rights, then one should support only a strict liability regime, so the arguable dilution of moral responsibility of clients becomes a non-issue. On the other hand, for those who believe, like me, that most clients are likely to be found liable under a fault regime, the advantage of a strict liability regime is that it saves the litigation costs of proving fault, whereas litigating fault would not change the result in most cases.

Lastly, it might be that civil strict liability of clients would better balance the interests of victims and clients. From this viewpoint, the criminalisation of the purchase of sex from forced CSPs is too harsh towards ignorant clients. Civil liability serves as a softer form of penalty – both in financial and expressive terms – while at the same time serving corrective and distributive justice by compensating victims. It is also possible that in terms of the law's potential to change its addressees' attitudes, the softer touch of civil liability is more effective than the harsher criminal responsibility.[34] Needless to say, that civil liability of clients is compatible with (and in fact might complement well) a reform which criminalises the purchase of commercial sex, either generally (from all CSPs) or from forced CSPs with or without knowledge or suspicion that the CSP is forced. It follows that those who support the recent criminalisation in the UK of purchase of sex from forced CSPs should easily support civil liability of clients. Indeed, following a conviction, civil suit by the victim is likely to face higher chances of success. But even those who oppose criminalisation of ignorant clients on the ground that criminalisation is too harsh to clients could still support strict liability in torts. I explain further the different effects of imposing civil and criminal liability in chapter 6.

## 5.2 Battery and apparent consent

Battery is the intentional and direct application of force to another person, and any physical contact with the claimant's body (with the exception of contact generally acceptable in the ordinary conduct of everyday life[35]) is sufficient

33 See T Keren-Paz, 'Liability regimes, reputation loss and defensive medicine', (2010) 18 *Med LR* 363.

34 See D Kahan, 'Gentle nudges vs. hard shoves: solving the sticky norms problem', (2000) 67 *U Chi LR* 607.

35 *Collins v Wilcock* [1984] 1 WLR 1172 (per Lord Goff).

to amount to force. While the claimant's consent to the contact negates liability in battery, such consent needs to be free.[36] Being forced into prostitution *ipso facto* negates the existence of free consent. Any woman who is subjected into forced prostitution is unable to form free consent to a sexual encounter with a client, since she does not have the alternative of saying no. The difficulty with imposing liability in battery on clients is that the client might not know that the CSP does not really consent to the sexual contact. If the mistake is unreasonable, no doubt that liability would be imposed. An unreasonable mistake would exist if the client failed to infer that the claimant was forced under circumstances that a reasonable client would have made such inference. A more controversial alternative, which I do not explore here, is to claim that the client's mistake about the victim's lack of consent was not reasonable under the circumstances, since it ignored the statistical chance that the CSP was forced, and despite the absence of concrete signs that the claimant was forced. It is unclear whether such a claim (which partially parallels the argument made in chapter 7 in the context of the tort of negligence) would be accepted. The two questions which have to be dealt with are whether a reasonable mistake about the lack of consent would exclude liability and whether the doctrine of apparent consent requires a conclusion that the victim indeed consented to the contact according to the objective test and, therefore, the client did not make a mistake about the woman's lack of consent.

Common law jurisdictions seem to give different answers to the question to what extent liability in battery is truly strict, and even within a given jurisdiction the position is not always clear. England seems to be relatively open to the idea that liability for battery should be strict. *Evans* is an authority in the context of false imprisonment that a reasonable mistake with respect to the legal authority to confine a prisoner is no defence to liability.[37] In *Hepburn*, in the context of assault, Sedley LJ stated more generally that 'an honest belief in a non-existent state of affairs does not excuse a trespass to the person'.[38] The position that a reasonable mistake about the victim's consent should not bar liability in battery is well accepted by English scholars.[39] Under that position, seemingly a victim who did not consent could sue successfully in battery (subject to the issue of apparent consent which will be discussed below) even if the client's mistake about the victim's lack of consent is deemed reasonable. However, recently in *Ashley v CC Sussex Police*[40] the

36 See *Latter v Braddell* (1881) 44 LT 369.

37 *R v Governor of Brockhill Prison ex p Evans (no 2)* [2001] 2 AC 19.

38 *Hepburn v Chief Constable of Thames Valley Police* [2002] EWCA Civ 1841, [24].

39 Clerk & Lindsell (n15) 989; Stevens (n26) 101; McBride and Bagshaw, *Tort Law*, 4th edn (Harlow: Pearson, 2012) 62. But see W Rogers, *Winfield and Jolowicz on Tort*, 18th edn (London: Sweet & Maxwell, 2010) 1132–3 (reasonable mistake, albeit in the context of apparent consent, is effective).

40 [2006] EWCA Civ 1085 (CA).

Court of Appeal decided that a reasonable mistake about the state of affairs does not deprive the defendant from the privilege of self-defence, and this approach is arguably incompatible with the approach in *Hepburn*. In the House of Lords different *dicta* were made. Lord Scott has voiced a strong preference towards strict liability (but formally left the possibility for adopting such a solution as open), unless the claimant is responsible for the mistake. Interestingly, Lord Scott specifically mentioned mistake about consent to sexual contact (and not only mistake about the existence of self-defence, the issue litigated in *Ashley*):

> I would start with the principle that every person is *prima facie* entitled not to be the object of physical harm intentionally inflicted by another. . . . Why, for civil law purposes, should not a person who proposes to make physical advances of a sexual nature to another be expected first to make sure that the advances will be welcome?[41]

Lords Rodger and Neuberger reserved their opinion on the issue without clearly indicating whether they support or reject strict liability.[42] Lord Carswell did not regard strict liability as 'possibly containing the correct principle'.[43] Lord Bingham was somewhat opaque but it seems that he thought that strict liability was not the rule and that the House should not change the existing rule.[44]

US jurisdictions are split with respect to the question of whether liability in battery should hinge on showing intent to injure or offend by the contact (such requirement will preclude strict liability), and such ambiguity is reflected in the *Restatement (Second) of Torts*.[45] Lastly, in Canada, the Supreme Court opined in *dicta* in *Scalera* that a defendant's reasonable mistake with respect to the claimant's consent for sex would exclude liability for battery.[46] Such an approach was criticised by Elizabeth Adjin-Tettey, for reasons which partially parallel mine, and which revolve around the importance of the protected interest of sexual autonomy, and the existence of distributive considerations about women's status in society in deciding whether reasonable mistake about the woman's consent to the sexual encounter should form a defence to the defendant.[47]

41 [2008] UKHL 25 [20].

42 Id, [55], [89]–[90].

43 Id, [76].

44 Id, [3].

45 See K Simons, 'A restatement (third) of intentional torts?', (2006) 48 *Ariz LR* 1061, 1066–70.

46 *Non-Marine Underwriters, Lloyd's of London v Scalera* [2000] 1 SCR 551 (Can), [24], [29].

47 Adjin-Tettey (n29). Adjin-Tettey's paradigmatic case of non-commercial sex is different, however, from the one examined in this book, and several possible conclusions might follow. First, it is less clear that in the context of non-commercial sex it is just to shoulder

In any event, all common law jurisdictions seem nonetheless to accept the principle of apparent consent, according to which, behaviour which appears objectively to show that the claimant consented to the touching would suffice as consent. Similar to contract law,[48] when a gap exists between a person's subjective lack of consent and the objective appearance of consent, it is that person making the representation of consent who bears the consequences of that gap.[49] Thus in the famous case of *O'Brien v Cunard*,[50] the claimant, an Irish immigrant teenager on a ship sailing to the US, who stood in the line for vaccination and extended her arm, was taken to consent to the vaccination according to the objective standard, so her battery claim against the ship's physician was precluded. Therefore, in order to impose liability on a client who purchased sex from a CSP in circumstances in which he could not have known she was a victim, there is a need to show why there is no apparent consent by the victim, or alternatively, why liability should be imposed despite the victim's apparent consent. The question which needs to be answered is whether third party duress, which the defendant should not have a reason to know of ('third party duress'), vitiates the claimant's consent.

In the context of battery, there is scant authority on this question. McBride and Bagshaw suggested there would be liability in such a case, but did not support this view with an authority.[51] The discussion of this point in both Clerk and Lindsell and in Winfield and Jolowicz is vague. Clerk and Lindsell maintain that

> consent affords no defence if the will of the consenting party was overpowered by force of the fear of violence. A claimant cannot give a real consent unless he has in fact the freedom to choose whether or not he should do so,[52]

men with the costs of the mistake. While I have no objection to such a rule, which could be supported by some of the arguments I present, I think there are stronger justifications for imposing strict (or fault-based) liability on clients than on men in general. One obvious difference is that the social value of non-commercial sex is much higher to men and consenting women than the social value of commercial sex. Another important difference is that the power gap between men and women in the non-commercial sex context is less significant than in our context. On the other hand, our context raises the difficulty of apparent consent to trade sex for money which is not necessarily raised in the general context. Lastly, the possibility of grounding strict liability in the tort of conversion discussed in section 5.3 is not open in the general context.

48 See e.g. *Paal Wilson & Co v Partnereederei Hannah Blumenthal* [1983] AC 854 (HL).

49 Cf Stevens (n26) 248.

50 28 NE 266 (Mass, 1891).

51 McBride and Bagshaw (n39, 2nd edn, 2005) 247–8. The current edition (at 62) does not discuss duress but its position on reasonable mistake induced by a third party allocates the risk to the innocent defendant. This is in accord with Lord Scott's view in *Ashley* (n40).

52 Clerk & Lindsell (n15) 1040.

while Winfield and Jolowicz maintain that 'the consent . . . must be freely given'.[53] Neither text mentions whether the claimant's lack of consent should be known to the defendant as a condition for liability. This goes to the heart of the role battery has to play in preserving human rights. According to the view that liability should be truly strict, the focus of the inquiry should be whether there was free consent to the contact, rather than whether the defendant was justified in believing that the claimant consented (even though she did not).

Third party duress has different effects in contract and restitution law.[54] In contract law the test for consent is objective, and accordingly if the pressure is not extreme and the third party had no notice of it, the contract cannot be rescinded. However, when the pressure is extreme the contract is void.[55] When softer pressures are involved, third party duress or undue influence can allow the claimant to rescind the contract if the other party has constructive notice of it. In restitutionary mistaken payment cases, the test for consent is subjective so third party duress (even if not extreme) can support a claim for restitution.[56]

This framework suggests that clients should be liable for battery towards victims based on at least two rationales: the pressure operating on the victim is extreme so the appearance of consent is ineffective, or that the client should be deemed to have notice of the duress, so he cannot rely on the appearance of consent. In addition, I will explore the possibility to set aside the victim's consent based on the Canadian version of the unconscionability doctrine. I end the discussion with yet another rationale that in battery the *subjective* test for consent should be applied.

### *5.2.1 Void transactions under extreme duress*

As the discussion in chapter 3 clarified, the pressures which typically operate on victims of trafficking are so extreme that they deprive victims of any choice, and English case law suggests that extreme cases of duress render the transaction void, not merely voidable.[57] While the relevant cases did not involve third party duress, the inevitable result of the contract being void is that the owner retains his title as against innocent third parties.[58] Applied to the battery context, at least third party duress which nullifies the consent (as opposed to less extreme pressures which merely deflect the will) should subject the innocent defendant to liability.

53 Rogers (n39) 1133.
54 Friedmann (ch3, n15).
55 Id, 81.
56 Id, 91.
57 See pp 40–1.
58 Note, however, that in *Barton* (ch3, n14), their Lordships concluded that they express no view as to what (if any) effect the result may have on the rights or obligations inter se of the other parties to the deeds.

The objective test for consent presumes the presenter's agency which justifies shouldering on her the results of the gap between her apparent and real consent. Without such agency, the conduct (such as signing a contract) is not hers, so the appearance of consent should have no effect. The approach that physical violence makes the contract void also against an innocent third party was adopted in the Scottish case of *Balloch*,[59] and the Maryland case of *Bond*.[60] Even according to the stricter *Bond* formula which restricts void contracts to (fear of) violence risking serious physical injury or false imprisonment, victims' consent should be considered as vitiated.

Both cases involved spousal abuse in the context of receiving a loan from the bank. The gender aspect of the violence should lead to a conclusion that battery claims against clients by victims – who suffer much more extreme pressure than the wives in *Balloch* and *Bond* – should be accepted. Moreover, both cases arose in the context of 'sexually transmitted debt' in which, as discussed below, English courts developed the constructive notice doctrine, which (in theory) allows wives to set aside voidable contracts against lenders, for reasons which are relevant also in the client–victim context.

### 5.2.2 Clients' constructive notice

In England, the objective test for consent is qualified in the 'sexually transmitted debt' line of cases – mainly *O'Brien* and *Etridge*[61] – by the doctrine of constructive notice. When the wife stands surety for her husband's debts, the bank is deemed to have notice of undue influence of the husband over the wife (real, or in exceptional circumstances, presumed) unless it takes reasonable steps to satisfy itself that the wife enters into a transaction with her eyes open so far as the basic elements of the transaction are concerned.[62] This doctrine can be justified on several grounds. First, the bank is best placed to minimise the risk of undue influence by insisting on procedure which will ensure that wives (and more generally non-commercial guarantors) will enter the transaction freely. Second, the power gap between the parties makes it just to allocate the risk of duress or undue influence by the third party to the bank, as a matter of distributive justice. Third, the bank benefits from the duress or undue influences extracted by the debtor on the claimant by being provided

59 *Trustee Savings Bank v Balloch* (1983) SLT 240.

60 *United States for the Use of the Trane Company v Bond*, 586 A2d 734 (Md, CA, 1990).

61 *Barclays Bank v O'Brien* [1993] 4 All ER 417; *Royal Bank of Scotland v Etridge (No 2)* [2001] 4 All ER 449.

62 *Etridge*, id, [44], [54]. This could be done by ensuring the wife received independent advice from a solicitor, id, [56]. Compare *Bond* (n60); D Post, 'Spousal abuse and the doctrine of duress', (2004) 26 *Hawaii LR* 469. The practical effect of *Etridge*, therefore, has been to provide lenders with a readily available immunity against the claim to set the contract aside. While I find this problematic, the principles underlying the result in *Etridge* mandate a finding of constructive notice by clients.

with a guarantor. This too supports allocation of the risk to the bank. These considerations could explain the doctrine as based on distributive considerations and strict liability.[63] They can also explain the doctrine as based on an implicit assumption of fault on the part of the lender, who has an interest to look the other way when the debtor pressurises his wife to mortgage her property.

These considerations apply also to a different extent in the commercial sex context. True, clients, unlike banks, are not good loss spreaders. More importantly, clients have more limited ability than banks do to insist on procedures which reduce the risk that the woman they purchase sex from is coerced. However, other important factors make the rationale behind the constructive notice doctrine applicable here as well. First, as explained in chapter 6, clients benefit from the fact that women are coerced into prostitution. As such, clients have an interest to blind themselves to the existence of trafficking and research shows that many clients do deceive themselves.

Second, a significant power gap exists between clients and most CSPs, let alone between clients and victims. A related point is that the creation of demand for commercial sex is factually linked to the fact that the claimants became sexually enslaved. While this can serve as an independent ground for clients' liability, as argued in chapters 6, 7 and 8, this fact is relevant for allocating to clients the costs of clients' mistakes about the victim's consent.

Third, clients are better placed than victims to prevent the purchase of sex from victims. In some circumstances, the client can deduce from the circumstances that the claimant is trafficked. In other circumstances, the client can prevent the risk by simply refraining from purchasing commercial sex at all; the victim has much less ability to prevent this encounter. Critics of this approach might argue that in the context of lenders, banks are able to enforce procedures that will minimise the risk that guarantors are unduly influenced, while clients cannot enforce procedures that will minimise the risk of duress.[64] This is probably true, but can hardly serve as a reason to impose the residual risk on victims, rather than on clients. A client found liable should be able to sue the trafficker for indemnity; the risk of failure to do so successfully, however, should lie with the client rather than with the victim. As discussed above, in this context it is fair that clients who purchase commercial sex will act at their peril. The distinction between the different social values of the risk-creating activities is crucial. In the lending context, there might be a way to almost eliminate the risk of vitiated consent. Regardless, given the social value of giving credit, it might be desirable (though this is by no means certain given banks' ability to spread the cost)

63 Note that these considerations might support imposing the risk on the bank, even if it made reasonable efforts to ensure that the wife's consent is freely given.

64 For reasons explained in section 5.3, and in chapter 6, regulating the sex industry, which in any event is beyond the control of individual clients, should not be considered as an adequate measure for minimising the risk of trafficking.

that the guarantor shoulders the residual risk, rather than the bank. Since the social value of purchasing sex is much lower, one should conclude, to paraphrase Lord Reid in *Bolton v Stone*,[65] that if commercial sex cannot be purchased safely, it should not be purchased at all.

### 5.2.3 Unconscionability

The objective test in the contractual context is further qualified by the doctrine of unconscionability. An instructive example is the Canadian Supreme Court decision of *Norberg v Wynrib* in which the claimant was a patient addicted to painkillers and the defendant a physician who exploited the claimant's vulnerability to enter into a sex-for-drugs relationship. The majority of the Canadian Supreme Court – La Forest, Gonthier and Cory JJ – allowed the patient's claim for battery, setting aside her consent based on the unconscionability doctrine.[66] The claimant's vulnerability and its exploitation by the defendant were the key factors in setting aside the claimant's consent and the Court took into account both the claimant's addiction and the power gap between the parties.[67]

In *Norberg*, the unconscionable behaviour was the product of the defendant's own behaviour, so this was not a case of third party duress. However, the power gap between the physician and the patient, coupled with the claimant's vulnerability (being addicted to painkillers), led to the conclusion that the patient could sue for battery. I take *Norberg* as further support to the claim defended in chapter 7 that the vast exploitation of CSPs by clients is another reason to impose the risk on clients. According to such an approach, the unconscionability involved in purchasing commercial sex from CSPs serves as a reason to put clients on constructive notice with respect to third party duress. Accordingly, such duress, which operates on victims, allows them to set aside the appearance of consent, even if clients did not know that the specific claimant was operating under duress. Note that clients' fault in exploiting the vulnerability of CSPs is different from the fault involved in the willingness to purchase sex despite the risk of submitting victims to non-consensual contact. Any client who purchases commercial sex should be aware, at least, that prostitution is often exploitative of CSPs (even if they are not forced). This exploitation should serve as a reason, according to the logic of *Norberg*, to allow victims to set aside the appearance of consent. Whether such exploitation is sufficient by itself to allow any CSP to set aside her consent is an issue I do not explore here.

65 [1951] 1 All ER 1078 (HL).

66 I leave aside the question of whether undue influence, rather than unconscionability, better supports the Court's result.

67 *Norberg* (ch1, n18) [40]–[45].

Justice Sopinka, in his concurring judgment,[68] opined that unconscionability in contracts operates to interfere in the contract despite the consent, rather than to set aside the consent. According to him, then, the battery claim should have failed. Even if Sopinka is right about the effects of unconscionability, still the apparent consent of victims of trafficking should be set aside, since they are subject to much more extreme pressure than that faced by Norberg, and this approach seems to be supported by Sopinka himself.[69] Sopinka also criticised the majority for using the contractarian doctrine of unconscionability in the context of battery given the different ramifications (from the defendant's perspective) of setting aside the claimant's consent in contracts and in battery. By contrast, I believe that the interest in bodily integrity deserves more protection than the interest in not being bound by unfavourable contract. Be that as it may, in the context of *duress* Sopinka's critique is irrelevant.

### *5.2.4 Reliance in torts, restitution and contracts*

The application of the subjective test to restitution claims, and the objective, to contracts,[70] is arguably based on the reliance interest of the other party to the contract, which is absent in mistaken payments. This might suggest that in battery claims, the objective test should be applied, since the defendant relies on the apparent consent of the claimant. On the other hand, two considerations support the adoption of a subjective test to battery claims. The first applies across claims for battery. The claimant's interest in bodily integrity is more significant than the claimant's interest in not being bound by a contract. Battery protects an interest that goes to the core of basic human rights of bodily integrity, personal autonomy and the interest in dignity. There is much to be said in support of a strict protection of this interest.[71] This might be even more so with respect to sexual autonomy. Violating sexual autonomy is one of the most serious violations of dignity. The second consideration applies to commercial sex (and has varying weight in other contexts of battery claims). The social value that should be accorded to the person relying on the appearance of consent changes with the context. In the contractual context, the need to ensure commercial stability weighs heavily to support the objective test. Purchasing commercial sex, on the other hand, is a much lower value activity, and accordingly, the client's reliance should receive less protection. This suggests that battery is more akin to mistaken

68 Despite the differences in approach, all the Justices in *Norberg* agreed that the physician should be liable. Sopinka J grounded liability in the physician's breach of professional duty, and JJ McLachlin and L'Heureux-Dubé grounded liability in breach of fiduciary duty.

69 *Norberg* (n67) [121], [122], [127].

70 Friedmann (n54).

71 Cf Adjin-Tettey (n29) 42.

payments than to contracts, in the sense that the legitimate reliance interest of defendants (at least in the commercial sex context) is much lower.

### *5.2.5 Conclusion and caveat*

The upshot of the analysis is that the victim should not be considered as consenting based on the apparent consent doctrine. Apparent consent is based on the logic of estoppel, which in turn is based on two complementing foundations. First, the claimant is at fault for creating a gap between her subjective preference and the objective appearance of her behaviour. At least, it is based on the assumption that it is fair to allocate the risk of a gap between apparent and real consent to the presenter, based on her responsibility for creating the gap.[72] The second foundation of apparent consent is that the defendant was justified to rely on the objective appearance of consent. The combination of these two factors makes it fair that the presenter, rather than the defendant, would bear the costs of the accident caused by the gap between real and apparent consent. In the context of trafficking, neither condition for imposing the risk on the presenter exists. First, the victim cannot be faulted or held responsible for creating the appearance of consent, since she would put herself at great risk if she conveyed the fact that she was forced (extreme duress logic). Second, given the realities of trafficking, the client's willingness (how convenient!) to take at face value the claimant's consent as real, could not be deemed as reasonable (constructive notice logic).

Arguably, the most faulty actor who is responsible for the gap between the victim's real lack of consent and appearance of consent is the trafficker. It might be just, therefore, that the client would have a cause of action against the trafficker to indemnify him for the former's liability towards the victim. As a matter of just allocation of the risk between the victim and the client, however, the risk should lie with the client.

One caveat is in order. In rare cases, the victim's behaviour might be considered as consent, or to amount to an estoppel. If, for example, the client tells the victim, 'please let me know if you are forced into prostitution. In that case I would not have sex with you and pay your fee nonetheless', and the victim tells him to go ahead, in such a case the victim (who is not likely to sue under this hypothesis anyway) should be estopped from suing the client in either battery or conversion. This is so since the client has created a possibility for the victim to refuse contact with him, without suffering any negative consequences. Under such conditions, the victim's consent is probably subjectively genuine and should be considered as such from an objective

72 Similar rationale supports the allocation of the loss to the original owner in cases of identity mistakes. See the dissenting views of Lords Nicholls and Millet in *Shogun Finance Ltd v Hudson* [2003] UKHL 62.

perspective, in order to protect the client's reliance which under these circumstances could be considered as reasonable. But these cases are likely to be rare. Most clients do not bother to think whether the CSP from whom they purchase sex indeed freely consents. In these don't-ask-don't-tell situations, the client should not be heard saying that by providing sex in exchange for money, the victim is estopped from claiming that her consent was not genuine.

## 5.3 Conversion

In this section I suggest that strict liability may also be grounded in the tort of conversion, which is an act of deliberate dealing with a chattel in a manner inconsistent with another's right, whereby that other is deprived of the use and possession of it. Since the quintessential experience of victims is that of being treated as property, the appropriate legal response is to allow them to benefit from the strict liability imposed on those who interfere with owners' dominion over their property. Accordingly, victims should be viewed as both subjects and objects. As subjects, they can sue clients for the violation of their sexual autonomy manifested in their treatment as objects. This approach is advantageous to victims, affording them protection that might not otherwise exist. Moreover, it is fair, since the ultimate response to the objectification of victims by clients should be to afford the former a proprietary-based claim against the latter. I further explain why the symbolic message of this solution – that the law treats women as property – is not problematic on conceptual grounds, anti-commodification sentiments or feminist concerns.

Section 5.3.1 provides evidence of the objectification of victims by traffickers and clients, conceptualises victims as simultaneously subjects and property, and explains why it is appropriate to analogise victims with property. Section 5.3.2 translates the conceptual apparatus into doctrinal ramifications. Section 5.3.3 responds to doctrinal and conceptual difficulties raised by this suggestion. Lastly, section 5.3.4 replies to feminist and anti-commodification challenges.

### *5.3.1 Conceptualising victims as subjects and property*

Liability under conversion is strict. The honest auctioneer in *Hollins v Fowler*[73] was liable for the value of the cotton he converted by selling it. The common law's position on conversion was summarised by Lord Diplock in *Marfani v Midland Bank* as follows:

> At common law one's duty to one's neighbour who is the owner . . . of any goods is to refrain from doing any voluntary act in relation to his goods which is a usurpation of his proprietary or possessory rights in them. . . .

73 (1875) LR 7 HL 757.

> it matters not that the doer of the act of usurpation did not know, and could not by the exercise of any reasonable care have known, of his neighbour's interest in the goods. This duty is absolute; he acts at his peril.[74]

Recall that the previous discussion suggested that the broader protection currently given to interests in property in comparison to interests in bodily integrity is unjustified. I contend, however, that if broader protection to property interests is justified, sex trafficking victims should benefit from this. The argument is based on the fact that the essence of forced prostitution is the ultimate objectification of victims by traffickers and clients. From the victim's perspective (as well as from that of traffickers and many clients), she is treated as property. As the following examples indicate, victims of trafficking are bought and sold like chattels, and deprived of both autonomy and agency. In the Australian case of *R v Tang*,[75] the accused was convicted of an anti-trafficking provision which punishes anyone who 'intentionally possesses a slave or exercises over a slave any of the other powers attaching to the right of ownership'.[76] In Israel, one complainant 'was subjected to an examination which could only be compared to one done to an animal sold in the market';[77] another was told by the trafficker that she 'must have sex with a condom and oral sex without a condom, and to allow the client do what he wants to do'.[78] Many were sold from one trafficker to another; two victims were sold for cash and a Fiat Punto car; one victim was rented by one trafficker from another; two victims reported they were inherited by family members of their trafficker who passed away; and others reported that they were used as collateral; yet others report they were 'stolen' (rather than 'abducted') from one trafficker by another. There are numerous instances in which the trafficker allowed the use of the victim's sexual services as a gift, without collecting money. Also common, of course, is the rape of the victim by the trafficker.[79]

Clients also treat forced CSPs as property. Research by Donna Hughes found that clients 'viewed all women and girls in prostitution as objects or commodities over which they had temporary powers of possession after they paid their money' and that an alarmingly high percentage of street CSPs are

74 *Marfani* (n17) 970–1.
75 [2008] HCA 39.
76 Criminal Code (Cth), § 270.3(1)(a).
77 *Rabi'ee* (ch3, n23).
78 *Yosef* (ch3, n23).
79 *Salsrevski* (ch2, n23) [6]–[49] (sale between traffickers); CrA 371/06 *Ploni v State of Israel* (Supreme Court, 30 April 2008), [2] (Fiat Punto barter); Levenkron and Dahan (ch1, n13) 24–5 (victims' swap, victims' being stolen from one trafficker by another); *Kuchick* (ch2, n23) [2] (rent); Nomi Levenkron, email correspondence with author, 1 October 2009 (inheritance, collateral, common practice of giving services as gifts); *State v Lifshin* (ch3, n23) [2] (rape by trafficker). For the experience of victims in general, see pp 41–3.

raped and attacked by clients.[80] Another piece of research with a telling title found that for clients, 'women's bodies and sexual services are regarded as commodities that are purchased in a similar fashion to other goods'. For these men, the increasing commodification of sex and women provides a context in which commercial sex not only is normalised, but also is associated with entitlement: 'with enough money, you can buy whoever (whatever) you want'.[81] Note that the research quoted above refers to the attitudes and behaviour of clients towards all CSPs, not only those who are forced. Victims of forced prostitution, whose varied experiences were documented in chapter 3, are even less able to refuse clients, and are subject to abject demands from clients. Martha Nussbaum identifies seven ways in which one can treat another person as a thing: instrumentality, denial of autonomy, inertness, fungibility, violability, ownership and denial of subjectivity.[82] Most or all of these aspects are manifested in the treatment of forced prostitutes by traffickers and clients.

Since it is clear that the essential experience of enslaved victims is that of being treated as property, the victim should be allowed to sue all those whose actions are incompatible with her inviolable right to dominion over her person. This inference requires a conceptualisation of the claimant as subject and object at the same time. As subject, the claimant is entitled not to be treated as property. Since this right has been violated, the victim could sue *as if* she were property with respect to violations of her agency. Conceptualising the victim as property would afford her all of the relevant proprietary causes of action, including trespass to goods.[83] My discussion focuses on conversion since the behaviour which establishes liability in conversion – the defendant's *acute* interference with the claimant's dominion over the property[84] – better reflects the experience of victims of trafficking. The claimant would be able to benefit from the rule that the defendant acts at his peril with respect to property. Accordingly, his reasonable mistake with respect to his right to deal with the claimant's property will not serve as a defence. Thus the client's liability is strict.

The argument does not require recognition of an *ex ante* right to self-ownership. This type of right, to the extent that it implies a right to sell oneself into slavery, is objectionable on several grounds (including the anti-commodification arguments discussed below). Rather, it requires the

80 D Hughes, *Best Practices to Address the Demand Side of Sex Trafficking* (Kingston, RI: University of Rhode Island, 2004) 12, 16, available at www.uri.edu/artsci/wms/hughes/demand_sex_trafficking.pdf (accessed 12 February 2009).

81 M Coy, M Horvath and L Kelly, *'It's Just Like Going to the Supermarket': Men Buying Sex in East London* (London: CWASU, London Metropolitan University, 2007) 19–20, 22, 24 ('Coy').

82 M Nussbaum, 'Objectification', (1995) 24 *Phil & Pub Affairs* 256, 257.

83 But see n17 for a possible caveat.

84 Rogers (n39) 824–6.

recognition of a right not to be owned by anyone else and not to be rendered into property. This position could be conceptualised as an *ex post* right to self-ownership: a person who has been rendered into property should be able to sue all those who have acted in a way that is incompatible with the right not to be owned, as if she had the *ex ante* right of self-ownership. Put differently, the violation of the right not to be owned should trigger at least the remedy which the tort of conversion affords to owners against violations of their dominion over the property. This is so because the right not to be owned shares at least one vital characteristic with an ownership right: the right to exercise dominion over the property and to exclude others from its unauthorised use.

The victim has a right to exclude the client from the unauthorised use of her body. The client, who has intentionally used the victim's body while being mistaken about his authority to have sexual relations with her, acutely interferes with her right to exercise dominion over her body. Given the reality of trafficking, the victim's body is conceptualised as property. Reasonable mistake about one's authority to deal with the chattel vis-à-vis the rightful owner is sufficient to establish conversion.[85] Therefore, the client should be liable towards the victim in conversion.

Further conceptual clarification is required before working out the doctrinal translation of this novel idea. Even though I presented evidence that clients have a sense of entitlement with respect to CSPs and victims, such evidence is not required to establish the victim's right to sue clients in conversion. To commit conversion, the defendant need not believe that he has a right over the chattel. Asserting dominion over the chattel is only one of many ways in which the defendant might convert the property. All that is required is that the defendant acts in a manner that is incompatible with the claimant's dominion over the chattel.[86] The basis for recovery against the client is *not* based on the fact that he owned the victim *de facto* while the victim had the *de jure* right not to be owned. Rather, it is based on the fact that the victim was unlawfully reduced to property by the trafficker (partially with the purpose and effect of benefiting clients) in violation of her right not to be owned, and that the client further acted in a way which is incompatible with that right.

As noted earlier, since liability for conversion is strict, the defendant's mistake with respect to his authority to use the property is irrelevant. But cannot the client argue that his mistake was about the *possibility* that the victim – as a human being – is property? I need not dwell on the general question of whether liability in conversion is excluded by a mistake as to the possibility that something is capable of being property. After all, as the

85 *Hollins* (n73).
86 Rogers (n39) 824–6.

foreseeability discussion in chapter 6 demonstrates, clients should be aware of the trafficking phenomenon. Thus the client's mistake is whether the CSP is a subject or property. This type of mistake is analogous to classic mistakes in conversion about title to the chattel. These mistakes do not preclude liability.

Lastly, this analysis explains why the data showing that the client himself objectifies the CSP should not necessarily lead to a right of a non-forced CSP to sue the client in conversion. It is possible to maintain that a non-forced CSP can, and in fact does, consent to the way she is treated by the client. Since her quintessential position is not that of property, she should not be able to sue the client in conversion. This could be conceptualised as the owner permitting the use of her property by the defendant, thus precluding liability in conversion.

The suggestion that victims should be allowed to sue clients in conversion is supported by the following considerations. First, the victim's lack of voice makes an analogy with property appropriate. Arguably, the distinction between strict liability for dealing with another's property and negligence liability for touching the person without her consent is justified by the fact that a person can express her lack of consent to the touching, while property (or its owner) cannot. If this is the rationale supporting the increased degree of protection to property, victims should be afforded the broader protection given to property owners, since their predicament prevents them from expressing their lack of consent. It could be argued that all people who act under duress by third parties are similarly disabled. Indeed, extreme instances of duress by third parties might invalidate the claimant's consent in battery claims, and the basic distinction between the different ramifications of varying degrees of duress noted above is a case in point. Perhaps less extreme forms of pressure would not be sufficient to overcome the reliance interest of the other party to the contract. However, the complete violation of the victim's autonomy and the totality of her enslavement justify the analogy with property in this case, without necessarily applying to other cases of serious duress.

Second, what makes the use of proprietary rules appropriate in the sexual enslavement context is not only the extent of the duress applied to the victim, but also its effects. Admittedly, extreme forms of pressure exist in other contexts (although they are quite rare). However, in the context of sexual slavery, the effect of duress is that the victim is being *treated* as (and rendered into) property. This is typically not true in other scenarios of extreme duress. While technically a CSP enters a contract with the client, the victim is rendered into property in two important ways. First, from the perspective of the traffickers, victims are sold, bought and used as chattels. Second, in the context of commercial sex, the woman herself is 'sold' (or rather 'let') to the client in exchange for money. Note that the first observation might support an extension of the possibility of suing in conversion to all enslaved people. (While the second observation might possibly support the extension of this possibility to all CSPs this is *not* an argument I make here and I think that such an argument should fail, since, and to the extent that, non-forced CSPs freely consent to the way they are treated by clients.) Be that as it may, the combined effect of these two observations renders the analogy between property and victims of sex trafficking especially convincing.

Third, this analogy is appropriate in light of the low social value of purchasing commercial sex discussed in chapter 7. In the general commercial context, priority is given to protecting entitlements to property despite the important social interest in facilitating free commerce. In the commercial sex context, society has far less interest in facilitating free sexual commerce and protecting clients' reliance. In addition, the victim's interest in not being treated as property is more important than the typical owner's interest in preserving his dominion over his property.

Victims of trafficking are wronged in two independent ways. First, they are denied their right to bodily integrity; second, they are denied their humanity by being treated as property. For the former violation they should be allowed to sue in battery; for the latter, in conversion.

### *5.3.2 Doctrinal translation*

Once the victim is conceptualised as property, the client can be seen as committing conversion by his temporary use or possibly by taking possession. When the temporary use denies the owner's right,[87] exercises dominion[88] or destroys the good,[89] liability in conversion is established. The client's use of the victim clearly denies her right not to be used as a sexual object; clients clearly exercise dominion over victims while purchasing sex;[90] and the cumulative effect of sexual contact between clients and victims seriously affects the victim's health.[91] Joyriding in a car is considered to be conversion.[92] If so, a client's 'joyride' of the victim should be considered as conversion as well. In general, taking possession which is temporary and trivial, which neither harms the property nor is accompanied by an intention to assert rights over the goods, will not lead to liability in conversion. However, it is not necessary for the defendant to assert ownership over the goods, and as the joyriding cases

87 *Lancashire and Yorkshire Ry v MacNicholl* (1919) 88 LJKB 601, 605.

88 *Hollins* (n73) 766, 782, 787, 790, 792.

89 *Roberts v McDougall* (1887) 3 TLR 666; *Mitchell v Ealing LBC* [1979] QB 1; *Toor v Bassi* [1999] EGCS 9.

90 If, contrary to my view, sexual contact were not considered by courts as amounting to conversion, it should at least amount to trespass to goods.

91 For health effects of trafficking, see Zimmerman *et al.* (ch3, n21); GAATW, 'Migration, trafficking and right to health', (2005) 23 *Alliance News*; *The IOM Handbook of Direct Assistance for Victims of Trafficking* (Geneva: IOM, 2007) 181–270.

92 *Rolle Abr Tit Action Sur Case* 5 (equine variety); *Aitken v Richardson* [1967] 2 NZLR 15. Cf *Schemmell v Pomeroy* (1989) 50 SASR 450.

demonstrate, any use which is not trivial will lead to liability.[93] An additional way to commit conversion is by abusing possession by disposing of the goods.[94] Possibly, at least in some cases, the client is responsible for conversion when he effectively returns the victim to the control or 'custody' of the trafficker.

The application of the conceptual apparatus of property law and proprietary remedies to human beings is not unprecedented. In the Ante Bellum American South, slaves were treated as property;[95] litigation based on the duty of bailees to take care of the slaves entrusted to them by the owner was common, and in Tennessee, for example, 'the master [was] at liberty to regard the wrongful act in a bailee as a conversion and sue in trover'.[96] The flip side of the coin – treating property as subject – exists as well: in maritime law, vessels are both property and legal persons, since the claimant and defendant in the litigation are the vessels themselves.

Strict liability for conversion has several exceptions, but none of them is applicable here. Estoppel is the most relevant of the qualifications to this kind of liability under the *nemo dat quod non habet rule*. In England, this exception[97] is very narrow, and is based on unconscionability or recklessness on the part of the claimant with respect to her absence of interest in the property. Mere negligence will not do.[98] As clarified earlier in this chapter and in chapter 3, except in the most extreme circumstances, a victim who fails to communicate her lack of free consent to a client could not be considered negligent, let alone reckless or unconscionable, since the extreme pressure she faces prevents her from communicating her lack of consent to the client.

Prior to 1994 in England[99] the common law doctrine of *market overt* allowed a buyer to acquire good title to stolen goods if they were purchased in good faith, without notice of any defect or want of title on the part of the seller, and sold in a market that is open, public and legally constituted by grant, prescription or statute.[100] This doctrine allowed the buyer to purchase a warranty against the seller's lack of title at the cost of some presumable

93 The approach of the *Restatement (Second) of Torts* (n14) § 222A, Ill, 24 is similar.

94 *Hollins* (n73); *Motis Exports v Dampskibsselskabet AF 1912 A/S* [2000] 1 Lloyd's Rep 211.

95 See K Orren, *Belated Feudalism: Labor, the Law, and Liberal Development in the United States* (Cambridge: Cambridge University Press, 1991). Cf R Steinfeld, *The Invention of Free Labor* (Chapel Hill, NC: University of North Carolina at Pembroke, 1991) 88 (actions in detinue in indentured servitude disputes), 90.

96 *Tallahassee v Macon*, 8 Fla 299 (1859).

97 Currently embodied in the proviso of Sale of Goods Act 1979 (c 54), s 21(1): '. . . unless the owner of the goods is by his conduct precluded from denying the seller's authority to sell'.

98 Rogers (n39) 844 (a plea of estoppel 'is extremely difficult to establish'). See also Sale of Goods Act 1979, s 11(1), which provides that contributory negligence is not a defence to a conversion claim.

99 Sale of Goods (Amendment) Act 1994 (c 32), s 1.

100 *Clayton v Leroy* [1911] 2 KB 1031. For the Israeli market overt doctrine, still in force but slightly differently constituted, see Sales Act 5728–1968 (Isr), § 34.

premium.[101] In open markets sellers are repeat players, so that the original owner is able to sue the seller and recover if her title is defeated. Similarly, the fact that the market is open and regulated decreases the chance that the goods are stolen. A buyer who refrains from buying in an open market takes the risk of being strictly liable towards the owner. One could argue, by analogy, that if prostitution were regulated, clients who purchase sex from a regulated CSP should not be liable to her if she happens to be a victim. Clearly, such an argument is not applicable to England, where market overt has been abolished and prostitution is not regulated. It is doubtful, however, whether market overt could ever apply, since it protects a buyer rather than a user from liability in conversion. The client does not buy the victim (who remains owned by the trafficker), but rather uses her. In any event, I oppose the legalisation of prostitution, since, as surveyed in chapter 6, research fails to show that it improves the well being of CSPs and reduces the number of victims. Women should not be further commodified by the creation of state-regulated markets for the sale of sex in order to shield clients who violate victims' rights from strict liability.

How should damages for conversion be computed in the trafficking context? In general, damages in conversion equate to the market value of the chattel at the time of conversion. The crucial point is that the relevant market value is that of the victim prior to her enslavement. Since, after the client's interference (and more generally after the enslavement is over) the victim is usually injured, damages should reflect the difference between the claimant's position prior to her enslavement and her post-enslavement position. This is consistent with courts' rulings in cases in which the subject matter of the suit in conversion was damaged, but eventually returned to the claimant who accepted it. In these cases the defendant had to pay the difference between the property's value pre- and post-interference.[102] Indeed, the House of Lords in *Kuwait Airways Co v Iraqi Airways Co* clarified that damages in conversion should always represent the true loss suffered by reason of the defendant's acts.[103] In this sense, the *practical* effect of damages for conversion will be similar to that of damages for battery and false imprisonment. Both will compensate the victim for the harm caused to her by the violation of her rights. In addition, punitive damages are available in appropriate cases for both conversion and battery and false imprisonment.[104]

Some might object that a remedy based on the market value of the subject matter confirms the inferiority of conversion from the symbolic perspective

101 H Dagan, 'Market overt as insurance', in S Lerner and D Lewinsoh-Zamir (eds), *Essays in Honour of Joshua Weisman* (Jerusalem: Sacher Institute, 2002) 15 (in Hebrew).

102 *Tucker v Wright* (1826) 3 Bing 601; *Solloway v McLaughlin* [1938] AC 247 (PC).

103 [2002] 2 AC 883, [68].

104 D Thomas and H McGregor, *McGregor on Damages*, 18th edn (London: Sweet & Maxwell, 2009) 1243; *Dulghieru* (ch2, n7).

inasmuch as it further commodifies the victim. The answers in section 5.3.4 are also relevant to this challenge. In addition, market value is only a proxy of the measure of recovery, which is the value of the goods.[105] Where no market exists, as is arguably the case with respect to each human's inalienable right not to be owned, measures such as replacement value are used. These alternative measures are both less problematic symbolically and closer to the quantum of damages in personal injury and battery cases.

*Kuwait Airways* highlights another important aspect of damages in conversion: damages can be awarded even against a defendant – a subsequent converter – who is able to show that the claimant would have suffered the same damage but for his interference.[106] This practical advantage is important for victims of trafficking. The fact that the victim was enslaved prior to the encounter with the client-defendant and was further enslaved afterwards should not prevent her from suing the client in conversion for the total difference between her condition prior to her enslavement and after the enslavement has ended.

> By definition, each person in a series of conversions wrongfully excludes the owner from possession of his goods. This is the basis on which each is liable to the owner. That is the nature of the tort of conversion. The wrongful acts of a previous possessor do not therefore diminish the plaintiff's claim in respect of the wrongful acts of a later possessor.[107]

This statement, however, was made in the context of a typical claim in conversion for the full value of the subject matter. In the trafficking context, the claim is for the difference between the value of the subject matter, the victim's person, before and after the series of conversions. This, some might argue, justifies apportioning the contribution of each converter to the damage or injury he has caused.

Some might view as unjust the interpretation of *Kuwait Airways* as mandating a client who purchased sex from a victim to compensate her for her entire loss from having been trafficked. This is a weighty objection but three reasons point to the opposite conclusion. First, to the extent that liability without but-for causation is unjust, the rule allowing for such recovery should be changed across the board. As long as it exists, it would be morally repugnant to afford stronger protection to the unauthorised use of 'real' chattels than to the unauthorised use of people who are treated like chattels. Second, contribution rules will allow the client who is found liable to seek contribution from all other clients and traffickers he can identify. The risk of inability to do so should lie with the client rather than with the victim. Lastly, a client's liability for all the losses involved in the enslavement could be justified on the

105 Thomas and McGregor, id, 1196.
106 *Kuwait* (n103) [81]–[86].
107 Id, [82].

ground that clients' indiscriminate demand for commercial sex is the cause of sex trafficking. Without this demand, trafficking for sexual purposes would cease to exist. However, while chapter 8 clarifies that the injury from being trafficked is indivisible, it also concludes that full liability for contribution to trafficking by creation of demand is too harsh. Whether the same conclusion is warranted with respect to liability for direct contact is less clear. But even if liability for conversion should be apportioned so that each client should be responsible only for the damage caused by his individual encounter(s) with the claimant, the measure of recovery is not likely to, and ought not, fall below what the victim would be able to claim in battery. Similarly, those convinced that each client should be liable only for the direct encounter and not for the entire injury of being trafficked have no good reason to oppose the option to sue in conversion since limiting the award to the damage caused by the individual encounter is consistent with *Kuwait Airways* and with principle. What *Kuwait Airways* clarifies and mandates is the following uncontroversial conclusion: that the fact that the victim has been and will be further sexually assaulted by other clients is not a reason to reduce the damages from what would have been awarded had the defendant's battery been the only violation of her rights.

The use of conversion as a cause of action, therefore, does not involve any practical downside, in comparison to the more straightforward battery claim, and might yield some practical benefits if damages for conversion are given for the entire loss from being trafficked, or if reasonable mistake is (wrongly) taken to exclude liability in battery.

I do not dwell on an alternative measure of recovery: the purchase price of a sex slave in the industry, which, as was documented in chapter 3, can amount to several thousand dollars. This sort of valuation is lower than the victim's loss from being enslaved (and is in all likelihood lower than the loss caused to her from the single encounter with the client) and is more problematic symbolically. Nonetheless, some might argue that a remedy in the range of several thousand dollars against an innocent client represents a better balance between the interests of the victim and the client than an amount reflecting liability for the loss caused by the encounter with the client or the trafficking experience as a whole.

### 5.3.3 Doctrinal and conceptual objections

The suggestion to allow victims to sue clients in conversion might be opposed on either doctrinal or conceptual grounds. According to the doctrinal challenge, the weight of authority is against viewing forced CSPs as property, since according to *Williams v Williams*[108] there is no property in a corpse,

108 (1882) 20 Ch D 659.

since according to *R v Bentham*[109] a person does not possess his body or any part of it, and since, until the recent Court of Appeals decision in *Yearworth v North Bristol NHS Trust*[110] there was no property in body parts in England or in many other jurisdictions according to the *Dobson* and *Moore* decisions.[111] But these cases raise different issues than those involved in a claim by a forced CSP. Even if correct (a point I do not explore here), they do not necessitate a denial of the victim's rights. Rights to a corpse are usually asserted by next of kin; therefore they do not raise the issue of whether the law should afford a person with a proprietary right with respect to her own body. Moreover, denying a deceased person (or her estate) a proprietary right in a corpse does not involve the same difficulties involved in denying a living person a proprietary right in her body. The effects of denying such a right on the living person's autonomy, dignity and well being are much more far-reaching. Lastly, as clarified above, my claim falls short of accepting a general proprietary right of a person over her body (an approach which might fall foul of anti-commodification sentiment). Rather, it is limited to instances in which the individual has been rendered into property by others. I return to this point in section 5.3.4.

One might suppose that there is authority against the position I am defending. In *Bentham*, for example, the defendant committed a robbery with his hand inside his zipped-up jacket, forcing the material out so as to give the impression that he had a gun. The House of Lords reversed his conviction for possessing an imitation firearm during the course of a robbery. 'One cannot possess something which is not separate and distinct from oneself'; '. . . no-one is to be regarded as the owner of his own limbs . . . Equally, we may be sure, no-one is to be regarded as being in possession of his own limbs'.[112] Even in its context this reasoning is unduly formalist, since it is clear that the purpose of the prohibition is to prevent the robber from falsely pretending to have a firearm. But even if a restrictive statutory interpretation in criminal law is justified, no such constraint exists in developing civil liability at common law. The context and consequences of possession in criminal and private law are different, as are the merits of recognising a right of self-ownership/possession in these different contexts (let alone, a right not to be possessed by others). Therefore, the reasoning in *Bentham* has little relevance to the forced-prostitution context.

In fact, case law provides weak support for the position defended here. In *Yearworth*, for example, the Court of Appeal ruled that the claimants (who had

109 [2005] UKHL 18.

110 [2009] EWCA Civ 37.

111 *Dobson v North Tyneside Health Authority* [1996] 4 All ER 474; *Moore v Regents of California University*, 51 Cal 3rd 120 (1990). Ownership of sperm for the purpose of bequest was recognised by the Californian Court of Appeal in *Hecht v Superior Court of Los Angeles County*, 20 Cal Rptr 2d 275 (1993).

112 *Bentham* (n109) [8] (Lord Bingham); [14] (Lord Rodger).

to undergo chemotherapy) owned sperm which was kept as a safeguard at a fertility unit and negligently destroyed. They were allowed to sue for the psychiatric injury which allegedly followed, based on theories of negligence and bailment, and notwithstanding the fact that the Human Fertilisation and Embryology Act 1990[113] had curtailed the claimants' rights with respect to the sperm. *Yearworth*, therefore, is a recent authority which suggests that a victim's right to sue a client in conversion fits with the increased recognition of proprietary interests in body parts. The Court referred in *obiter* to the traditional common law principle:

> a living human body is incapable of being owned. An allied principle is that a person does not even 'possess' his body or any or part of it . . . One consequence of the principles, albeit not recognised until the nineteenth century, is that, if our bodies cannot be our own property, it follows that they cannot be the property of other persons; and that therefore we cannot sell ourselves, or be sold, to others. Another consequence is that, if we do not own our bodies, we have no right to destroy them, i.e. to commit suicide; in this respect it was necessary for Parliament, by s.1 of the Suicide Act 1961, to legislate the necessary reform to the criminal law.[114]

But these statements do not stand in the way of recognising the victim's right to sue in conversion. In the first place, the decriminalisation of suicide indicates that the idea of self-ownership is acceptable. More importantly, the Court states the obvious: *ex ante* we cannot be sold to others. Once such a sale occurs, however, nothing in the decision suggests that self-ownership will be denied *ex post*. On the contrary, the Court's willingness to recognise ownership in sperm suggests that it might be willing to give the victims of trafficking the right to sue clients in conversion. Both the ruling and the reasoning in *Yearworth* demonstrate sensitivity to context, careful examination of the merits of the case and a strong and healthy sense of practical justice. The contexts of *Yearworth* and forced prostitution reveal important parallels. The claims are based on the injury to the claimant and do not involve a voluntary attempt by the claimant to sell the object with respect to which a property right is asserted.

Unlike *Williams* and *Bentham*, and to a greater extent than *Yearworth*, *Moore* raises questions analogous to claims by forced CSPs. In *Moore*, allegedly the physician did not disclose to the patient that cells taken over a long period of time from his body were being used for a lucrative research project which culminated in patenting a cell line that produced big profits for the physicians and other related defendants. The majority of the Californian Supreme Court

113 (c 37).
114 *Yearworth* (n110) [30].

held that even though the claimant could have a valid cause of action for breach of a fiduciary duty and a duty to receive the patient's informed consent, the claimant did not have a proprietary right in his own cells and therefore could not sue in conversion. Judges Broussard and Mosk filed strong dissenting opinions which recognised a right to sue in conversion. The similarity between forced prostitution cases and *Moore* is that the bodily integrity of both claimants has been violated for profit-seeking motives. However, even if the majority view could be defended, it does not follow that sex slaves should be equally barred.

The majority reasoned that the social utility of biomedical research necessitates the protection of innocent third parties. To the majority, the protection afforded by conversion was unnecessary, since the breach of fiduciary duty afforded sufficient protection to the autonomy of patients. Neither consideration applies in the context of forced prostitution. The social utility of commercial sex is much lower than that of medical research, and thus cannot serve as justification to trump the claimant's rights. Furthermore, the majority is concerned with the interests of innocent third parties. Clients who ignore the risk of purchasing sex from a forced CSP cannot be considered as innocent as those involved in medical research. As Judge Broussard mentioned, the facts of *Moore* are atypical,[115] while forced prostitution is rampant. This fact affects the extent to which third parties can truly be innocent. Moreover, according to common wisdom – challenged in chapter 4 – the forced CSP cannot base her claim on breach of fiduciary duty and some might doubt whether she could base her claim against arguably innocent clients in battery.

Three further distinctions between *Moore* and forced prostitution come to mind. First, the invasion of bodily integrity and its effect on the claimant's dignity and autonomy are more far-reaching in the context of prostitution. After all, Moore was not enslaved in order to provide the precious cells. This fact weighs in favour of extending more protection to victims by affording them with a conversion claim. Second, removing the cells from Moore's body did not harm him in any way (and in fact probably improved his health).[116] By contrast, sexual contact with the client harms the victim in many ways. Unlike *Moore*, which was a profit-based litigation, victims' claims against clients are harm-based, even when conversion is the relevant cause of action. The interest in preventing harm should receive more protection from the legal system than the interest in making profit. Third, Moore's contribution to the profits made at his expense was the result of fortuity, and his claim was not supported by a labour-desert theory. This possibly weakened his claim. While the victim's claim against clients is harm-based, her claims for any profit made at her expense are based on her (forced) labour.

115 *Moore* (n111) 158–9.
116 Id, 180.

Arguably, the statutory definition of property in the Torts (Interference with Goods Act) 1977[117] (the Act) which refers specifically to 'chattels personal other than things in action and money' is a further indication that this area of law does not embrace notions of people as property. Similarly, the House of Lords in *OBG v Allan* refused (by 3:2 majority) to extend the protection of conversion to contractual rights.[118] Seemingly, then, it is insufficient for the victim to show that she has been rendered into property, since conversion protects the owner only against interference with chattels (and documents evidencing a debt).

At one level, it is indisputable that people are not and should not be treated by the law as property. My argument is that *if* humans are treated like chattels, *they* should be afforded the option to sue in conversion in order to vindicate their right not to be rendered into property. The argument cannot be fairly evaluated if the link between its two parts is severed: viewing the victim as both the *de jure*, *ex post* owner of her body and as *de facto* property. In fact, there is no doubt that the trafficker exercised dominion over the victim. But on the normative level, since the victim should have had the right not to be rendered into property, we give her the right to sue with respect to all instances in which she was so rendered. The Act, as indeed the modern common law, does not purport to exclude human beings from being considered as property since the reality of slavery did not cross the collective mind of Parliament when the Act was enacted.[119] Indeed, the Act can support the view that sex slaves should be able to sue in conversion, since in the relevant aspects victims are akin to chattels rather than to things in action and money. Likewise, the Act does not prevent classifying the sperm in *Yearworth* as property.

Similarly, none of the substantive reasons to reject liability in conversion for interference with contractual rights mentioned by the majority in *OBG* are relevant in the sex trafficking context. Lord Hoffmann was concerned with the creation of strict liability for pure economic loss, which traditionally requires at least negligence.[120] But the interests of bodily integrity, sexual autonomy and dignity deserve, and are routinely afforded, protection from innocent violations. Lord Brown's objection could be understood as either focusing on the need to limit conversion to the 'taking of physical possession of property' (why?) or on the difficulty of identifying the 'real and ascertainable value' of the claimant's chose in action at the time of the interference.[121] Victims of trafficking, as documented above, are treated like chattels and possession in them is a crucial aspect of their enslavement and the interference with their rights. As for real and ascertainable value, the violation of the right not to be

117 (c 32).
118 [2007] UKHL 21.
119 For similar reasoning, see Baroness Hale's dissent in *OBG*, id, [313]–[315].
120 Id, [99].
121 Id, [321].

rendered into property leads to a real and significant loss. As the previous discussion demonstrated, this loss is as ascertainable as any unauthorised interference with chattels that causes damage to property.

These somewhat formalistic doctrinal quibbles are rooted in a conceptual critique according to which the venerable distinction between non-property and property-based interests cannot allow the classification of the victim's interest as proprietary and should not be compromised in order to accommodate the needs of victims. I disagree. To begin with, the correct conceptualisation of victims of sex trafficking is as both subject and object. As human beings, they *should* be treated as humans. The reality of their victimisation is that they *were* treated as property. Concepts are helpful as analytical tools which help to explain why certain policy considerations are relevant (or not) in a certain context. Affording victims property-based remedies is conceptually justified, since it corresponds to an essential aspect of the violation of their rights: their treatment as property. No conceptual transgression occurs by affording victims the benefits of property law to remedy the violation involved in treating them as property.

At a deeper level, the elasticity or rigidity of concepts is the result of value-based decisions. My approach is rooted in a legal realist and pragmatic tradition which gives priority to the attainment of just results and the preservation of human rights and dignity over formalist distinctions, conceptualist zealotry and fetishism with respect to principles and coherence. Legal rules are a human creation whose aim is to promote human flourishing and justice. Concepts are meant to serve jurists, not to control them,[122] and it would be most unfortunate if in the twenty-first century the clanking chains of concepts replaced those of the forms of action in the path of justice.[123]

### 5.3.4 Symbolic message and poetic justice

We must distinguish between two separate normative critiques of allowing victims to sue clients in conversion; both are concerned with law's symbolism. The first and more serious critique is that allowing victims to sue in conversion demeans them, and perhaps women in general, since the law conceives of them as property. Nearly everyone concedes that objectification of humans is morally wrong.[124] Much ink has been spilt by (mainly radical) feminist thinkers in identifying and condemning the objectification of women in general and for sexual purposes in particular.[125] While Nussbaum acknowledges the possibility

122 F Cohen, 'Transcendental nonsense and the functional approach', (1935) 35 *Colum LR* 809.

123 Cf *United Australia* (ch3, n86) 29.

124 See I Kant, *Lectures on Ethics* (London: Methuen, L Infield trans, J Macmurray rev edn, 1979) 165; M Radin, 'Market inalienability', (1987) 100 *Harv LR* 1849.

125 Classic examples include C MacKinnon, *Feminism Unmodified* (Cambridge, MA: Harvard University Press, 1987) 174, and *Toward a Feminist Theory of the State* (Cambridge,

of benign objectification in the sexual context, the required conditions do not apply in the context of forced prostitution. These include lack of instrumentalisation, symmetry, and context of mutual respect and rough social equality.[126] Seemingly, a legal response which conceives of women as property is demeaning, insulting and pernicious. Moreover, it might be understood as the law's imprimatur to the objectification of victims, and thus to the normalisation of their enslavement. Furthermore, the symbolic message that women are commodities might permeate and negatively affect women's status in society. This critique targets the aspect of my argument which conceptualises the victim as property.

But this critique fails for the following reasons. First, it would be disingenuous to deny victims an advantageous remedy based on the argument that conceptualising them as property would harm or demean them, while the purpose and effect of this conceptualisation is to afford victims the better protection given by proprietary torts. In any event, each victim would be free to choose whether to pursue such a claim in court; no one should be the victim's guardian with respect to the claim she should advance. Second, it is clear that the system regards the victim as property only in order to afford her increased protection, and that this conceptualisation is both advantageous to the victim and conforms to her preference. Thus the social meaning of such conceptualisation is beneficial to the victim.[127] Third, the victim is not conceptualised merely as an object, but as a subject as well: as the owner of the right *not* to be treated as property. The victim is not viewed as property in litigation between two traffickers over their respective rights to the victim. Rather, it is the victim who sues those who treated her as property. In this sense, accepting the claim has an empowering symbolic effect (aside from its beneficial practical aspects). Fourth, even if it were true that conceptualising the victim as property is problematic symbolically, the practical advantage should tilt the scales towards accepting the claim when it is submitted by the victim herself.

Most important of all is the following observation. The objectification, denigration and dehumanisation of victims result from the way in which they are treated in reality and are *not* the result of conceptualising them as property for the purposes of legal proceedings. These women *were* treated as property, and refusing to afford them with an appropriate remedy would not undo this horrible truth. Rather, it would allow clients to benefit from this objectification instead of assisting victims to recover from it. Strangely enough, disallowing this cause of action might contribute to the objectification of victims by denying them a more effective remedy and hence decreasing deterrence. Moreover, battery and negligence take place on a daily basis and range from

MA: Harvard University Press, 1989) 124; A Dworkin, *Intercourse* (New York, NY: Free Press, 1987) 122–3.

126 Nussbaum (n82) 275.

127 Cf Keren-Paz (n20) 152–4.

serious attacks to relatively innocuous violations of bodily integrity. We might depreciate the unique and horrific experience of sexual slavery by channelling the claims of victims towards battery or negligence. Affording victims a proprietary cause of action with respect to their sexual abuse highlights their unique experience as slaves. This sends a desirable symbolic message that sexual enslavement actually happens, that it is especially repugnant and that it merits an exceptional response.

The second critique concerned with the law's symbolic message is the familiar anti-commodification argument. This critique attacks the other aspect of suggested conceptualisation: by affording victims with proprietary rights. According to this critique, there are interests which are inalienable and should not be subject to market mechanisms, logic or rhetoric. The interest in bodily integrity is such an interest; therefore, victims should not be allowed to sue in conversion for its violation. This argument has been advanced in several contexts, including slavery,[128] sale of body parts, prostitution, adoption of babies and surrogacy.[129] Margaret Radin presents a powerful and eloquent account of the pitfalls of universal commodification, which undermines personhood and represents an inferior conception of human flourishing. Nonetheless, Radin's powerful anti-commodification argument should not be invoked to oppose my suggestion. Given the imperfections of the world in which we live, Radin supports incomplete commodification of prostitution rather than market inalienability.[130] More importantly, the tenor of her argument in 'Market inalienability' (with few exceptions) is directed against an *ex ante* consensual alienation, and does not target *ex post* compensation for non-consensual infringements of inalienable rights. Radin is correct to limit her argument to consensual settings, since, as we will see, non-consensual contexts raise different issues.

Yet others make the misconceived argument that allowing a proprietary-based remedy for violations of an inalienable right commodifies and hence depreciates the interest. Judge Arabian's concurring opinion in *Moore* is typical of this line of argument:

> Plaintiff has asked us to recognize and enforce a right to sell one's own body tissue *for profit*. He entreats us to regard the human vessel – the single most venerated and protected subject in any civilized society – as equal with the basest commercial commodity. He urges us to commingle the sacred with the profane. He asks much.[131]

128 A Seboc, 'Reparations, unjust enrichment and the importance of knowing the difference between the two', (2003) 58 *NYU Ann Surv Am L* 651.

129 Radin (n124).

130 Id, 1921–5.

131 *Moore* (n111) 148. See Seboc (n128) for a statement of this argument in the context of restitution for slavery. For a response which parallels mine, see Dagan (ch3, n128) 250–4.

But this concern totally misses the mark. 'Defendants' position that plaintiff cannot own his tissue, but that they can, is fraught with irony'.[132] Cases of objectification (by slavery or by taking body parts) raise only a distributional question. The commodification has already occurred; the only issue is whether the wrongdoer or the victim should be allowed to keep the profits. Redistributing the profits from a past violation of an inalienable interest does not commodify that interest. Indeed, by better deterring such behaviour it is likely to decrease the incidence of these violations. But regardless of the deterrent effect of such a rule, justice requires that the profits be given to the victim rather than the wrongdoer.

Granted, an even more radical anti-commodification argument might be developed. It opposes tort compensation for violation of bodily integrity since damages for pain and suffering 'commodify our unique experience' and damages for injuries to relationships 'commodify love'. The jury 'must simulate a market in sadomasochism'; tort law 'transforms an involuntary past experience (injury) into future gain (damages), reflecting bourgeois notions of delayed gratification and an instrumental view of the self'.[133] This view is incompatible with my argument. Note, however, that this approach, if taken seriously, would deny victims compensation for causes of action in battery or negligence. As long as tort damages continue to be based on the principle of full compensation, forced CSPs should not be excluded. Since Abel's argument targets tort damages in general rather than proprietary responses, one could reject his radical anti-commodification argument (based on grounds of either fit or justification) while also rejecting *Moore*-like anti-commodification arguments based on their failure to distinguish between voluntary transactions and forced violation of interests. To be sure, Abel suggests that no compensation should be given to negligently caused property loss. But his reason is distributive. It would be most unbecoming to adopt Abel's opposition to compensating property damage, which is based on egalitarian commitment to protecting the interests of the marginalised, in order to deny sex slaves – perhaps the most vulnerable group in society – a better remedy.

Lastly, Abel's proposal to significantly curtail tort damages for bodily integrity could be questioned on pragmatic and principled grounds. On the pragmatic side, denying damages based on their symbolic message might impede the well being of victims (a point conceded by Radin[134]). On the principled level, damages for infringement of an inalienable right could serve to vindicate the right, rather than to provide a substitution.[135] Moreover, especially in a capitalist society which values things in monetary terms, it is

132 *Moore* (n111) 166 (J Mosk, dissenting, citing the Court of Appeal).

133 R Abel, 'A critique of torts', (1990) 37 *UCLALR* 785, 803–6.

134 See (n124) 1877.

135 N Witzleb and R Carroll, 'The role of vindication in the law of remedies', (2009) 17 *Tort LR* 16; Stevens (n26) 59–62; Weinrib (ch3, n128) 34.

crucial to place a high price tag on violations of inalienable rights in order to convey their importance. A commitment to the value of the interest without the backing of a financial sanction might be deemed hollow.[136] Once damages are understood to represent vindication rather than compensation, their social meaning changes, and they do not (necessarily) commodify the interest any longer.

To conclude: we should distinguish between the symbolic effects of deciding that a given interest is alienable and of deciding to afford a given remedy for the infringement of an inalienable interest. The problem with the former is that law's constituents who now sell (since the law permits such transactions) what should be inalienable will devalue the interest. This problem is irrelevant in the context of forced prostitution, since the sale and objectification of women remains prohibited. The potential risk of the latter – that law's constituents would think of women as property since the law conceptualises them as such – is unlikely once it is understood that the conceptualisation only responds to the illegal reality in which women were treated as property and that victims seek this conceptualisation only in order to receive better protection. Moreover, this fear is also based on a contested and somewhat implausible assumption about the potential of legal *reasoning* to mobilise the views of the law's constituents.

In short, I argue that it is fair and that it serves poetic justice that the response to the ultimate objectification of victims should be to afford them the more generous protection given by proprietary torts. Note that this approach is both *advantageous* to victims and *fair*. It is advantageous since it might afford victims better protection than is currently available under the law of battery. It is fair since it does not objectify victims; rather, objectification occurs through the reality of trafficking. My suggested solution merely allows victims to alleviate the consequences of this horrid objectification instead of letting clients and traffickers benefit from it. Lastly, the solution serves poetic justice, since the ultimate response to the objectification of victims by clients should be to afford the former a proprietary-based claim against the latter. Clients who treat victims as property are met with the onerous burdens imposed by the common law on those who seriously interfere with the owner's dominion over her property.

## 5.4 Conclusion

It is both normatively defensible and doctrinally feasible to hold clients ignorant of the fact that they bought sex from a victim liable in torts towards

136 Cf L Jaffe, 'Damages for personal injury: the impact of insurance', (1953) 18 *L & Contemp Probs* 219, 224; M Radin 'Compensation and commensurability', (1993) 43 *Duke LJ* 56, 61, 73–4.

that victim. Fairness and equality demand that clients would compensate victims even if one refuses to acknowledge that purchasing sex from a CSP who might be a victim is a faulty behaviour. Imposing strict liability will preserve (or bring) consistency into the English law of trespass and is likely to reduce demand for (forced or otherwise) prostitution. Such strict liability could be grounded in battery, despite the appearance of apparent consent by the victim to sell sexual services to the client; it might even be grounded in conversion, since the quintessential experience of victims of trafficking is that they are treated as property.

One way or another, based on either notions of fault or distributive justice, the client must pay. If the percentage of victims among CSPs is sufficiently high, the risk imposed on victims by clients purchasing commercial sex is unreasonable. This conclusion is bolstered if one adheres to the view that prostitution itself is exploitative. These propositions are examined in the next two chapters. But even if one adheres to the rosy description of the sex industry pictured by some – in which the vast majority of CSPs are happy and free – still winners should compensate losers. These losers are the tiny minority of victims whose suffering is the inevitable cost needed to be incurred in order for the sex industry – which according to such account is socially desirable, empowering to CSPs and unexploitative – to continue to thrive.

Chapter 6

# Clients' negligence in contributing to trafficking

## Duty

In this chapter and chapters 7 and 8 I defend the imposition of negligence-based liability on clients who buy commercial sex indiscriminately, that is, without the ability to ensure that their demand is *not* satisfied by victims of sex trafficking. The argument is that by creating demand, the client negligently contributes to the future recruitment of victims and their transfer to the site in which he buys (or bought) sex; he likewise contributes to the continuation and prolongation of the trafficking experience of victims already exploited in that site. This risk is distinct from the risk, discussed in chapter 5, that by buying sex indiscriminately the client might commit sexual battery of any victim from whom he bought sex. If successfully defended, this cause of action will allow a victim to sue clients who did not have direct contact with her (or even with any other victim); however, it will not avail itself to non-victims, since it is the contribution of indiscriminate demand to trafficking (rather than to exploitation of non-victims) which makes the behaviour a breach of duty. Even within this constraint, such theory raises complex problems with respect to duty of care, breach and causation. This chapter deals with duty, chapter 7 with breach and chapter 8 with factual and legal causation. In practical terms, I suggest that liability will be limited to clients buying sex in the same city (or cities) in which the victim was exploited in the period of time ending when her exploitation ended and beginning at a date calculated by detracting the duration of the claimant's exploitation from her date of recruitment; and that each such client will be severally liable to damages at large or a conventional award which could be set at around a £5,000 benchmark.

Sections 6.1 to 6.3 examine whether, for purposes of establishing a duty of care, the damage to the claimant is reasonably foreseeable, whether sufficient proximity exists and whether it will be fair, just and reasonable to impose liability.[1] The chapter concludes that all three elements are satisfied,

1 I analyse the duty question according to the English formula. For the Canadian test, see *Cooper v Hobart* 2001 SCC 79; *Childs v Desormeaux* 2006 SCC 18. Nothing in the analysis below hangs on the difference between these formulas.

although some geographical and temporal limitation of liability is justified as a matter of either duty or legal causation – a point explored further in chapter 8.

## 6.1 Foreseeability

The prospect that indiscriminate demand for commercial sex will lead to trafficking does not raise problems of foreseeability. To begin with, there is ample evidence that clients (as well as the general public) are in fact aware that trafficking exists. Bridget Anderson and Julia O'Connell Davidson in their multi-country pilot study found that between 77 per cent (Japan) and 100 per cent (Sweden) of clients surveyed in five countries were aware of women being trafficked into prostitution.[2] Many other studies find high awareness as well. Among London clients (n = 103) 55 per cent believed that a majority of women in prostitution were lured, tricked or trafficked; 36 per cent thought that the women in prostitution they used had been trafficked to London from another country; 48 per cent believed that most women in prostitution are victims of pimps; 50 per cent said that they had used a woman in prostitution whom they knew was under the control of a pimp; 25 per cent had encountered a woman in the sex industry whom they believed was forced into prostitution; and 43 per cent said that it was their impression that one-half or fewer of all those in prostitution were fully informed about the nature of prostitution. In another study (n = 223) 56 per cent of men who bought sex in the US and 63 per cent in Scotland said that they also believed that a majority of all those in prostitution are lured, tricked or trafficked into it.[3] Yet another study exploring demand in Italy, the Netherlands, Romania and Sweden found that punters 'look for their pleasure though they are aware of exploitation and trafficking'.[4] Another study about London men found much lower explicit awareness of trafficking: 6 in 139.[5] Anecdotal data about clients' awareness of trafficking is available from other studies, including by Sanders who is a vocal pro-sex work researcher.[6] PunterNet – a UK online network in which clients exchange information about commercial sexual services – frequently refers to

2 B Anderson and J O'Connell Davidson, *Is Trafficking in Human Beings Demand Driven? A Multi-Country Pilot Study* (Geneva: IOM Migrant Research Series No. 15, 2003) 23. The data available from three of these countries on awareness among non-clients ranged between 67 per cent (Japan) and 95 per cent (Sweden).

3 Farley *et al.* (ch1, n11) 15–6.

4 A Di Nicola and P Ruspini, 'Learning from clients', in A Di Nicola, A Caduro, M Lombardi and P Ruspini, (eds), *Prostitution and Human Trafficking: Focus on Clients* (New York, NY: Springer, 2009) 227, 233.

5 Coy *et al.* (ch5, n81) 23. The same study found, however (at 34), that none of the men arrested for kerb crawling reported that they would stop paying for sex if they knew a woman was forced into selling sex. Other studies are consistent with this finding.

6 Sanders (ch1, n35) 52–6, 59.

men buying sex with women who are clearly unhappy, unwilling, frightened and/or in pain.[7] Moreover, clients' awareness (which still underestimates the real figures) that most CSPs enter prostitution as minors[8] should be considered as a further indication of actual awareness of trafficking, since, according to the Palermo Protocol definition of trafficking, any recruitment of a minor into prostitution, even if no unlawful means is used, is defined as trafficking.

But of course, unlike criminal law which (with the exception of strict liability offences) requires subjective awareness to the risk, the test for foreseeability in tort law is objective. It is *reasonable* foreseeability that matters, so the defendant would be judged against the knowledge that someone in the defendant's position would be expected to possess.[9] The fact that so many clients are aware of trafficking provides an inconclusive indication that those who do not, should have. To be sure, determinations of reasonable foreseeability (and fault) are, partially, normative and not merely factual. They are not based on empirical observation of what people in fact foresee; rather, they are based on an evaluative judgement about what people should foresee. The fact that many clients do foresee the risk is, therefore, inconclusive. But prevalent actual foresight by people in the defendant's position is a strong indication that the defendant did foresee the risk (an issue which is unobservable directly and with respect to which the client has a clear incentive to lie during litigation) and ought to have foreseen it. Moreover, the popularity of PunterNet (and equivalent mechanisms) as an information-sharing mechanism among clients suggests that the documented concerns uttered by some clients about involuntariness of some CSPs could and should alert other users to these risks.

More generally, reasonable foreseeability to the existence of sex trafficking and forced prostitution is a function of the media coverage of the problem. The more acute the problem in a given society, the more likely it is to be discussed in Parliament, by the Government and courts, and be covered in the media. In both the UK and Israel, for example, the sex trafficking phenomenon enjoys high visibility.[10] Public campaigns alerting the public and potential clients to the risks of trafficking and (at times implicitly) to the relationship between demand and abuse of victims' rights are common.[11] Indeed sex-work

7 S Dickson, *Sex in the City: Mapping Commercial Sex Across London* (London: Poppy, 2004) 10, 52.
8 See ch1, n11.
9 *Donoghue v Stevenson* [1932] AC 562, 580; Clerk & Lindsell (ch5, n15) 423.
10 During 2005–06 British newspapers published 6,840 news items dealing with trafficking in women; in the same period the three leading Israeli newspapers published 224 articles about sex trafficking. See http://news.google.com/archivesearch?q=sex+trafficking&btnG=Search+Archives&num=10&ned=us&lr=lang_en&as_ldate=01%2F05&as_hdate=12%2F06&lr=lang_en (accessed 23 February 2008). The terms 'sex trafficking' and 'trafficking in women' appeared 39,000 and 16,900 times on UK web pages searched on Google on 23 February 2008. The equivalent search in Hebrew brought 37,600 hits.
11 In 2008 the Home Office launched a poster campaign to raise awareness about trafficking in human beings among those who pay for sexual services. Advertisements were placed

feminists generally criticise anti-demand campaigns as excessive and as fuelling (and being fuelled by) moral panic.[12] These campaigns should alert clients to the problem of trafficking and therefore reasonable foreseeability exists. It is incongruent to argue that the problem of trafficking is exaggerated, and at the same time that clients ought not to be aware of the problem. I therefore find the view that 'the acquisition of [the relevant] knowledge and the execution of the required deductive steps to the conclusion presume a great deal of the average client' entirely unconvincing.[13]

A possible objection to the conclusion that foreseeability exists is that all the evidence can establish is that clients are aware of the trafficking phenomenon and that they might buy sex from a victim. But liability for contribution to trafficking is based on the causal connection between creating demand in the market and the trafficking of some victims and this connection is arguably not foreseeable. But the argument that clients ought not to foresee that indiscriminate demand contributes to victims' recruitment and transport to the site of exploitation is disingenuous.[14] The observation that demand and supply are interconnected so that demand for commercial sex is connected *also* to the recruitment and transport of victims (whose existence is undisputedly foreseeable) is straightforward; from a normative perspective an evaluative judgement that a client ought to foresee this connection should be considered as uncontroversial. Indeed, the contrary assertion is surprising: that clients who are aware that trafficking exists should not be expected to foresee that their indiscriminate demand fuels the supply of both non-forced and forced CSPs. It ignores the reality that clients do understand this connection, or at least could understand it upon short reflection; and it promotes ethics of inconsideration and obliviousness to the interests of others. Given the obviousness that demand and supply are interconnected (albeit in complex ways), and the reasonable foreseeability that part of those supplying sex are forced to do so, the contribution of indiscriminate demand to trafficking ought to be considered as reasonably foreseeable.

in pubs and clubs, depicting a brothel with the caption: 'Walk in a punter. Walk out a rapist.' GRETA (ch1, n32) 42. A conscious-raising campaign by actress Emma Thompson was run in the UK in 2007; it was watched more than 90,000 times on YouTube. Other campaigns included Truth Isn't Sexy (see http://feminenza.org/the-truth-isnt-sexy (accessed 1 January 2013)), and the Crown Prosecution Service Violence against Women campaign, which tackled also prostitution and human trafficking.

12 See p 10.

13 D Archard, 'Criminalising the use of trafficked prostitutes: some philosophical issues', in Munro and Della Giusta (ch1, n56) 149, 152. Archard's view is uttered in the criminal context (in which subjective awareness is required) and with respect to the risk of direct contact with a victim, which raises the additional difficulty of identifying a victim as such or being aware of the impossibility to identify victims.

14 For evidence of Dutch clients' denial (which ironically establishes actual awareness) that they are among the forces that create demand for trafficked prostitution, see Di Nicola *et al.* (n4) 104.

Whether clients are *actually aware* of their contribution to trafficking through their indiscriminate demand is unclear. Research shows that clients develop elaborate denial mechanisms that convince them that 'their' CSPs are consenting,[15] but that clients simultaneously hold many diametrically opposed attitudes about prostitution, including on their own roles and women's roles in it.[16] But doubts about this actual awareness are normatively irrelevant. The only relevant question is whether it is reasonably foreseeable that creating demand in the market will contribute to some women being trafficked. For the reasons explained above, the answer is (emphatically) in the affirmative. As we shall see, there are serious doubts about whether clients ought to avoid buying sex in the market due to awareness of the connection between demand and trafficking, but these are questions about proximity, not foreseeability.

## 6.2 Proximity

Since the harm to the victim caused by indiscriminate demand is mediated by traffickers and the market, and is hence indirect, questions about proximity and whether the imposition of the duty is fair, just and reasonable arise. I am one of those who believe that proximity is merely a label used by courts to reach a conclusion on whether the imposition of duty is just.[17] Indeed, what amounts to proximity as a distinct and independent requirement from both foreseeability and what is fair, just and reasonable is a hugely underdeveloped theme in the case law and the literature. I will take proximity to refer to considerations of interpersonal justice – whether the relationship between the parties is such that the defendant ought to have taken the claimant's interests into account – as opposed to broader considerations of the effects of liability on society, the courts and third parties (although this distinction is at times blurred).[18] Proximity considerations usually revolve around closeness between the parties in terms of time and space, the nature of the relationship between them (circumstance proximity) and the directness of causal connection between the creation of the risk and the claimant's injury (causal proximity).[19] The last element is highlighted by Christian Witting, who views proximity as indicating that 'there existed at some stage prior to the failure in care

15 Di Nicola *et al.*, id, 102–5, 230, 233; N Bridget Busch, H Bell, N Hotaling and M A Monto, 'Male customers of prostituted women: exploring perceptions of entitlement to power and control and implications for violent behavior toward women', (2001) 8 *Violence Against Women* 363.

16 M Farley, J Macleod, L Anderson and J M Golding, 'Attitudes and social characteristics of men who buy sex in Scotland', (2011) *Psychological Trauma: TRPP*, doi: 10.1037/a0022645.

17 See e.g. *Caparo Industries v Dickman* [1990] 2 AC 605, 633 (Lord Oliver); Rogers (ch5, n39) 179–81.

18 This approach is adopted by the Canadian Supreme Court in *Cooper* and *Childs* (n1). Cf A Robertson, 'Policy-based reasoning in duty of care cases', (2013) 33 *LS*, 119.

19 *Sutherland Shire Council v Heyman* (1985) 60 ALR 1, 55–6; Clerk & Lindsell (n9) 423–4.

significant *causal pathways* by which such a failure might have resulted in harm to the claimant'[20] (note the redundancy with legal causation). The factors relevant for determination of proximity include:

> the extent of the defendant's control over the risk, whether the defendant created the risk, the extent of the defendant's knowledge of the risk, the magnitude of the risk, the degree of foreseeability of the harm, the extent of the claimant's vulnerability to harm arising from the risk, the extent to which the claimant relied on the defendant, whether the defendant knew of that reliance and whether the defendant can be said to have assumed a responsibility, either to the claimant or for a particular task.[21]

Applying these factors to the relationship between the client and a victim leads to conflicting conclusions; while some factors indicate that proximity exists, others lead to the opposite conclusion. In what follows I attempt to analyse the indicators suggesting that proximity exists, and then explain why the contravening indicators are ultimately unconvincing, despite having a strong initial intuitive appeal.

### 6.2.1 Active creation of risk

Our situation involves *active creation of risk* (as opposed to omission) leading to foreseeable *physical* harm. These two factors weigh in the direction of sufficient proximity. True, the creation of the risk is indirect and mediated by the traffickers; however, without the active act of placing indiscriminate demand in the market, traffickers would not have responded to the demand and enslave victims. In this sense, trafficking involves a degree of proximity falling short of that existing in situations in which the defendant *directly* creates the risk which harms the claimant (and therefore also controls it) and exceeding that existing in situations involving pure omission, in which the defendant merely failed to control the intermediary who harmed the claimant, or otherwise protect the claimant.

Before dwelling further on the classification of indiscriminate demand as an active creation of risk and explaining the features of the trafficking market which establish sufficient causal, circumstance and spatial proximity, it is useful to explain away the relevance of several indicators of proximity. Within Witting's analytical framework of situations involving proximity difficulties, the closest for purposes of comparison seems to be misstatements indirectly

20 C Witting, 'Duty of care: an analytical approach', (2005) 25 *OJSL* 33, 37.

21 Robertson (n18) 5. Note that these considerations somewhat conflate the role of proximity with that of foreseeability, standard of care and legal causation.

causing physical harm. While in this context Witting argues that 'ordinary *Donoghue v Stevenson* principles generally are insufficient to ground a duty of care',[22] the factors he summarises as indicating the existence of proximity are irrelevant to our context, since they all deal with establishing reasonable reliance: control over the activity in which the claimant was engaged, inducing the claimant to rely on the statement, request for information by the claimant from the defendant and special (actual) knowledge of the risk by the defendant coupled with comparative ignorance of those risks by the claimant.[23] Since the risk in our context is not created by reliance on a statement, inducement and requests are irrelevant.

The *directions and control factor* – often exercised by the defendant over the intermediary[24] – usually involves general reliance by the claimant and omission by the defendant; both factors are irrelevant to our context. (The discussion below demonstrates, nonetheless, that the client's control over the risk supports a finding of sufficient proximity.) For similar reasons the *actual knowledge factor* (whether the defendant had actual knowledge of the relevant risk) and the *comparative ignorance factor* (that the claimant is ignorant of the risk compared to the defendant) – are irrelevant to the trafficking context: the proximity is based on active creation of risk so reliance is not needed in order to establish proximity. In any event, if relevant at all, these factors suggest that proximity exists: the data presented in section 6.1 suggest that many clients have actual knowledge of the risk of trafficking (albeit rarely of the specific claimant); in contrast, at the relevant moment, the victim, who has not been trafficked yet, does not have any knowledge that demand for prostitution puts her at *specific* risk of being trafficked. But the comparative ignorance factor should be rejected altogether in our context as a basis to determine whether proximity and duty exist: any attempt to apply comparative knowledge analysis to trafficking comes close to blaming the victim for being trafficked. It is not in the mouth of the client, who, at times consciously, ignores the risk that his purchase of sex might cause future victims to be trafficked, to argue that the victim should have been more careful so that she would not be trafficked in order to satisfy the client's demand. If at all, such a claim should be raised (but rejected) as part of contributory negligence, but it should not exclude duty.

*Victims' vulnerability*, in the sense of being exclusively dependent on another to take care, is considered as a classic factor creating proximity between the defendant and the claimant. Indeed, based on the Australian High Court decisions, Jane Stapleton has described the protection of the vulnerable as the

22 Witting (n20) 49.
23 Id, 48–51.
24 See e.g. *Perrett v Collins* [1998] 2 Lloyd's Rep 255, in which the inspector who certified the aircraft as fit for flying was found to owe a duty to the claimant.

golden thread at the heart of tort law.[25] In the context of forced prostitution the victim is exclusively dependant on the client to take care not to expose her to the risk of being trafficked in order to satisfy the client's demand. In many situations involving proximity difficulties the risk is not created by the defendant, so to justify liability it needs to be explained why the defendant should protect the claimant from a risk he did not create. In this context, victims' vulnerability can explain why a duty is imposed on the defendant if his action is the only way which could have protected the claimant, and in these cases either real reliance or some type of general reliance (or assumption of responsibility by the defendant) is required. In our context, clients actively contribute to the risk of trafficking (although, granted, indirectly) so given the victim's inability to otherwise protect herself from the risk of being trafficked, proximity seems to exist. It should be plain enough that victims do not have alternative means of protection: these (and the corollary status of non-vulnerability) typically exclude liability in the context of economic loss where the claimant could have protected herself by a contractual warranty or insurance.[26] These measures are unavailable to victims.

*Active creation of risk and control of the intermediary*. In cases involving omission, where the defendant (unlike the defendant in *Home Office v Dorset Yacht*[27]) did not have clear control over the intermediary or clear obligation to protect the claimant's class, courts tend to hold that sufficient proximity is absent.[28] In these cases it is debatable whether the defendant increased the likelihood that the claimant would be injured from the intermediary's conduct. This might depend on whether the intermediary just seized an opportunity created by the defendant's negligence to cause an injury by an activity which the intermediary would not have otherwise engaged in (increase of risk) or that he would have engaged in this or similar activity in any event (and the defendant's negligence just displaced the risk from one potential claimant to another).

*Control over the risk* – a relevant indicator of proximity – exists in the risk increasing scenario, but not in the risk displacement one. According to such

25 J Stapleton, 'The golden thread at the heart of tort law: the protection of the vulnerable', (2003) 24 *Aust Bar R* 1, 20. For a list of Australian cases which exemplify this notion see id, n46. These cases include *Rogers v Whitaker* (1992) 175 CLR 479 and *Perre v Apand Pty Ltd* (1999) 198 CLR 180. Cf Robertson's discussion of English and Canadian case law (n18) 6.

26 *Murphy v Brentwood District Council* [1991] 1 AC 398; J Stapleton, 'Duty of care: peripheral parties and alternative opportunities for deterrence', (1995) 111 *LQR* 301.

27 [1970] AC 1004.

28 *Childs* (n1); *Topp v London Country Bus South West* [1993] 3 All ER 448, in which the Court ruled that there was no sufficient proximity between the defendant's assumed negligence in leaving the keys in the bus and the claimant who was killed when an intermediary stole the vehicle. Query whether this result is consistent with *Dorset Yacht*. The Israeli Supreme Court imposed liability in an equivalent case in which leaving the keys in an unsupervised car was in breach of a statutory duty. CA 704/71 *Agabria v Hame'iri*, PD 26(1) 743 (1972).

understanding, clients exercise control over the risk since the demand leads to acts of trafficking which would otherwise not exist. This is just another way to restate the conclusion that clients actively put victims at risk of being trafficked, rather than merely omitting to prevent traffickers from trafficking victims. As the discussion below demonstrates, the complicity between traffickers and clients creates proximity and might be considered as manifestation of control over either the risk or the intermediary.

### 6.2.2 Indirect contribution and complicity

There are three main factors which suggest that sufficient proximity is absent and a related concern of line-drawing. The first objection is that the injury caused by consumption is *not direct* but rather mediated by traffickers and the market. This objection can also be rephrased as (or bolstered by) a concern with respect to maintaining well-functioning markets and preserving the autonomy of potential defendants–consumers. This relates to both circumstance and causal proximity. But the fact that the injury is mediated through traffickers is not a conclusive reason to deny proximity; indeed, in appropriate cases proximity exists even for pure omissions when the active risk is created by a third party. For current purposes, of importance is the fact that the relationship between clients and traffickers is (or very close to) that of complicity:[29] traffickers recruit and exploit victims in response to the impinged act of creating indiscriminate demand in the market. It is not only that a causal pathway could be established (no indiscriminate demand, no trafficking). This exists also in cases in which proximity is more tenuous (had the bus company not left keys in the bus, the unauthorised user would not have run over the claimant). Rather, the trafficker caters to the client's request (although in a way not necessarily approved of by the client – an element absent in the stolen bus example) and clients as a group benefit from the phenomenon of trafficking and therefore have an interest in turning a blind eye to this phenomenon. Clients benefit from trafficking – one instance of patriarchal dividend[30] – not only in the trivial sense that it increases supply which leads to a drop in price but also since victims' limited ability to refuse certain practices makes these practices available to clients from victims themselves, and possibly from non-victims due to race-to-the-bottom market pressures.

29 Cf M Madden-Dempsey's argument from complicity for the criminalisation of buying sex, 'Sex trafficking and criminalization: in defense of feminist abolitionism', (2010) 158 *U Pen LR* 1729, 1752–62.

30 R Connell, 'Change among the gatekeepers: men, masculinities, and gender equality in the global arena', (2005) 30 *Signs* 1801.

### 6.2.3 Indeterminate liability?

A classic duty-denying factor (the second objection) is that the ensuing liability will be to 'an indeterminate amount for an indeterminate time to an indeterminate class'.[31] To this relates the (third) objection about the absence of spatial and temporal proximity: the potentially tenuous connection between the demand from a client in, say, London, and the recruitment of victims in Moldova and their exploitation in Milan. Indeed, in *Home Office v Dorset Yacht*, the House of Lords restricted the defendants' scope of responsibility to the damage caused by the escaping borstal youth to property owners in the immediate vicinity in the course of the escape. This was so, even though hypothetical damage exceeding the temporal and spatial restriction would be a consequence attributable to that which made the act wrongful (responsibility within scope of duty rule)[32] and out of concern to limit the defendant's liability. At first blush, indeterminate liability is indeed likely in the context of demand-based contribution to trafficking: due to the nature of markets in general, and markets of (forced) sexual services in particular, a client might be liable to an unknown number of victims and for an unknown period of time to victims recruited from all over the world. However, upon reflection, the twin concerns of avoiding indeterminate liability and promoting time and space proximity fail to establish lack of proximity between creating demand and some victims' injuries. It is trite law that the indeterminacy concern is not about the size of liability (or number of claimants) but rather with *indeterminacy*.[33] Indeed, defendants' exposure in mass torts litigation is huge but no one suggests that liability is indeterminate so no duty is owed. The indeterminacy concern revolves mainly about the fact that, unbeknown to the defendant, potential claimants might rely on information provided by the defendant and in this respect, the genealogy of the injury is not sufficiently clear. But the genealogy of trafficking and its relationship to the demand is sufficiently clear (though complex). Traffickers, whose identity is unknown to the client, but this is irrelevant, will enslave some victims (same caveat) in order to partially respond to the demand. An auditor has no direct and real interest in investors relying on his audit; a client has an interest in supply chains responding to his demand; the suppliers do exactly what the client wishes them to do.

*Donoghue v Stevenson*[34] has taught us that proximity could be found to exist when the claimant's injury by the defendant's product is separated in time and space from the defendant's negligence in manufacturing the product.

31 *Ultramares Corp v Touche*, 174 NE 441, 444 (NY, 1931).

32 *SAAMCO v York Montague* [1996] 3 All ER 365, 371; cf *Restatement (Third) of Torts: Liability for Physical and Emotional Harm* (2010), § 29.

33 *Perre v Apand* (n25) 221.

34 See n9.

One way to explain the rule is that the existence of the market – the reality that products produced at a certain time and place might harm a consumer at a different time and place – replace time and space proximity with circumstance and causal proximity. An alternative explanation is that spatial proximity (which is the one which is harder to establish in such cases) exists since the product with its accompanying risk moves, due to the dynamics of the market, from the defendant-producer to the claimant-consumer. Both explanations are equally applicable in our context. The market dynamics are the same, and they create circumstance proximity, and the victim spatially moves from the place of recruitment to the place of exploitation in response to clients' demand. That in our context, the claimant is the 'product' rather than the consumer does not make the risk created indirectly by the consumer (and directly by the supplier) any less proximate. In fact, the discussion below illustrates that due to certain features of the sex industry, there is greater proximity between the client and a victim than between a consumer and the producer.

This leads me to the last response to the indeterminacy and time and space objections. I do agree that a legal rule allowing a victim to sue any client whose demand contributed to her recruitment and exploitation in another venue creates indeterminate liability which should be avoided. So, if the client's demand in London contributed to the recruitment of a victim in Russia but the victim was sent to Milan and exploited there, it is only the clients in Milan (but not in London) who should be liable to the victim. This proposition is explained more fully in chapter 8. But whether this limitation is perceived as a limited duty rule, or as legal causation limitation, the result is the same. The fear of indeterminate liability could and should shape the scope of clients' liability towards their victims, as do concerns about limiting liability in terms of time and space. But these fears and concerns fail to justify a flat denial of duty. As chapter 8 demonstrates, sensible limitations with respect to indeterminacy in time, and the financial scope of liability could also be crafted.

### 6.2.4 Drawing a line

The companion concern to these objections is one of drawing a line. In many markets supply involves an illegal component, so demand arguably fuels also the illegal acts contributing to the supply. If contribution to trafficking gives rise to a duty, how about a contribution to stealing cars and their sale in second-hand markets? And how about clients who buy non-fair-trade chocolate? Should they owe a duty to those enslaved to pick the cocoa beans?[35] With respect to the first example, the different type of damage, property loss

35 K Bales, *Ending Slavery* (Berkeley, CA: University of California Press, 2007) 181–8; Anderson and O'Connell Davidson (n2) 10–11.

to the owner, as opposed to the claimant being trafficked herself, can justify a denial of duty. It makes perfect sense and is sufficiently principled to say that a defendant ought to take the claimant's interest into account when the defendant is buying in a market which might cause the claimant to be trafficked, but ought not to have the claimant in contemplation with respect to her property loss. This is hardly revolutionary: generally, the type of interest threatened (i.e. the damage) is a crucial factor in deciding whether a duty is owed and if so what its scope is. Considerations of proximity balance the interests of the classes of potential victims and injurers under the assumption that the injurer is negligent. Similar to standard of care analysis, then, they are based on a balancing approach (which in neither case is based on narrow economic calculus). The following factors could, and in my opinion do, justify recognising a duty with respect to trafficking but not with respect to stolen property: the claimant's interest is much more weighty in cases of trafficking; first party insurance is available in cases of property loss; and property is apparently stolen much more frequently than people are trafficked; therefore, the burden on consumers from owing a duty of care with respect to stolen property is possibly more onerous in comparison to that created by owing a duty to victims of trafficking.

Nor does the argument defended here necessitate recognising a duty with respect to consumption which is met by supply chains involving risks to bodily integrity or exploitation, provided that the injured or exploited individuals consent to the practice. Consumers of American football or rugby presumably contribute to the serious injuries suffered by some players. But since the players accept the risk (and in this example at least, but not in others, are handsomely compensated for it) there should be no duty (and no finding of sub-standard behaviour). As consumers, we also consume products which involve exploitation of some individuals – employees or others – who are involved in the supply chain. But as long as those exploited consent to the practice (although reluctantly and lacking better options) a conclusion that the consumer owes a duty to those exploited is not warranted. To be sure, such consumption might be morally problematic and a decision to avoid consuming or to protest against the exploitation might be commendable, but this course of action would be considered as supererogation by moral philosophers and by lawyers. So the Harvard students who protested against the exploitative working conditions of cleaners (usually supplied by contractors) did well to do so,[36] but those who have continued to consume higher education at Harvard cannot be considered as owing or breaching a duty to those exploited.[37]

36 D Lamas, 'Harvard protesters declare victory upon exit', *Harvard Crimson*, 9 May 2001.

37 There is also a remoteness issue here. The students consume mainly higher education and only indirectly cleaning services.

The issue could thus be narrowed to instances in which the consumer consumes in a market in which the supply chain is infiltrated with trafficking. From a proximity perspective,[38] there are several distinctions which could (and probably should) justify singling out sex trafficking from consumption of chocolate and shirts[39] whose supply chains involve forced labour, so that only with respect to the former a duty will be recognised. First, in sexual exploitation the labourer, rather than merely the product, is shifted to where the demand comes from, and this also creates the risk of forced direct contact. Therefore, there is a greater spatial proximity than the one existing between the consumer of a chocolate bar and the forced labourer. Furthermore, only in the case of sexual exploitation does the consumer create not merely the risk of the claimant's trafficking, but also the distinct risk of subjecting the claimant to direct contact to which she does not consent. This creates circumstance proximity absent in other forms of trafficking. Indeed, in terms of spatial proximity, what closer proximity could be envisioned than the one in which the defendant's act brings the claimant to bed (against her will) with himself or with other clients?

Second, some, but not all, will agree that trafficking for sexual exploitation is worse than any other type of trafficking since it adds to the indignity of being enslaved and forced into labour the horrors of sexual assault and sexual enslavement. All victims are enslaved but only victims of sexual exploitation are inevitably and repeatedly raped as part of their exploitation.[40] If one buys into this argument it is easy to explain why a defendant ought to have a victim of sex trafficking in contemplation but not necessarily the victim of other forms of exploitation.

Third, in sex trafficking there is another type of circumstance proximity which is absent in other forms of trafficking. Since the victim of trafficking is also the 'product', clients' preferences shape the identity of victims in a manner consumers' preferences to shirts and chocolate do not. The consumer of shirts does not enjoy more or less from the product, and in this sense is indifferent, if labourers along the supply chain (be they forced or not) are men or women, old or young, blond or brunette, South Asian or black, virgin or not, with big breasts or small and so on. Therefore, his consumption does not contribute to

38 From a standard of care perspective it might be that consuming sex is negligent while consuming other products whose supply chain is infiltrated with trafficking is not. This would depend on the relative incidence of trafficking in each sector and on different normative evaluations about the social value of buying the specific service or commodity.

39 See Bales (n35) 182–4.

40 Female victims of other forms of trafficking, mainly for domestic labour, often report sexual exploitation as part of their ordeal. M Barnhart, 'Sex and slavery: an analysis of three models of state human trafficking legislation', (2009) 16 *Wm & Mary J of Women & L* 83, *91*. But these assaults, which are obviously horrible, are incidental to the main form of trafficking and occur less frequently than the sexual assault of victims of sex trafficking. For a different view see Barnhart, id.

any particular type of victims having been enslaved. The opposite of course is true with respect to clients of sexual services. Their preferences are not only the cause that some people are trafficked, but rather the reason that those chosen to be trafficked were trafficked. This obviously creates circumstance proximity absent in other forms of trafficking.

I would not like to overstate this point. As discussed in chapter 8, the relationship between supply and demand is complex and to some extent supply-led demand does exist. This means that either some clients buy sex from whoever is selling (still, probably within certain limits) or that their preferences are shaped due to the available supply. But it is equally clear that clients do have preferences with respect to the looks, age and ethnicity of the women from whom they buy sex[41] and evidence also exists that some traffickers make decisions on where to exploit victims (and by implication where from and how many to recruit) based on sophisticated analysis of demand.[42] In addition, regardless of a taste for a specific body type or ethnicity, many clients buy sex to have a variety of sexual partners.[43] This also means that there is a need for a fresh supply of CSPs, including victims, in order to meet this demand. This contributes not only to fresh recruitment of victims, but also (in many markets) to frequent transportation of victims from one venue to another (a practice which serves other goals as well).[44] Research suggests that some clients have a taste for victims since they are more submissive;[45] this creates another type of circumstance proximity (albeit one which is relevant only to an identified portion of clients), since such demand, which is not strictly indiscriminate since it assumes that clients both prefer victims and partially know how to identify them, is a direct cause of trafficking in order to satisfy such demand. Unethical consumers of shirts might be happy that some labourers are enslaved to the extent that this reduces the retail price (and according to Bales, it does not[46]). But these consumers' enjoyment of the product does not otherwise necessitate trafficking. In contrast, clients with a preference for victims need them not only for lower prices but also to satisfy part of their specific taste for control (and possibly all clients benefit from the existence of victims due to the race-to-the-bottom phenomenon).

Fourth, the difference in market structure might justify a conclusion that while sufficient proximity exists in sex markets, it is absent in other markets. In the shirt example, the cotton picked with slave labour is mixed with cotton from neighbouring farms (the equivalent of a sex market comprised of forced and non-forced CSPs), and only then does the farmer get paid. Then the cotton

41 Dickson (n7) 21.
42 Kara (ch3, n4) 11.
43 Dickson (n7) 21.
44 See pp 49–50.
45 Anderson and O'Connell Davidson (n2) 25.
46 Bales (n35) 182–3.

is ginned and packed into bales, and sold for carding, spinning and weaving into a shirt. Then the shirt is sold to wholesalers and retailers and only then bought by the consumer.[47] This process involves many more intermediaries than in the case of sex trafficking and this suggests a lower circumstance, and possibly a lower causal proximity. Crucially, intermediaries are better placed than clients to ensure that cotton is bought only from farmers who do not exploit slaves. The closer the intermediary in the chain is to the farmer, and the more significant its market power, the better it is placed to prevent trafficking. Accordingly, while intermediaries (or at least some of them) might have sufficient proximity with the forced labourers, consumers of shirts do not. Moreover, the fact that intermediaries in the confection, chocolate or car industries are both lawful entities (unlike traffickers) and repeat players, suggests that if they owe a duty to forced labourers and are found negligent, it is likely that the victims will be able to collect the awards from the intermediaries. This suggests that recognising a duty against consumers is less crucial. In other words, the fact that the victim has available an alternative remedy is a reason not to recognise a duty by consumers towards victims. This well-entrenched principle could be viewed as the manifestation of either proximity (i.e. interactive justice) or broader considerations, to which I now turn.

## 6.3 Is liability fair, just and reasonable?

Even if proximity is established, duty can still be denied if the prospect of liability might bring about undesirable results to either class of litigants (claimants or defendants), third parties, courts or, more broadly, society in general. At the outset, it is useful to note that the prominence of such considerations in judicial decisions about the existence of duty is disputed (and this relates to the normative debate about the role of policy, and distributive justice considerations in private law, tort law and negligence law). Some decisions are clearly based on broad policy considerations, while others clearly reveal disapproval of a broad use of such considerations.[48] Recently, it has been suggested that the role of policy considerations is quite limited.[49] Some judges express the view that policy-based arguments against liability should be accepted only in instances in which the negative consequences arguably resulting from recognising a duty are supported by

47 Id, 182.

48 Policy considerations were relied upon to deny duty in *Hill v Chief Constable of West Yorkshire* [1989] AC 53; *Marc Rich & Co AG v Bishop Rock Marine Co Ltd* [1996] 1 AC 211; *Gregg v Scott* [2005] UKHL 2. Policy-based claims were rejected in *Capital & Counties PLC v Hampshire County Council* [1997] QB 1004, 1043–4 (arguments are unsubstantiated); *Barrett (AP) v Enfield London Borough Council* [2001] 2 AC 550, 568, 589.

49 Robertson (n18).

clear evidence.[50] As the discussion below demonstrates, the consequential arguments against recognising a duty are lacking in evidence and do not support a denial of duty which should otherwise be imposed as a matter of interactive justice. To be clear, my own view is that policy arguments should be taken into account by courts in developing private law and in making duty determinations.[51] The problem with the arguments, then, is not that the concerns mentioned are irrelevant for determinations of duty, but rather that the existing evidence and educated conjectures fail to convince that liability should not be imposed.

### 6.3.1 Shaky anti-criminalisation evidence

The main argument against clients' liability is that liability might negatively affect both victims and non-victims. It has been made by sex-work feminists in the context of the bitter debate with abolitionists over the regulation of prostitution, including, in particular, whether the abolitionist Swedish model which criminalises clients, but not CSPs, is better than regulationism, which calls for regulating and normalising sex work, and is adopted (to different degrees) in the Netherlands, Germany, some states in Australia and (most of) Nevada.[52] The relevant questions are as follows. First, do abolitionist regimes reduce the number of victims in comparison to regulationist regimes? Second,

50 In *Spring v Guardian Assurance plc* [1995] 2 AC 296, 326 Lord Lowry was of the opinion that if a prima facie duty exists at the very least 'public policy ought not to be invoked if the arguments are evenly balanced'; possibly the defendant needs to demonstrate 'based on tangible grounds instead of on mere generalities' that 'the potential harm to the public is incontestable'.

51 Keren-Paz (ch5, n20) ch 6.

52 Following common terminology, the classification includes also *prohibitionism*, under which the sale of sex is also criminalised, and *decriminalisation* which entails minimal policing and non-intervention and usually prohibits all forms of communication for the purposes of prostitution. The literature on the prostitution debate is enormous; the following focuses only on work including factual claims (as opposed to purely normative arguments) with respect to the conditions of CSPs under different regimes. For abolitionist views, see M Sullivan, *Making Sex Work: A Failed Experiment with Legalised Prostitution* (Melbourne: Spinifex Press, 2007); M Farley, 'Theory versus reality: commentary on four articles about trafficking', (2009) 32 *Women's Stud Int'l Forum* 311; J Bindel and L Kelly, *A Critical Examination of Responses to Prostitution in Four Countries: Victoria, Australia; Ireland; the Netherlands; and Sweden* (London: London Metropolitan University, 2003) 13; M Waltman, 'Sweden's prohibition of purchase of sex: the law's reasons, impact and potential', (2011) 34 *Women's Stud Int'l Forum* 449.

For sex-work feminists' views, see Sanders (n6) chs 7, 8; R Weitzer, 'Prostitution as a form of work', (2007) 1 *Sociology Compass* 143; Agustin (ch1, n59); J Scoular, 'Criminalizing punters: evaluating the Swedish position on prostitution', (2004) 26 *J Soc Welfare and Fam L* 195; S Dodillet and P Östergren, *The Swedish Sex Purchase Act: Claimed Success and Documented Effect*, conference paper presented at the International Workshop: Decriminalizing Prostitution and Beyond: Practical Experiences and Challenges, The

do remaining victims under criminalisation suffer from increased levels of violence due, for example, to the effect of the industry going underground? Third, is the well being of non-victims reduced under abolitionist approaches due to: (a) the underground effect producing increased risk of being subject to violence from clients and pimps and increased harassment from the police; (b) increased stigmatisation of CSPs; and (c) lost business due to decreased demand?

In examining the data the following points should be borne in mind. First, there is a dearth of evidence with respect to the effects of the regime chosen on the well being of CSPs. Second, the methodological difficulties inherent in researching prostitution and trafficking are relevant to evaluating the results of the studies.[53] Third, the studies complete the evidentiary gaps with some form of more or less rigorous theoretical modelling or conjectures about those effects. At times, the validity of these modelling and conjectures could be doubted. Fourth, generally there is a link between the researchers' normative stance in the prostitution debate and the findings of the study.

There is certainly no evidence that criminalisation increases the number of victims. If at all, the number of victims is expected to be lower since criminalisation increases traffickers' costs of doing business. The claim that regulationist regimes increase trafficking is often made by abolitionists.[54] A recent study by economists which included both a theoretical model and analysis of available data found that

> using cross country data we find clear support for our theoretical predictions: trafficking of persons for commercial sexual exploitation is least prevalent in countries where prostitution is illegal, most prevalent

Hague, 3 and 4 March 2011; most of the contributors in Munro and Della Giusta (n13) take the same view.

For a more nuanced, yet critical, evaluation of the Swedish model, see N Levenkron, 'Could the master's tools dismantle the master's house? Sweden's criminalisation of punters as a case study on the potential of legislation to transform the sex industry' (Masters thesis, Tel Aviv University, 2011) (in Hebrew). See also the Ontario Court of Appeal's decision, striking down Canada's criminalisation of brothels, limiting the criminalisation of 'living on the avails' of prostitution to those doing so in circumstances of exploitation and upholding the constitutionality of the criminalisation of solicitation. *Canada v Bedford* 2012 ONCA. Leave to appeal to the Supreme Court of Canada has been filed and is likely to be given.

53 See Waltman's methodological critique, id, 460–2, of Weitzer, Scoular, Dodillet and Östergren. In particular, Östergren's work, on which Anglo-American sex-work feminists rely to demonstrate the failings of the Swedish model, is problematic in terms of biased sampling. For Weitzer's critique of Farley and Raphael and Shapiro and their reply, see (2005) 11 *Violence Against Women* 934–77. For the debate in the context of the 'numbers game', see pp 176–7.

54 Sullivan (n52) 206–11, 219–21; for further references, see MacKinnon (ch1, n10) n113, and Madden-Dempsey (n29) 1771 n131. For a finding that 50 per cent of CSPs working in legal brothels in Nevada interviewees (n = 45) were controlled by pimps outside the brothel, see M Farley, *Prostitution and Trafficking in Nevada: Making the Connections* (San Francisco, CA: Prostitution Research and Education, 2007) 31–2.

> in countries where prostitution is legalized, and in between in those countries where prostitution is legal but procuring illegal . . . [In] Sweden and Norway, which have both introduced harsher laws, . . . as predicted, trafficking seems to have been reduced.[55]

The effects of the regulatory regime on both the number of victims and the ways victims are treated (but *not* the effects on non-victims) were examined in a study produced by Transcrime for the European Parliament.[56] The study distinguished between four types of regimes. After giving due allowance to the dearth of evidence and methodological difficulties, the study made several tentative conclusions including the following. The regimes that seem to 'produce' more victims are those not prohibiting or those even regulating outdoor and indoor prostitution whilst the model that seems to 'produce' less victims is the one prohibiting indoor and outdoor prostitution. Generally speaking, violence in the trafficked prostitution market does not seem to be strictly dependent on the model on prostitution. Nevertheless, if one were to express a general rule it seems that the models allowing for outdoor and indoor prostitution (but prohibit either profiting from another person's prostitution or brothels) are those which can develop a slightly higher level of violence than other models. While the conclusions are tentative, it is clear that this study does not support a denial of a duty as unfair, just or reasonable. If at all, civil liability for the creation of demand, assuming it is most akin to a prohibition, seems to reduce the number of victims without increasing, and perhaps even slightly reducing, the level of violence remaining victims endure.

The merits of the Swedish model in general and its arguable negative effects on the well being of (mainly street) non-victims are hotly debated. This debate spills over to the general question of whether non-victims fare worse under abolitionist models. The Swedish Government in a 2010 review of the Prohibition of Purchase of Sex Act[57] claims that it has been successful and among other things that the law serves as a barrier to human traffickers; that it halved street prostitution without evidence of displacement into indoor prostitution; that the law has a deterrent effect so that demand was decreased; and that there was no indication of either increased risk or worse living conditions of CSPs; it also claimed that the ban is supported by those who

55 N Jakobsson and A Kotsadam, 'The law and economics of international sex slavery: prostitution laws and trafficking for sexual exploitation', (2011) *European J L & Econ*, doi: 10.1007/s10657-011-9232-0, 1–21. As the authors mention, previous studies reached similar conclusions. Jakobsson and Kotsadam did not investigate the total welfare consequences of an abolitionist regime but nod towards the standard economic prediction (critically examined below) that harsher laws might lead to increased violence and stigmatisation.

56 A Di Nicola, I Orfano, A Candoro and N Conci, *Study on National Legislation on Prostitution and the Trafficking in Women and Children* (Milan: Transcrime Research Institute, 2005).

57 See ch1 (n17). The Act was passed in 1998 and amended several times. Norway (in 2008) and Iceland (in 2009) enacted equivalent Acts.

extricated themselves from prostitution while criticised by those still in prostitution.[58]

The report has been criticised as lacking in evidence and methodology.[59] Some of this critique, however, is inconsistent. For example, critics of the Swedish model and, more generally, abolitionist models, find insufficient evidence of a reduction in consumption, deterrence and effect on clients' behaviour, yet accept that the industry is going underground (a claim contested by some abolitionists[60]) and that this has detrimental effects on CSPs.[61] But if there is no deterrence, how come there is an underground effect? There is also a discrepancy between the predictions of economic models, which suggest that criminalisation should lead to decreased demand, supply and equilibrium price, and some empirical research suggesting an underground effect without decreased demand, but merely displacement.[62] And yet, according to the Malmö Prostitution Knowledge Centre, there has been an estimated drop of 20 per cent in the overall number of CSPs in Sweden (from 1,850 to 1,500) in the relevant period, a point obfuscated by Dodillet and Östergren, who describe the figures as 'similar' before and under the ban.[63] Others came with a much lower estimation (650) of the total number of CSPs after the ban (compared with around 5,500 in the equivalent period in Denmark in which prostitution is legal).[64]

58 SOU 2010:49b, *Inquiry on the Evaluation of the Prohibition of the Purchase of Sexual Services* (English translation), available at www.sweden.gov.se/sb/d/2093 (accessed 1 May 2011). Following the evaluation, the Act has been amended (in effect from 1 July 2011) to increase the maximum penalty from 6 to 12 months in prison, available at www.sweden.gov.se/sb/d/13420/a/151488 (accessed 12 October 2011). For other positive evaluations, see G Ekberg (who was involved in the enactment of the law), 'The Swedish law that prohibits the purchase of sexual services: best practices for prevention of prostitution and trafficking in human beings', (2004) 10 *Violence Against Women* 1187; Waltman (n52) at 458–60; and sources in MacKinnon (n54) n109. A Situation Report on trafficking made by the Swedish National Criminal Police (cited by Waltman, id, at 459) cited wiretapping showing traffickers and pimps disappointed with low demand in Sweden.

59 Dodillet and Östergren (n52) at 12; cf L Agustin, The Naked Anthropologist Blog, 15 July 2010, available at www.lauraagustin.com/smoke-gets-in-your-eyes-evaluation-of-swedish-anti-prostitution-law-offers-ideology-not-methodology (accessed 8 July 2012). Note that neither source is peer reviewed.

60 Waltman (n52) 462.

61 See e.g. Dodillet and Östergren (n52) 14 (Act does not affect behaviour), 22 (sex-workers experience higher levels of vulnerability in their contact with clients). Curiously, the authors cite anecdotal evidence that Swedish men buy sex abroad and, hence, are unbothered by the Act, as evidence of no effect, while neglecting the possibility that this displacement might be one effect of the Act. The same critique could be made against Sanders's analysis (n6) at 177.

62 See M Della Giusta, 'Simulating the impact of regulation changes on the market of prostitution services', (2010) 29 *Eur J of Econ* 1, 7.

63 Dodillet and Östergren (n52) 11.

64 Waltman (n52) 458–9.

The likelihood of displacement relates also to the persuasiveness of the concern that criminalisation increases fears for the safety of (mainly street) non-victims, due to either a sorting effect, in which the proportion of dangerous clients increases due to a decrease in demand or displacement of other clients, or a lesser ability to screen dangerous clients, since criminalisation requires a quick conclusion of negotiation.[65] The evidence that such an effect exists is not strong,[66] and no member of PRIS, a Swedish CSP organisation, has encountered any negative effect from the law. According to PRIS, the law might improve women's bargaining power since 'theoretically women then have a way to tell the buyers that if they don't pay or are violent, the woman can call the police'.[67] There are also claims that it is *legalisation* (at least in the form of toleration zones) that increases the risk of physical danger to CSPs[68] (and leads to other undesirable results since 'the governmental apparatus to address [the illegal market] erodes because the industry is decriminalized'; 'prostitution will become part of [the prostituted woman's] official life story' and legalisation attributes 'agency . . . ignoring the unequal and violent material conditions of the life, [and this] can be a desperate grab toward lost dignity'[69]).

65 Sanders (n6) 175; Dodillet and Östergren (n52) 22–3; H Kinnell, *Violence and Sex Work in Britain* (Cullompton: Willan Publishing, 2008) 77–80; A Collins and G Judge, 'Differential enforcement across police jurisdictions and client demand in paid sex markets', (2010) 29 *Eur J of Econ* 43, 52–3.

66 In the context of the Swedish model, Dodillet and Östergren ((n52) 22–3) rely on anecdotal reports from sex-workers about fear from increased violence and an actual increase but 'there has not been any specific research done on the level of violence'. In Germany and New Zealand, governmental evaluations of legalisation failed to find 'measurable improvements to prostitutes' social protection' (Germany) or significant improvement in the lives of prostitutes (New Zealand). See *Report by the German Federal Government on the Impact of the Act Regulating the Legal Situation of Prostitutes (Prostitution Act)* (Berlin: Federal Ministry for Family Affairs, Senior Citizens, Women and Youth, 2007) 79; and *Report of the Prostitution Law Review Committee on the Operation of the Prostitution Reform Act 2003* (Wellington: Ministry of Justice, 2008).

67 Levenkron (n52) 135.

68 See M Farley, '"Bad for the body, bad for the heart": prostitution harms women even if legalized or decriminalized', (2004) 10 *Violence Against Women* 1087, 1094. MacKinnon (n54) 305 claims that legalisation is more dangerous to the vulnerable women operating in the illegal sector which continues to exist (and arguably expands) under legalisation: however, MacKinnon's argument is in fact about displacement (or its absence), namely, that the more dangerous practices, such as unprotected sex, are being performed by vulnerable CSPs in the illegal section of the market.

69 MacKinnon, id, 306–7. For documented opposition by Dutch CSPs to legalisation due to loss of anonymity, see Waltman (n52) 458. Earlier studies finding that legalisation fails to improve the well being of CSPs include A Albert, *Brothel Mustang Ranch and its Women* (New York, NY: Random House, 2001); N Bingham, 'Nevada sex trade: a gamble for the workers', (1998) 10 *Yale JL & Fem* 69; N Levenkron, *The Legalization of Prostitution: Myth and Reality – A Comparative Study of Four Countries* (Tel Aviv: Hotline for Migrant Workers, 2007) (in Hebrew). For Levenkron's current (and somewhat different) view, see n52.

But even if the risk to street non-victims indeed increases, this phenomenon cannot be used to oppose criminalisation, since it fails to show that the *overall* level of violence is increased under criminalisation, rather than violence being merely displaced from victims to non-victims or from indoor non-victims to street non-victims. The dangerous and violent clients do consume sex (and injure CSPs) under regulationist regimes.[70] If they purchase sex under both regimes from the same group of non-victims, criminalisation does not increase the risk to these women. If they previously purchased sex from victims (a likely possibility given the fact that victims are generally less able to screen out clients) than the harm does not increase but is simply shifted from victims to non-victims. The difference is that non-victims consent to this occupational risk – and it is the premise of sex work advocates that sex-workers can and do form meaningful consent to work in the industry – while victims do not. Similarly, the findings that under criminalisation CSPs lower their prices, are prepared to take more clients, and are prepared to give the service without protection,[71] are typical of victims' experiences,[72] so if indeed criminalisation decreases the supply of victims, the harm might just be shifted from non-consenting victims to consenting sex-workers.

In addition, sex-work feminists largely argue that off-street prostitution involves less risk to CSPs than street prostitution;[73] yet at the same time they criticise criminalisation for the ensuing underground effect, despite the fact that a major part of this effect is displacement of prostitution from the street indoors. The claim that such a move increases the isolation of CSPs and their risk of injury, and decreases the reach of service provision is inconsistent with the claims about reduced risks in indoor prostitution. Indeed, there is some evidence that in recent years the use of the Internet by indoors Swedish CSPs has increased their control in negotiations with clients, and improved the overall clients' profile by adding a segment of courteous and co-operative clients; more generally, PRIS is positive about the law's effects.[74]

70 According to the New Zealand 2008 Prostitution Report (n66) 14, 57, the majority of both sex-workers and all respondents, including brothel operators, felt that the Prostitution Reform Act could do little about the violence that occurred; according to a brothel operator 'clients getting stroppy will always happen. This was the case before the Act and after it'.

71 Ministry of Justice and the Police (Norway), *Purchasing Sexual Services in Sweden and the Netherlands: Legal Regulation and Experiences* (2004) 13, available at www.regjeringen.no/upload/kilde/jd/rap/2004/0034/ddd/pdfv/232216-purchasing_sexual_services_in_sweden_and_the_nederlands.pdf (accessed 6 July 2012) (citing the Malmö Prostitution Knowledge Centre).

72 See pp 41, 202, 211.

73 Sanders (n6); Weitzer (n52).

74 Levenkron (n52) 145–7.

In tension with the common belief that off-street prostitution is less risky to CSPs, there are somewhat conflicting findings by Bettio and Nandi that:

> overall, trafficked women working in secluded places other than bars and nightclubs are more at risk of experiencing the worst cases of violation of our five rights than are those working on the streets. The worst locations in this respect are private apartments, followed by massage parlours and saunas, whilst working on the streets brings some (comparative) improvement. The least worse working locations are bars and nightclubs, whilst no clear pattern was found for escort girls.[75]

If correct, this finding suggests, somewhat ironically, that if criminalisation displaces both victims and non-victims from the street to brothels, the well being of victims decreases (according to Bettio and Nandi's study), while that of non-victims improves (according to findings of sex-work feminists that in general street prostitution involves more violence than off-street prostitution). In any event, for reasons explained in section 6.3.4 and in chapter 7, the thwarted expectations of non-victims to have the demand for their services remain intact (if indeed recognising a duty will decrease demand) cannot serve as a reason to deny a duty if proximity exists and the client's active creation of risk negligently injures victims.

### *6.3.2 Tort liability different from criminalisation*

As mentioned earlier, it is uncertain that criminalisation decreases demand or involves displacement, but even if it does, it is not clear that negligence-based liability in torts will bring about the same deterrent effect. First, deterrence depends on the level of enforcement;[76] in the absence of routine tort claims by victims against clients, the tort deterrence is not likely to be significant. Second, some (but not all) research interviewing clients suggests that only significant sanctions such as imprisonment or shaming sanctions would act as an effective deterrent.[77] Since negligence liability is akin to a fine, with the added factor that the social stigma it produces is lower than the one achieved by a criminal conviction, the deterrence might be lower. However, it is possible that due to the social stigma involved in buying sex and the potential negative effects to clients who are in long-term relationships, the main deterrent effect of criminalisation or tort liability stems from the increased likelihood that the client will be indentified, rather than from the severity of

75 Bettio and Nandi (ch1, n24) 36; see also id, 32–3.
76 Collins and Judge (n65).
77 Madden-Dempsey (n29) 1773.

the legal sanction (at least as long as the legal sanction is not too harsh). Some empirical research supports such a hypothesis.[78]

The difference in the potential of tort and criminal law to stigmatise is also relevant in evaluating the objection that criminalisation of *clients* further stigmatises and marginalises *CSPs*. To begin with, this assumption is not intuitively compelling: if criminalisation is based on the exploitation of CSPs it is far from evident that it will stigmatise those the legislation attempts to protect.[79] But be this as it may, the argument is even less plausible when liability is based on the injury to *victims*. Such liability is not necessarily based on the vulnerability of *non-victims* (although the discussion below suggests that liability could be further supported if one concedes that a significant portion of non-victims are exploited), so it does not stigmatise them. True, accepting the logic of the argument of increased stigmatisation *might* suggest – the point is not clear – that liability which is based on contribution to trafficking stigmatises *victims*. But denying a duty owed to victims in a litigation initiated by them based on such reasoning is at best paternalistic and at worst hypocritical.

Interestingly, regulationists oppose criminalisation due to the fear that the status of victims is imposed on sex-workers.[80] But this concern is misplaced with respect to civil litigation which is controlled by the victim herself. Related to this, even if criminalisation should be opposed based on doubts concerning its deterrent and transformative effects, and based on its paternalistic nature, such concerns are misplaced as regards to civil liability. Civil liability vindicates victims' rights, hence it is remedial rather than punitive; its legitimacy does not hinge on showing that it creates effective deterrence or is likely to bring about an attitude change; it is based on the harm indiscriminate demand causes to victims and therefore is not paternalistic; it is controlled by the victim, not the state, and therefore does not raise the spectre of being sinisterly used as part of improper anti-CSP and anti-immigration sentiments; lastly, the ensuing sanction is moderate and liability involves a lesser stigma to the client. Given the inconclusive nature of the evidence about the overall effects of criminalisation (or equivalent civil measures which reduce demand) it might be that criminalisation should be avoided, since the onus should lie on those asking to criminalise a certain activity, and yet, once proximity has been established, duty should be

78 Cf Waltman (n52) 460; Dodillet and Östergren (n52) 21; Levenkron (n52) 110–11.

79 Cf MacKinnon (n54) 301, 306. More generally, the Special UNESCO Rapporteur on Violence against Women observed that the 'highly stigmatized' social status of prostituted women is not measurably improved by legalisation (id, n122). A similar conclusion, that the social stigma continues after legalisation, was reached by the New Zealand 2008 Prostitution Report (n66) 154. The CSP organisation (PRIS) argues that criminalisation of clients alone reduces CSPs' stigma. Levenkron (n52) 135.

80 See e.g. Phoenix (ch1, n59) 35–50, 46 and *passim*.

recognised to victims whose harm from the practice of indiscriminate demand is indisputable, since the onus should lie on those claiming that the imposition of duty is not fair, just and reasonable.

To conclude, there is no credible evidence that even criminalisation of demand, let alone tort liability, will either increase the number of victims or decrease their well being. Indeed, some research tentatively suggests that the opposite is more likely. Sex-workers' lost business is not a convincing reason to oppose liability for creation of demand, if the client indeed negligently contributed to the injury of a victim having been trafficked. There is no credible evidence that an underground effect increases the overall level of violence suffered by CSPs; it is more likely at most to displace it from non-consenting victims to consenting sex-workers and possibly from indoor to outdoor CSPs. Lastly, duty which bases liability for purchase of sex from any CSP on the contribution to trafficking of victims is not likely to stigmatise non-victims.

### 6.3.3 No floodgates concern

The other possible argument against the fairness of a duty is that of floodgates and the related fear from unmerited claims which might succeed due to the difficulties in disproving the claimant's evidence.[81] Even if the floodgates argument is valid in principle, the experience with respect to victims' claims thus far suggests it is quite far-fetched. Victims face many access-to-justice barriers and while these might be partially overcome, the dominant concern is that an insufficient number of victims will sue, rather than that too many of them will. More crucially, the scope of liability demarcated in chapter 8 ensures that the gates would not be flooded. Limiting liability to clients purchasing sex in the same city for a limited period of time and victims' practical inability to identify all (or even most) clients who could be liable according to the suggested rule ensures that the number of claims will be held in check. Moreover, the British and Israeli experience suggests that victims will sue only after their trafficker has been convicted. This suggests both that the number of claims is not likely to be high and that claims brought forward are likely to be genuine and easy to litigate.[82]

### 6.3.4 Concern for markets

I have rejected earlier the claim that from a proximity perspective, duty should not be imposed since the injury was mediated by both traffickers and the

81 However, the floodgates argument is on the decline and is often met with some judicial disapproval; see *McLoughlin v O'Brian* [1983] 1 AC 410, 425, and Witting (n20) 39.

82 The last point is explained on pp 248–9.

market. The equivalent, and equally unconvincing, policy arguments are that liability is not fair since it is disproportionate to the fault[83] (a variant of the indeterminacy concern) and since it unduly threatens the operation of a well functioning market. While interference in allocation of risk is an accepted ground to deny duty,[84] it is invoked almost only in economic loss cases, while the trafficking context is very different: the loss is not merely economic and the claimant does not have alternative measures to protect herself. To the extent that the argument is reformulated as interference with the contracts between clients and non-victims, or a threat to a thriving prostitution market, the focus shifts to the social value of having such an unconstrained market. This is discussed further in chapter 7 while evaluating the benefits and harms to non-forced CSPs from prostitution. As further explored below, the liberty interest of clients and non-victims to exchange sex for money should hardly be considered as justification to contribute to the enslavement of victims resulting from the operation of such a market, if the imposition of risk by the client is negligent. Lastly, the argument in chapter 5 supporting strict liability for direct contact based on considerations of fairness and equality could also be used to explain why recognition of fault-based duty for creation of demand is fair, just and reasonable.

However, it would not be fair, just and reasonable to make the client fully liable for the entire injury suffered by the claimants of whose trafficking his indiscriminate demand was a legal cause. Several factors make unlimited liability disproportionate to the client's fault. Some of these factors have just been mentioned: the indirect mode in which the client contributes to trafficking; the supply of commercial sex by non-victims; and the reduced culpability of clients in comparison to traffickers who are the direct cause of trafficking.[85] Other factors will emerge from the causation discussion in chapter 8: that the contribution of each individual client to the trafficking of the claimant is small (and neither necessary nor independently sufficient), and that each client is exposed to claims by several victims. This limitation of liability is explored further in chapter 8. But the fact that full liability is unfair does not mean that any liability is unfair. On the contrary, the availability of a solution which is not all or nothing and which was adopted in other circumstances to limit the scope of compensable damage[86] makes a denial of duty an unfair solution.

83 Cf *Topp* (n28) 460.
84 See (n26).
85 For the relevance of the defendant being a peripheral party as a reason to deny a duty, see Stapleton (n26).
86 *Rees v Darlington Memorial Hospital* [2003] UKHL 52.

## 6.4 Conclusion

That indiscriminate demand would lead to some women being trafficked is reasonably foreseeable. In fact, the evidence suggests that many clients are actually aware that trafficking exists. By creating demand, clients positively create risk – albeit indirectly – that some women will be trafficked in order to partially satisfy this demand. Traffickers' behaviour which directly injures victims is done in order to respond to clients' indiscriminate demand and clients benefit from the trafficking phenomenon. Special features of the sex industry indicate both that sufficient proximity exists, and that recognition of duty in this context is immune from slippery slope and floodgates concerns. Most crucially, in trafficking for sexual exploitation claimants are both the victims and the product. Clients' demand brings victims from the place of recruitment to the site of exploitation and exposes victims to the related risk of having non-consensual direct sexual contact with the client himself. Moreover, the client's sexual preferences shape to a large extent the identity of those trafficked. All these elements create sufficient circumstance and causal proximity in this context, but are absent in other contexts of trafficking. Lastly, in the absence of clear evidence that liability towards victims will threaten the well being of both victims and non-victims, imposing a duty is fair, just and reasonable. Indeed, some research tentatively suggests (by implication from the decriminalisation of prostitution debate) that tort liability to victims might decrease the number of victims without increasing (and even possibly decreasing) the overall level of violence towards victims and non-victims. That tort liability gives control of the process to claimants also allays concerns about stigmatising CSPs and enforcing the status of victim upon them.

## Chapter 7

# Breach

The basis for judging the client's conduct as unreasonable is simple: the client is taking a risk (in many cases consciously) that in order to satisfy his preference for commercial sex he subjects some women to the risk of being trafficked. The willingness to purchase sex services is unreasonable when the client knows, or should have known that: (a) women are forced into prostitution; and (b) his demand might be met by forced CSPs and he has no way to rule out the possibility that it would. When these conditions exist, not only does the client expose victims to the risk of non-consensual sex (which materialises randomly), but he also contributes to some victims being recruited and others continuing to be trafficked in order to satisfy his demand. If the risk is substantial, the behaviour should be considered as unreasonable. Evaluation of a given conduct as unreasonable usually means that the actor failed to balance the claimant's interests with the interests of others (usually, but not always, the defendant himself). In common law jurisdictions the evaluation is based on a cost–benefit analysis which is not equated with efficiency. This evaluation compares the risk arising from the defendant's conduct against the conduct's benefits, so it takes into account the social value of the activities involved.[1] This means that the costs of precaution take into account the costs of forgoing the activity with its associated benefits. The following discussion lists the factors which support the conclusion that purchasing sex indiscriminately is unreasonable. The first factor concerns the magnitude of the risk involved in creating indiscriminate demand and the next five factors are relevant elements in assessing the social value of buying sex: the proportion of victims to non-victims; the characterisation of buying sex as a self-serving imposition of risk which arguably satisfies a basic human need; the benefits to non-victims from the activity; the (contested) vast exploitation of non-victims in prostitution; and the fact that the risk targets those who to begin with are vulnerable.

1 See e.g. *Tomlinson v Congleton BC* [2003] UKHL 47, [34]–[37]; *Young v Bella* [2006] SCC 3; Keren-Paz (ch5, n20) 125–9.

## 7.1 The magnitude of the risk

Typically, the magnitude of the risk is determined by the magnitude of the injury if the risk materialises multiplied by the chance that the risk will materialise. Due to the dynamics of the market, in which discrete acts of consumption contribute to demand which is partially met by victims, each client contributes to the trafficking of a certain unknown number of victims. The magnitude of the risk is therefore determined by the magnitude of the ensuing injury which depends on the number of affected victims. In this sense, there is no question of likelihood that the risk will materialise.

The magnitude of the risk, therefore, derives from the degree of injury suffered by each victim and the number of victims affected by the client's behaviour. With respect to the first element, given the importance of the victim's underlying right (bodily integrity) and degree of violation (enormous intrusion of the victim's dignity and autonomy by violating her sexual autonomy),[2] the risk-taking is unreasonable. With respect to the second, clearly, the more victims are trafficked in response to indiscriminate demand, the less reasonable the behaviour becomes. It is one thing to contribute to demand which produces five victims; it is quite another if the contribution produces 5,000.

Two complications exist in assessing the number of affected victims. First, the overall number of victims (as opposed to the number of identified victims) is unknown and to a large extent unknowable. The sticking point is the gap between the confirmed number of identified victims for sexual exploitation and the estimated number of victims, which tries to account for what criminologists call the 'dark figure', namely the gap between the reported and all cases of the same criminal activity.[3] The number of identified victims is around 500 in the UK and less than 10,000 globally; estimated figures are 4,000 in the UK according to the Conservative Government estimation and between 1.2 and 1.35 million globally. According to the *IOM Trafficking Database* – which refers to cases assisted by the IOM between 1999 and 2009 – the number of assisted victims was 13,809 of which 71 per cent (9,804) were exploited for the purpose of sexual exploitation.[4] The ILO estimates that globally there are 12.3 million victims of forced labour, 11 per

2 For a description and summary of conditions of victims and extent of violation of rights, see pp 41–3. In addition to the sources mentioned there, see Di Tommaso *et al.* (ch5, n23). For findings of the injuries suffered by victims, see Zimmerman *et al.* (ch3, n21) 47 (57 per cent of women reported suffering between 12 and 23 concurrent physical health symptoms when they entered care after their trafficking had ended; symptoms suggestive of post traumatic stress disorder (PTSD) in 56 per cent of participants).

3 K Bales, 'International labor standards: quality of information and measures of progress in combating forced labor', (2004) 24(2) *Comp Labor L & Policy* 321, 331.

4 *IOM Trafficking Database* (ch3, n114). The other major global source of the identified number of victims is the United Nations Office on Drugs and Crime, *Global Report on Trafficking in Persons* (Vienna: UNODC, 2009) 10. The number of assisted victims (for all purposes of

cent of which (1.353 million) are estimated to be victims of forced commercial sexual exploitation, both transnationally and within countries.[5] Siddharth Kara estimates 1.2 million sex slaves at the end of 2006, and 500,000 to 600,000 new victims trafficked for sexual exploitation each year.[6] Other estimates exist – at the global, regional and national level – with respect to both human trafficking and sex trafficking.[7]

Estimated figures like these have been challenged with one commentator concluding that the estimation of modern forms of slavery 'is a pseudoscience, little better than astrology'[8] and another lamenting that 'numbers take on a life of their own, gaining acceptance through repetition, often with little inquiry into their derivations'.[9] The main critiques mounted against 'the national, regional, and international statistics proffered by activists, organizations, and governments'[10] are about lack of methodological transparency and source documentation,[11] extrapolating data from identified victims who are unrepresentative of the victim population[12] and the lack of a standard definition of 'victims' as a basis for estimates of the magnitude of the problem.[13]

These are of course serious challenges. And yet, as Kevin Bales reminds us 'the conversion of difficult-to-measure phenomena into measures that can be

exploitation) in 2006 was 14,909 but due to the methodology double counting is likely. A Gould, *From Pseudoscience to Protoscience: Estimating Human Trafficking and Modern Forms of Slavery*, paper presented at the Second Annual Interdisciplinary Conference on Human Trafficking, Nebraska, 2010, 13.

5 ILO, *Combating Forced Labour: A Handbook for Employers & Businesses* (Geneva: ILO, 2008) 13, 15. See also Belser (ch3, n3) 4 (1.7 million estimation based on adding the proportionate share of victims whose purpose of exploitation was not ascertained); *ILO Action Against Trafficking in Human Beings* (Geneva: ILO, 2008) 3; P Belser, M de Cock and F Mehran, *ILO Minimum Estimate of Forced Labour in the World* (Geneva: ILO, 2005) (explaining the methodology).

6 Kara (ch3, n4) 17, 264–6. Kara provides only limited explanation about his methodology which includes both ethnographic visits in several places, interviews with CSPs, victims in shelters and experts, and extrapolations of data according to business and economic methodology.

7 For a useful survey of other estimations and the methodological debate, see M Segrave, S Milivojevic and S Pickering, *Sex Trafficking: International Context and Response* (Cullompton: Willan Publishing, 2009) 12–16. For Kevin Bales's estimation (27 million in forced labour, country breakdown but no specific breakdown for sex trafficking), see (n3) 343.

8 Gould (n4).

9 J Sanghera, *Churning Out Numbers: Trafficking and Statistics*, Office of The High Commissioner for Human Rights, Working Paper No. 16, 2004, available at www.unece.org/fileadmin/DAM/stats/documents/2004/10/gender/wp.16.e.pdf (accessed 6 July 2012).

10 Weitzer (ch1, n26) 456.

11 L Kelly, 'You can find anything you want: a critical reflection on research on trafficking in persons within and into Europe', (2005) 43 *Int'l Migr* 237.

12 G Tyldum and A Brunovskis, 'Describing the unobserved: methodological challenges in empirical studies on human trafficking', (2005) 43 *Int'l Migr* 17.

13 El Gozdziak and E Collett, 'Research on human trafficking in North America: a review of the literature', (2005) 43 *Int'l Migr* 99.

statistically manipulated is common in sociology. Many of these phenomena are much less visible than slavery and yet are generally and readily accepted by the public and social scientists'.[14] More specifically, the fact that victims cannot be sampled randomly does not suggest that careful estimations, even based as they are on some method of extrapolation, are devoid of any value. The alternative, which is sometimes implicit in the critique offered by sex-work feminists, is to erroneously conclude that since the ratio of forced to non-forced CSPs is unknown or unknowable, it should be treated as zero. However, as Ronald Weitzer concedes 'it would be mistaken to assume that coercion and deception are myths'.[15]

Moreover, research brought as support by sex-work feminists seemingly suggesting low numbers of victims which is based on clients' reports (such as PunterNet) or even on interviews with sex-workers[16] will necessarily suffer from under-reporting bias and would be skewed against a finding of coercion. PunterNet, for example, does not file any reports on a sex-worker when there is suspicion she is coerced and coerced CSPs are not likely to agree (or to be allowed) to participate in a survey or to say that they have been forced into prostitution if they do participate. Similarly, studies done by groups such as the UK Network of Sex Work Projects[17] are likely to consistently suffer from report bias, since victims are less likely to seek their services. Most victims are not allowed to go out without supervision[18] and some of them, especially those suffering from language barriers, are not likely to be aware of these services. Indeed,

> judging from the experiences of the trafficked women the Poppy Project is working with, even in boroughs with one or even two support agencies, some women in the sex industry do not get the opportunity to link into any sexual health services.[19]

As the discussion below demonstrates, estimations of the absolute number of victims and their proportion among all CSPs can be made, and these estimations suggest that the risk is significant. Moreover, given the numbers of known victims (presented immediately below), the enormous harm each suffers and the likelihood that the number of unidentified victims is much higher than those identified (even if one insists to be agnostic about the correct multiplier between known and overall number of victims), a conclusion that the risk is significant is warranted.

14 Bales (n3) 334.
15 Weitzer (n10) 454.
16 For one UK example, see Sanders (ch1, n35).
17 See www.uknswp.org (accessed 8 July 2012).
18 According to Bettio and Nandi (ch1, n24) 21–2, 26, only 6.5 per cent of victims could leave the premises unaccompanied.
19 Dickson (ch6, n7) 49.

Lastly, even the number of identified victims (as opposed to an estimation of the overall number of victims) is significant. According to the UK Human Trafficking Centre, the results of the National Referral Mechanism (NRM) between 1 April 2009 and 30 June 2011 found 231 victims of sex trafficking (of whom 68 were minors) and 67 further cases awaiting conclusive grounds decisions.[20] Previously, the confirmed number of UK victims of sexual exploitation found in the Pentameter 1 and 2 operations in 2006–07 was 252.[21] The NRM and Pentameter statistics deal only with confirmed cases of trafficking and are not based on estimation. Even if one looks only at confirmed cases statistics, UK clients consuming sex during and prior to 2006–11 are contributing to the trafficking of at least 483 victims (252 + 231). The significance of that risk cannot be seriously doubted. In addition, the Anti-Trafficking Monitoring Group report mentioned 'more than 130 individuals who were identified by support organisations between 1 April 2009 and 1 April 2010 whose cases were not referred to the system for a variety of reasons'.[22] Indications of trafficking exist also in several reports, some of which are discussed below. It is not clear if the figures reported there[23] are additional to the NRM statistics. This suggests that the number of identified victims might be even higher.

A second complication in assessing the magnitude of risk relates to the possibility that different consumption patterns contribute to a different extent to trafficking (a point explored in more detail in chapter 8). Consider the hypothetical defendant Charles. The only available evidence with respect to Charles is that he bought sex only from Spanish women. The available NRM data suggests that no victim was trafficked from Spain.[24] Can Charles claim he is not at fault since his conduct did not create a significant (or even real) risk of trafficking? In answering this question several distinctions have to be made. As is explained in chapter 8, the client contributes to trafficking by triggering a supply of victims from traffickers in response to the demand to which the client contributes. Unless Charles buys sex only in closed markets, namely establishments in which all women are from Spain,[25] his consumption is still indiscriminate in the sense that it triggers supply which is not free from

20 UKHTC, *NRM Statistical Data, April 2009 to June 2011* (London: UKHTC, 2011).

21 L Cusick, H Kinnell, B Brooks-Gordon and R Cambell, 'Wild guesses and conflated meanings? Estimating the size of the sex-worker population in Britain', (2009) 29 *Critical Soc Po'cy* 703, 707; UKHTC, *United Kingdom Pentameter 2 Statistics of Victims Recovered and Suspects Arrested During the Operational Phase* (London: UKHTC, 2009).

22 Arocha (ch1, n60) 7. Note that this figure relates to victims of all forms of trafficking.

23 For example, 24 victims according to the ACPO report: Jackson *et al.* (ch7, n47).

24 UKHTC (n20) 5.

25 While ethnic-based closed markets do exist they are hard to locate and obviously would not exist for every ethnic (let alone national) identity. A Google search (conducted in September 2011) looking for 'massage parlour only Spanish women' failed to find UK establishments offering sexual services exclusively from Spanish women.

trafficking. For example, if Charles buys sex from several massage parlours and in some parlours few non-Spanish women are trafficked, he contributes to demand which is met by supply involving the trafficking of women. With the *possible* exception of closed markets (to which I return in chapter 8), traffickers respond to the overall level of demand in deciding how many women to recruit, transport and exploit in a certain locality.

Would the answer change if Charles bought sex only from Spanish women after he looked at the NRM statistics, since he wanted to avoid contributing to trafficking (and the risk of subjecting a victim to non-consensual sex)? On the one hand, Charles clearly attempts not to contribute to trafficking. On the other hand, if the analysis offered above is correct, he still contributes to trafficking. Since the standard of care in negligence is objective, Charles is nevertheless negligent. Note, however, that even a contrary conclusion would only rarely shield the defendant from a finding of negligence. The typical client is not likely to be able to show that his consumption pattern was chosen in order to reasonably and reliably eliminate the risk that it would contribute to trafficking (a point further explored in chapter 8).

A similar analysis could be made with respect to consumption of sexual services in different market segments. As the data presented in chapter 8 suggests, victims exist in all market segments, although probably to different extents. It is believed, for example, that the number of victims and their proportion to non-victims is lower among escorts than among women in brothels. The analysis in chapter 8 suggests that since markets are porous – so demand in one segment might affect supply to another segment – a client buying sex in a relatively victim-free market still contributes to trafficking. But the lower risk imposed by certain consumption patterns might be relevant to the question of fault and *legal* causation. If the number of victims in a given market is sufficiently low, although not nil, and the segregation between the markets is significant, but not complete, fault-based liability might be inappropriate due to the absence of fault (rather than due to a lack of factual contribution to trafficking). Arguably, the ensuing risk is so small that the behaviour which created it – purchase of sex in a relatively 'clean' market – is not negligent, or that the contribution is so small that it does not justify the attribution of liability. Since the test for fault is objective, such a client should still be found liable, if the risk is not sufficiently low, even if the client consciously consumes sex only from escorts in order to reduce the risk he will contribute to trafficking (and the related risk that he would buy services from a victim).[26]

26 Cf Madden-Dempsey (ch6, n29) 1755–6, who supports criminal responsibility of escorts' clients based on the existence of trafficking in escort services and the fact that market segments are porous.

## 7.2 The proportion of victims to non-victims

A decision to purchase sex in a market in which 90 per cent of CSPs are forced is much less reasonable than when only 0.1 per cent are. The proportion of victims to non-victims is relevant, since indiscriminate demand is met by both illegal supply of victims and lawful supply of non-victims. If buying sex for itself is morally neutral, and we have no reason to accord it low social value, the client derives a legitimate benefit from the purchase of sex from non-victims; moreover, the fact that his demand creates a continued and future supply of non-victims is unproblematic; in fact, it might even be considered as beneficial to non-victims and therefore as increasing the social value of the activity. The benefit to the client (and possibly also to non-victims) should be weighed against the inevitable injury caused to victims trafficked to partially meet this demand. The more significant the portion of victims in the market, the less reasonable the consumption, since at once, the total risk from the activity increases and the total benefit to clients and victims, which should be accorded social value, decreases.

The question, therefore, boils down to the acceptable level of risk-taking. Should 20 per cent be considered as too high? Should 3 per cent? Should 1 per cent? The more one: (a) devalues the social value of purchasing commercial sex (for the reasons discussed below); and (b) stresses the dehumanisation involved in the sexual enslavement of victims, the lower the ratio needed to support an unreasonableness verdict. Usually, determinations about the size of risk that renders the activity negligent (as well as determinations about the other elements relevant for determination of reasonableness) are done in an intuitive manner and obviously there is no precise line with respect to a threshold of risk beyond which the activity is deemed negligent. Still, case law reveals that even small risks can render the relevant behaviour negligent, if running the risk was unreasonable.[27]

As will be surveyed immediately below, some UK reports and studies estimate that between 4 per cent and 9 per cent of all UK CSPs are forced. This surely should be sufficient to be considered as a significant unjustifiable risk. While the methodological debate between abolitionist and sex-work feminist researchers canvassed above demonstrates that estimations are contested, it also demonstrates that there are reasons to be somewhat critical of the *critiques* of the estimations presented below. It should also be recalled that other, possibly less reliable estimations, would set the said proportion at 33 per cent or more (in Italy)[28] and 70 per cent (in the UK).[29]

27 *Wagon Mound (No 2)* [1967] 1 AC 617 (PC). Cf, in the context of informed consent, *Chester v Afshar* [2004] UKHL 41 (not informing about a 1–2 per cent risk of adverse response to a procedure is negligent).

28 Kara (n6) 265.

29 A Travis and A Sparrow, 'New law to criminalise men who pay for sex with trafficked women', *The Guardian*, 16 November 2008, available at www.guardian.co.uk/society/

The estimation by the British Government in 2007 was that about 4,000 women were trafficked to the UK for sexual exploitation.[30] A similar estimation of between 4,000 and 5,000 was made by Kevin Bales.[31] The estimations regarding the overall number of CSPs in the UK vary. In 1999, Hilary Kinnell's research estimated the total number of sex-workers in the UK at 80,000. This included both street and off-street workers, men, women and transgender.[32] A 2009 study by the UK Network of Sex Work Projects estimated 17,081 sex-workers in contact with specialist projects, extrapolated to 35,870 where there are specialist projects and 'it is possible that two or even three times this number of sex-workers are operating in the UK'.[33] Using these figures suggests that about 4–5 per cent of CSPs are forced (4,000 out of 80,000–100,000). In Sweden, the estimation of the number of forced CSPs between 2002 and 2006 by the National Police Board was between 400 and 600. The estimation of the total number of CSPs prior to the ban was 1,800–3,000 and after the ban 1,500.[34] Taking the lowest two figures suggests that over 25 per cent of CSPs in Sweden are forced.

A recent study by Nick Mai on the experience of migrant CSPs in London found that 6 per cent of female interviewees 'felt that they have been deceived and forced into selling sex in circumstances in which they felt they had no share of control or consent'.[35] According to ACPO 2010 Project Acumen's findings, out of 210 migrant women in the off-street prostitution sector sampled in the study, 24 were found to be trafficked, 113 were found to be vulnerable migrants and the rest did not meet the trafficked or vulnerable

2008/nov/19/prostitution-justice (accessed 12 March 2013) (citing the Metropolitan Police estimation). For other unsound estimations and their critique, see Cusick *et al.* (n21) 707. If, as estimated by some, the number of forced CSPs in the UK is 10,000, the proportion of victims among all CSPs would be around 10 per cent to 15 per cent.

30 *UK Action Plan* (ch3, n23) 14. But the source of the 4,000 victims figure is not clear. See Cusick *et al.*, id.

31 Bales (n3) 363.

32 H Kinnell, *Sex-workers in England and Wales: Europap-UK Briefing Paper for Department of Health, National Sexual Health Strategy* (London: Department of Health, 1999).

33 Cusick *et al.* (n21) 714. Using Kinnell's 1999 study methodology would have led to an estimation of 101,625.

34 Dodillet and Östergren (ch6, n52) 8, 11, 13. For lower post-ban estimations, see p 166. See also Levenkron (ch6, n52) 142 who mentions a 20 per cent estimation (600 out of 3,000).

35 Mai (ch1, n47) 32. Thirteen per cent of female interviewees felt that they had been subject to different perceptions and experiences of exploitation, ranging from extreme cases of trafficking to relatively more consensual arrangements. Due to the study's two-phase methodology, Mai (at 10–11) disclaimed that 'the actual number of interviewees who feel that they have been exploited is higher than the one which has occurred randomly (9 per cent) and which would be closer to a statistical representation'. Note that no information is available about British nationals.

thresholds and were considered to have relatively few barriers preventing them from exiting prostitution.[36]

The limitations of the ACPO study should not be ignored. First, it is important to be clear of the figures that are not available: there was no attempt to find out the extent of trafficking in the on-street sex market and among off-street nationals. Second, the report does not cover closed markets in the off-street sector (in which the likelihood of trafficking is arguably higher). Third, due to reporting bias the real number of trafficked people might be higher, and it is not clear that the methodology chosen satisfies the random selection requirement; although this for itself should not render the report valueless. As a result of the previous three points, the overall number (or percentage) of forced among all CSPs is unknown and there is no easy way to extrapolate this figure from the existing estimations (if considered as sound). Fourth, the estimated figure of off-street CSPs in England and Wales is much lower than other estimations (presented above). Lastly, there is some lack of clarity with respect to the ways in which the findings were reached; accordingly, the percentage of trafficked among all migrants ranges between 9 per cent and 15 per cent.[37]

Still, the study suggests that 11.4 per cent (24 out of 210) of all foreign CSPs are victims. When one takes into account the extraordinarily high number of vulnerable CSPs who are not trafficked (113 out of 210 immigrants), the conclusion about the unreasonable nature of the risk-taking is strengthened, since it bolsters the conclusion (examined below) that buying sex has low social value, or alternatively, that the total injury suffered from that activity is bigger. The study, which did not attempt to find out the extent of trafficking among off-street nationals, noted that 'none of the 44 British nationals exhibited any of the "dimensions of the trafficking definition"'.[38] But even under the assumption that no British national is forced, the study suggests that 8.66 per cent of all CSPs in the off-street market are victims, based on the extrapolated numbers of 2,600 victims out of all 30,000 off-street CSPs. Note, however, that the NRM statistics reveal that domestic trafficking does exist: 53 British nationals were found conclusively to be victims (although it is not discernable how many were victims of sexual exploitation).[39]

36 Jackson *et al.* (ch1, n47). The researchers extrapolated this data to estimate that there are approximately 17,000 migrant women (out of 30,000) in off-street prostitution in England and Wales, out of whom 2,600 are trafficked, 9,200 are vulnerable migrants and 5,500 are women who do not exhibit any of the dimensions of the trafficking definition.

37 For the report's qualifications, see Jackson *et al.*, id, 24–5. For the 'methodological debate', see section 7.1 and ch6, section 6.3. For a critique that the ACPO's estimation derived 'from ridiculously crude, subjective and evidence-free methods', see L Agustin, The Naked Anthropologist Blog, 17 August 2010, available at www.lauraagustin.com/police-quarrel-about-which-bad-method-to-use-to-estimate-trafficking-victims-uk (accessed 8 July 2012).

38 Jackson *et al.* (n36) 23.

39 UKHTC (n20) 1.

## 7.3 Client's self-interest in risk-creating activity

The client's activity which imposed the risk on victims was undertaken to promote the client's self-interest. Other than the fact that this characteristic can support strict liability (as explained in chapter 5), it can be taken into account in the balancing process so that the social value given to the risk creation is deemed lower. Richard Wright, in his interpretation of *Bolton v Stone*[40] and *Wagon Mound (No 2)*,[41] as well as American case law, argues that when the defendant put the claimant at risk in order to advance the defendant's interest, liability is not based on a risk-utility test, but rather on the creation of a significant, foreseeable and unaccepted risk.[42] According to such a view, which does not take the utility of the client from purchasing sex into account, it seems that a conclusion that the risk was unreasonable is straightforward. This reading, however, of *Bolton* and *Wagon Mound* is contested, and in my opinion, mistaken, for the reason that it ignores the fact that two of the Law Lords in *Bolton* based their decision on the traditional balancing approach,[43] and since even Lord Reid's view in *Bolton* could be understood as being based on a balancing approach.[44] But even though cost–benefit analysis still applies, no doubt the advancement of self-interest will affect the evaluation of the risk in the direction of a greater likelihood of finding it unreasonable.[45]

According to Wright's interpretation of *Wagon Mound*, risk-utility balancing is limited to instances of small risk (real) which is neither significant nor far-fetched. But Lord Reid's distinction between small and significant risks in *Wagon Mound* did not have much impact on decided cases and tort textbooks, to the extent that it purported to create two qualitatively different tests for negligence. Even when the risk is significant, the benefits from the activity are taken into account.[46] Wright is correct, however, that the

40 *Bolton* (ch5, n65).

41 *Wagon Mound (No 2)* (n27).

42 R Wright, 'The standards of care in negligence law', in D Owen (ed), *Philosophical Foundations of Tort Law* (Oxford: Clarendon Press, 1995) 249, 261–3. Note, though, that 'significant' and especially 'unaccepted' beg the question of balancing the act's risks and benefits. Presumably, a significant foreseeable risk is acceptable only if it serves a legitimate purpose which should be balanced against the risk it generates to others.

43 *Bolton* (n40) 1082e–f (Lord Normand), 1087e–g (Lord Radcliff).

44 See e.g. R Heuston and R Buckley, *Salmond and Heuston on the Law of Torts*, 21st edn (London: Carswell, 1996) 230, n30; A Linden, *Canadian Tort Law*, 7th edn (Markham: Butterworths, 2001) 122; cf. T Keren-Paz, 'Is the reasonable person the efficient person? The role of efficiency in Israeli standard of care jurisprudence', (2008) 23 *Bar-Ilan U L Rev* 793, 815–16 (in Hebrew).

45 Compare *Watt v Hertfordshire County Council* [1954] 2 All ER 368, 371 (CA); A Porat, 'The many faces of negligence', (2003) 4 *TIL* 105, 116–21, 144.

46 *Watt*, id; *Tomlinson* (n1) [34], [39], [41].

purpose for which the risk-creating activity was imposed (i.e. whether it is self-serving or not) is relevant for the evaluation of the social value that should be accorded to the activity, and hence for the result of the balancing, that in this sense is not wealth-maximising (or possibly, strictly utilitarian).

Of course, that an activity is self-serving does not preclude it from being reasonable even if it creates significant risks to others. Arguably, buying sex, despite the significant risk it poses to victims, is not unreasonable since it satisfies a fundamental human need.[47] It should be recalled, however, that male demand for commercial sex is socially constructed,[48] so the existence of such demand, and hence the need to satisfy it, should not be taken for granted.[49] The social value that should be accorded to buying sex is obviously value-laden, and normatively contested. To be sure, from the client's subjective perspective, a requirement to avoid buying sex in the market is burdensome. Moreover, the extent to which the requirement is subjectively perceived as burdensome might change depending on the client's personal circumstances. But should we normatively embrace the proposition that the fewer alternatives to commercial sex are available, the more burdensome the requirement to avoid buying sex becomes, to the extent that purchasing sex becomes reasonable? Some would answer in the affirmative. But even in the paradigm case of 'legitimate' interest in buying sex – the disabled client who arguably cannot form long-term relationships – the client still contributes to trafficking by his indiscriminate demand, and if exploitation of CSPs is rampant he also contributes to that exploitation. Whether the imposition of significant risk on victims could be justified in order to fulfil this important need is open for debate.

In Israel, the question was raised in the context of personal injury litigation. In *Ploni v Migdal* the Supreme Court ruled that as a general rule, and also in the specific case, the claimant cannot be awarded special damages for the purchase of sex where the injury arguably prevents the claimant from forming sexual relationships outside the sex market.[50] Justice Rivlin, in the leading opinion, based his decision not only on lack of sufficient evidence to support

47 For a critical presentation of this view, see M McIntosh, 'Who needs prostitutes? The ideology of male sexual needs', in C Smart and B Smart (eds), *Women, Sexuality and Social Control* (London: Routledge, 1978) 53–64; Jeffreys (ch1, n52) 35–64.

48 See B Anderson and J O'Connell Davidson, *Trafficking: A Demand Led Problem?: A Multi-country Pilot Study* (Stockholm: Save the Children Sweden, 2002) 25–6, 29–30; Marttila (ch5, n24) 5–6; Hughes (ch5, n80) 7. That sexual preferences are socially constructed is a major theme in the writings of radical feminists. See e.g. MacKinnon *Feminist Theory*, 131–2, and Dworkin 47–61 (ch5, n125).

49 Compare the critique by M Jacob of the demand for organ donation in 'Another look at the presumed-versus-informed consent dichotomy in postmortem organ procurement', (2006) 20 *Bioethics* 293, 293.

50 *Ploni* (ch2, n32). As surveyed in the decision, the issue has been raised in District Courts before and received inconsistent answers.

the claim that the claimant can have sex only with 'escort girls' and on the conceptual difficulty of classifying the use of escort services as a remedy for the damage involved in the loss of the ability to enjoy sexual relations, but also on public policy. Such compensation does not sit well with the unrelenting war of the law enforcement authorities against the serious incidents that accompany the prostitution industry in Israel, including the particularly grave and widespread phenomenon of sex trafficking. The purpose of denying compensation is to prevent the encouragement and financing of phenomena that involve, at least in a large number of cases, exploitation, damage and dependence. The courts that denounce the phenomena with which the prostitution industry in Israel is tainted, including trafficking, must speak with one voice. In view of Israeli law and Israeli realities, the use of prostitution services should not be recognised by courts as 'compensation' to the injured party, and there is no basis for the court to order a payment of money that is most likely to find its way into the pockets of those persons who earn their livelihoods from the profits of prostitution. Instead, courts should award non-pecuniary damages to compensate the claimant for his loss of sexual functioning.[51] Chief Justice Beinisch agreed that in principle such an award should be avoided based on public policy considerations but left open the question of whether such a rule should have an exception. Former Chief Justice Barak concurred in the result based on the absence of sufficient evidence to justify the award but reserved his opinion on the question of principle.

The decision in *Ploni* is important for two reasons. First, it supports the view that the reasonableness of buying sex should be determined regardless of the alternatives to commercial sex available to the defendant. I return to this point below. Second, it comes very close to accepting that buying sexual services in an industry in which trafficking and exploitation are rife is unreasonable. That financing the buying of sex contravenes public policy because it enriches traffickers and pimps and because it supports exploitation and the causing of injury strongly implies that indiscriminate demand both contributes to trafficking (and exploitation) and is wrong for that reason. True, the decision could be understood as based on: (a) the need for courts to speak with one voice or not to be perceived as giving their imprimatur to such phenomena; or (b) the policy of preventing traffickers and pimps from profiting from prostitution rather than preventing injury to victims. However, given the overview of the trafficking phenomena and the explicit mention of the injury caused to CSPs (alongside exploitation and dependency) as a reason to deny compensation, my overall reading of the case is as follows: it is the contribution of indiscriminate demand to trafficking and the exploitation of victims (or CSPs) which make the award of damages whose purpose is to buy sexual services to be against public policy.

51 Id, [11], [14]–[19], [24]–[25].

Moving away from *Ploni*, deciding whether buying sex is reasonable based on the client's available alternatives is at once straightforward and deeply problematic. It is straightforward in that it employs a standard of care logic: given the lack of alternatives, the benefit to the defendant from running the risk-creating activity is more significant and therefore the activity is more likely to be deemed overall reasonable. But such calculus, which is so endemic to reasonableness determinations, is problematic from several normative perspectives. From a liberal (let alone libertarian) perspective, an alternatives-based determination of reasonableness seems to be impermissibly committed to a certain understanding of the good about sexual mores, and might be mistaken for a condemnation of casual sex (i.e. monogamy is good, therefore men in long-term relationships act unreasonably when they buy sex, but if they are single, or incapable of establishing a long-term sexual relationship, their consumption of sex is reasonable). To be clear, my problem with prostitution is not that it involves casual sex but that it contributes to trafficking (and, arguably, but this is more contested, to exploitation of non-victims).

From certain feminist and philosophical quarters, an alternatives-based determination of reasonableness is problematic since it accepts that commercial sex and non-commercial sex are substitutes for each other.[52] According to such a view, resort to commercial sex is problematic regardless of the existence or absence of alternatives to the client. Some research on clients suggests, however, that in fact clients view these types of sex as substitutes, not only in the sense that some (but not all) clients buy sex only or more so when they are not in a sexual relationship, but also since some clients look for a 'girlfriend experience' when they buy sex.[53] Lastly, the assumption that disabled people cannot have alternatives to commercial sex is both factually speculative and expressively unpalatable, and might be opposed by disability rights advocates as grossly insulting.

To summarise, the promotion of self-serving interests might be reasonable despite imposing significant risks on others, but whether buying sex should qualify as such an interest should be doubted. Sexual gratification is an important human need, and its pursuit in a manner respecting the dignity and sexual autonomy of partners is a worthy goal. But sexual autonomy and dignity are extremely important values, and activity which risks individuals losing their liberty and sexual autonomy to satisfy another's sexual needs is suspect. The assumption that since the pursuit of sexual gratification is important so is an attempt to pursue it by buying commercial sex is problematic; it ignores the fact that there are other ways to reach sexual

52 Cf Radin (ch5, n124) 1921–5.

53 Sanders (n16) 40–1, 46–7. For PunterNet forum discussion of the term, see www.punternet.com/forum/index.php/topic/2999-what-does-gfe-include/ (accessed 9 August 2011).

gratification and that these ways pose a lesser risk that women will be enslaved and subject to sexual assault in order to satisfy the defendant's sexual needs. It also ignores the fact that men's need (read 'right') to have access to sexually available women as long as they are willing and able to pay for it is a social construct of patriarchal societies. At the end of the day, the client, in pursuing a self-serving activity, poses a significant risk that some women will be trafficked in order to satisfy his sexual needs.

Recall that when all things are equal, significant risks to others are more likely to, and should be, considered as negligent if they derive from self-serving activity. The corollary to this proposition is that where the demand is on rare occasions motivated by other-regarding motivation, a conclusion that the risk was not negligent is more likely. So a relative who buys sex in order to try and track down a trafficked family member, or a reporter who buys sex as part of research on the sex industry can fend off a claim that he was negligent, even though his demand did contribute to the trafficking of some women.[54]

## 7.4 Effect on non-victims

The demand for commercial sex is supplied by non-victims as well ('workers'). It could be argued that purchasing commercial sex should not be classified as a self-interest creation of risk, since it also benefits workers. But the fact that the defendant advances the interest of a third party as well, does not change the basic characteristic of the situation as one in which the victim's interests are put at risk for the defendant's (and third party) interests. Indeed, Ariel Porat, who examined determinations of negligence in situations in which the claimant's interest is balanced against different sorts of interests, concluded that even when the defendant failed to balance the victim's interest solely with that of a third party, imposition of liability is crucial from both deterrence and justice perspectives. When the failure is to balance the victim's interest against the defendant's, imposition of liability is *very* crucial from these two perspectives.[55] In sex markets, the purchase of sex predominantly serves the defendant's interests and only secondarily the interests of workers. This is clear in terms of motivation: clients buy sex in order to achieve sexual gratification, not out of concern for workers' interest in making a living. Therefore, in evaluating the social value of the activity, and related to this, the burden to the defendant of forgoing the activity, the focus should be on the fact that the activity is self-serving.

Still, arguably, the benefit from the practice which needs to be balanced against its risks is not only the benefit to clients from buying sex, but also the benefit to workers from selling sex. As a preliminary point, I accept the

54 Madden-Dempsey (n26) 1760–1.
55 Porat (n45) 144.

proposition that valuations of the reasonableness of the defendant's activity should take into account effects on third parties (including positive externalities).[56] Nonetheless, I find the claim that the benefits to workers (combined with the benefits to clients) outweigh the loss to victims unconvincing for two reasons. First, to those, like me, who believe that buying commercial sex involves a vast exploitation of non-victims, the net gain to workers from the practice of buying sex is smaller than that which the current argument posits; this proposition is explored below.

Exploitation aside, it is unclear whether the well being of non-victims would be reduced due to the anticipated decrease in demand if liability were imposed on clients. Recall that the evidence surveyed in chapter 6 is inconclusive about whether criminalisation results in negative effects on all CSPs and on non-victims in particular; and that observable negative effects under criminalisation might reflect only a displacement of risk, rather than its increase. The welfare effects of a decrease in demand (assuming imposition of duty will have a deterrent effect) on non-victims depends on the *relative* decrease of supply of sexual services by victims vis-à-vis non-victims. Presumably, the decrease of supply of victims will improve workers' bargaining power, since the existence of victims reduces the bargaining power of workers by creating a race to the bottom. Moreover, to the extent that some clients can sometimes tell victims from non-victims, liability towards the former will increase the attractiveness of the latter. It might be, therefore, that the general reduction of demand for commercial sex is compensated for by better working conditions of non-victims which results from reducing demand for and supply of victims. Without knowing how significant the decrease in supply of victims would be in the commercial sex market, it is impossible to know whether an increased share of non-victims in the market compensates for the general decrease of demand for commercial sex.

I stress, however, the speculative nature of the assumption that the commercial sex market works like any free market. On the demand side, it has been argued that some of the demand is inelastic. If true, this means that sex addicts are not likely to be responsive to legal sanction, including tort liability.[57] More importantly, on the supply side, the prevalence of economic and other kinds of coercion operating on many CSPs and the pool of potential

56 Keren-Paz (n1) 121–2. Cf *Watt* (n45); *Restatement (Third) of Torts* (ch6, n32) § 3 Comment e; *Restatement (Second) of Torts* (ch3, n58) § 295.

57 See S Månsson, 'Men's practices in prostitution and their implications for social work', in S Månsson and C Proveyer (eds), *Social Work in Cuba and Sweden: Achievements and Prospects* (Göteborg: Department of Social Work, Göteborg University, 2004). This does not mean that liability should not be imposed, but rather that the deterrent effect of the tort sanction, and hence its potential to change the well being of non-victims by changing the pattern of consumption, might be limited. Similar findings can be found in Di Nicola *et al.* (ch6, n4). Contrast with Kara (n6) 33–7, 89, 255, who found that demand for commercial sex is highly elastic.

CSPs, casts doubt on the assumption that the decrease of demand for victims will improve the conditions of non-victims. But as some of the research surveyed in chapter 6 indicates, the same factors cast doubt on the assumption that imposition of liability will be detrimental to workers.

I turn now to the second reason why the benefits to workers should not change the conclusion that buying sex indiscriminately is negligent. The risks to victims and the benefits to workers from the demand for commercial sex are not of the same order, and should be weighted differently. The thwarted *expectation* of workers to make a living cannot outweigh the *right* of victims not to be trafficked. In a rights framework, a worker's privilege to sell her body (and the corresponding privilege of clients to purchase commercial sex from her) cannot trump a victim's right to bodily integrity. In a consequentialist framework, the harm to victims from non-consensual sex must be deemed to outweigh the benefit to workers from increased demand due to the immunity granted to clients from being responsible for their contribution to victims' trafficking. This is not to say that the benefit to workers should be completely disregarded. It does mean, however, that the weight given to it from a social perspective should be reduced; in other words, the benefit should be devalued.

There are several ways to state this intuition. One is to stress that the benefit to clients and workers is one and the same – the interest in entering into mutually beneficial transactions. We should be careful then not to double count this interest with respect to both clients and workers. Another way to look at the matter is to realise that the fact that the transaction did not harm (and in fact benefited) both clients and workers is no justification to impose risks on third parties: the victims.[58] Recall that when the defendant fails to balance the victim's interest with that of a third party both justice and deterrence support liability, and that the interests of victims are qualitatively different and superior to that of workers. According to an old joke, the schoolmaster told a pupil 'John, there are five pupils who saw you smashing the window with a stone' to this John retorted 'But, Sir, 500 pupils did not see me smashing it'. Like John, the client should fail to demonstrate his case that risking the victims is not negligent since it did not risk workers.

## 7.5 Exploitation of non-victims

Sections 7.3 and 7.4 proceeded on the sex-work feminism's assumption that buying sex in itself has neutral social value. In particular, section 7.4 assumed that indiscriminate demand benefits non-victims and that this benefit should be taken into account in determining whether the risk associated with the

58 As Madden-Dempsey ((n26) 1761–2) argued, there is no need to stretch this argument to its logical conclusion and view workers as complicit (alongside clients) with traffickers in bringing about the trafficking of victims.

activity is unreasonable. But arguably, the activity which creates the risk – the purchase of commercial sex – has low social value. Since courts take the social value of the risk-creating activity into account, the result of a finding that such activity has low social value is likely to be (as a prediction), and should be, that buying sex indiscriminately, with its associated risk of contributing to trafficking, was unreasonable. One can think of at least three good reasons why the purchase of commercial sex has low value: (a) it commodifies sex, while we tend to think of sex as an intimate activity which should not be traded in the market;[59] (b) it commodifies CSPs and objectifies all women;[60] and (c) the practice is founded on the vulnerability of many non-victims and contributes to their exploitation.[61]

I would like to say few words on the last reason. I adhere to the view that prostitution is vastly exploitative. While I do not question the existence of sex-workers who live up to the myth of the 'happy hooker', I question the interpretation that this group is significant in numbers. To say the least, many women, at least in the street sector,[62] who are not forced into prostitution according to the way defined in this book, are nevertheless drawn into prostitution out of extreme economic and social pressures, usually when they are minors, and often against a background of previous abuse. These women have very limited, if any, real chance to exit; some have a drug addiction which impinges upon their ability to form consent to have sex, and in any event to exit the profession. They are often subject to pressures from pimps, a fact which casts doubt on the voluntariness of their choice of profession, and they are subject to frequent sexual and physical abuse by clients.[63] Similarly,

59 See e.g. C Stark and R Whisnant, *Not for Sale: Feminists Resisting Prostitution and Pornography* (Melbourne: Spinifex Press, 2004).

60 MacKinnon (ch1, n52).

61 According to M Farley, A Cotton, J Lynne, S Zumbeck, F Spiwak, M E Reyes, D Alvarez and U Sezgin, 'Prostitution & trafficking in nine countries: an update on violence and post-traumatic stress disorder', in M Farley (ch1, n55) 55–66, 92 per cent of the CSPs surveyed would like to leave prostitution, but cannot do so due to a lack of other options.

62 For the debate about whether abolitionists illegitimately extrapolate from the experience of street CSPs to all CSPs, see sources in ch6 (n53).

63 For data about clients' violence, see e.g. S Church, M Henderson, M Barnard and G Hart, 'Violence by clients towards female prostitutes in different work settings: questionnaire survey', (2001) 322 *BMJ* 524–5; H Ward, S Day and J Weber, 'Risky business: health and safety in the sex industry over a nine-year period', (1999) 75 *Sex'ly Trans Inf* 340. For data about prior sexual abuse leading to prostitution, usually when the woman is a minor, see J James and J Meyerdin, 'Early sexual experience and prostitution', (1977) 134 *Am J Psychiatry* 1381; R Simons, 'Sexual abuse as a precursor to prostitution and victimization among adolescent and adult homeless women', (1991) 12 *J Fam Issues* 361. For data about drug dependency as a barrier to exit prostitution, see e.g. T May, A Harocopos and M Hough, *For Love or Money: Pimps and the Management of Prostitution* (London: Police Research Series 134, 2000) 8. For an extensive collection of data about the harm in prostitution, see MacKinnon (n60). Needless to say, the background conditions of victims and workers vary. According to Levenkron (private correspondence with the author 21 December 2011),

sex-work feminists who concede that child prostitution is wrong and should be prohibited

> seem to miss . . . that in the sex trade, adults and children are . . . the same group of people at two points in time . . . If there is nothing wrong with prostitution . . . what on earth is wrong with children doing it . . .? And if something is problematic here, how does it change suddenly when she reaches seventeen years and three hundred sixty-six days old?[64]

This reality suggests that, first, the distinction between forced and non-forced prostitution is only too often a matter of degree;[65] and, second, that the harm caused to non-victims from the phenomenon of purchasing commercial sex should be taken into account when evaluating the reasonableness of a client's purchase of commercial sex.

To be clear, the conclusion that buying sex has low social value is based on the normative assumption that prostitution in general is problematic and harmful to its participants and to women in general. As discussed in chapters 1 and 6, such a view, which is mainly associated with radical feminism, is contested, both normatively and empirically. The less exploitation of non-victims one finds, and the more 'happy hookers' exist, the less reason there is to devalue the benefit to clients and workers from buying sex, and accordingly, a finding that the activity is reasonable is more likely.

Critics of the view that prostitution is rife with exploitation often mention that prostitution is no different from other low-end jobs which poor people have to take in order to survive where conditions are exploitative and most of those doing the job would like to leave it. There are important differences, however, between prostitution and other low-end jobs. First, the fact that prostitution typically begins when the woman is under age is a factor which vitiates consent. Some would add that prior sexual abuse, to the extent it exists and which arguably led the CSP to prostitution, is likewise a vitiating factor. Second, exploitative jobs, while often involving health and safety risks, do not typically expose employees to the risk of being exposed to physical violence.[66]

almost without exception, the victims she met arrived in Israel as adults, with the purpose of working as prostitutes and without having been CSPs in their country of origin.

64 MacKinnon, id, 297–8.

65 See Huda's observation (ch1, n16) that prostitution usually satisfies the elements of trafficking.

66 Compare MacKinnon (n60) 295–6 and n16 (evidence of incomparable mortality rates of CSPs), 32 (evidence of incomparable rate of injuries including research observing that 'the women are injured far more often than workers in occupations considered the province's most dangerous, like mining, forestry and firefighting'), id, with K Ford, 'Evaluating prostitution as a human service occupation', in J Elias, V L Bullogh, V Elias, G Brewer and J Elders (eds), *Prostitution: On Whores, Hustlers, and Johns* (Amherst: Prometheus, 1998) 420, 426, 430 (orderlies were more likely to have been subject to physical violence than sex-workers but overall hospital workers are much more likely to be satisfied with their work than sex-workers).

Similarly, not many exploitive jobs subject the employee to degrading requests by clients such as those faced by CSPs. Lastly, while exit from all exploitative jobs is limited due to economic pressures, in prostitution the exit is further limited by threats of violence from pimps, drug addiction, social stigma and propensity to self-destruction.

The argument defended here – that clients who ignore the risk that indiscriminate demand contributes to victims' trafficking should be liable in negligence – could be supported also by those who do not share the belief that purchasing commercial sex has *no* value. It is sufficient to concede that the purchase of commercial sex has low social value. This view enables the possibility of limiting tort liability of clients towards victims, without *necessarily* extending it towards non-victims. The argument for negligence-based liability is not based on the assumption that the purchase of commercial sex is or should be criminally prohibited, although of course it is compatible with such a view. A given activity could be non-criminal and yet have low value. Therefore, a finding that the activity is low valued could lead to a conclusion that the behaviour is negligent even though it is not criminal. This distinction in a sense echoes Guido Calabresi's distinction between specific deterrence (criminal prohibition) and general, market, deterrence (tort liability).[67] Not all conduct leading to liability in negligence (or in torts) does or should lead to criminal responsibility.

Of course, in countries in which buying prostitution is illegal (and the same should be true where buying and selling is illegal, since the claimant is forced to prostitute herself) the conclusion that buying sex is negligent is self-evident (although the question of whether there should be civil liability for such violation is not). In England, making or promising payment for the sexual services of a prostitute who is forced has been rendered criminal by s 53A of the Criminal Offences Act 2003, regardless of whether the client was, or ought to have been, aware that the prostitute was forced. This provision is not directly determinative since the offence relates to attempted purchase of sex from a forced CSP and since the criminal responsibility is strict while liability for creation of demand is fault-based and is founded on an attempt to purchase sex from any CSP. However, s 53A supports the conclusion that buying sex has low social value. Criminal responsibility, even though strict, clearly conveys the conclusion that the behaviour is anti-social.[68] Moreover, the fact that the inability to know that the CSP was forced does not serve as defence and supports the proposition that it is the indiscriminate nature of the demand which makes the demand socially undesirable. Section 53A, therefore, supports a finding that indiscriminate purchase of sex has low social value and is unreasonable.

67 G Calabresi, *The Costs of Accidents* (New Haven, CT: Yale University Press, 1970) 68–9.
68 Compare Madden-Dempsey (n26) 1756–7.

Some critics of the conclusion that buying sex has low social value have suggested that commercial sex provides an outlet for male sexuality and as such reduces rape.[69] But such arguments are speculative and contested.[70] For example, perhaps the increased objectification of women due to the existence and acceptability of prostitution increases the incidence of rape in society. Moreover, from a feminist instrumentalist perspective, the availability of commercial sex reduces the bargaining power of women in long-term (or short-term) relationships. In any event, even if there is any merit in the outlet for the male sexuality argument, it goes only to establish the social value of *supplying* commercial sex, rather than of the demand for it. Surely, the argument 'if I can't go to a prostitute I will rape a (decent) woman' cannot prove that the demand for commercial sex is socially valuable.

Lastly, it is somewhat peculiar that the practice of purchasing commercial sex, which contributes to the sexual enslavement and rape of some women, is defended based on the unfounded hypothesis that it might reduce the incidence of rape of other women. At best, therefore, the instrumental argument amounts to a claim to privilege the rape of victims of forced prostitution – possibly the most vulnerable individuals in society – in order to spare local and 'normative' women. Such ethics are problematic, even when we ignore the speculative nature of the argument. To begin with, the risk of being sexually abused is so serious that conscious attempts to shift it from one group to another can hardly be justified. Therefore, an identified potential victim has a right not to be exposed to the risk, even if this means that an unidentified alternative victim might be exposed to that risk.[71] Alternatively, if channelling this risk according to distributive criteria is at all legitimate, the outlet argument leads to a regressive redistribution of the risk – exposing the most vulnerable members in society to the risk of being sexually abused in order to protect local 'normative' women – and as such is problematic.

## 7.6 Victims' vulnerability

Courts should, and do, take into account the victim's foreseeable vulnerability when evaluating the reasonableness of the risk created by the

69 See e.g. K Davis, 'The sociology of prostitution', (1937) 2 *Am Socio'l R* 744, 755. While this theory is out of favour in current scientific research, it is very much present in popular beliefs, as can be seen in talkbacks attacking abolitionist reforms. Cf N Levenkron, '"Since not everyone is good looking, so they wouldn't go and rape women in the street": reflections on policemen, prostitutes, and what's between them' (unpublished manuscript, in Hebrew) 1. The title's quote came from a Tel-Aviv policeman patrolling in the red light district and asked by a woman why the police did not crack down on brothels which are illegal.

70 M Monto, 'Why men seek out prostitutes', in R Weitzer (ed), *Sex for Sale: Prostitution, Pornography and the Sex Industry* (New York, NY: Routledge, 2000) 68.

71 Keren-Paz (n1) 125.

tortfeasor.[72] Courts can do this by either reducing the social value accorded to the risk-creating activity, since it risks the vulnerable, or viewing the magnitude of the risk as greater, if the injury is suffered by the vulnerable. This is justified, since typically, injuring the vulnerable will generate a greater disutility to them than would injuring the better-off. The valuation of reasonableness should be, and usually is, based on (intuitive) balancing of utilities rather than money. Since a loss of equal economic value will decrease more significantly the utility of the poor, vulnerability should be taken into account. Moreover, a decision to risk the vulnerable seems more despicable, and less fair, than a decision to risk the better-off.[73] Indeed, as canvassed above, vulnerability is an important factor in establishing proximity and duty which otherwise would not exist. Sensitivity to the claimant's status as vulnerable in making negligence (and liability) determinations is revealed in several common law jurisdictions, including, for example, in England and Canada: the House of Lords' decisions of *Paris v Stepney Borough Council*[74] and *Phelps v London Borough of Hillingdon*;[75] and the Canadian Supreme Court decisions of *Young v Bella*[76] and *Norberg v Wynrib*.[77] In *Paris*, the claimant's foreseeable vulnerability (having only one eye) made the litigated practice of not providing the employee with goggles a negligent one, even though exposing a two-eyed employee to the same risk might be reasonable. In *Phelps*, the vulnerability of a child with learning disabilities was a factor in determining the educational psychologist's liability towards the child. In *Young*, the power gap between the claimant, a student, and the defendant, a university professor, can account (at least partially) for both the existence of duty and the finding of negligence. In *Norberg*, the power gap between the physician and the patient and the latter's vulnerability due to her addiction were crucial for the finding of liability in a sex for painkillers deal. In Israel, the Supreme Court has endorsed in *obiter* in several cases the approach I defended elsewhere that power gaps between the parties should influence findings of negligence and damages.[78]

72 Id, ch 5. The propositions in the next sentences are discussed particularly on pages 92–101, 105–114, 123, 127–8.

73 A few cultural examples of this sentiment include the outrage commonly felt when robbers prey on old or disabled people, and the biblical poor man's lamb proverb (Samuel 2:12).

74 [1951] 1 All ER 32 (HL).

75 [2000] 4 All ER 504, 529 per Lord Nicholls.

76 *Young* (n1) [33]–[34].

77 *Norberg* (ch1, n18).

78 See CA 5604/94 *Hamed v State*, PD 58(2) 498 (2004) (per Justice Rivlin, [3]); CA 1678/01 *State v Weiss*, PD 58(5) 167 (2004) (per Justice Dorner, [8]); CA 10064/02 *Migdal v Abu Hanna*, Takdin-Elyon 2005(03) 3932 (2005), [38]–[40]; CA 89/07 *Noodelman v Sheranski* (4 August 2008), [67]; Keren-Paz (n1). See also CA 2625/02 *Nahum v Dorenbaum*, PD 58(3) 385 (2004) in which the vulnerability of the unrepresented borrower was relevant for liability of the lender's lawyer according to the alternative reasoning of the Supreme Court.

While many CSPs are vulnerable, victims of forced prostitution are particularly vulnerable. This vulnerability is twofold: background vulnerability and present vulnerability. The former is manifested in the fact that those forced into prostitution almost always come from deprived (at times extremely) socio-economic backgrounds, and are often (illegal) immigrants.[79] Present vulnerability is the result of the totality of the enslavement experience, its horrific nature and outcomes, its undignified nature, its deprivation of the victim of agency and the lack of hope it produces.

For current purposes, what matters is the background vulnerability; the vulnerability caused by trafficking merely reflects the importance of the protected interest and the extent of its violation and relates to the significance of the risk discussed above. Victims' background vulnerability bolsters the conclusion that contributing to the risk (or injury) that they would be trafficked is unreasonable. It follows, then, that the decision to purchase commercial sex, despite the risk that this would contribute to victims' trafficking, is unreasonable, partially since it risks those who are already especially vulnerable (and those who are vulnerable with respect to their ability to protect themselves from the defendant's activity).

## 7.7 Conclusion

The existing evidence suggests that the number and proportion of victims among all CSPs are significant. The former finding suggests that the risk in creating demand in the commercial sex market is significant; the latter, that relative to the benefits from the activity, the risks are unreasonable. Pursuing sexual gratification is an important and worthy human need. But it does not follow that the interest in buying sexual services has high social value, or should be legitimised, when it significantly contributes to trafficking. The fact that the activity is self-serving further suggests that it is unreasonable and the benefits it arguably confers on non-victims should not change the conclusion. If one accepts the evidence that exploitation of non-victims is rife, the consequent devaluation of the social value of buying sex further bolsters the conclusion that indiscriminate demand is unreasonable. Lastly, victims' background vulnerability reinforces this conclusion.

79 See ch5, n23.

# Chapter 8

# Causation

In chapters 6 and 7 I argued that the indiscriminate purchase of sex is unreasonable and that clients who do so owe a duty to affected victims. But to be liable in negligence the defendant's fault needs to cause the claimant's injury. As is seen below, contribution to trafficking by creating demand is almost a textbook example of conceptual and evidentiary difficulties: very little is known about the way traffickers supply victims in response to clients' demand; the litigation involves both multiple victims and multiple tortfeasors, i.e. each client contributes to the trafficking of several victims and each victim is trafficked due to the demand created by numerous clients; any individual contribution is neither necessary nor independently sufficient to cause the claimant's trafficking. In addition, it is not always clear whether the defendant contributed to the trafficking of any particular victim and the extent of any identified contribution to trafficking is always unclear. To make things worse, it is not clear whether the injury from trafficking should be considered as indivisible and what ought to be the scope of liability for contributions which are neither necessary nor independently sufficient.

Despite these formidable problems, I attempt to defend a solution which imposes liability which is fair to both victims and clients, reasonably principled and easy to litigate. The discussion focuses on the two big uncertainties which are partially evidentiary and partially normative and conceptual. One, how to determine who has factually contributed to the claimant's trafficking, and who should be considered as the legal cause of the trafficking among the big group of potential factual causes. The other uncertainty is the extent of contribution of those considered to be the legal cause of trafficking and the related appropriate scope of liability.

Section 8.1 provides a roadmap of supply and demand of prostitution in different markets and their interconnection with trafficking. Section 8.2 presents the doubts about whether the defendant has contributed to trafficking. Section 8.3 explores solutions to the problems of factual uncertainty and the appropriate scope of legal attribution. It explains why both a pure risk-based proportional liability approach and liability which is imposed only on those who had sexual contact with the victim should be rejected. It then suggests that liability should be imposed on all clients who purchased sex in the city in which the victim was exploited within a certain time frame, which is a function of the length of the victim's trafficking. Sections 8.4 and 8.5 turn from identifying those liable to the scope of liability. Section 8.4 presents the conceptual, evidentiary and normative difficulties involved in ascertaining the appropriate scope of liability. Sections 8.5 explains why neither no-liability, proportional liability, nor full liability should be adopted; it then defends the award of damages at large or a conventional award payable by each client found liable, which could revolve around a £5,000 benchmark and should accumulate.

## 8.1 Patterns of demand in non-forced and forced sex markets

### *8.1.1 The supply*

Sex services are sold, across jurisdictions, in different market segments and the prevalence of forced prostitution within these segments might vary. A theory of liability for contribution to trafficking, therefore, should begin with mapping prostitution markets and their relationship with forced prostitution. A basic distinction is between street and off-street prostitution and it is largely accepted that the latter is by far the biggest segment of the market – often estimated at around 65 per cent to 80 per cent of the market in Europe and the US.[1] Indoor markets include massage parlours, private flats, saunas, clubs, hotels, brothels and escort services.[2]

How does forced prostitution fit within this picture? First, the little evidence existing suggests that there are victims in all segments of the market, although probably the number and proportion of victims in brothels (including private flats, massage parlours and saunas) is higher than in escort services (and possibly also on the street).[3] Kelly, for example, reports that 'there is a small

1 For estimations of street prostitution in the US as around 20 per cent, see R Weitzer, 'New directions in research on prostitution', (2005) 43 *Crime, L & Soc Change* 211; J Porter and L Bonilla, 'The ecology of street prostitution', in Weitzer (ch7, n70). TAMPEP, *Sex Work in Europe* (Amsterdam: TAMPEP, 2009) 33, available at http://tampep.eu/documents/TAMPEP%202009%20European%20Mapping%20Report.pdf (accessed 18 July 2011) estimates the outdoor sector in Europe as 35 per cent and the indoor, 65 per cent. The UK Network of Sex Work Projects, *Briefing Re: Criminal Justice and Immigration Bill & Review of Demand (Paying for Sexual Services)* (London: UK Network of Sex Work Projects, 2008) estimates that 70 per cent of UK prostitution is indoors.

2 TAMPEP, id, 32; T Sanders, *Sex Work* (Cullompton: Willan Publishing, 2005) 13–20; Kara (ch3, n4) 12. In a private flat there is usually only one woman selling sexual services at a time but there might be rotation of different women at different times. See Coy *et al.* (ch5, n81) 13.

3 According to the *IOM Trafficking Database*, as analysed by Di Tommaso *et al.* (ch5 n23), 48.0 per cent of victims (n = 2,493) worked in bars/nightclubs, 11.9 per cent on the streets, 10.8 per cent in private houses/apartments, 7.2 per cent in saunas/massage parlours,

"high class" end of the market, and some trafficked women are located there, but this is not the reality for the majority'.[4] Similarly, a Poppy report suggests that 'it may be the case that women selling sex as escorts are less likely to be trafficked' and that 'women trafficked from outside the United Kingdom are rarely found on the street'.[5] However, some escorts and street CSPs are trafficked.[6]

Second, it is widely accepted that in destination countries, domestic trafficking occurs, but its incidence is negligible in comparison to transnational trafficking.[7] Third, a crucial question relates to the ways in which forced prostitution is arranged within each venue or segment: would establishments be either victim-based or victim-free or rather would there be a mix of forced and non-forced CSPs in a given establishment? The limited evidence suggests that both models (either/or and mixed) exist. Kara found, for example, that bungalow brothels in Mumbai, club or house brothels in Italy and Thai sex-establishments will always contain a mix of victims and non-victims, while massage parlours in the US are primarily filled with East Asian victims.[8] Anecdotal evidence gathered by Poppy suggests that the venues (whether closed-market or not) in which victims are exploited might include both non-forced and forced CSPs.[9]

The extent to which victims and non-victims work in the same establishment will be determined by the relationship between the traffickers who supply the victims and those who manage the sale of the sexual services ('pimps'). Trafficking occurs in many formats ranging from the small (sometimes family) business, through medium-sized networks, to sophisticated and big organised

3.6 per cent in escort/call-girl agencies, 3.2 per cent in motels, 2.4 per cent in hotels and 12.9 per cent in other venues. Cf Bettio and Nandi (ch1, n24) 26, 33 (trafficking exists in all segments of the sex industry including both upper-scale segments of the prostitution market, a 'small group' of escort girls as well as locations in bars and nightclubs, and street prostitution); Kara, id, 12–15 (observing *inter alia* that hotels are less frequently used as venues to exploit sex slaves).

4 L Kelly, *Journeys of Jeopardy: A Review of Research on Trafficking in Women and Children in Europe*, IOM Migration Research Series no 11 (Geneva: IOM, 2002) 35.

5 Dickson (ch6, n7) 27, 31.

6 Madden-Dempsey (ch6, n29) 1755–6; Aronowitz *et al.* (ch1, n15) 23, 39, 50; Bettio and Nandi (n3) 36.

7 For the UK data see p 181. Whether overall more victims of sex trafficking are trafficked internationally or domestically is less clear. The *IOM Trafficking Database* for the years 1999 to 2006 as analysed by Bettio and Nandi (n3) 23 suggests that 71.1 per cent of cases had been subject to international trafficking. Curiously, a more updated version of the same database tells a different story: 23 per cent in-country trafficking, 15 per cent transnational, 68 per cent not available. This also raises some doubts about the accuracy of the database – the number of victims trafficked internationally dropped from 3,816 in the 1999–2006 database to 2,057 in the 1999–2009 database. *IOM Trafficking Database* (ch3, n114) 7.

8 Kara (n2) 255–6.

9 Dickson (n5) 8, 16.

crime networks which might also be involved in other types of criminal activity including money laundering.[10] Networks of the latter type are likely to vertically integrate the sale of sex so that the sex establishments owned by them are likely to include only (or perhaps almost only) victims.[11] For example, a Poppy report found that 88 flats, parlours and saunas selling sex across the UK are probably operating in an organised manner as either being under the control of one organised criminal network, or an agreement between many different criminal groups to share women; the report's authors estimate that between 865 and 1,076 women were involved in these linked flats, parlours and saunas.[12]

A small trafficking business might use the victim in a private flat, sell her to traffickers controlling one or more sex establishments[13] or make the victim work in a sex establishment (say, a massage parlour) which is not homogeneously victim-populated. In such a case, the pimp would not necessarily know (or at least could theoretically be ignorant) of the fact that the CSP is forced.[14] In such cases, the profit would be divided between the brothel owner and the victim according to the regular practice (usually 50:50[15]) but the trafficker will control the victim's share.[16] There is also evidence that Romanian trafficking rings operating in Italy began leasing victims to pimps so that they were paid all the profits in the first 3 months and split the profits evenly with the pimps after this period; similar arrangements exist in India[17] and a variety of arrangements in Israel.[18]

There is ample evidence to show that it is not uncommon for victims to be exploited in more than one place, either by being sold from one trafficker to another or by being moved between different establishments controlled by the same criminal ring. This might also involve sexual exploitation in different countries.[19] There is also evidence that victims are moved between different venues. Poppy's 'Routes In' report found that the women surveyed (n = 117) were trafficked on average in three sites and in nearly two types of venue

10 Aronowitz *et al.* (n6) 21–2, 44–6; Levenkron and Dahan (ch1, n13) 33–5. The summarised case studies in Aronowitz *et al.*, while lacking sufficient details, give a weak indication as to the existence of both in-house exploitation (e.g. cases 5, 6, 15, 17, 22 at 90–1, 95–6, 98) and 'outsourcing' exploitation in brothels which are not necessarily controlled by the traffickers (e.g. cases 8, 14, 17, 18 at 92, 94, 96).

11 Aronowitz *et al.*, id, 21, 46.

12 Dickson (n5) 37.

13 Aronowitz *et al.* (n6) 21.

14 Id, 46–7.

15 Kelly (n4) 31.

16 Aronowitz *et al.* (n6) 46–7.

17 Kara (n2) 93.

18 Levenkron and Dahan (n10) 14 (describing barter, package deals, joint ownership and hiring of victims).

19 Kelly (n4) 33; Dickson (n5) 17, 39; Aronowitz *et al.* (n6) 45, 55, 91; Levenkron and Dahan, id, 14.

(n = 205).[20] That many women had experience of more than one type of sex market is a finding which is not limited to victims.[21] As discussed below, the evidence that victims (and non-victims) move between different venues is important in examining (and largely rejecting) claims by clients that 'their' demand was neither negligent nor did it contribute to the claimant's enslavement.

### 8.1.2 The demand

Clients differ significantly in the frequency and amount of sexual services they consume.[22] In fact, some distinguish between regular hard-core clients and experimenters.[23] It also appears that the majority of clients purchase sex in more than one venue. According to one research studying London clients, the vast majority (96 per cent) bought sex indoors and 36 per cent also bought sex on the street. Four out of five (81 per cent) had bought sex in more than one location.[24] According to another study, a very small number of men reported buying sex only on the street (6.6 per cent) but four times as many respondents buy sex in both street and off-street locations (25.5 per cent). Thus just under one-third (32.1 per cent) bought sex on the street.[25] While it is clear that closed markets of prostitution exist, their size and the percentage of men who buy only in closed markets are unknown. The variance in clients' demand in terms of frequency, venues, geographical scope and engagement in closed (and racialised) markets might be relevant for purposes of establishing causation and fault.

Clients' abilities – well intentioned as they might be – to rule out the possibility that the CSP is trafficked are limited. According to one Poppy report, a Soho flat recommended by a punter in PunterNet as slave-free – 'the girls here are well established pros and not East European sex slaves like in many of the other places' was in fact 'a flat in which two of the trafficked women currently housed by the POPPY Project worked in for four and two years respectively. They were both in this flat in the time period this field report was written'.[26]

20 Stephen-Smith (ch2, n1) 17 (women worked both on street 6 per cent (n = 7) and off street 81 per cent (n = 95), in flats 51 per cent (n = 66), saunas, massage parlours/brothels 23 per cent (n = 29), as well as hotels, clubs and restaurants 6 per cent (n = 7) and lap dancing clubs 0.8 per cent (n = 1)).

21 T Sanders and R Campbell, 'Designing out vulnerability, building in respect: violence, safety and sex work policy', (2007) 58 *Brit J Soc* 1, 7.

22 M Della Giusta, M L di Tommaso, I Shima and S Strøm, 'What money buys: clients of street sex workers in the US', (2009) 41 *App Econ* 2261, 2267; Månsson (ch7, n57); Coy *et al.* (n2) 14.

23 Månsson, id.

24 Farley *et al.* (ch1, n11).

25 Coy *et al.* (n2) 13.

26 Dickson (n5) 23–4.

### 8.1.3 The interaction between demand and supply

Migration, prostitution and trafficking are explained as reflecting both push and pull factors.[27] The former are socio-economic pressures in source countries that cause people to seek migration, and in the trafficking context, to fall prey to recruitment. The latter are reasons drawing migrants (and more generally job-seekers) to the particular employment in a particular destination. In this context, the client and his preferences form part of the pull factors, drawing usually individuals with very limited options into the '3D' jobs – dirty, dangerous and demeaning. Recall that demand is socially constructed; indeed, Donna Hughes has stressed the contribution of culture and those profiting from the demand – apart from individual acts of consumption by clients – to its creation. Culture socially constructs the understanding of both men's demand for commercial sex and women's willingness to engage in prostitution as 'natural'; several actors encourage the demand and profit from it either illegally, such as traffickers, or otherwise, such as source and destination states.[28] But whether the contribution of others to the creation of demand should lead to legal or moral obligation to victims is not addressed here,[29] and in any event should not undermine the legal liability of clients for the creation of demand, if otherwise defensible.

The relationship between demand and supply is complex. 'Classical economists have argued that the supply of a product alone creates its own demand'.[30] The possibility that the demand for sexual services is, at least partially, supply-driven was raised by several researchers, some of whom view this interaction as an argument against imposition of criminal liability on clients. Anderson and O'Connell Davidson in their pilot study examining whether trafficking is a demand-led problem, mention both that in general 'a supply of workers who are willing or forced to undertake certain tasks or provide certain services can generate demand for such labour/services rather than *vice versa*' and that it is not clear that:

> demand for cheap and vulnerable sex workers . . . acts as a stimulus for trafficking. It could equally be that a supply of cheap workers stimulates demand. In some places, the growing presence of migrant sex workers over the past decade is believed to have led to a fall in the price of both street and off-street prostitution. It could well be that as a result, more men are buying sex and/or that established clients are buying sex more frequently.[31]

27 Anderson and O'Connell Davidson (ch7, n48) 22–3.

28 See D Hughes, *The Demand for Victims of Sex Trafficking* (Kingston, RI: University of Rhode Island, 2005), available at www.uri.edu/artsci/wms/hughes/demand_for_victims.pdf (accessed 15 August 2012).

29 See Keren-Paz (ch1, n39).

30 Kara (n2) 270.

31 Anderson and O'Connell Davidson (n27) 22, 32.

Similar conclusions were reached by Kara, according to whom the use of slaves in the sex industry allows the reduction of price, which in turn increases clients' demand. Kara found that the demand for sexual services is highly elastic; this suggests that demand for sex services has increased as a result of the increased use of slaves. Kara procured 'tangible evidence' that the average price of a sex act was decreasing over time as a direct result of the increased use of slaves: 'as prices in some parts of Asia and Europe dropped by half, new customers entered the market'. 'The price of a sex act for apartment and street prostitution is typically 25 to 30 percent lower than it is in a club brothel, and for the same reason, these slaves typically perform more sex acts per day'.[32]

Poppy's 'Sex in the City' report notes the difficulties in deciphering the ways supply and demand interplay in explaining the fact that the sex industry in London is now mainly populated by non-British national women. 'The question is whether demand for women who are racially different to the dominant culture has contributed or led to trafficking of non-British national women into the sex industry'. If such demand does not exist:

> then has the ethnic profile of London's sex industry come about because traffickers and pimps are using the most profitable source of women? If so, do British men buy sex with non-British nationals simply because they are available? [While] it is difficult to respond to such questions from this research project . . . it seems that many men buy sex particularly with women from particular racial or ethnic backgrounds because they believe that the racial stereotyping used to advertise women, and women's vulnerability is definitely part of this.[33]

More broadly, other researchers highlight the social context affecting the interaction between supply and demand in which the use of sex, in particular the female body form in advertising, has produced an increasing acceptance for men to pursue these desires.[34]

Naturally, due to the clandestine and illicit nature of the trafficking industry, there is very little evidence on the ways in which trafficking rings respond to demand in general and to ethnicity-led demand in particular. Kara reports in his study that 'sophisticated market assessments [were] made

32 Kara (n2) 33–7, 89, 255. The findings of Sanders (ch1, n35) 37 with respect to the English market are somewhat different and suggest a steep difference in average price between indoor (£123 for a visit as gleaned from clients' reports on PunterNet) and outdoor markets (£10–£20).

33 Dickson (n5) 52.

34 E Bernstein, 'The meaning of the purchase: desire, demand and the commerce of sex', (2001) 2 *Ethnography* 389.

regarding which ethnicity was demanded in certain brothels in certain countries . . . then receive orders from brothels owners across Europe for more Russian slaves'.[35] The above account suggests the inter-relationship of demand and supply. The initial indiscriminate demand for prostitution causes some women to be trafficked; this in turn reduces prices which in turn increases the demand. Presumably, this cycle continues so that the increased demand leads to more victims (and workers) being recruited to satisfy (and further increase?) the demand.

## 8.2 Difficulties in identifying causation

A client's consumption of sex could be a cause of a victim's trafficking only to the extent that the trafficker takes it into account in his decision to recruit, transport and exploit a victim in prostitution. The consumption is a mediated cause of trafficking, and it is mediated by traffickers' decisions. In general, current patterns of consumption create in the minds of traffickers anticipation of future demand; this anticipation, in turn, is the cause of recruitment of victims, and their initial and subsequent transport to specific sites of exploitation. Victims' continued exploitation is also caused by the contemporary demand at the site of exploitation.

The chain of trafficking includes recruitment, transition and exploitation. The victim might be exploited in more than one locality and more than one market segment. During the period of exploitation, she might, or might not, be sold from one trafficker (or trafficking ring) to another. A client's consumption might contribute to just one link in the chain of the claimant's trafficking, to some, or to all. The question of attribution (whether liability should be imposed and to what extent) should be distinguished from the question of causation. In order to contribute to the claimant's trafficking, the defendant's consumption should be in an area to which the trafficker supplies, within a certain time limit and, possibly, of a certain type. After examining the difficulties in identifying factual contribution along these lines in sections 8.2.1–8.2.3, this section concludes by rejecting two claims intending to establish the absence of legal causation between the consumption of sex and the claimant's injury from trafficking.

### *8.2.1 Traffickers' geographical boundaries*

To be a cause, the act of consumption needs to be in markets to which the trafficker is capable of supplying directly or indirectly. Consider a hypothetical trafficker who is insistent that his victims will be exploited only in Europe, and is capable of making sure his victims would not be sold outside

35 Kara (n2) 11.

Europe.[36] The cause of trafficking of all this trafficker's victims is the combined demand for commercial sex in Europe. In contrast, the demand outside Europe is not a cause of any of his victims being trafficked, since such demand did not serve as a reason for the recruitment, transport and exploitation of its victims. But care needs to be taken not to reach too quickly an erroneous conclusion about lack of causation. For the right amount of money, most, if not all, trafficking rings will happily sell the victim for exploitation in another venue, even if that ring does not operate in that market. Since a victim recruited in the Ukraine for the initial purpose of being exploited in Italy might end up being exploited in the US, UK, Turkey or Israel, the demand in these (as well as other countries) might have contributed to her trafficking experience.

#### *8.2.1.1 Determining causation in a chain of trafficking*

Kara's findings illustrate the difficulties in ascertaining causation between demand for prostitution and trafficking. Kara found in one site of inquiry a two-step process of movement from rural areas in Russia from which victims were recruited to a Russian urban centre followed by the international transportation of selected victims. The second stage was the product of sophisticated market assessments regarding which ethnicity was demanded in certain brothels or certain countries.[37] Let us assume that the victim spent 6 months in a Moscow brothel and following market assessment was sent to London. Is the London demand responsible only for the period of exploitation in London or also for the recruitment and exploitation in Moscow? Does it matter whether the market assessment was based on demand occurring before the victim was recruited or between her recruitment and the date in which the traffickers decided to send her to London? Arguably, 'London demand' relied upon to transport the victim to London which preceded the recruitment could be considered as the cause of recruitment while demand subsequent to the recruitment could not.

However, one could make two arguments against such a conclusion. First, if at the time of recruitment the traffickers did not know that the victim would be transported to London,[38] could it really be said that the London demand was the cause of the victim's enslavement? The alternative potential causes would be: (a) merely the domestic demand; (b) the total international demand; or (c) the total domestic and international demand. Second, in all likelihood, the market assessment whose result is the transport of the victim to London is based on demand which both preceded the recruitment and was subsequent

36 This would usually mean that the brothels are vertically integrated within the same organisation which recruits and transports victims.

37 Kara (n2) 11.

38 Kara's description suggests that the market assessment occurs after the victim arrives at the domestic urban centre.

to it. Accordingly, the London demand, alongside the domestic demand and probably alongside the other international demand, is the cause of the initial enslavement.

#### *8.2.1.2 Traffickers' business model 1: responding to general demand*

Kara's findings fall into what I term a general demand model in which the trafficker first recruits the victim under the expectation (which is later confirmed) that the total demand existing for prostitution will allow him to transport victims to the most profitable venue. Under this model, it is the total demand for prostitution to which the trafficker was willing to respond and capable of responding that is the cause of trafficking, regardless of the specific place to which the victim was eventually sent.

It follows that the trafficker's anticipation that there would be demand for the victim's services in foreign brothels could be considered as the cause of the victim's enslavement, despite the fact that at the time of recruitment the final destination of that victim was unknown. According to the general demand model, the demand in Israel and Germany for Russian women apparently materially contributed to the sexual exploitation of a victim in Moscow (stage 1) and London (stage 2). Should the correctness of this conclusion depend on whether the victim would have been recruited and exploited in Moscow but for the international demand? If, as a matter of fact, the stage 1 demand was sufficient for the recruitment, standard but-for analysis suggests the following. Only those contributing to the local demand (in Moscow, in our example) would be responsible for the sexual enslavement in stage 1. The clients producing the demand in London (but importantly, not those in Israel and Germany) would be responsible for the sexual enslavement at stage 2. The initial recruitment and taming process is apparently the over-determined result of the demand in Moscow (stage 1) and London (stage 2), for which, accordingly, the clients who contributed to the demand in both places should be liable.

The following qualifications apply. First, the scope of liability in cases involving multiple tortfeasors depends on whether the damage is indivisible. This point is analysed in section 8.4.1. Second, the example probably involves over-determined causation. If international demand (like domestic demand) is a sufficient cause of the recruitment, so that victims would have been recruited and sent directly to London (or other venues) had domestic demand not existed, the international demand is a pre-empted cause of the stage 1 exploitation (in addition to being an over-determined cause of recruitment). In theory, however, domestic and international demand might work cumulatively. It might be that only the expectation of profits from both stages 1 and 2 make the operation of the business profitable so that without either domestic or international demand victims would not be enslaved. In that case each demand is a but-for cause of the entire period of enslavement and the international demand is not a pre-empted cause of the stage 1 period of exploitation.

It might also be that the overall length of the exploitation period increased due to the combined effect of domestic and international demand. Assume that the victim would have been enslaved even if only one kind of demand had existed but in that case her period of exploitation would have been only 10 months (either wholly in Russia, or wholly in London) while in effect it endured 15 months (6 months in Russia and 9 months in London). This scenario necessitates a decision whether the total demand in each city is responsible for the entire 15-month period of exploitation, for the actual length of exploitation in each city or (based on the understanding of the damage as both divisible and over-determined) for 10 months with an overlapping period of 5 months for which the claimant cannot doubly recover.

#### *8.2.1.3 Traffickers' business model 2: responding to specific demand*

The general demand model under which the traffickers, reported by Kara, operated is not the only *modus operandi*. Traffickers might work under a specific demand model, under which they respond only to demand in a specific place. The Hungarian ring which trafficked Hungarian women to the Netherlands and the women who trafficked Mexican girls into the US[39] seem to have responded only to the domestic demand in the Netherlands and US respectively, so the demand for commercial sex in the UK or India does not seem to have contributed to the trafficking of their victims. But even here caution is warranted. For example, the Hungarian ring (ten to 15 men) might have also been involved in trafficking Hungarian women to other places but this fact would not be easily detected by the Dutch authorities which exposed its operation in the Netherlands. Another difficulty is the need to identify the relevant market at the domestic level. Was it the demand in San Antonio, Texas, the US South, or the US which led to the trafficking of the Mexican victims to San Antonio?

The conclusion thus far is that if victims are recruited with only a specific venue in mind, or as a response to a specific demand-led request from the retailer end in the trafficking chain, then probably it is only the demand in that venue which is the cause of trafficking. The following clarifications are in order. First, as just illustrated by the Mexican–San Antonio case study, 'specific venue in mind' might vary greatly in terms of geographical coverage. The relevant causative demand would vary accordingly. Second, a victim might be recruited with the purpose of supplying the need in one place (say, London), but then be resold to another geographical area (say, Sheffield). On one account,

39 Both reported in Aronowitz *et al.* (n6) 90, 97.

the demand in Sheffield cannot be the cause of the trafficking from recruitment until the moment the victim was sold to the Sheffield trafficker.

On another account the prospect of resale of the victim, even if the specific transaction is unforeseeable at the moment of recruitment, is just one example of general demand which is the cause of the victim having been trafficked. This would be the prediction of conventional income theory within financial valuation according to which an asset's value is based on the present value of the future income streams expected from the asset under consideration.[40] This means that the total pay-off from enslaving a victim includes also a component attributable to future sales of victims to markets to which the recruiter (and his immediate associates) does not directly supply. This conclusion holds true, even in cases in which the retailer pimp to whom the victim was sold initially is not vertically integrated in the business of the traffickers who recruited and transported the victim. The victim's price is increased by the opportunity to resell her further. The conclusion is evidently correct when the retailer pimp is so integrated since in that case it can be said that the post-resale venue is part of the market whose demand is causative to the recruitment decisions.

### *8.2.2 Time limits: past consumption creates anticipated demand*

In order to be a cause, the act of consumption should be made within a certain time bracket. If it is too recent it could not have influenced the trafficker's decision to recruit the victim or send her to that particular venue; if it is too remote in time, (say, 30 years ago) it is likewise not likely to have influenced the trafficker's decision.

Consider future and cyclical demand first. In theory, future acts of consumption which confirm traffickers' anticipation that there would be future demand could be considered as causes of recruitment. So the client who purchased sex for the first time from the claimant could be the cause of her recruitment, since the victim was recruited and sent to the site in order to meet also this client's demand. On my account, the factual cause for this victim's recruitment is the past acts of consumption in that city, which gave rise to traffickers' anticipation that there would be future demand in that place. However, as explained below,[41] the indivisible nature of the injury from trafficking, and the fact that demand contributes to recruitment, to the transport of victims to the sites of exploitation and to the continuation of their exploitation in these sites, enables, ultimately, to hold the client in our example liable to the victim for her injury from trafficking (which includes also the injury from the recruitment).

40 J Hitchner, *Financial Valuation*, 2nd edn (Hoboken, NJ: John Wiley & Sons, 2006) 107–26.

41 pp 223–5.

Demand for prostitution during football World Cups is an apposite example. It is well documented that the increased demand for commercial sex during World Cups is met by an increased supply of CSPs. It is equally known that the arrival of CSPs at the World Cup venue largely precedes the commencement of the event.[42] It is clear that the decision of any trafficker to send a victim to the venue is caused by the anticipated future demand. The pattern of past increased cyclical demand in certain venues (which created the traffickers' expectation) is the cause of the decision to transport victims to the specific venue. However, according to common wisdom, the cause of recruiting victims to meet the 2006 World Cup demand or transport victims already recruited to Germany is *not* the consumption of sex in the 2006 World Cup itself (which confirmed the traffickers' expectation for consumption of sex was formed based on cyclical demand in previous World Cups). Accordingly, the demand for CSPs in World Cups in the past (say, between 1990 and 2002) is the cause for the transport of CSPs to Germany in 2006.

As the World Cup example demonstrates, an act of consumption might *not* be the cause of future recruitment because it is too dated (and not only because it is too recent). The assumed increased demand for commercial sex during the 1934 World Cup in Italy is not a factual cause of trafficking in anticipation of the 2006 World Cup, to the extent that traffickers' market assessments were not based on that increase. Contemporary traffickers are not likely to rely on 1934 data in making market assessments for two reasons; first, they are not likely to know the pattern of demand in 1934; second, the relevance of patterns of demand diminishes as time passes due to changing market conditions (e.g. average purchasing power and likelihood of travelling) and societal attitudes (e.g. acceptability of buying sex).

A few clarifications are in order. First, sex-work feminists and abolitionists debate whether the number of victims among all CSPs in these events is significant.[43] My point here is not to argue that it is. Rather the point is to clarify the temporal boundaries on patterns of consumption as causes of trafficking. Second, there is the issue of displacement versus fresh recruitment. The anticipated demand for commercial sex in the 2006 World Cup is the

42 Council of the European Union, German Delegation, *Experience Report on Human Trafficking for the Purpose of Sexual Exploitation and Forced Prostitution in Connection with the 2006 Football World Cup in Germany*, 19 January 2007, No. 5006/1/07 (Brussels: Council of the European Union, 2007) 4 ('*Experience Report*').

43 The *Experience Report*, id, 5, did not find 'significant increase' in the number of illegal stays in connection with the practice of prostitution but did find that five cases of human trafficking 'were assumed to have a direct link to the 2006 World Cup'. For an argument that the Germany 2006 event did not increase trafficking, see J Hennig, S Craggs, F Larsson and F Laczko, *Trafficking in Human Beings and the 2006 World Cup in Germany* (Geneva: IOM, 2006). For comparable debate with respect to the 2010 South African event, see M Mannak, 'Will soccer world cup attract human traffickers?', IPS News, 27 May 2010, available at http://ipsnews.net/africa/nota.asp?idnews=51605 (accessed 9 August 2011).

cause of the displacement of non-victims and victims from other countries to Germany and for the recruitment and transport of new victims. With respect to displaced victims, the 2006 World Cup demand is possibly the cause of the continuation of the trafficking experience, a point which is explored further below. Moreover, it might be that the decision to recruit victims is based on some anticipated average demand, and this average includes cyclical demand. In that case, past cyclical demand which gave rise to such anticipation could be the cause, which is probably over-determined, of victims recruited prior to the event, exploited elsewhere and then displaced to the venue immediately before the event begins. And of course, the past cyclical demand is the cause of trafficking of victims who were recruited specifically in order to meet this demand.

### *8.2.3 Special types of consumption*

#### *8.2.3.1 Demand in closed markets*

Seemingly, clients who have an exclusive ethnic preference cannot contribute to trafficking of victims from other ethnicities, so, for example, clients in London who buy sex only from Chinese women cannot contribute to trafficking of victims from Russia, since traffickers in Russia cannot hope to profit from supplying non-Chinese victims to this market. But a few factors complicate this conclusion. To begin with, the extent of a given client's contribution to trafficking is the result of his total consumption. Moreover, recall that acts of consumption are causative to recruitment and transport decisions by traffickers through their influence on traffickers' market analysis decisions. So if the Russian trafficker fails to know of the existence of such exclusive preference, and his market analysis is (erroneously) based only on an estimation of the general demand in London for prostitution, the consumption of sexual services from a Chinese woman might cause the trafficking of Russian women into London in order to satisfy this general demand.

Traffickers will find it hard to know whether the purchase of sexual services from Chinese women in London is simply the result of these women happening to be there (so that the client does not have any ethnic preference), of a preference for Chinese women which is not absolute (so the client prefers Chinese women but will diversify) or of an exclusive preference for Chinese women which is not likely to change. Only the last option renders the transport of non-Chinese women futile. Moreover, before a clear pattern of consumption is established, not even sophisticated and well-informed traffickers can know to which category the consumption from a Chinese CSP should be classified. Consider a client who bought sex only once, and it happened to be from a Chinese CSP. His consumption contributed to the specific demand in London, but it is impossible to know whether, if inclined to buy sex again, he will do so only, or preferably, from a Chinese CSP.

Therefore, a pattern of exclusively buying sex from victims from a specific ethnic origin could be ruled out as a cause for trafficking of women from other ethnicities only if that pattern is known to all the relevant trafficking rings supplying to that venue. Only then can we be sure that the trafficking of the victims from other ethnic origins did not come as a response to that demand and therefore the ethnic-specific demand is not the cause of trafficking of women from other ethnicities to that venue.[44]

### *8.2.3.2 Demand in different market segments*

The analysis with respect to market segments demand is similar to that of closed markets with the important distinction that for the victim, a move from one segment to the other is possible, unlike a change of ethnicity. Therefore, the likelihood that the demand in one segment did not contribute to trafficking in another segment is even less likely to be true. To rule out factual causation between consumption of sex and trafficking of victims, the client needs to buy sex only in a market segment which is victim-free. The problem is that there is no such segment. As seen in section 8.1, while the likelihood that a CSP will be a victim might be lower in the escort segment, there are documented cases of employing victims as escorts. Moreover, evidence suggests that all CSPs, including, crucially, victims, shift between different market segments. This means that demand for escorts might contribute to victims being exploited in other market segments.

Research on clients suggests that many of them buy in different market segments. A client who buys sex from both escorts and CSPs in brothels obviously contributes to trafficking in both sectors. But even a client who buys sex only from escorts might contribute to victims having been trafficked in brothels. First, victims might be moved from brothels to escort services or be sent directly to these services in order to meet the demand. Second, if non-victims shift from brothels to escort services to meet this demand, victims might replace them in brothels in order to meet the demand for sex bought in brothels. Lastly, similarly to the analysis made with respect to closed markets, traffickers' market assessments might be based on the total demand within a geographical unit, without heed to its market segment breakdown. After all, whether a victim would be exploited as an escort partially depends on the training she will receive by the retailer-pimp at the end of the chain of trafficking. It is possible, therefore, that the trafficker decides how many victims to send to a given venue based on the total demand at a specific place, rather than on the market segment breakdown.

44 The trafficker's mistake of not knowing about the exclusivity of the client's preference should not sever the legal causation. The mistake is created due to the client's behaviour. Part of the risk which is inherent in buying sex is that the preferences of the client would not be well understood.

That presumably the proportion of victims to all CSPs is lower in the escort sector than in brothels is relevant to the extent of contribution to trafficking, not to its mere existence. A client who buys sex only (or mainly) from escorts contributes less to trafficking than a client with the reverse pattern of consumption. This involves evidentiary uncertainty about the *extent* of the contribution rather than to its *existence*, and as discussed in chapter 7, might cast doubt on the conclusion that the consumption was unreasonable.

Segment demand might intersect with local demand so that in theory, a certain market segment at a certain locality might be victim-free. It might be that escort services in Stoke are victim-free. But even a client who consumes only escort services in Stoke might contribute to trafficking if its contribution to the general demand in Stoke is taken into account by traffickers in deciding how many victims to send there. Only if all the relevant traffickers do not take his consumption into account can it be said that he did not contribute to trafficking. For this to happen we need also to exclude the possibility that a victim will substitute a non-victim who displaced her activity in response to this demand.

#### *8.2.3.3 Clients' preferences with respect to the service bought*

Presumably, some services demanded are more likely to be supplied by victims, if such services are considered as risky or unwelcome, since victims have less ability to refuse such demands. It is well documented, for example, that victims are pressured by traffickers to provide sexual services without protection.[45] This suggests that clients who consume unprotected sex contribute more to the demand for victims than clients without such a preference. But this again goes only to the extent of contribution rather than to its existence. Clients preferring protected sex still contribute to trafficking since traffickers still respond to their demand. Demand for unprotected sex does not translate into two isolated markets in which all victims and only victims provide unprotected sex and no other CSP does. Therefore, both types of demand contribute to the supply of victims (and non-victims) to the market, although to a different extent.

### *8.2.4 Unconvincing legal causation challenges*

#### *8.2.4.1 Traffickers' response to demand is not an intervening cause*

The fact that traffickers are the immediate cause of victims' trafficking does not sever the client's responsibility. While usually the intentional conduct by a third party does amount to intervening cause, this is not the case when the

45 Aronowitz *et al.* (n6) 23.

conduct is probable, and not merely foreseeable.[46] Moreover, when what makes the defendant's behaviour a breach of duty is the prospect of the third party operating and immediately harming the claimant, the third party's behaviour is not an intervening cause. For this reason, the intentional behaviour of the prisoner who committed suicide in *Reeves*,[47] of the fleeing inmates from youth borstal in *Home Office v Dorset Yacht*[48] and of the burglar in *Stansbie v Troman*[49] did not break the chain of causation between the defendants' negligence and the claimants' damage. It was the defendants' duty to act reasonably in order to reduce the risk of the inmate's suicide attempt in *Reeves*, the running away of the inmates in *Dorset Yacht* and the burglary in *Stansbie* (in the last case, by the contractors locking the house).

What makes the creation of indiscriminate demand a breach of a victim's right is exactly the risk that victims will be trafficked by traffickers in order to respond to that demand. Arguably, the trafficker's response is even less deserving of being considered an intervening cause since it provides the clients with exactly what they want: a supply of women who would satisfy the demand for commercial sex. No defendant in the cases above stood to profit from the third party behaviour which was allegedly breaking the chain of causation. True, most clients would (presumably) prefer a supply of CSPs who are not forced; nonetheless, the fault in their behaviour is exactly the indifference to the fact that indiscriminate demand does cause victims to be trafficked.

### *8.2.4.2 Supply-led demand*

As documented in section 8.1, possibly, push pressures which cause women to enter prostitution (both domestically and across borders) increase demand for prostitution. Arguably, then, some women did not enter prostitution due to clients' demand and therefore the demand-based claim is doomed to fail. But the fact that supply and demand interact in intricate and complex ways fails to disestablish the causation between a client's current consumption, which might be supply-driven, and both the recruitment of new victims and the continued exploitation of existing victims. Clearly, the process in which the victim is recruited by traffickers and tamed into submission is the result of traffickers' expectation, which is confirmed *ex post*, that there would be

46 Whether, in the context of deliberate intervention, probability displaces foreseeability or manifests it is not clear. The former view is evident in Lord Reid's view in *Dorset Yacht* (ch6, n27) and Watkins LJ in *Lamb v Camden* [1981] QB 625, 647; the latter in Oliver LJ's view in *Lamb* at 644 and Lord Mackay in *Smith v Littlewoods Organisation* [1987] AC 241.

47 *Commissioner of Police of the Metropolis v Reeves* [2000] 1 AC 360.

48 See n46.

49 [1948] 2 KB 48.

demand for the victims' services. This expectation is based on patterns of past consumption. That arguably the demand is partially responsive to the supply of CSPs is not an adequate response to the victims' plight.

The client's argument seems to be that of an entrapment: had there been no supply of sexual services he would not have purchased them.[50] But this entrapment argument – if morally convincing at all – has purchase against traffickers, pimps and sex-workers; namely, against all those who voluntarily created supply that led to purchase of sex which would not have been purchased otherwise. But the fact remains that the client did purchase sex and that based on the knowledge or expectation that he would, some women were trafficked. The entrapment claim, if convincing, should be assessed with respect to the client's fault in purchasing sexual services. It does not affect the existence of causal connection between the act of consumption and the exploitation of victims.

Even if the 'supply defence' were to be accepted in principle it should still be subject to at least two significant constraints. First, the supply chain should be clean from forced prostitution. For example, a client purchasing sex after seeing a sex-worker who is pimped by someone who traffics victims, or after being exposed to an advertisement for a massage parlour in which some victims are trafficked, should be liable to victims even though his purchase was supply-driven. His demand, although supply-driven, still contributes to victims having been recruited or remaining as victims.

Second, since what is at stake is the cumulative effect of any client's purchase of sex on women having been trafficked, in order not to contribute to trafficking the entire defendant's purchase of sex needs to be supply-driven. This would not be an easy pattern to follow especially since it is true that supply and demand relate to each other in intricate ways. Let us say that the client first bought sex due to the allure of an ad for a massage parlour he has been visiting, that this parlour was coercion-free, but that later on the client patronised other parlours in which some women were trafficked. At some level, it might be true that but-for the initial exposure to the allure of victim-free commercial sex the client would not have supported trafficking-enhancing parlours. But the fact remains that his overall purchase activity did enhance trafficking. Moreover, due to the potential porous boundaries between markets (and businesses) which involve trafficking and those which do not, any purchase of sex, even if it happened to involve trafficking-free supply chains, might contribute to some women's trafficking.

50 Cf in the criminal context the institutionalised entrapment claim against the state based on the state partly sanctioning the sex markets in J Lowman and C Atchison, 'Men who buy sex: a survey in the greater Vancouver regional district', (2006) 43 *Can J of Soc and Ant* 281, 288.

## 8.3 Establishing factual and legal causation

The previous discussion showed at length that in some cases it is unclear whether the client contributed to the claimant's trafficking. In theory, the following solutions are available:

(a) Categorically denying liability due to the claimant's inability to show that the client materially contributed to the injury, or the risk of injury.
(b) Shifting the burden to each client to show he did not contribute to the claimant's trafficking.
(c) Imposing liability which is based on material contribution to the risk of injury. This acknowledges that an attempt to discern which demand was causative to the trafficking of the claimant is futile.
(d) Imposing liability on all clients who had direct contact with the claimant for their contribution to the trafficking of the claimant (and not only for the direct contact itself).
(e) Imposing liability on all clients in the route of exploitation. Such solution insists on contribution to injury, as opposed to contribution to risk, but views all those along the claimant's route of exploitation as contributing to her trafficking. This solution necessitates setting temporal and geographical boundaries.

In choosing between the possible solutions, the following considerations are relevant. First, the solution should be fair to both claimants and defendants. Second, it should be practical. Therefore, solutions which are based on unverifiable information and those necessitating high litigation and administrative costs should be discarded. Lastly, in choosing between solutions that are filtered through the previous considerations, the court (or legislature) should pay attention also to considerations of fit, and not only justification. The extent to which a rule presents a lesser deviation from existing principles or can draw a better analogy with existing principles could be taken into account by the court.

### *8.3.1 No liability*

The justice requirement seems to rule out general denial of liability. Since clients' demand does cause trafficking and is unreasonable, and since the claimant's inability to prove causation is systemic and does not involve any fault on her part, leaving her without any compensation is unfair. Indeed, the increased tendency of courts in England, the US and Israel to impose liability in cases of indeterminate causation, which is documented below, is motivated exactly by such sentiment. Moreover, the claimant's inability to prove the causation between the clients' demand and her trafficking is due not only to her traffickers' fault but also due to the clients' fault in creating indiscriminate demand for the purchase of sexual services. Liability for uncertainty, which is essentially a form of proportional liability, could therefore be justified.[51]

### *8.3.2 Reversing the burden of proof*

Reversing the burden of proof is both somewhat problematic on grounds of justice and not very practical. As for justice, clients are not likely to know more than the victim whether their sex consumption contributed to the claimant's trafficking. They do not know the traffickers' business plan, the way prostitution and trafficking markets are organised and the consumption patterns of other clients who might influence traffickers' decisions about recruitment and transfer of victims. To the extent that reversal of burden is generally justified by the defendant's better access to relevant information and providing incentive to reveal that information to the court,[52] this justification fails to support a reversal of burden. Given the practical inability to reverse the burden in many circumstances, arguably reversing the burden casts the net of liability too wide: clients from cities and indeed countries in which the claimant was not exploited could be sued based on the assumption that the traffickers were responding to general demand. Indeed, if the logic behind reversing the burden is taken to the extreme, any client could be sued by any victim for buying sex, if the traffickers' business model is not known to the client (as is likely), since in theory, the trafficker might have responded to demand from all over the world.

Such acute indeterminacy is even exacerbated due to an absence of clear temporal boundaries. In theory, traffickers might respond to patterns of demand created a few years before the victim was recruited. Reversal of burden, then, might result in clients being liable to victims despite the fact that their consumption pattern did not in fact contribute to the claimant's trafficking. The problem of indeterminate liability in terms of time, space, number of claimants and amount[53] is exacerbated due to the fear of selective and multiple law suits. Since it is not easy to find clients, those who are found, especially if they have deep pockets, might be sued by hundreds of victims. This cannot be right.

In terms of practicality, such a broad scope of liability will either cause forum shopping, if the rule is adopted by many countries, so the problem of

51 A Porat and A Stein, *Tort Liability Under Uncertainty* (Oxford: Oxford University Press, 2001) 160–216. Note that the doctrine is yet to be adopted by courts. As will be clarified below, while all proportional liability solutions are not applicable to contribution to trafficking, they share with my suggested solution the idea that partial liability is better than none, or full.

52 Id, 97, 155–8, 165–7.

53 Cf *Ultramares* (ch6, n31) in which the fear from indeterminacy led to the denial of duty of care in the context of pure economic loss.

biased enforcement is exacerbated, or will cause some co-ordination problems in terms of private international law, since foreign victims will be able to sue clients in countries adopting such a rule. Lastly, the costs involved in adopting such a solution in terms of both justice to clients and administration of justice are unnecessary for assuring victims with compensation. A much more tailored rule, casting the net of liability much narrower, will still provide a claimant with a sufficient number of potential defendants whose involvement in her trafficking is much more certain and from whom she can recover.

### *8.3.3 Contribution to risk*

Where the defendant increased the risk that the claimant will be injured but on balance of probabilities he did not cause the injury, and there is no way to know for sure whether the injury resulted from the defendant's risk or not, courts' results diverge. In England, full liability was imposed, under the doctrine of material contribution to the risk of injury, in *McGhee v National Coal Board*,[54] *Fairchild v Glanhaven Funeral Services Ltd*[55] and in *Sienkiewicz v Greif*.[56] In the latter case, the Supreme Court, applying s 3 of the Compensation Act 2006[57] which reversed *Barker v Chorus*[58] on the point of proportional liability, made clear that such full liability in mesothelioma cases is a special rule which will not be easily expanded. In medical malpractice cases, the House of Lords refused to impose liability, either full or proportional.[59] In *Barker*, the majority viewed the liability in *McGhee* and *Fairchild* as based on the defendant's material contribution to risk, and, therefore, classified the relevant damage as divisible, leading to proportional liability. This aspect of the decision was overturned by s 3 of the Compensation Act 2006, which is limited only to mesothelioma cases. It follows then, that if liability for material contribution of risk be extended to other situations (presumably where the causative agent is identical or operates in the same way), liability, according to *Barker*, will be proportional as long as Parliament does not intervene.

54 [1973] 1 WLR 1.
55 [2002] UKHL 22.
56 [2011] UKSC 10.
57 (ch 29).
58 [2006] UKHL 20.
59 *Hotson v East Berkshire AHA* [1987] AC 750; *Wilsher v Essex AHA* [1988] AC 1074; *Gregg v Scott* [2005] UKHL 2. I discuss below the same agent requirement which is the basis for distinguishing between asbestos and loss of chance cases. The loss of chance doctrine, largely unsupported in the commonwealth, is adopted in France, Israel and some US jurisdictions. The Israeli approach to proportional liability is quite expansive but was recently put under check in CFH 4693/05 *Carmel Hospital v Malul* Tak-El (2010) (3) 2674 (Supreme Court).

In *Summers v Tice*,[60] the Californian court reversed the burden of proof, so in effect imposed full liability on two negligent hunters who both shot negligently, and one of them, who could not have been identified, injured the claimant.[61] This doctrine of alternative liability was adopted in the *Restatement* and currently appears in s 28(b) of the *Restatement (Third) of Torts*. The doctrine was applied only when all the potential causes were joined as defendants, and when each defendant acted tortiously and exposed the claimant to the risk of injury.[62]

Proportional liability for negligent exposure to risk was imposed in the innovative yet limited applied market share liability (MSL) cases.[63] The doctrine was applied almost only to the DES cases in which the products of all producers were fungible. Since all defendants were repeat players, they all caused injury to some claimants (as opposed to one of the two one-shot defendants in *Summers* who was found liable despite not causing any physical injury). The extent of total liability imposed on each defendant under MSL equals (under the non-trivial assumption of full enforcement) the expected loss his negligent behaviour causes, which is commendable from an efficiency perspective. Since (again, under full enforcement assumption) all victims are compensated in full and solvent defendants pay the total damage they caused, no more, no less, the doctrine is commendable also according to some worthy understandings of corrective justice which do not insist that the defendant compensates only his victims.[64]

Courts adopting MSL differed with respect to the definition of the relevant market, and to whether the defendant is allowed to disprove specific causation. The New York court in *Hymowitz* based liability on the national market. In Florida, *Conley*, following the Washington decision in *George*,[65] held that liability is based on the narrowest local market that could be established such as a specific pharmacy, county or state. The *George* decision was explicit that national figures can be relied upon when local figures are unavailable or unreliable.

60 199 P2d 1 (Cal, 1948).

61 The same result was achieved three years later in Canada: *Cook v Lewis* [1951] SCR 830.

62 See ch6 (n32) § 28 Comments h–j. *Doe v Baxter Healthcare Corp*, 380 F3d 399 (8th Cir, 2004); *Goldman v Johns-Manville Sales Corp*, 514 NE2d 691 (Ohio, 1987). Whether or not liability is joint and several depends on whether the relevant jurisdiction meddled with the joint and several liability rule. See *Restatement*, id, § 28 Comment n.

63 A few of the leading cases are *Sindell v Abbott Labs*, 607 P2d 924 (Cal, 1980); *Hymowitz v Elli Lilly* 539 NE 2d 1069 (1989); *Conley v Boyle Drug Co*, 570 So 2d 275 (Fla, 1990); *George v Parke-Davies*, 733 P2d 507 (Wash, 1987); *Restatement*, id, § 28 Comment p.

64 C Schroeder, 'Corrective justice and liability for increasing risks', (1990) 37 *UCLA LR* 439; D Rosenberg, 'The causal connection in mass exposure cases: a "public law" vision of the tort system', (1984) 97 *Harv LR* 851, 881–7; Porat and Stein (n51) 133–6.

65 All three cases are cited in n63.

Practical considerations, conceptual clarity and possibly also justice-based considerations militate against adopting risk-based liability for contribution to trafficking. Why full liability should be denied for creation of risk which led to trafficking is explained in section 8.5.1. Indeed, alternative liability, which leads to joint and several liability, is denied when the claimant has not joined all the possible defendants. This rule is based on the normative concern that the defendant should be given the opportunity to seek contribution. Obviously, an attempt to join all relevant contributors to trafficking, clients and traffickers alike, is hopeless.

But there are also good reasons why a general market share liability doctrine should not (or at least cannot) be adopted. First, the aetiology of trafficking is different from that of typical cases of MSL. In the latter group, the actual harm did result, or could have resulted, from the activity of only one defendant. The problem is to know whose activity – among all those who put the claimant at risk – injured the claimant. In trafficking, it is the combined effect of individual demand which caused the trafficking. So the demand was either causative – although unnecessary and independently insufficient – to the injury itself, if it contributed to traffickers' decisions along the chain of trafficking, or it did not even put the claimant at risk if the trafficker did not respond to it. Clients whose demand did not contribute to the trafficking also did not expose the claimant to the risk of being trafficked, although they did risk other victims and contributed to their trafficking. Put differently, if the clients did not contribute to the trafficking itself, they cannot be part of the relevant market for purposes of contribution to risk, at least according to the traditional understanding of the doctrine.

Consider a claimant trafficked from Moldova to London by traffickers who did not respond to North American demand and a defendant who posed demand in Toronto. It would be inappropriate to hold the defendant liable to the claimant under MSL, since the defendant did not expose the claimant to the risk of being trafficked. This relates to the question discussed above of the definition of the market. If the whole world is considered as one market, the Torontonian client whose demand did not in fact contribute to the claimant's trafficking could be considered as putting her at risk. But the big advantage of defining markets broadly in the DES litigation is absent here. The award of damages cannot reflect the expected damage caused in fact by the defendant since it is impossible to calculate the defendant's share of the market; and litigation costs could not be saved by defining the market broadly. As seen below, unlike the DES context, a sufficiently narrowly crafted injury-based liability is available as an alternative.

This leads us to the second reason for the limited applicability of the MSL to contribution to trafficking: the absence of sufficient data about the defendant's statistical contribution to the total damage. The justifications for the MSL doctrine, from both corrective justice and deterrence perspectives, are based on the ability to ascertain the relevant contribution of each defendant. When the court is able to ascertain these contributions, each defendant pays the expected loss which he, as repeat player, statistically caused, neither more, nor less. This necessitates knowledge of both the overall and the defendant's risk-creating behaviour – sales of medicine in the DES context and length of employment in *Barker*.[66] Neither figure is available in the context of commercial sex. The overall size of the market and the number of sex acts performed is unknown, and could hardly be guessed with accuracy. The defendant's level of consumption is known to the defendant himself but given the proportional character of MSL liability he has a clear incentive to lie and play down the figure and the consumption pattern is not otherwise observable or verifiable to the claimant or the court. An attempt to quantify the liability of each client will have to be merely an unfounded guess. It has been argued that in that case the deterrence and corrective justice justifications behind proportional liability significantly diminish, to the extent that liability might not be justified.[67]

The concern for accuracy also led American courts to limit the MSL doctrine to situations in which the products are fungible and, therefore, pose equivalent risks. A similar sentiment appears in several speeches in *Barker* and *Fairchild* and led to distinguishing the *Fairchild* line of cases from loss of chance cases on the basis that only in the former group was the causative agent identical or operated identically.[68] While this limiting mechanism might be accused as arbitrary, the logic behind it is that this requirement helps to ensure that liability reflects accurately the damage caused statistically by the defendant. Reasonable minds can differ on whether all acts of consuming sexual services should be considered as the same agent or not. At a high level of abstraction they are, since victims are recruited and exploited in order to satisfy all of them. But some patterns of consumption might contribute to trafficking more than others (e.g. brothels v escort services, unprotected v protected sex). Therefore, at a lower level of abstraction one might argue that the same agent requirement is not satisfied in the context of trafficking.

### 8.3.4 Direct contact as a hook

This solution casts the net of liability too tight. It uses as a proximity mechanism the direct contact between the victim and client. The direct

66 Under the assumption that mesothelioma might be caused by single exposure, *Fairchild* is an alternative liability case and *Barker* an MSL. That under *Barker* not all defendants need to be joined bolsters this conclusion. Lord Hoffmann in *Barker* (n58) [44] refers to MSL as analogous but (curiously) opined that the doctrine 'obviously has no application to injury caused by exposure to asbestos'.

67 *Malul* (n59) [31] (per Rivlin J).

68 *Restatement (Third) of Torts* (n62) § 28 Comment p; see e.g. *Skipworth v Lead Indus Ass'n*, 690 A2d 169, 173 (Pa, 1997); *Fairchild* (n55) [22] Bingham, [115] Hutton, [149], [170] Rodger; *Barker* (n58) [24] Hoffmann, [64] Scott, [114] Walker. In *Sienkiewicz* (n56) [187] Lord Brown disapproved of this distinction but Lord Phillips [104] endorsed it.

contact serves not only as a reason to compensate the victim for the single non-consensual sexual contact with the defendant client, but also as a hook on which to hinge liability for the client's contribution to the claimant's trafficking.[69] The rule has a practical advantage in that it offers a workable test for casting liability; it also has the normative advantage in that it imposes liability only on those sufficiently implicated in the wrongful behaviour. These advantages, however, come at a cost which is both conceptual and normative. Clearly, the direct contact was not causative to the victim's *recruitment* (although as will be clarified later on, this point is not determinative). Using direct contact as a hook also blurs the conceptual distinctiveness of liability for contributing to trafficking by creating demand, which is not based on the direct contact with the victim.

The most acute problem, however, is normative. This solution leaves out too many relevant contributors and distinguishes between those who are liable and those who are not, based on the morally irrelevant criterion of whether the client happened to have direct contact with the victim. The direct contact limitation effectively limits the scope of liability for contribution to trafficking, which is otherwise very broad and indeterminate. But this apparent advantage is in fact a serious drawback as it leaves all clients who did not happen to have direct contact with victims not liable. Since the risk leading to trafficking of women is imposed by all clients to whose demand the traffickers respond, and since this risk is conceptually different from the risk of having direct contact with a victim, it seems arbitrary and under-inclusive to impose demand-based liability only on those found independently liable for direct contact with the claimant. True, as long as liability is not full, the sting of this objection fades, since those found liable are not subsidising other tortfeasors.[70] Yet, that a rule exculpates most of those contributing to a given injury based on a morally irrelevant distinction out of a motivation to find a workable solution should be considered as unacceptable. The question boils down to a trade-off between justice and practical considerations. It could also be viewed as trading off different aspects of justice. A broader casting of the net will either impose liability on those not necessarily involved in contributing to the claimant's injury, or will necessitate the use of arbitrary control mechanisms which again are hard to justify in terms of principle. As the discussion immediately below clarifies, the demand in route of exploitation solution is workable, sufficiently narrow and more principled.

69 Lord Hope's dissenting view in *Gregg* (n59) [117] is based on a similar reasoning. To him, the physical injury from the delayed diagnosis of cancer justified compensating the claimant for the consequential reduction in the prospects of recovery.

70 Cf Keren-Paz (ch5, n20) 33–40.

### *8.3.5 Demand in route of exploitation*

This solution reasonably avoids imposition of liability on those whose behaviour did not contribute to the claimant's trafficking. As such it satisfies the justice criterion. Whether the trafficker responds to specific or general demand, the fact that the claimant ended up in a particular site proves that the demand in this site contributed to the victim's trafficking. The route of exploitation solution still necessitates a practical demarcation of contribution in terms of time and space and in order to be practical, the demarcation has to be somewhat arbitrary. Given lack of knowledge about traffickers' business models, it is impossible to know the cut-off point beyond which a client's demand is not causative in terms of time and space.

#### *8.3.5.1 Factual and legal causation*

The rule developed below both imposes liability in circumstances where there could be almost no doubt that the defendant factually contributed to the claimant's trafficking and denies liability, based on remoteness or proximity considerations, of defendants whose contribution, if factually existing at all, is too remote in space and time to justify liability to the claimant. Exculpating contributing defendants from liability is fair given the following three factors: (a) other defendants whose contribution to the claimant's trafficking is more direct are available to be sued; (b) exculpated defendants are likely to be sued by victims to whose trafficking they contributed more directly; and (c) litigating the contribution of exculpated defendants to the claimant's trafficking is very costly. The suggested rule shields contributing defendants from indeterminate liability to a potentially large and unknown number of claimants for a long and indeterminate period of time. It likewise protects non-contributing defendants from being erroneously found to be contributing, and hence liable. Such legal policy considerations for curtailing the scope of liability are well accepted at common law and are manifested in denial of either duty of care or legal causation due to remoteness.[71]

These reasons suggest both that a claimant should not be allowed to prove that 'shielded' defendants did in fact contribute to her trafficking and a 'captured' defendant should not be allowed to show that he did not in fact contribute to the claimant's trafficking. Clients presumed to contribute to the claimant's trafficking most probably did contribute. At the very least, they did put the claimant at risk of being trafficked and probably contributed to the trafficking of other victims. This, combined with the fact that the extent of liability is not crushing, makes the rule sufficiently just with respect to clients as well.

71 *Dorset Yacht* (n46); *Sams v Oelrich*, 717 So2d 1044 (Fla Dist Ct App, 1998); *Grover v Eli Lilly & Co*, 591 NE2d 696 (Ohio, 1992); *Ultramares* (n53); *Restatement (Third) of Torts* (n62) § 29 Comment m; Stapleton (ch6, n26).

### *8.3.5.2 Geographical limit*

Using consumption of sex in the same city as a geographical limit is a practical solution which prevents overly broad imposition of liability, although it might leave some clients who contributed to the trafficking out of the reach of liability. So a victim recruited in rural Russia and exploited in Moscow and then London will be allowed to sue all clients in these two cities she was able to indentify (within the relevant time limit explained below), but not clients from other cities. Considerations of reducing litigation costs suggest that this limitation should remain, even if the victim is able to show that the traffickers were operating under a general demand business model, so that the demand posed by clients in other cities, or countries, was causative to her recruitment. As explained above, clients in other cities are likely to be sued by victims who were exploited in their cities. So in the broader scheme of events, under the suggested rule all clients contributing to trafficking stand an equal theoretical chance to be successfully sued. In any event, it is practically impossible to calculate the exact extent of individual contributions to the claimant's trafficking (a point discussed below), and therefore liability has to be limited to damages at large falling well short from the claimant's full damage from being trafficked. This also makes the suggested cut-off point defensible. The under-inclusiveness of the rule's reach in terms of the individual claimant is fair to both victims and defendants. The former are left with an adequate number of potential defendants, with an easy-to-meet burden of proof and with reduced litigation costs; the latter are not selected in a manner which is overall under-inclusive and arbitrary, and are free from the burden of seeking contribution from other defendants.

### *8.3.5.3 Multiple sites of exploitation*

Where the claimant has been exploited in more than one city, consumption of sex in the first city occurring after the victim was moved into the second city contributed to neither recruitment nor exploitation. Therefore, if the only evidence existing against the defendant is acts of consumption after the claimant was moved, liability should be denied. But the reverse is not true; consumption in the second city occurring before the victim was transferred is an over-determined cause of recruitment and the cause of the victim's transfer from the first to the second site of exploitation and therefore should lead to liability.

### *8.3.5.4 Market segments*

The porous boundaries between different segments of the sex market make it impossible to rule out (or verify) the possibility that consumption in one market segment contributed to trafficking in another segment. The logic behind the geographical cut-off point for liability – limiting liability to those whose demand very likely contributed to the claimant's trafficking – could be applied also with respect to market segments consumption. There is more room for doubt whether buying sex from an escort contributed to a claimant's trafficking in a massage parlour than whether buying sex in a massage parlour did.

Still, even such a narrowly tailored rule should permit cross-segment suits if the claimant can prove that the market segment in which the defendant consumed sex includes victims. Consider a defendant who bought sex from an escort who was not forced herself, but in a city in which some escorts are forced, and who was sued by a victim exploited in a brothel. The defendant's consumption in the escort segment clearly contributes to trafficking in that segment. Moreover, the defendant cannot reasonably come up with evidence that his consumption in the escort segment, in which trafficking is proven to exist, did not contribute to trafficking into the brothels segment in which the claimant was exploited. Therefore, proving that exploitation exists in the escort market should suffice to allow victims from other segments to sue.

But one can reasonably support a broader rule still. Given the built-in liability curtailing elements of the suggested rule in terms of space, time and scope of liability, and the fact that the evidential gap was caused by defendants' voluntary risk-creating behaviour, a rule allowing any victim exploited in the city to sue any client consuming sex in that city would be fair, even if the evidence available about the client's consumption relates to a segment different from the one in which the claimant was exploited. The research findings that victims and non-victims often shift between segments[72] bolster this conclusion.

### *8.3.5.5 Temporal boundaries*

With respect to temporal boundaries, one workable solution is to limit liability to consumption of sex in the period beginning at a date calculated by deducting the claimant's total length of exploitation (since recruitment) from the date of recruitment and ending when her exploitation ends. To illustrate, if the claimant was trafficked for 8 months, and recruited on 1 September 2010, any demand occurring before 1 January 2010 is not causative. The logic behind this liability cut-off rule is that current acts of consumption not only prolong the trafficking of the victim already exploited in the city in which the client consumed sex, but also, by indicating future demand, necessitate the recruitment of a new victim who would substitute the existing one. Demand which is too far removed in time probably led to the trafficking of a previous victim, not the claimant. Using the length of the claimant's exploitation

72 pp 199–200 above.

period as a proxy for the estimated period in which consumption prior to recruitment was causative to the recruitment is, while inevitably arbitrary, both workable and sufficiently principled.

A reasonable alternative, yet practically inferior, cut-off point would use as a proxy the average (rather than individual) exploitation period in that city. On the plus side, this alternative is slightly more principled, since the claimant is recruited and sent to the specific venue based on traffickers' estimations which are based on average figures (and in any event, could not be based on the figures relating to claimant's future exploitation). On the other hand, using individual figures sits well with the principle that the tortfeasor takes the victim as he finds her. Claimants who were trafficked for a longer period can sue clients for a longer period of time, and presumably more of them. This individual approach then is arguably more compatible with corrective justice by taking more into account than the claimant's individual features. A second advantage is practical: finding the claimant's length of enslavement is likely to be easier than finding the average length.

I turn now to justify the flip side of the rule: that the claimant can sue clients for contemporaneous consumption, namely consumption happening after the victim was recruited and while she was at the site of exploitation. First, such consumption not only contributed to the recruitment and transfer of future victims, but also to the prolongation of the claimant's trafficking. If all demand stopped at once, the exploitation of victims would likewise stop. Especially if the injury from trafficking is understood to be indivisible, imposing liability on contemporaneous consuming clients for their contribution to the injury from the entire trafficking experience is principled, just and practicable. Such clients contributed to the victim having been trafficked; therefore, it is just that they would be held liable.

Second, linking liability for contribution to trafficking with contemporaneous consumption might be justified based on an analogy with MSL. MSL could be understood as a victim-swap scheme, in which a specific defendant 'A' pays only a part of the damages to victims he injured alone, but partially compensates victims whose injury was caused by another defendant ('B', or 'C' and so on). Eventually, each defendant pays the expected damage he caused, neither more, nor less. Similarly, each current act of consumption contributes to an unknown number of unidentified future victims to be recruited and exploited. Each victim who is currently providing sexual services to clients was recruited due to the contribution of past consumption by unknown clients. Linking liability for contribution to trafficking with contemporaneous consumption ensures that the extent of liability would respond to contributions to both exploitation and recruitment, by a conceptual time-shifting manoeuvre, similar to the victim-swap under MSL. Clients who did not cause the recruitment of the victim with their contemporaneous consumption 'pay the bill' of previous clients who did contribute to that victim's recruitment. However, they do not 'pay the bill' for their contribution to the recruitment of future victims. This bill is paid by the clients who will have contemporaneous consumption of sex from future victims.

An obvious objection to the analogy with MSL is the inability in our context to identify the exact contribution of clients to the trafficking of victims. While clients probably contribute to a different extent to victims being trafficked, the exact contribution cannot be observed.[73] But the analogy is used to solve another problem, which is distinct from the problem of quantification of damages. This problem is about imposing liability on a defendant who cannot be proven to cause the relevant injury – from recruitment – to the specific claimant but who can be proven to cause, statistically, the relevant injury to someone else.

Another objection to the validity of the analogy is that in MSL the defendant could have caused the claimant's injury; indeed, some courts hold that defendants who can prove that the claimant was not exposed to their product are not liable. Seemingly, a client who contemporaneously consumed sex from the claimant could not have been the cause of her recruitment. The objection is unconvincing for two reasons. First, the client necessarily does contribute to the continuation of the victim's trafficking (a certainty absent in the MSL context). Moreover, the client might have contributed also to the recruitment of the claimant and her transfer to the current site by prior acts of consumption which are not observable. Therefore, the analogy with MSL remains valid. Second, considerations of reducing administrative costs, promoting efficiency and giving appropriate incentives for disclosure of information all support adoption of a broad definition of the market and not allowing defendants to disprove causation. Fragmenting the market necessitates recurrent litigation on the defendants' size in the different markets. While defendants might have records about their market share in different markets, they only have incentive to provide information leading to denial of liability. Allowing defendants who posses information asymmetrically vis-à-vis claimants to disprove specific causation will therefore cause under-deterrence of defendants. Moreover, MSL is based on the logic of a move from specific to statistical proof. It is therefore incoherent (and counter-effective) to undermine this logic by allowing defendants to show that in any specific case they did not cause the damage. The doctrine's advantages in terms of deterrence and corrective justice depend on consistent application of statistical liability.

## 8.4 Extent of contribution: uncertainties

Even when a reasonably narrow group of potential defendants who contributed to the claimant's trafficking has been identified, still the appropriate scope of liability of each is not clear. I do not examine here the possibility that all clients will be considered as joint tortfeasors acting in concert. The chances of

73 See p 234 for the problem and section 8.5 for the suggested solution.

such a finding are slim. While tacit agreement is sufficient to establish common design,[74] *CBS Songs Ltd v Amstrad Consumer Electronics plc* clarified that mere foreseeability, and even knowledge, that others will act in a similar manner will not.[75] It is also hard to see how tacit agreement could exist when the defendant does not even know the identity of the other tortfeasors.[76] From a normative perspective, viewing clients as joint tortfeasors will lead to full liability of each of them to all victims of the joint tortfeasors; such a result is overkill.

It also seems that as long as *CBS* is considered as good law, the client could not be considered as a joint tortfeasor with the trafficker as either procuring or engaging in common design. In *CBS*, the refusal to hold the seller as joint tortfeasor with the infringing buyer was based on the fact that non-infringing use is possible. By a similar token, an attempt to hold the buyer-client as joint tortfeasor with the infringing seller-trafficker will be rejected based on the fact that sex is sold by both victims and non-victims. From a normative perspective, again, full liability is unjustified, as is equating clients' responsibility to trafficking with that of traffickers.

The uncertainty about the appropriate scope of liability is threefold. First, whether liability of independent tortfeasors is several or joint depends on whether the resulting injury is divisible or not.[77] As will be seen below, the answer to this question in the context of trafficking is in dispute. Second, even when the damage is indivisible it is not clear what is, and what should be, the appropriate scope of liability of defendants whose contribution is neither necessary nor independently sufficient. Lastly, if one concludes that liability should be several (whether because the damage from trafficking is found to be divisible or because one believes that liability for contributions neither necessary nor independently sufficient should be several) no yardstick exists to calculate the relative contribution of each client to the claimant's trafficking.

### *8.4.1 Is the injury from trafficking divisible?*

The answer to this question is contested. A divisible injury can be apportioned to multiple tortfeasors based on causation. If the damage is comprised of distinct

74 *Uniliver plc v Gillette (UK) Limited* [1989] RPC 583, 609.

75 [1988] AC 1013.

76 Cf J Dietrich, 'Accessorial liability in the law of torts', (2011) 31 *LS* 231, 256–8, who believes that there could be no accessory liability in negligence, despite his critique of the limited scope for accessory liability under English law. Dietrich opines (at 240–1) that there could be no accessory liability based on knowledge that the product supplied is used commonly, or even mainly, for criminal activity, nor could there be liability where it was reasonably foreseeable to the defendant that the purchaser would use the goods to assault the claimant.

77 *Barker* (n58) [31], [35]. For (US) qualification, see *Restatement (Third) of Torts: Apportionment of Liability* (2000), § 17 ('*Restatement Apportionment*').

units, it is divisible. If it is one and the same, it is indivisible. At the outset, it is important to distinguish the trafficking period and the injury it causes. The trafficking period itself, from recruitment to end of exploitation, is not the injury in itself but is rather the mode in which the victim's rights were violated and her injury came about. It is the injury only which is the subject of the indivisibility inquiry. One aspect of injury which always exists in trafficking cases is dignitary: the victim is subject to prolonged false imprisonment, numerous sexual assaults and is forced into labour. For those who did not contemplate work in the sex industry there is another indignation involved in being prostituted against their wish. A second type of injury is very common: physical and mental. The former includes venereal diseases, gynaecological problems and recurrent headaches; the latter, PTSD.[78] At first glance, these types of injury from trafficking are indivisible, since like death, blindness or a broken leg, they cannot be divided into distinct components. The victim's injury is not merely the sum of distinct units of injuries stemming from specific sexual encounters to which she did not consent. Rather, the sexual enslavement is about losses of autonomy, dignity and bodily integrity. The injury from the trafficking experience cannot be broken artificially according to, for example, the duration of the exploitation in each venue.

What stands in the way of such conclusion is the approach, prevalent in England, that cumulative diseases are divisible. Cumulative diseases (like asbestosis) are dose-related. While a threshold needs to be met in order for the disease to develop, further exposure increases the disease's severity.[79] If the overall injury from trafficking is positively correlated with the size of the total causative demand, arguably, trafficking is like a cumulative disease and hence divisible. This might mean that the extent of each client's liability will be very small since it will reflect his contribution to prolonging the victim's enslavement, or possibly, will have to be apportioned based on the number of clients who are considered as the legal cause of her trafficking (or more accurately, the proportion of the defendant's consumption to all causative consumption).[80]

But even if there are good reasons to treat cumulative diseases as divisible,[81] it is far from sure that trafficking should be treated the same. Recall that liability for contribution to trafficking is *not* based on direct contact between the client creating the demand and the claimant. It might be true that being

78 See p 175.

79 *Holtby v Brigham Cowan (Hull) Ltd* [2000] 3 All ER 421 (CA); *Sienkiewicz* (n56) [17].

80 To illustrate, if in a certain city there are 1,000 clients whose consumption pattern is identical and 20 victims, each client contributed 2 per cent of the *total* injury from trafficking. If each client is sued successfully by all victims and each pays 0.1 per cent of her damage, each client will eventually pay the total damage he caused.

81 My doubts are based on the facts that some of the disease's effects are indivisible and that such approach ignores the over-determined character of exposure before the threshold is met. For the first point, see *Dingle v Associated Newspapers* [1961] 2 QB 162, 189; for the second, *Restatement (Third) of Torts* (n62) § 27, reporter's notes to Comment d. By contrast to

trafficked for a longer period of time, or having to provide more sexual services causes more injury than a trafficking experience which is shorter in time, or involves less 'tricks'. Seemingly, then, trafficking, once 'contracted', can vary in severity and is therefore cumulative. But neither a victim's length of enslavement nor the number of direct contacts she had overall with clients is reliably connected to the size of the demand which led to her recruitment and exploitation. To be a truly dose-related condition, one needs to show that the greater the total demand which led to the victim's recruitment or exploitation in a given site (or several sites) the worse her injury is. No evidence exists, however, suggesting that if the relevant demand to which traffickers respond is doubled, the length of enslavement, or the number of clients served by the claimant is doubled as well. It might be that the traffickers' response to a doubling of demand is to increase the number of victims recruited or moved. It does not seem from the existing anecdotal evidence that victims cease to be trafficked due to lack of demand for their services. If this is true, the assumption that greater total demand leads to longer duration of trafficking is unsubstantiated. More crucially, to be considered a cumulative condition, the size of causative demand should correlate with the victim's *injury*, not merely with the length of enslavement or the harshness of its conditions. Evidence of such correlation does not exist, and given that typically the injuries caused by trafficking reflect diminishing marginal disutility from being trafficked,[82] the size of the injury is not likely to correlate with the length of enslavement or the number of clients served, and even less with the size of the causative demand.

The view that the injury from trafficking is divisible faces two other challenges. First, its understanding as a dose-related condition sits uncomfortably with the finding of any individual act of creating demand as independently insufficient. If no single abstained act of buying sex would prevent the victim from being recruited or shorten the length of her enslavement, how can it contribute to a defined stand-alone part of the injury from trafficking? Second, trafficking typically results in physical and mental conditions which are themselves indivisible. A prominent example is psychiatric injury which is both a very common condition of victims and was correctly characterised (in *obiter*) by the Court of Appeal as indivisible.[83] Other prevalent conditions such as headaches and venereal diseases are also non-cumulative and indivisible.[84]

the English approach, the Israeli Supreme Court concluded that physical injuries are essentially indivisible and therefore imposed full liability in a case involving a vicious attack by several dogs owned by different owners. *Melekh* (ch3, n134); Porat and Stein (n51) 80.

82 See p 33.

83 Cf *Dickins v 02 plc* [2008] EWCA Civ 1144, [40]–[47] (Smith LJ with whom Sedley LJ concurred).

84 Correctly understood, the last two challenges in the text are variations of the critique of viewing cumulative diseases as divisible (n81).

And yet, characterising trafficking as indivisible is not straightforward. One reason is that the justice considerations behind the classification of cumulative diseases as divisible are not wholly without merit. They prevent holding a defendant, whose contribution to the total injury was small, liable for the entire damage. Indeed, the same sentiment led the House of Lords in *Barker* to interpret the *McGhee* line of cases as based on liability for creation of risk to injury which is inherently divisible in order to achieve a result which is also fair to defendants.[85] Several justices in *Sienkiewicz* clearly disapproved of full liability of a defendant whose contribution to the overall risk (most of which was non-tortious) was small.[86]

The conclusion that the injury is indivisible could be questioned for another reason. The victim's trafficking experience, such as the length of enslavement or its conditions, is likely to affect the victim's injury, albeit in a non-linear manner. While there is no clear evidence that the total demand correlates to the victim's trafficking experience, and hence, the injury, there is no conclusive evidence ruling out such correlation. It could also be asked whether the injury could be divided according to the length of exploitation in different cities, to which the demand posed by some clients was causative while the demand posed by others was not. The problem with this view is that it is much harder, in comparison to the case of a cumulative disease, to conclude that without any specific act of demand the victim's damage would be any different. As explained above, the recruitment and exploitation of victims, including the move between sites of exploitation, are the result of the combined acts of creating demand *together*, rather than of simple aggregation of individual (usually sequential) and unrelated acts. Specifically, there is no way to tell whether and to what extent any individual act of buying sex in Birmingham led to the victim being moved to Birmingham and if so, to what extent this contributed to the victim's injury, either in Birmingham or overall.

Under the assumption, which I find unfounded, that the injury from trafficking could nevertheless be theoretically divisible according to the length of exploitation in each city, three conclusions follow. First, the recruitment and taming of the victim is the over-determined effect of the total demand from all the places to which the claimant was trafficked (or, more broadly, all places to which the claimant might have been trafficked). The brutality of the taming process with the drastic and abrupt loss of control over one's life, and the realisation of what awaits the victim contribute disproportionately to the injury from trafficking. If this is accepted, any individual client should be found liable to a significant proportion of the victim's overall losses, even if one accepts the proposition that the injury from trafficking is divisible.

85 *Barker* (n58) [40]–[43].

86 *Sienkiewicz* (n56), most notably Lord Brown [174]–[187]. See also Lord Mance [189]. Other judgments are more equivocal, see e.g. Lord Phillips [103]–[105] and Lady Hale [167].

Second, if the injury from exploitation, as distinct from recruitment, could be divided according to cities of exploitation, still, the apportioned part of the injury from the exploitation in a given city is indivisible as regards all clients who contributed to the victim's exploitation in that city.

Lastly, even if the injury from trafficking is theoretically divisible, it is still *practically* indivisible. This is clear as regards apportionment between individual clients, a point discussed in section 8.4.3. But even the simple assumption that any further move between sites increases the total injury from trafficking, a crucial assumption for the thesis that the injury could be divided according to the length of exploitation in each city is not entirely obvious. The extent of the injury from trafficking is likely to be determined by several factors: how the victim is treated by traffickers and clients, number of clients served, level of control exercised by traffickers over the range of sexual services the victim must provide and over her freedom of movement and lastly, the length of the period of enslavement. Such factors are likely to change between cities, and in theory, a move from a city in which the conditions are very harsh to a city in which the conditions are better will not necessarily increase the victim's injury. In any event, given the diversity of conditions in different cities, it is hardly accurate or fair to use the length of exploitation in each city as a sole criterion for apportionment.

### 8.4.2 Scope of liability for contributions neither necessary nor independently sufficient is unclear

Any client's negligent act of creating demand by indiscriminately purchasing sexual services is insufficient to cause alone the claimant's trafficking with its ensuing injury. Clients' demand is not only insufficient (necessary and insufficient contributions are routinely held to be the injury's legal cause), it is also unnecessary: no one client's demand is the but-for cause for any victim being trafficked. To use Richard Wright's terminology, each client's contribution is neither strongly necessary nor independently strongly sufficient.[87] It is well accepted, however, that such contribution is considered as a factual cause. In *Warren v Parkhurst*,[88] for example, the pollution by each of the 26 defendants led to (several) liability, despite the finding that no one defendant's pollution was independently sufficient for the 'fixed threshold of stench' and would not support any liability had it been alone.

A similar result was achieved by English courts in *Lambton v Mellish*,[89] which dealt with noise pollution as the result of aggregate noise level assumed

87 R Wright, 'The Ness account of natural causation: a response to criticisms', in R Goldberg (ed), *Perspectives on Causation* (Oxford: Hart Publishing, 2011) 286, 303.

88 92 NYS 725 (NY Sup Ct, 1904). For analysis of this and other cases, see R Wright, 'The grounds and extent of legal responsibility', (2003) 40 *San Diego LR* 1425, 1442–5.

89 [1894] 3 Ch 163, 165–6 (Chitty J).

to be non-tortious when examined separately. While in *Lambton* each source was necessary (but insufficient) for the infringement of right,[90] the holding clearly applies (based on *Thorpe v Brumfitt*[91]) to situations in which 'one person leaves a wheelbarrow standing on a way, that may cause no appreciable inconvenience, but if a hundred do so, that may cause a serious inconvenience'. It should be noted that the correctness of such results is accepted both by those who embrace the NESS test for causation and those opposing it.[92] According to the NESS test, to be a cause, the defendant's act or omission needs to be a necessary element in a set of conditions jointly sufficient to produce the result. According to such an analysis, if 400 men are needed to consume sex in order to have a victim trafficked and 1,000 do so, each of the 1,000 is a necessary element in any set of 400 men which is jointly sufficient to cause the trafficking.

A common objection to NESS analysis is that it creates false positives and brings about a proliferation of causes. This objection is really about legal attribution – what the appropriate scope of liability for such contribution is – and not factual causation. The questions should remain separate, and the scope of liability aspect will be discussed below. Moreover, the examples given in the literature for the undesirable proliferation of positive causes – such as adding a teaspoon of water to a flooding river – are based on an intuition comparing the *relative* negligible contribution of the defendant. Such a challenge is misconceived where

> the same flood . . . [was] caused by a million (or many more) different people all contributing a teaspoonful of water. . . Denying that any of the teaspoonfuls . . . contributed to the destruction of the property that was destroyed by the flood . . . would leave its destruction as an unexplained, non-caused miracle.[93]

There is little authority on the scope of liability where the defendant's contribution to a theoretically indivisible injury is neither necessary nor independently sufficient, but in such cases liability is probably joint and several.[94] The issue is usually raised in *dicta* in nuisance cases in which the

90 Id, 165. Chitty J considered each contribution alone to be a nuisance. However, he continued the analysis based on the assumption that each contribution alone was insufficient. Since the combined effect was a nuisance, each contribution has to be necessary as well.

91 (1872–3) Law Rep 8 Ch 650, 656.

92 E.g. Wright (n87) 303; Stevens (ch2, n53) 136–7, 142.

93 Wright (n87) 305, responding to David Fischer's example in 'Insufficient causes' (2006) 94 *U Kentucky LR* 277, 290–1. See also *Restatement (Third) of Torts* (n62) § 27 Comment I and § 36 (discussed in n102).

94 The vitality of joint and several liability: *Amici Curiae Brief* of American law professors in support of respondents, *Norfolk & Western Railway Co v Ayers*, 538 US 135 (2003), 15 August 2002, available at http://works.bepress.com/richard_wright/30 (accessed 12 January 2012) concluded that many courts have imposed in such situations joint and

damage is arguably divisible.[95] In *Woodyear v Schaefer*,[96] a river pollution case in which an injunction was issued against each polluter, the Court observed:

> One drop of poison in a person's cup, may have no injurious effect. But when a dozen, or twenty, or fifty, each put in a drop, fatal results may follow. It would not do to say that neither was to be held responsible.

Two other American cases involve multiple tortfeasors causing an indivisible injury: *Northup v Eakes*[97] and *Tidal Oil Co v Pease*.[98] In *Northup*, the emission of oil by several defendants into the river caused a fire damaging the claimant's property. One defendant was sued and found liable for the entire damage. In *Tidal Oil*, the emission of salty water into streams by several defendants caused the death of livestock which drank from the water. In both cases the courts observed that 'each [contributor] is responsible for the entire result, even though his act or neglect alone might not have caused it'.[99] Note that in these cases there was no positive finding that the defendant's contribution was insufficient (but the fact that no such finding was deemed to be required might suggest that mere contribution is sufficient to be a legal cause).[100] US

several liability while others treated (erroneously) the injury as divisible in order to impose proportionate liability. However, the cases covered in the main work referred to which supposedly stand for joint and several liability are inconclusive for the same reasons mentioned in n100 with respect to Fischer's list. See especially F Harper, F James and O Gray, *The Law of Torts*, 2nd edn, vol 4 (Boston, MA: Little Brown, 1986) 121.

It is also noteworthy that due to tort reform legislation many American jurisdictions do not impose joint and several liability for indivisible injury, see *Restatement Apportionment* (n77) § 17. As mentioned in the *Amici Curiae Brief*, id, 23 environmental and toxic torts – which bear resemblance to liability for contribution to trafficking – are two areas for which joint and several liability is maintained in many statutes otherwise dispensing with it.

95 See *Warren* (n88) which Fischer (n93) 284 analyses as imposing liability for divisible harm and indivisible injury, since once the threshold for recognising nuisance is met, each contribution increases the stench suffered by the claimant. See also Stevens's discussion (n92) at 137, of *Lambton v Mellish* (n89). Wright (n87) 304 views the damage in *Warren* as (characteristically to many nuisance cases) indivisible, based on the court's observation that no person's single contribution would 'cause any material change to the plaintiff by way of noxious smell' which he interprets as no difference in the nuisance-related harm. Similar controversy exists whether or not some types of physical injuries are theoretically divisible. See n81.

96 57 Md 1, 1881 LEXIS 2, 9–10 (Ct App MD 1881).

97 178 P 266, 268 (Okla, 1918).

98 5 P2d 389, 391 (Okla, 1931).

99 *Northup* (n97) 268; *Tidal Oil*, id, 391. While in *Tidal Oil* a new trial was ordered, Fischer (n93) at 285 reads this case as imposing liability for a contribution which is neither necessary nor independently sufficient.

100 Fischer, id, at 286 mentions other cases imposing liability 'based on possibly unnecessary and insufficient contributions' but with one possible exception these cases are less relevant for my purposes (and arguably are problematic examples of this judicial tendency)

asbestos litigation, which (fictionally) treats all related diseases as both requiring threshold of exposure and being dose-independent (and hence indivisible) does not allow defendants to avoid liability based on the ground that the plaintiff would probably have suffered the same disease from exposure to other potential defendant's products.[101]

The *Restatement (Third) of Torts* recognises that trivial contributions to over-determined harm should be excused, but its implicit position is that the excused contribution should be trivial in comparison to other *individual* contributions, rather than in comparison to the total contributions:

> The exception applies only when there are multiple sufficient causes and the tortious conduct at issue constitutes a trivial contribution to any sufficient causal set. In general, this limitation will apply when the causal contribution *of various actors* is susceptible to being compared on a common metric . . . *It may be particularly appropriate when another tortious actor's conduct is sufficient* (with background causes) to cause the harm.[102]

This interpretation is bolstered by illustration 1 in which the excused exposure was for 1 day compared to the other exposures which were each for several years.

There is no direct English authority on the scope of liability (and indeed the satisfaction of a factual causation requirement) of a defendant whose contribution is neither necessary nor independently sufficient. Here too, the more prevalent cases litigate nuisance in which the harm is (arguably) divisible.[103] But it is well established that liability for indivisible injury is

for one of two reasons. They either have only two contributors, and in such case the defendant's contribution might be necessary or sufficient (which is clearly not the case with respect to any client's contribution), or they deal with mesothelioma in which the contribution is to the risk, not the injury. Similarly, the cases on Fischer's list at 286 supposedly rejecting liability for unnecessary and insufficient contributions do not in fact clearly reject liability for such contributions. In the most relevant case, *Bockrath v Aldrich Chem Co*, 980 P 2d 398, 403 (Cal, 1999), which dealt with exposure to multiple toxins uniting to cause a disease, the Court remanded and allowed the claimant to amend his claim to include the required elements. Moreover, the quote to which Fischer refers only rules out 'an "infinitesimal" or "theoretical" part in bringing about injury, damage, or loss' but explicitly holds that 'a very minor force that does cause harm is a substantial factor'.

101 *Borel v Fibreboard Paper Prods*, 493 F2d 1076, 1094 (5th Cir, 1973); *Eagle-Picher Indus Inc v Balbos*, 604 A2d 445, 459 (Md, 1992); *Restatement (Third) of Torts* (n62) § 27, reporter's notes, Comment g; J Stapleton, 'Two causal fictions at the heart of U.S. asbestos doctrine', (2006) 122 *L Q Rev* 189.

102 *Restatement (Third) of Torts* (n62) § 36 Comment a. Emphasis added.

103 See nn 89–91.

joint and several, and *Baker v Willoughby*[104] is widely taken to adopt joint and several liability for over-determined harm.[105] Since (as demonstrated above) there is little dispute that contributions which are neither necessary nor independently sufficient but which are not trivial when compared to any other individual contribution, are factual and legal causes, legal orthodoxy suggests that when the harm is indivisible, liability is joint and several.

### *8.4.3 No yardstick for division*

The extent of the contribution by each client to the claimant's trafficking is unknown, and to a large extent unknowable. One reason is that individual apportionment should be based on dividing the client's aggregate number of sex acts bought in the relevant market by the overall consumption of sex acts in that market. Neither figure is likely to be observable to the court. It will be almost impossible for a claimant to know (and to prove) how many sex acts were bought by each client *overall*. Recall that the theory is not based on the direct contact between the client and the claimant. In theory, any victim could sue any client whose consumption contributed to her trafficking. Yet, claimants would find it practically impossible to find a client's total consumption of sexual services. Arrests (which predominantly occur on the street for kerb crawling and soliciting) give no indication of the client's overall level of consumption. Moreover, even a claimant suing a client who had a sexual encounter with her under a contribution to trafficking theory cannot know the client's overall level of consumption, although she might know about his level of consumption with her (or in the venue she inhabits). Likewise, the total number of sex acts bought by all clients is unknown as well.

The extent of contribution to the trafficking phenomenon is probably not merely a function of the intensity of demand by each client but also of its qualitative nature. For example, assuming that the escort segment is relatively victim-free compared to the brothel segment, a client who uses only or mainly escort services contributes less to the trafficking of victims than a client with the reverse pattern. If the demand for unprotected sex is more likely to be met by victims,[106] clients with such preference are likely to contribute more to trafficking than clients without such a preference. Clients with a specific ethnic preference are likely to contribute more to the trafficking of women from that ethnicity than clients without such a preference, and so on. Therefore, there is no reliable way to try and estimate the client's relative contribution to trafficking for purposes of apportionment.

104 [1970] AC 467.

105 Stevens (n92) 139 is a notable exception based on his different interpretation of the facts.

106 See Aronowitz *et al.* (n45).

## 8.5 Scope of liability

The possible solutions to the difficulty in ascertaining the extent of a defendant's contribution to the claimant's injury range from rejecting the claim for failing to prove damage to imposing full (joint and several) liability on each client found liable. Three intermediate solutions are several liability, damages at large or the obligation to pay a conventional award. For reasons explained in section 8.3, rejection of liability is unjust; for reasons explained in section 8.4, an exact apportionment exercise is impossible. The choices are therefore full liability, damages at large, which are based on the court's best estimation (read guess) of the defendant's contribution, or a conventional award which is the payment of a uniform amount.

### *8.5.1 Full liability?*

Full liability is too harsh for the following reasons. First, full liability means that in legal terms the liability of each individual client equals that of the trafficker. This does not seem to be right: the client's contribution to the trafficking is mediated by the trafficker's actions; while the trafficker is implicated directly, the client is implicated indirectly. The client's level of fault is much lower than the trafficker's since the demand might be met by (and the direct contact might be with) non-forced CSPs. Recall that some dispute that the client's behaviour amounts to unreasonable behaviour at all. Even though I believe the behaviour to be unreasonable, the client's level of fault is quite different from the intentional enslavement of victims by traffickers. The client's contribution is also neither necessary nor independently sufficient for the trafficking to occur.

Second, the client has a very limited chance of recovering contribution from other responsible tortfeasors. The client is unlikely to recover a judgment from the trafficker, and to identify all the other responsible clients. While the point of joint and several liability is to shift the risk of insolvency from the victim to the tortfeasor, a result that a peripheral party is responsible for the entire damages is troubling.[107] Third, due to the dynamics of the market, full liability might mean that each client will be liable to numerous victims. This remains true even when the control mechanisms discussed in section 8.3 are operative, so full liability is both potentially oppressive (especially given the low level of fault involved) and indeterminate. In big cities, there might be numerous victims who will all be able to sue a given client but the exact number of potential claimants is unknown. A related problem is the

107 Cf Stapleton (n71). This perceived unfairness is partially behind the reforms to joint and several liability documented as tracks C–E in the *Restatement Apportionment* (n77) and in particular track C, which reallocates pro-rata the shares of insolvent defendants to all other parties (including the claimant) according to comparative responsibility.

existence of deep pocket and/or high profile defendants to whom many claims will be channelled, without the defendant effectively being able to sue for contribution.

### 8.5.2 Damages at large

Where the extent of the contribution to an injury which is theoretically divisible is unknown, English courts tend to apportion the damage – whether or not all the contributions are tortious – by using a broad brush common sense approach and avoid accepting or rejecting the claim in full based on the burden of proof. In doing so they make the best estimate they can in light of the evidence and make the fullest allowances in favour of the plaintiffs for the uncertainties known to be involved in any apportionment.[108] The approach in the *Restatement* is similar, at least with respect to damage caused partially by innocent exposure. While US courts are split as to the bearer of the burden of proof,

> the preferred approach is to employ a modest threshold for the party with the burden of proof to satisfy the burden of production on the magnitude of harm . . . mak[ing] a causal apportionment . . . is preferable to making whichever party bears the burden of proof bear the entirety of the loss.[109]

When a divisible damage was caused by multiple tortfeasors and the extent of each tortfeasor's contribution is unknown, US courts largely shifted to imposing the burden of proof on the defendant to show his share, so in effect liability is joint and several.[110] There is limited support in some US jurisdictions for a per capita apportionment rule when evidence does not permit apportionment among the tortfeasors according to causal contribution to the harm which is theoretically divisible.[111]

As seen in section 8.4, at the very least trafficking cannot be viewed as a purely theoretically divisible injury, due to over-determined causation with

108 *Holtby* (n79) [20], [21], [37]; *Thompson v Smiths Shiprepairers* [1984] 1 QB 405, 443G; *Allen v British Rail Engineering* [2001] EWCA Civ 242. The pro-claimant approach was evident in *Holtby*, in which the trial court reduced merely 25 per cent of the general damages to reflect a 50 per cent period (which was in fact longer) in which the claimant was working for other employers, which presumably contributed equally to the progression of his asbestosis.

109 *Restatement (Third) of Torts* (n62) § 28 Comment d(2).

110 Id, § 28 Comment d(1). See also *Restatement Apportionment* (n77) § 26 Comment h; Harper *et al.* (n94), vol 3, § 10.1, 25–9.

111 *Loui v Oakely*, 438 P 2d 393 (Haw, 1968); *Campione v Soden*, 695 A 2d 1364 (NJ, 1997). As mentioned by the reporters of the *Restatement Apportionment*, id, § 26 Comment h, commentators (including Keeton and Prosser writing separately) generally favour this approach; the *Restatement* does not expressly endorse this view due to sparse judicial support.

respect to recruitment as well as for other reasons. This suggests that liability should be neither purely several nor purely full but rather *sui generis*. For reasons discussed above, full liability is too harsh. However, a mechanical attempt to apportion the defendant's liability according to the estimated number of clients who legally contributed to the claimant's trafficking, or even more correctly according to the estimated relative weight of the defendant's consumption out of all the causative consumption, is not only impractical but also unprincipled and unjust. It is unprincipled, since such apportionment does not fit well with the findings that clients contribute to the injury from trafficking (and not only to the risk of being trafficked) and that this injury is largely indivisible. Consequently, it is unjust, since by overlooking both indivisibility of damage and over-determination, divisibility would lead to too small an award to victims. The appropriate award should therefore be either damages at large whose size is determined based on broad brush estimation of the court about what is just in the circumstances, or a conventional award.

The fact that there is no one correct amount that can be logically or mathematically defended should not serve as a reason to oppose such solution. To begin with, the entire exercise of compensating for non-pecuniary damages is arbitrary in the same way. How much is a loss of life or limbs worth? The compensation for dignitary interests is likewise theoretically incommensurable with money. What is the worth of being free from false imprisonment or from defamation? Indeed, the fact that damages for defamation are at large proves the point that when an important interest is at stake courts do not shy away from providing compensation despite the need to put an arbitrary figure on the value of the interest infringed.

As documented in chapter 2, following *Plonit (K) v Jaack*, Israeli courts award general damages at large, without hearing testimony from the claimant.[112] In this line of cases the missing evidence was about the claimant's individual damage from being trafficked, rather than about clients' individual contribution to the claimant being trafficked. This laudable flexible approach should be imported to deciding the client's contribution.

### *8.5.3 Conventional award*

The conventional award given by the House of Lords in *Rees v Darlington Memorial Hospital*[113] is another example of awarding an arbitrary amount, in deviation from traditional principles of compensation, in order to give partial compensation for violation of an important interest. In *Rees*, the House put a gloss on its previous decision in *McFarlane v Tayside Health Board*[114] refusing to

112 See pp 31.
113 See ch 6 (n86).
114 [2000] 2 AC 59.

compensate parents for the costs of raising an unwanted child. The gloss was that in recognition of the fact that the birth of an unwanted child involves a serious interference with the parents' reproductive autonomy, the defendant will have to compensate the parents by way of a conventional award of £15,000.[115]

It is useful to see the similarities and differences between the wrongful conception and the trafficking contexts. *Rees* did not involve any difficulty to apportion liability among several defendants who all contributed to the claimant's injury. Rather, the question was the appropriate scope of protecting an interest (reproductive autonomy) not hitherto directly protected by the tort of negligence. To complicate things further, the claimants in *McFarlane* and *Rees* did not ask for an unorthodox compensation for the injury to their autonomy per se; what they asked for was compensation for their economic loss from the need to raise an unplanned child.

It is not my purpose to fully evaluate here the merits of the decision to give a conventional award in *Rees*. For current purposes I would like to note that to the extent the decision is deficient, it is *not* due to its deviation from settled principles about compensation and corrective justice, the related institutional concern about courts' power to adopt such rules, or the arbitrariness ingrained in setting a figure for the size of the award.[116] One ground to criticise the decision is that the Court should have awarded either (or both) the costs of raising the child or compensation which is calculated, as always, on an individual basis for the loss of reproductive autonomy.[117] But this 'no need for second-best solution when best solution is available' critique does not seem to apply to contribution to trafficking, in which, as we have seen, there are no superior alternatives to this solution. The second convincing and related ground to criticise *Rees* is that the size of the award is much too low so it neither provides compensation which nearly approximates the injury to the parents' reproductive autonomy nor serves a vindicatory purpose.[118] Arguably, it might achieve an opposite result of conveying that the interest is not

115 See n113. The award is given in addition to the mother's pain and suffering from the unwanted pregnancy and labour and the financial costs involved in lost earnings which immediately follow the labour.

116 *Rees* (n113), dissenting opinions by Lord Steyn [46] and Lord Hope [73]–[77].

117 Whether, and if so how, loss of autonomy could be awarded in negligence and whether such an award should accumulate with the costs of raising the child bring up interesting and complex questions. For a framework, see T Keren-Paz, 'Nicolette Priaulx, the harm paradox: tort law and the unwanted child in an era of choice', (2008) 16 *Fem LS* 269. At least with respect to the mother, given the correct classification of the unwanted pregnancy and labour as physical injury, the loss of autonomy (including its significant non-pecuniary component) could be awarded as consequential damage. Alternatively, a new protected interest in autonomy could be recognised but this requires a careful demarcation of the scope of liability for its infringement.

118 Cf Lord Hope in *Rees* (n113) [75], [77].

valued by society and the legal system. But this does not suggest that the conventional award is wrong. It only means that the size of the award should be much higher.

### 8.5.4 Individual assessment or a uniform sum?

The size of the damages awarded is bound to be somewhat arbitrary whether it is assessed individually or paid as a uniform sum. From a corrective justice perspective, and possibly from a deterrence perspective, individual assessment is to be preferred and such a solution enjoys a better fit with existing doctrines. It allows courts to set the damages at a level influenced by both the individual experience of the claimant (length of trafficking and its conditions), and the defendant's behaviour (level of fault, nature and incidence of consumption). Taking defendants' behaviour into account allows for variance under which defendants who were likely to contribute more to the trafficking will pay more. The advantage of a uniform award is that it obliterates the need to litigate over the client's individual behaviour which is largely unverifiable, and to delve into the assessment of the victim's overall damage. As long as courts begin with a robust benchmark which does not necessitate a long and costly litigation over the defendant's (and the city's overall) consumption pattern, an individual approach is preferable by allowing courts to take into account exceptional behaviour by the client which was observed and the victim's trafficking experience.

### 8.5.5 Cumulative award

One aspect of the nature of the suggested rule as *sui generis* is its departure from the venerable principle prohibiting double recovery of awards for the same injury. The damages paid by each client should be, and are likely to be, relatively small in comparison to the victim's total damage; I have in mind a £5,000 benchmark which should be compared with an average award of around £120,000 for each of the victims in *AT v Dulgheiru*[119] as compensation for their entire trafficking experience. This means that the awards should accumulate. If not, the claimant is deprived of a chance to recover amounts that *in toto* approximate her real damage, a result mandated not only by corrective justice but also due to the limited likelihood that awards against traffickers would be recovered. However, the fact that this benchmark is set above the amount presumably required by a pure several approach means that, depending on the number of solvent tortfeasors detected and sued successfully

119 *Dulgheiru* (ch2, n7).

by the claimant, her total recovery might exceed her estimated damage from being trafficked.[120]

For several reasons this result should be tolerated. First, the alternative rule prohibiting over-recovery requires a layer of litigation dealing with contribution claims among clients if the overall amount awarded to the claimant in law suits against clients exceeds the court's estimation of her total damage from the trafficking experience. The alternative rule will also involve the administrative cost of ensuring the claimant does not over-collect. Second, the fact that the valuation of non-pecuniary losses is to some extent inherently subjective and that sexual enslavement is such a serious violation of one's rights and far removed from other serious violations of rights make a result of over-compensation unproblematic. Third, the problem of over-recovery might be purely theoretical. If the victim is unable to identify sufficient clients she will not over-recover. In addition, any benchmark for damages could be adjusted with time, after sufficient data is available about the number of clients who are typically identifiable for purposes of such suits, so that the total recovery will approximate the total damage.

On a more theoretical level, given the unique features of trafficking with its extraordinary conceptual, normative and evidentiary difficulties, it is impossible to come up with a solution which will respect principle in full. The suggested solution is, given the considerations discussed above, the best available. Lastly, those subscribing to the role of vindication in tort law might classify the damages – be they a conventional award or damages at large – as unflinchingly non-compensatory; hence they would be unmoved by the fact that the overall amount collected from all clients either falls below or exceeds the total damage from the trafficking experience.[121]

## 8.6 Conclusion

Proving causation between any single act of consuming sexual services and the ensuing trafficking of a claimant seems at first glance an insurmountable task. However, when the issues are unpacked, the following unfolds. Those who bought sex in the city in which the victim was exploited contributed to both the recruitment, and the exploitation of the victim. For several reasons, the appropriate solution for the need to demarcate causative demand within

120 However, if the victim succeeded in recovering tort damages (as distinct from restitution) from the trafficker, she should not be allowed to recover damages from clients.

121 The conventional sum awarded in *Rees* (n113) could be understood as non-compensatory and was declared as such by one of the majority judges, Lord Bingham at [8]. For the role of vindication in tort law, see ch9, section 9.2.2. The deviation from compensatory principles and the implied adoption of vindicatory damages seems to be at the heart of Lord Steyn's unarticulated objection to the award (at [46]) and a significant part of Lord Hope's objection (at [73]–[74]).

temporal boundaries is to double the actual period of the exploitation so those buying sex in the exploitation period, and the equally long period preceding the victim's recruitment, should be considered as contributing factors. Liability might be limited to those exploited in the same market segment in which the defendant consumed sex. However, given the porous boundaries between segments the better option would be to remove the same-segment limitation. The injury from trafficking, while hard to conceptualise, seems to be indivisible. This suggests that liability should be joint and several. However, such result is too harsh to defendants, whose contribution is neither necessary, nor independently sufficient to cause any single claimant to be trafficked. Given the nature of liability, which is based on actual contribution to trafficking by affecting traffickers' decision processes, a theory of liability for material contribution to risk is misplaced. Moreover, several liability is neither practical nor fair. Accordingly, I support a *sui generis* rule of damages at large or a conventional award which will revolve around £5,000 and which the claimant can accumulate from each defendant found liable. While such liability is novel, it is not unprecedented, as the House of Lords' decision in *Rees* demonstrates.

Chapter 9

# Practical challenges

## Access to justice, evidence, recovery

A private law response to trafficking faces a general challenge: that it is not likely to be effective. According to such critique, an insufficient number of claims will be brought and many of those filed will not succeed. Undeniably, victims face considerable practical barriers to suing defendants successfully and recovering the awards. Nonetheless, the inquiry offered in this book is not a mere intellectual exercise. Section 9.1 describes the major hurdles faced by victims which cast doubt on the potential for civil litigation to become a useful or significant victims' protection strategy: first, the problem of access to justice; second, the problem of adducing sufficient evidence to win the claims; and third, the problem of recovering the awards, especially from traffickers. Read in light of the Israeli experience of claims against traffickers, surveyed in chapter 2, section 9.1 demonstrates not only the force of the impracticability critique, but also its limits. Despite formidable obstacles, tort claims against traffickers are viable in Israel. By implication, equivalent claims against traffickers in England, restitution claims against traffickers and second-generation claims against the state and clients are viable as well. At the same time, the discussion highlights the necessary conditions for successful private law claims and sketches some potential solutions to existing problems. Section 9.2 suggests that litigation might have a transformative potential and that the availability of causes of action has some intrinsic value as a form of vindication. Accordingly, assessing private law's effectiveness as a response to trafficking only in terms of the number of successful claims and their immediate effect is misconceived.

### 9.1 Overcoming barriers to effective recovery

The extent to which it is possible to overcome problems of access to justice, insufficient evidence and recovery of awards changes with the context. Two important variables are the substantive cause of action and the defendant's identity. Some difficulties are more pronounced in certain types of claims but not in others. For example, it is more difficult to identify clients than traffickers. On the other hand, traffickers, more so than clients, are likely to intimidate claimants and to dissipate assets. Other important factors are jurisdictional, and perhaps cultural, differences. The fact that legal aid is more readily available to victims in Israel than in England definitely explains the larger volume of successful claims in Israel. Similarly, civil procedure rules and the level of constitutional protection afforded to the rights of the accused in criminal proceedings will also significantly determine the likelihood of success of civil claims against traffickers.

### 9.1.1 Access to justice

#### 9.1.1.1 Challenges

Consider the following experiences of victims trafficked to Israel as reported by Levenkron:[1] one claimant was deported before an opportunity to testify; another testified in Romanian but the testimony's tape disappeared from the District Court's safe; a third committed suicide a few days after filing a civil suit; a fourth was intimidated by the defendant's family members and friends when she came to testify; the lawyer of a fifth's claimant was threatened as well; a sixth claimant did not get a visa and was afraid she would be arrested if she came to testify; a seventh claimant reached a US$1,000 settlement with the claimant but was not paid; another victim did not file a suit since the trafficker absconded from Israel after conviction.

As these examples demonstrate, victims face considerable barriers to filing a claim in civil courts. One issue could be roughly described as involving self-selection. Due to a combination of reasons, those who have a perfectly viable claim against a defendant (usually the trafficker) might not be interested in suing. The reasons include lack of awareness of such a possibility,[2] mistrust of law enforcement bodies, psychological conditions causing the victim to be drained and uninterested in pursuing a claim, the related fear from re-living the trauma during testimony and litigation, the fear of retaliation from traffickers and defence mechanisms causing the potential claimant not to view herself as a victim.[3] Those victims wishing to sue face another set of barriers including the need to finance the claim and difficulties of proving their case if they are deported or have returned to their home countries and are uninterested or cannot afford to come back in order to testify.[4]

1 Levenkron (ch1, n38) 471–2.

2 This was raised in the UK context as a special concern, which partially results from language barriers, by GRETA (ch1, n32) 66.

3 GRETA id 66–8; OSCE/ODIHR (ch1, n41) 11, 13, 31–2, 164; Anti-Slavery and Eaves (ch1, n41) 15; Arocha (ch1, n60) 9; Levenkron (n1) 469–76; Levenkron (ch3, n75); K McCabe, *The Trafficking of Persons: National and International Responses* (New York, NY: Peter Lang Publishers, 2008) 47.

4 GRETA, id, 66. Levenkron (n1) 473–4 mentions as a further barrier the civil procedure requirement that the statement of claim included the claimant's address (even if represented)

These are of course significant hurdles and yet they could be alleviated to some extent. For one thing, if it is accepted that private law litigation is not mainly a regulatory mechanism (but rather a mode of vindicating rights), and that it is not the main regulatory mechanism, self-selection is not necessarily a problem. It is unclear whether society has an interest in encouraging claims from those fearing the trauma involved in litigation or those who do not conceive themselves as victims. Indeed, a similar point is mentioned in chapter 10 – the concluding chapter – as an advantage of a private law framework in response to the critique of anti-trafficking measures amounting to a 'rescue industry'. What victims should get is psychological support and legal advice which will allow them to decide whether they would like to sue or not. Such support and advice are crucial to victims in any event, regardless of the prospect of civil litigation. It should also be recalled that victims almost always sue only after the trafficker has been convicted. This both reduces the fear of retaliation and involves the opposite type of self-selection – victims who have usually already co-operated with law enforcement to assist in the conviction of the trafficker. With respect to such victims, most of the concerns surveyed above are applicable to a lesser extent.

#### *9.1.1.2 Legal aid and contingency fees*

Problems of both a lack of awareness and lack of financial means could be alleviated by the provision of legal aid. Article 12(2) of the 2011 EU Trafficking Directive[5] imposes for the first time in international instruments an obligation to ensure

> victims of trafficking have access without delay to legal counselling and . . . to legal representation, including for the purpose of claiming compensation. Legal counselling and legal representation shall be free of charge where the victim does not have sufficient financial resources.

As the Israeli experience suggests, the provision of legal aid to victims is both necessary and an effective measure in bringing about a significant number of claims (around 35) by victims.

In England, following the recent reform to legal aid,[6] and probably due to the influence of the EU Trafficking Directive mandating legal aid to civil claims by victims, legal aid is available with respect to 'Civil legal services provided in relation to a claim for damages' or 'under employment law' 'arising in connection with the trafficking or exploitation of' a victim of trafficking.

and passport number. The former deters victims from claiming out of fear they would be approached by the trafficker; the latter is a barrier since victims' passports are often taken by the traffickers and the cost of issuing new ones is prohibitive.

5 See ch1 (n30).

6 Legal Aid, Sentencing and Punishment of Offenders Act 2012 (c 10).

This covers claims (generally excluded) in battery, false imprisonment, personal injury, negligence, damage to property and trespass to goods, but (curiously) excludes claims for compensation under the Criminal Injuries Compensation Scheme.[7] While, strictly speaking, a claim in restitution is neither damages[8] nor a claim under employment law, it is unlikely that the interpretation of this provision will exclude legal aid to victims suing in restitution. A claim against a client who bought services from a forced CSP under the English model[9] also seems to be eligible for legal aid, even if there was no criminal conviction and even if the contact occurred prior to the provision criminalising such purchase coming into force.[10]

Prior to the UK reform, legal aid had not been available as a matter of course to victims of trafficking with respect to civil claims.[11] The success of a particular request was far from clear and depended, among other things, on the claimant's means; prospects of success; the public interest in pursuing the case or the overwhelming importance of the litigation to the client (both seem to be satisfied); whether financing is reasonable given the resources available and likely future demands on those resources; and on the availability of conditional fee funding.[12] According to the Government, 'identified victims are provided with information as to their rights and the services and support available to them, including their options regarding claiming compensation, as part of the support package provided to them during their recovery period'.[13] However, according to the recent GRETA evaluation of the UK, 'British authorities should . . . ensure that victims of trafficking are systematically informed in a language that they can understand of the right to seek compensation and the procedures to be followed' and 'enable victims of trafficking to exercise their right to compensation by ensuring their effective access to legal aid'.[14]

7 Id, Sch 1, Part 1, s 32(2), (3), (4), Part 2, para 16. Eligibility to legal aid depends also on determination (s 9(1)(b)) that the individual qualifies for services; the criteria for qualification are set out in s 11 and include the individual's financial resources (s 21). There is also discretion to accommodate exceptional cases (s 10).

8 In fact, as explained in chapter 4, this might depend on whether the restitution claim is a gain-based remedy to a wrong, in which case it could be considered as restitutionary damages, or a claim in unjust enrichment or vindication of property, in which the characterisation of the award as damages is more contested.

9 See pp 12, 107.

10 Legal Aid, Sentencing and Punishment of Offenders Act 2012, Sch 1, Part 1, s 39(3)(a), (5), (6).

11 Drew (ch1, n36) 8.

12 J Peysner, 'Expropriation, access to justice (and Wikileaks): a comparative case study of funding difficult cases in England and the United States', (2012) 31 *Civil Jus Q* 113, 119–21. Similar criteria appear in Legal Aid, Sentencing and Punishment of Offenders Act 2012, s 11.

13 J Currell, 'Response to the OSCE report on human trafficking' (London: Home Office, 11 November 2011).

14 GRETA (n2) 68.

The other variant in increasing victims' access to justice is the availability of a contingency fee. This allows victims with reasonable likelihood of success to sue, even if they do not have money to pay for legal representation and free legal aid is not available. A contingency fee is available in Israel and was recently introduced (under the name of Damages Based Agreements) by the reform to litigation financing in England[15] and is going to be capped at 25 per cent of damages. A further change eliminates the obligation of the losing defendant to pay for the success fee under conditional fee agreements as part of the recoverable legal costs. This reduces access to justice by imposing on the claimant the financial burden of paying the success fee.[16]

#### *9.1.1.3 Class actions*

Class actions, or more generally some sort of collective redress, are thought to be instrumental in increasing access to justice. Class action as such is not available in England, and is not available in Israel for tort claims. For a number of reasons, it could be doubted whether collective redress should be introduced in the context of trafficking, although, ultimately, the decision would depend on one's view about the relative weight that should be given to the goal of deterrence, both generally in the context of trafficking, and as a goal of private law litigation in this field.

First, the true rationale behind class actions is the need to solve a collective action problem in situations where individual damage is too small to be pursued in an individual litigation. However, the value of victims' claims (whether loss- or gain-based) is high. The typical obstacles mentioned above preventing victims from filing a suit have little to do with the problem of collective action. Second, typically, class actions are brought against deep pocket tortfeasors who harm a large number of victims and would be able to pay the aggregate amount awarded against them. Clients definitely do not have deep pockets in this sense, and probably the same is true of most traffickers. Third, in all claims except possibly the one against clients for contribution to trafficking, the damage is individual. This makes a class action an inappropriate tool, although in theory, an English court might allow a representative claim for purposes of liability with a second stage individual litigation with respect to individual damages.[17]

Fourth, the size of the group (i.e. how many victims are trafficked) is an especially contested issue, which will need to be resolved for purposes of calculating damages. It seems, then, that collective litigation undermines one

15 Legal Aid, Sentencing and Punishment of Offenders Act 2012, s 45.

16 Id, ss 44(4), 44–7. For evaluation of the current framework and the reform, see Peysner (n 12) 122–6.

17 CPR r 19.6; *Prudential Assurance Co Ltd v Newman Industries Ltd* [1981] Ch 229 Ch D; [1982] 1 Ch 204, CA.

of the big advantages of a private law claim (with the exception of claims based on contribution to trafficking): that it does not depend on resolving the methodological debate about the overall number of victims. As for claims based on contribution to trafficking, in all likelihood, the alleged negligence of each client in purchasing sex will need to be litigated separately (since determinations about the standard of care depend on the individual circumstances) so the procedural advantage of collective redress is not significant.

It has been argued that collective redress is designed to solve also the problem of having too many claims arising in mass torts, when the same activity injures many in similar ways (and not only the problem of not having enough claims due to the claim's low value).[18] But for the reasons surveyed above, even if the overall number of victims is high, the prospect of hundreds or thousands of claims being filed and clogging the courts is unlikely.

An area in which a class or reprehensive action might be appropriate is a claim against the state for restitution of what it confiscated from traffickers.[19] As chapter 4 clarifies, an individual claim is generally limited by the claimant's ability to trace the money. It is clear, however, that collectively, victims should have priority over the state with respect to money confiscated from traffickers as proceeds of crime.[20] A collective redress, then, might be appropriate especially since it will ensure that the money will be returned to victims in its entirety, even if at the individual level, some victims will receive more or less than what they should have received if no evidentiary problems had existed.[21]

### *9.1.2 Evidence*

Victims might find it hard to prove some constitutive elements of the cause of action and the extent of the damage or the amount subject to restitution. There are two different difficulties. First, victims who were repatriated might lack the immigration status to come and give evidence or be unwilling to do so. But in claims against traffickers, which are based on battery and false imprisonment, general damages are likely to be significant even without

18 G Wagner, 'Collective redress – categories of loss and legislative options', (2011) 127 *LQR* 55.

19 Israel's Class Actions Law 2006, SH 264 enumerates in the second addition, item 11: 'A suit against an authority for the restitution of sums collected illegally, as tax, Agra fees or other obligatory payment' as a suit which could be submitted as a class action.

20 See also Keren-Paz (ch1, n39) 176–8.

21 Examining whether this is possible according to the representative claimant rule of CPR r 19.6 exceeds the scope of this work. Israeli law, following American law, allows for flexible solutions at the remedial stage. See Class Actions Law, n19, s 20(c); *Tnuva* (ch2, n41) [49]–[60].

evidence regarding special damages.[22] Moreover, since civil claims almost always follow previous conviction of the trafficker, the findings in the criminal proceedings could be relied upon, whether the conviction follows trial or a guilty plea to the charge sheet.[23] It could be hoped that once the prospect of civil claims becomes clearer, the charge sheet would include details that will allow civil courts to make findings with respect to the victim's loss, and the profit made at her expense. In Israel, s 77 of the Courts Law (Consolidated Version) 1984[24] further alleviates victims' claims by allowing a procedure of a civil claim attached to a criminal conviction which is heard by the same court convicting the offender. Attached claim proceedings have been used by some claimants in Israel.[25]

Victims will obviously find it hard to prove the size of the profit made at their expense. As demonstrated in chapters 2 and 3, these difficulties could be overcome in several ways, including a resort to average figures as known or estimated in relevant reports and by making any reasonable inference against the trafficker who created the evidentiary uncertainty by his unlawful conduct.[26] The experience thus far has revealed that while victims receive less than they argue for, and possibly less than they deserve, the difficulty of proving the exact profit made at their expense hardly ever served as the reason to reject the claim for restitution[27] (and, as I suggest in chapter 3, even when it did, it should not have).

Chapter 4's main argument is that victims can vindicate their property right to money confiscated by the state which they can trace. This requires a show of transactional links and will be hard to prove. If indeed such difficulties make a successful claim fanciful – and this is possible, although we currently lack sufficient information to know whether this is the case – there might be a need to develop other theories of recovery which do away with transactional links.[28]

The scope of liability I defend for contribution to trafficking through creating indiscriminate demand would require the claimant to show that she was a victim (and after a criminal conviction of her trafficker, or being identified as such by the NRM, establishing the status is easy), that the client purchased sex, not necessarily from her, in a period of time double that of the duration of her exploitation, and that the client was at fault. There is no need for complex factual causation inquiries and if a conventional award is adopted,

22 See *K*, *Moaiseyv* and *Shivas* (ch2, n23).
23 Civil Evidence Act 1968 (c 64) s 11 (UK), Evidence Ordinance [New Version] 1971, NV 421, S 42A (Isr).
24 SH 198.
25 Including in *K*, *Moaiseyv* and *Shivas* (n22).
26 See pp 65–73.
27 See pp 26–8, 72–3.
28 See pp 79–80.

there is no need to quantify a victim's individual damage (which, in any event, does not pose any unique difficulty). Moreover, since determination of fault is likely to be made based on data which is largely not victim or client specific, the litigation costs of fault are not likely to be prohibitively high.

While, no doubt, it will be impossible to identify the majority of clients who consumed sex in the relevant time and geographic boundaries, there is no reason to believe it will be impossible to find some who did. First, clients are detained by the police both on streets and in brothels quite regularly. Second, some pimps have 'black books' with details about clients which enable their identification.[29] Lastly, private investigators are likely to be able to find clients who purchased sex in the recent past in a certain geographical area. While it might be difficult for claimants to identify clients in order to sue them, successful unmerited suits, based on evidence mistakenly identifying a non-client as a client, are unlikely.

It will probably be harder to identify clients who had direct contact with the claimant, for purposes of a battery claim. But while no victim will be able to identify all (or the majority) of her clients and most victims might not be able to identify any, there is reason to assume that some victims will be able to identify some clients. First, when black books exist, the clients might be tracked. Second, police raids (and criminal proceedings against clients in jurisdictions criminalising the purchase of sex) will provide a source of information on clients, so victims might identify them. In the UK, for example, as of June 2011, 40 offences had been charged for paying for the sexual services of a prostitute subjected to coercion since the amendment to the Criminal Offences Act 2003 came into effect on 1 April 2010.[30] The 40 or so accused could be identified and sued by the victims of that offence. Third, clients who are celebrities might be identified by victims during the contact or *ex post facto*. Indeed, anecdotal data supports such a conclusion.[31] Victims (as well as CSPs in general) often report that corrupt policemen use their services.[32] They too are often identifiable defendants.

### 9.1.3 Recovery

Claims in torts and restitution against traffickers are doctrinally straightforward and relatively uncontroversial normatively. For victims who cross the barrier of suing a trafficker, the road for judgment in their favour is practically

29 See Levenkron (ch6, n52) 110, 112 for the Swedish experience.

30 See ch1 (n43); *Human Trafficking: The Government's Strategy* (ch1, n36) [94].

31 Keren-Paz and Levenkron (ch1, n38) 462.

32 Levenkron and Dahan (ch1, n13) 43–5 (victims' experience in Israel); Cr (Tel-Aviv) 45757-07-10 *State v Masuri* (Magistrates' Court, 21 March 2012); Levenkron (n29) 46 (citing studies based on reports by New York CSPs); Stephen-Smith (ch2, n1) 17 (victims' accounts in England).

guaranteed. Even though, as the Israeli experience indicates, victims are usually awarded less than they sued for, victims are still awarded significant amounts. The main hurdle is that of recovering the awards. There are two issues here. First, since tort damages and restitution should accumulate, and since the profits from trafficking might often be the defendant's main source of income, even a trafficker who does not dissipate assets would in all likelihood not be able to pay in full both tort damages and restitution to all victims. Second, the more organised trafficking rings will dissipate assets and launder the money, so the traffickers on the sites of exploitation – those who are most likely to be sued – are unlikely to have sufficient assets from which the judgment could be satisfied. According to the Criminal Prosecution Services, 'most often in trafficking cases, the assets are sent out of the country and are not recovered/restrained'.[33]

Unsurprisingly, there is generally a reverse correlation between the size of the award and the chances of recovery. Indeed, some of the highest amounts have been awarded so far in cases in which the defendants did not bother to defend themselves.[34] This is a bad sign; it suggests that the trafficker is indifferent to the judgment since there is no way to satisfy it.

And yet, here too, the Israeli experience suggests it is too soon to despair. Not all traffickers dissipate assets and those who do not are subject to debt collection mechanisms, including the sale of the trafficker's home as part of bankruptcy proceedings.[35] Similarly, in several cases a settlement was reached and the amounts were paid, at times after attachments have been imposed.[36] Undoubtedly, the gap between what victims should have received and do in fact receive is enormous, and frustrating. In *Bousolevitz*, the two claimants eventually received only 18 per cent of what they had been awarded, despite obtaining an attachment on the trafficker's jointly-owned apartment and initiating bankruptcy proceedings.[37] On the negative side, this gap shows the limited potential of a private law response from a regulatory perspective; although, as the facts demonstrate, it was the added threat of debt collection mechanisms which enforced a financial sanction on the trafficker which the criminal law alone failed to enforce. On the plus side, the amounts received by victims, however small in comparison to what they should have received, will still be significant for them. This is so especially when one bears in mind

33 Currell (n13).

34 See *Dulghieru* (ch2, n7) and *Lifshin* (ch2, n23).

35 B'cy 4197/07 *Adv Shoshany as Special Manager v Bousolevitz* (District Court, Jerusalem, 14 March 2010).

36 *Makeyevski* and *Argantir* (ch2, n23).

37 *Bousolevitz* (n35). The District Court ruled that the flat should be sold as vacant and the trafficker's share should be used in full to satisfy the claims. Based on comments of Supreme Court Judges on appeal hearing, the parties reached a settlement according to which each claimant received NIS 75,000, reflecting together one-third of the flat's value. Zohar (ch1, n67).

that victims typically do not have any other capital, and all the more so when victims return (as they often do) to their country of origin in which the standard and costs of living are often much lower than in the country of destination. In *Bousolevitz* itself, the amount received by one claimant who returned to the Ukraine (the other returned to Moldova) would allow her to buy an apartment and to finance her higher education.[38]

Still, there is much to be done to improve victims' recovery from traffickers. To begin with, a restitution claim against the state with respect to confiscated profits could be instrumentally supported based on the assumption that the state stands in a better position relative to victims to prevent the dissipation of assets and to trace money laundered. Beyond that, it is crucial to understand that within the limit of the trafficker's profit from trafficking, non-payment of damages is predominantly a problem of motivation, not of inability to pay. While the trafficker will almost certainly not have enough assets to pay both full restitution and tort damages (at least to all of his victims), the trafficker should be able to pay what is awarded against him (in the form of either tort damages or restitution) within the limits of his overall profit from the trafficking activity. The convicted trafficker will know either where the money is, or who should know better than himself where it is.

This reality requires a reform which will increase traffickers' incentive to pay the award made against them. One way to go would be to impose a significant conditional period of incarceration in case the trafficker has not paid a civil verdict or a settlement to his victims. It is already believed that in the criminal process courts trade off a longer incarceration of traffickers for the imposition of a compensation order.[39] What is needed is to use this trade-off as a stick, rather than carrot, and to expand the trade-off to *recovery* of *civil* awards, rather than to have it limited merely to the sentencing stage of the criminal process (i.e. deciding the amount to be paid in a compensation order without heed to the question of whether the amount was in fact paid). The court should first decide what the appropriate sentence is ignoring issues of compensation (say, 6 years' incarceration) and then should add a conditional sentence (say, 3 years) in the event there is an unsatisfied claim by a victim. A slightly different way to induce the desired incentive is to enforce the civil verdict with civil incarceration, which could be imposed for an indeterminate period until the damages are paid, if the court is not satisfied that the trafficker is unable to satisfy the award. The civil imprisonment should be served before the criminal sentencing, so while imposed, service of the criminal sentence is stayed until the civil imprisonment is over.[40]

38 Zohar, id.

39 OSCE/ODIHR (n3) 117; Levenkron (n1) 461. For UK prosecutors' related concern regarding victim's credibility see OSCE/ODIHR, id, 25.

40 Israeli Penal Law 1977, SH 1366, s 47 defines civil incarceration as non-criminal incarceration, sets the priority of civil incarceration over criminal incarceration and sets the

England, like many other countries, has justly moved away from the idea that incarceration, whether civil or criminal, is generally accepted as a means to enforce debtors to pay their debts. In brief, incarceration is possible only as a response for contempt of a court order, rather than for the non-payment itself, and the maximum sentence for civil contempt is limited to 2 years in prison (which is effectively halved due to mandatory release of short-term prisoners after half the sentence is served).[41] However, there might be some scope for (well hidden) manipulation by the creditor with respect to the maximum length of incarceration for civil contempt, by making separate contempt applications for breach of separate items of the disclosure order.[42]

Both measures suggested above deviate from English law as it stands in two respects. They extend the ground for incarceration for non-payment over and above civil contempt and, importantly, cover situations in which it is not clear that the defendant can, but is unwilling to, comply with the order. By this, they subject the defendant to effectively a strict liability rule with respect to the non-payment of the civil debt to the victim. Moreover, they are not committed to the 2-year cap currently existing for civil contempt. These significant extensions of the scope of sanctions against defaulting debtors, which will require a statutory reform, should be considered as an acceptable exception in the context of trafficking to the modern trend mentioned above, for the following three reasons.

First, as explained above, the most acute problem in the trafficking context is that of concealment of assets rather than that of inability to pay. The suggested rules would give traffickers an adequate incentive to pay, or to lead the claimant to those from which the debt could be collected. Second, such rules would give traffickers *ex ante* incentive not to waste the profits so that they can use it as 'ransom' in case they are caught.[43] This, of course, further increases the recoverability of the awards. Lastly, and most crucially, when traffickers cannot pay damages to their victims, the consequences of their anti-social behaviour are more serious; therefore, a greater sanction, in the form of longer incarceration, is justified. The traffickers are not innocent, or even fraudulent, defaulting debtors, but rather criminals who forced the victims into prostitution and deprived them of their liberty for greed. It will be only

priority between several types of civil incarceration, the first being imprisonment to compel compliance with a court order and the third being imprisonment to compel payment of any other civil debt. I am not aware of the use of civil imprisonment in the context of collecting a judgment debt from a trafficker and will not analyse the availability of such a measure here.

41 Contempt of Court Act 1981 (c 49), s 14(1).

42 *Ablyazov v JSC BTA Bank* [2011] EWCA Civ 1386. For some guidelines on the proper sentence for civil contempt and the distinction between punitive and coercive elements of such a sentence, see *JSC BTA Bank v Solodchenko* [2011] EWCA Civ 1241.

43 Chapter 3 (pp 45, 68–9) discusses further the (contested) potential to deter traffickers by adjusting the scope of private law liability.

fitting that traffickers' liberty would be further curtailed if they do not pay full compensation and restitution.[44] This logic should lead both to preferring the conditional criminal sentencing model over the civil imprisonment model and to a willingness to impose a significant additional incarceration period for a failure to compensate the victim, even if the court is convinced that the trafficker is unable to pay the full amount awarded against him.

For those doubting the normative appeal of such a radical suggestion, or fearing that it might fail constitutional and European Convention on Human Rights challenges, a more limited and less controversial reform is offered. The Israeli experience reveals that many traffickers are convicted in plea bargains. A third way to improve the recoverability of awards is to include a compensation element in the bargain (something which is sometimes done) and to insist that the money be deposited in an account prior to the bargain's approval.

## 9.2 Beyond short-term effectiveness

### *9.2.1 The transformative potential of a private law response*

Private law litigation might have some transformative and awareness raising potential and by this makes some contribution to prevention of trafficking – over and above any direct deterrent effect – and to better protect victims by improving the ways victims are treated before their enslavement ends. The argument from *reputation loss* suggests that for normative defendants, such as clients, the involvement in a civil litigation over their consumption of sex is likely to create deterrence over and above that created by the prospect of paying damages to the claimant, due to the stigma attached to buying sex and potentially also due to the added stigma from being labelled as negligent (or committing battery) in doing so. This, of course, assumes that sufficient number of claims will be filed, which assumes in turn that either the prospects of suing successfully is sufficiently high, or that victims will sue clients even if they know that the prospects of success are slight.

The argument from *internalisation of norms* suggests – following Hart's analysis of the law as giving a reason to behave in a certain way – that legal norms might make an endogenous change in social norms and individuals' value judgments.[45] So, for example, a norm viewing indiscriminate demand as unreasonable might make clients believe that there is something wrong in

44 Cf Weinrib's argument discussed in ch3, n128 of a corrective justice argument for disgorgement of profits from a conscious tortfeasor, and my poetic justice argument, in ch5, section 5.3, for allowing victims to sue in conversion.

45 See H Hart, *The Concept of Law*, 2nd edn (Oxford: Clarendon Press, 1994) 79–91; C Sunstein, 'On the expressive function of law', (1996) 144 *U Pa LR* 2021; O Bar-Gill and C Fershtman, 'Law and preferences', (2004) 20 *JL Econ & Org* 331.

buying sex, so this would cause them to cut down or stop buying sex, rather than the fear from legal penalty and reputation loss. In this respect, I have mentioned the possibility that in terms of the law's potential to change its addressees' attitudes, a softer touch – a gentle nudge – is more effective than a hard shove.[46] It might be, therefore, that the softer touch of tort liability, symbolically, and potentially also practically, will be more effective in changing attitudes than the harsher criminal responsibility.

The argument from *raising awareness* is that civil liability, and even civil litigation, against all potential defendants, traffickers, clients, the state, and potentially others, will raise further awareness to: (a) the trafficking phenomenon; (b) the fact that it involves serious violations of victims' rights; and (c) the contribution and responsibility of the different defendants to these violations. A private law framework might increase public concern for victims – for example due to media coverage of the litigation – in the following ways: first, by expanding the volume of litigation against traffickers (with respect to whom criminal proceedings also exist); second, by extending claims against defendants hitherto not captured by criminal responsibility (such as the state and, in many countries, clients); lastly, by focusing on the violation of victims' rights. Recall Bettio and Nandi's finding that violations of victims' rights were most severe in countries where the population was least concerned about the phenomenon of human trafficking.[47] Indeed, some anecdotal data suggests that as a possible consequence of general anti-trafficking measures traffickers change their conduct by treating victims less brutally and somewhat increasing the share of the profits they leave in victims' hands.[48] An increased awareness of the rights of victims of trafficking generated by a private law framework might then decrease the extent of victims' rights violation. By this a private law framework contributes to victims' protection during the period of exploitation, over and above ensuring compensation to victims after their exploitation has ended or contributing to the prevention of trafficking of potential victims.

A variant of the raising awareness argument maintains that even a failed attempt to translate the claim for recovery into a private law cause of action might bolster the claim and ultimately lead to a *sui generis* legislative compensation scheme.[49] Indeed, a framework of private law response to

46 Kahan (ch5, n34).

47 Bettio and Nandi (ch1, n24) 33–4, 36.

48 Aronowitz *et al.* (ch1, n15); N Levenkron, email correspondence with the author, 4 November 2011.

49 The following are examples of special schemes which were enacted against a failed litigation background. The Compensation for Victims of Ringworm Law 1994, SH 1478 (Israel) (compensation for immigrants injured by irradiation against ringworm of the scalp disease); Restitution for World War II Internment of Japanese American and Aleuts, 50 USC 1989 (US); CBC News, 'Japanese who contracted hep C from tainted blood to be compensated', 11 January 2008, available at www.cbc.ca/health/story/2008/01/11/

trafficking can highlight the shortcomings in the current protection framework, and by this increase the chance that a legislative remedy will be crafted. For example, the lesson from the private law analysis offered in chapters 3 and 4 is that even if individual victims cannot trace their money, confiscated proceeds are in essence victims' money and therefore should be used solely to compensate victims (and possibly for other protection activities) but not to finance other anti-trafficking measures. In other words, even if tracing rules should continue to be applied, so that a failure to satisfy them would block an individual victim's claim, the use of this money for any other purpose than compensating (and possibly protecting) victims is wrong. Similarly, a failed negligence claim against clients based on the contribution to trafficking theory might increase the chance that a statutory civil remedy will be enacted.

### 9.2.2 Vindication

From a rights-based perspective the fact that a civil response is not likely to deter clients or to benefit many victims is not a reason to deny a right which should otherwise exist. From a perspective focusing on vindicating the claimant's rights,[50] the number of successful claims is irrelevant and no one should be the victim's guardian and decide for her whether she should try and sue. Of course, sexual abuse in general is an area in which serious violations of victims' rights occur but private law claims are rare; and yet, no one suggests that the difficulties victims face ought to disqualify victims from suing the perpetrators. Rather, efforts should be (and have been[51]) invested to increase victims' access to justice. The same is true with respect to potential claims brought by victims of trafficking.

Moreover, the process itself of filing a claim might be therapeutic to some victims,[52] even if victims will not be able to recover the award, and possibly, even if the claim should fail. It is instructive that the four claimants in *Dulghieru* sued, even though their traffickers had been previously issued unsatisfied confiscation orders and were apparently judgment-proof.[53] Recently, the House of Lords confirmed (by majority) in *Ashley* that the

japan-compensation.html (accessed 11 November 2009); CBC News, 'Duplessis orphans get $26M from Quebec', 28 November 2006, available at www.cbc.ca/canada/montreal/story/2006/12/21/qc-duplessisorphans.html (accessed 11 November 2009) (compensation for children taken from home and put in Catholic orphanages in the 40s and 50s, in which they suffered serious abuse).

50 See Witzleb and Carroll; Stevens; and Weinrib (ch5, n135).

51 See ch10, n8.

52 For general claims of the therapeutic role of tort law, see D Shuman, 'Making the world a better place through tort law?: through the therapeutic looking glass', (1993) 10 *NYL Sch J Hum Rts* 739, and 'The psychology of compensation in tort law', (1994) 43 *Kan LR* 39.

53 See p 36.

interest in vindicating one's right is sufficient to allow a claim to proceed, and prevents the classification of the litigation as abuse of process, even though the claimant did not stand to derive any practical benefit from pursuing the battery claim in terms of the remedy requested.[54] This is another indication of the project's viability. Victims of trafficking, like any other litigant with an established cause of action, 'may, quite legitimately, wish to use the proceedings to try out another novel, and more doubtful, cause of action'. Indeed, as Lord Rodger concluded, '[w]here parties have a valid cause of action, justice is unlikely to be served by preventing them from advancing their cause of action on the ground that their motive for doing so is somehow improper'.[55] That their chances of recovery are slim, or that litigation is not a sufficiently effective response to trafficking, is even more beside the point. Victims who wish to vindicate their rights ought to be allowed to do so, without heed to speculations (yet to be confirmed) about the very limited regulatory potential of this response.

## 9.3 Conclusion

The answer to the question of whether civil liability is an effective regulatory response – in terms of either providing sufficient protection to victims or deterring traffickers and clients from violating victims' rights – is simply unknown and we should not assume that the answer is necessarily in the negative. A sceptical approach is a self-fulfilling prophecy so should not be relied upon to pre-empt initiatives to impose liability. Otherwise, due to the belief that private law claims are hopeless, insufficient resources will be spent in improving victims' access to justice.

While victims who contemplate civil litigation face formidable obstacles, these obstacles might be overcome. As chapter 2 demonstrated, the Israeli experience regarding claims against traffickers suggests that such claims are viable. There is no reason to assume that equivalent claims in other jurisdictions, or a second-generation litigation against clients and the state are doomed to fail. Moreover, private law might bring about some long-term transformative change so its effects should not be examined only in terms of the number of successful claims or of collected awards. Lastly, private law claims have intrinsic value, at least to interested victims, as they serve the goal of vindication.

54 *Ashley* (ch5, n40). In that case, the claimants were the father and the son of someone wrongfully shot and killed by a police officer. The defendant conceded negligence but the claimants wished to establish the defendant's liability for battery.

55 *Ashley*, id, [70].

Chapter 10

# Conclusion

## The promise of private law

This chapter suggests that the inquiry conducted in this book has something to offer both those interested in the regulation of trafficking and prostitution and those interested in private law scholarship and theory. Section 10.1 suggests that a private law framework has something to add to anti-trafficking measures. Such a framework might enhance the protection of victims and the prevention of trafficking, it is empowering to victims, it might either supplement or supplant criminalisation of clients and might serve as a way to partially transcend the feminist debates about the regulation of prostitution. Section 10.2 suggests that such a framework can also contribute to some perennial debates in private law scholarship, and especially, private law theory, by developing private law's doctrines, challenging its concepts, if not the conceptual framework itself, and refining competing understandings of the roles of private law.

### 10.1 Private law response empowers victims

Seemingly, from a protection-centred approach, the use of private law to compensate victims has no special value. If, for example, the amounts victims received in compensation from public funds equalled what they received through private law claims, there would be no reason to use private law as a response to trafficking. I think this view is mistaken for several reasons. First, it assumes that state-based compensation would equal what victims can recover in private law litigation. This is doubtful. It is generally acknowledged that the international protection provisions are soft and that the level of spending on protecting victims is inadequate.[1] The current European economic climate makes an increased public expenditure on victims' protection unlikely. The assumption is especially questionable where claims against the state are concerned, due to the state's conflict of interests as both the provider of compensation and a potential defendant. One advantage of private law

1 See ch1, section 1.2.

litigation is that, despite all the barriers for claiming and recovering awards, it might increase the total amount otherwise received by the victim in compensation.

Second, from a corrective justice perspective, as well as from the perspectives of distributive justice and retributive justice, and possibly deterrence, it is better that those who were involved in the violation of victims' rights should pay for it, rather than that the same amount is paid by the public. Specifically, clients' fault-based liability for their demand-based contribution to trafficking, and strict liability for direct contact with a victim, advance the fulfilment of and are certainly compatible with, although not required by, the obligation to 'discourage the demand that fosters all forms of exploitation of persons . . . that leads to trafficking' appearing in the international anti-trafficking framework as one measure of prevention.[2] Private law liability, then, potentially advances prevention in ways that compensation from the state would not.

In general, private law empowers victims in at least two ways. First, it gives them control over the decision whether and whom to sue, and under what cause of action. Since the different causes of action have different symbolic meanings, this choice of 'menu' can help victims, make sense of their experiences. Some would not view themselves as victims; some would but would be discouraged from suing. Indeed, some victims refuse to entertain the possibility of civil litigation, despite a pleading to do so by activists, since they have 'no energy' to do so and not because they fear traffickers' retaliation.[3] But the big advantage of a private law approach to trafficking is that it lets each individual decide[4] whether she considers herself to be a victim, whom she considers to be involved in the violation of the rights,[5] whether she is interested in pursuing remedies for such violations, and which remedies and causes of action she finds practically promising and expressively palatable. In this sense, private law's menu is not only empowering, it also sits well with a liberal and pluralist society accepting the existence of legitimate yet incompatible moral and ontological claims about the nature of trafficking and the responsibility of different actors to trafficking.

I would like to dwell on the qualities of private law's menu as empowering and pluralistic while tying it to the feminist debate which I discussed in

2 See p 9.

3 Levenkron (ch3, n75).

4 The correct observation that in forming these opinions the claimant is influenced by service providers, including those who provide legal aid, has no normative implication. All of us are socially constructed and manipulated to a certain extent with respect to the naming, blaming, claiming process; it would be inconceivable to deny, based on these influences, our right to sue those we perceive have wronged us. Victims of trafficking should not be singled out as those denied such a right.

5 Recall that many victims will not want to sue clients since they conceive of them as 'normal men who did what normal men do' and not as victimisers. Levenkron (n3).

chapter 1 on the regulation of prostitution. An important advantage of a private law framework is that it suggests a way to partially transcend this debate. Perhaps most importantly, a private law framework is immune from the charge – most notably made by Laura Agustin – that the anti-trafficking movement is a rescue industry which forces the status of victims upon consenting migrants.[6] Even if correct in the context of criminalisation and other state-co-ordinated responses to trafficking, such a claim has no merit when directed against a private law response. Private law gives a perfect assurance against false positives – a false finding of a non-victim as a victim: given the claimant's control over the process, only those who view themselves as victims will sue in torts and restitution; hence the empowering nature.

Recall that the prostitution debate is both normative and empirical. Both whether there is something inherently exploitative in prostitution, and the extent of exploitation are disputed. As explained in chapter 1, another advantage of a private law response is that *some* claims do not hinge on taking a stance in this debate. The case for strict liability (of clients for battery and of the state for restitution of confiscated profits) does not hinge on accepting an abolitionist (or even middle-ground feminist) account of prostitution or the estimations about the number of victims and their proportion among all CSPs. This book offers a menu, with respect to both potential defendants and available causes of action, from which anti-trafficking activists (and through them victims), practicing lawyers and law makers can choose.

Yet another advantage of private law is that liability under it is less harsh and less stigmatising than criminal responsibility. Therefore, even if criminalisation of the demand for prostitution is too oppressive, one can still support tort liability, at least for direct contact, but also for demand-based contribution to trafficking. A private law response, then, might be a superior regulatory response in a pluralist 'mixed society' – to echo Guido Calabresi's argument[7] – to that of both criminalisation and laissez faire. As explained in chapters 6 and 7, tort liability is compatible with the Swedish model, but could be supported by those opposing criminalisation of demand. For the reasons explained there, civil liability for buying sexual services is likely to create less stigmatisation of CSPs and other adverse effects than those arguably created by criminalisation.

Moving back from the feminist debate on prostitution to empowerment, private law litigation is empowering in a second sense. Unlike or more so than alternative victims' compensation modes, it is based on victims' *rights*. In this respect, the distinction between tort compensation for harm and restitution for gain is crucial. The suggestion to use confiscated assets to compensate victims for their harm is not only conceptually confused and practically

6 Agustin (ch1, n59).
7 G Calabresi, 'Torts – the law of the mixed society', (1978) 56 *Tex LR* 519.

deficient by using victims' money to compensate them for their harm. It is also disempowering by falsely presenting the payment as some kind of benevolent act on the part of the state in order to assist vulnerable victims. Private law helps us understand that the confiscated money belongs to victims, not the state. This helps to forge consensus that the money should be returned to victims (while at the same time reducing the need for such consensus); moreover, it should help to build consensus that if indeed the state is under an obligation to compensate victims, this compensation should be added to what victims ought to receive as restitution.

For some, basing restitution (as I largely do in chapter 3) on the value of the forced labour extracted from the victim, rather than on restitution of gain made by committing a wrong against the claimant is also empowering, by being based on the claimant's active (though forced) labour rather than on her being merely the passive victim of crime. The extent to which such conceptualisation is empowering, however, might depend on one's view of whether prostitution is inherently degrading and disempowering.

## 10.2 'Retaining legitimacy': challenged concepts and innovative solutions

This book has twin purposes: normative and analytical. The normative claim is that victims should receive compensation from clients, restitution from the state and both compensation and restitution from traffickers. The analytical claim is that this could be done by private law, albeit sometimes through a considerable departure from accepted concepts and considerable change to existing doctrines. Some will dispute the normative desirability of certain claims made in this book. Others might accept the desirability of the suggestions but maintain that private law cannot, or should not, be used (some would call it manipulated) in order to achieve the normative goals I designate. For example, the claim against clients which is based on demand-based contribution to trafficking is controversial, not only since it provides a civil equivalent of the abolitionist Swedish model criminalising the purchase of sex from *any* CSP (a normative challenge), but also since it is a radical deviation from the tort of negligence in terms of causation and damages and is based on innovative yet contested analysis of proximity and standard of care (an analytical challenge).

From a normative perspective, and in terms of subject matter, this book's argument could be located within several projects, conversations and debates. Most narrowly, it could be affiliated with attempts to broaden the scope of tort recovery to victims of sexual assault[8] and to provide restitution to victims of

8 Examples include B Feldthusen, 'Civil liability for sexual assault in aboriginal residential schools: the baker did it', (2007) 22 *Can JL&S* 61; K Sutherland, 'Measuring pain:

slavery and the Holocaust.[9] More broadly, given the conspicuous gender identity of victims of sex trafficking as overwhelmingly women,[10] this book corresponds with feminist tort scholarship highlighting gender-based injuries and the need for reforms which will better protect these interests.[11] While part of this scholarship argues that existing tort law has an androcentric bias or is discriminatory in effect,[12] this is not my main claim in this book. Rather, I argue that the scope of liability should be reformed and imagined in new ways, which will better protect the interests of disadvantaged groups, along the lines of what I would term the pro-active or optimistic prong of progressive tort scholarship. Such a prong believes that tort law has a role to play in protecting the interests of the disadvantaged, and usually calls for expansion of tort liability to achieve this better protection.[13] Lastly, at the highest level of generalisation, this book intersects with a law and society scholarship which examines law's actual effects (as opposed to imagery), attempts to use law as a tool to further social change, or is sceptical of such an endeavour.[14] It belongs

quantifying damages in civil suits for sexual assault', in K Cooper-Stephenson and E Gibson (eds), *Tort Theory* (New York, NY: Captus Press, 1993) 212–34 ('*Tort Theory*'); Adjin-Tettey (ch5, n29).

9 Contrast Verdun (ch3, n42), Armstrong (ch3, n42) and Dagan (ch5, n131) with Seboc (ch5, n128) and C Rounds, 'Proponents of extracting slavery reparations from private interests must contend with equity's maxims', (2011) 42 *U Tol LR* 673. For the broader reparation debates, see the following Symposia in (2004) 24 *Boston C Third World LJ* 1–185, (2004) 84 *BULR* 1135–465, (2003) 58 *NYU Ann Surv Am L* 447–698 (slavery), and (2001) 25 *Fordham Int'l LJ* 1–176 (Holocaust). Cf M Bazyler and R Alford, *Holocaust Restitution: Perspectives on the Litigation and its Legacy* (New York, NY: New York University Press, 2006) Part III, which deals with slave labour litigation.

10 See ch1, section 1.2.

11 See e.g. A Bernstein, 'Treating sexual harassment with respect', (1997) 111 *Harv LR* 445; T Koenig and M Rustad, 'His and her tort reform: gender injustice in disguise', (1995) 70 *Wash LR* 1; J Goodman, E F Loftus, M Miller and E Greene, 'Money, sex, and death: gender bias in wrongful death damage awards', (1991) 25 *L & Soc R* 263, 263–82; E Handsley, 'Mental injury occasioned by harm to another: a feminist critique', (1996) 14 *L & Ineq* 391; M Chamallas and J Wriggins, *The Measure of Injury: Race, Gender, and Tort Law* (New York, NY: New York University Press, 2010).

12 See e.g. Goodman *et al.*, id, and M Chamallas, 'The architecture of bias: deep structures in tort law', (1998) 146 *U Pa L R* 463.

13 See e.g. T Koening and M Rusted, *In Defense of Tort Law* (New York, NY: New York University Press, 2001); Chamallas and Wriggins (n11); the contributions of Ken Cooper-Stephenson and Ted Decoste in *Tort Theory* (n8); Handsley (n11). As I explain in *Torts, Egalitarianism and Distributive Justice* (ch5, n20) 71–9, an egalitarian approach might call for a restriction of liability of typical defendants who are disadvantaged relative to typical claimants.

14 For 'tort law and society' and its evaluation, see e.g. M Galanter, 'An oil strike in hell!: contemporary legends about the civil justice system', (1998) 40 *Ariz LR* 717; T Baker, *The Medical Malpractice Myth* (Chicago, IL: University of Chicago Press, 2005); M Saks, 'Do we really know anything about the behavior of the tort litigation system – and why not?', (1992) 140 *U Pa LR* 1147; D Engel and M McCann (eds), *Fault Lines: Tort Law as Cultural*

to the 'inquiry and activism' prong realising that because 'tort law gives voice to people who have suffered injury, it has the capacity to redistribute money and power in a progressive direction' and while doctrine 'may never occupy the whole of tort . . . it does matter'.[15]

I turn to the analytic purpose of this book. From a victims' protection perspective, a legislation adopting the normative thesis advanced throughout this book about the proper scope of liability of traffickers, clients and the state would be adequate, and welcome. But the analysis in this book manifests a jurisprudential approach I adhere to and have attempted to defend in my previous work:[16] that the normative should (and does) influence the analytical, that private law should be understood in functional terms and that judge-made law should and can be developed without being overly shackled by a formalist, conceptualist approach. This continues a legal realist tradition which is instrumental, anti-conceptualist and sensitive to distributive questions.[17]

This book deals with some important and lasting debates in private law scholarship and challenges some accepted wisdom. One issue resurfacing throughout is competing understandings of private law as reflecting only corrective justice or as also based on some instrumentalist foundations;[18] in this regard, my underlying instrumentalist stance is accompanied by the insight that interpersonal justice (or a right-based approach) can justify liability to victims of trafficking even if instrumentalist justifications for such liability are weak, or contested (a point made most clearly in chapters 6 and 9). Indeed, similar to my previous work, but perhaps even more so, this book demonstrates the centrality of rights and their vindication in tort law. As Hedley has observed 'much "externalist" writing goes little beyond the demand that internalism should be tempered with the occasional reference to the real world, or that the role of external preferences when choosing between internal theories should be more openly acknowledged'.[19]

*Practice* (Palo Alto, CA: Stanford University Press, 2009); A Bernstein, 'Distributive justice through tort (and why sociolegal scholars should care)', (2010) 35 *L & Soc Inq* 1099.

15 Bernstein, id, 1130–1.

16 Keren-Paz (n13).

17 K Llewellyn, 'Some realism about realism' in K Llewellyn (ed), *Jurisprudence: Realism in Theory and Practice* (Chicago, IL: University of Chicago Press, 1962) 42; Cohen (ch5, n122); R Hale, 'Coercion and distribution in a supposedly noncoercive state', (1923) 38 *Pol Sci Q* 470. For an evaluation, see H Dagan, 'The realist conception of law', (2007) 57 *U Toronto LJ* 607.

18 For a review of the debate, see S Hedley, 'Looking outward or looking inward? Obligations scholarship in the early 21st Century', in A Robertson and H Tang (eds), *The Goals of Private Law* (Oxford: Hart Publishing, 2009) 193. Focusing on torts and restitution, corrective justice views include Ernest Weinrib, Robert Stevens, Alan Beever, Peter Birks and Bill Swadling. Instrumentalists include Patrick Atiyah, Jane Stapleton, Peter Cane, Ken Oliphant, Hanoch Dagan, Craig Rotherham, Steve Hedley and proponents of economic analysis of law.

19 Hedley, id, 198.

Another perennial debate pertains to the choice of liability regime, fault-based or strict, and its rationales and consequences.[20] The scope of liability defended in this book is a mix of both. This in turn relates, within the instrumentalist tradition, to doubts about the ability of tort law (and restitution) to deter,[21] and the debate, which is mainly economically oriented, of whether tort law should be used within a regulatory framework, as a complement to regulation, an alternative to it, or not at all.[22] Similar to my previous work, the analysis was partially informed by law and economics methodology – while being aware of the limitations inherent to some of its assumptions – and gave deterrence only a secondary role in the analysis, viewing it as a possible associated benefit, but not as the ultimate justification of a private law response to trafficking.[23] A private law response should complement other protecting and prevention mechanisms; specifically, it should accompany criminalisation of traffickers and might either supplant or supplement criminalisation of clients.

Perhaps most significantly, from a jurisprudential perspective, this book is an exercise of challenging or stretching fundamental concepts in private law, so it sets the ground for a debate about the feasibility and desirability of such an approach.[24] In the tradition of legal realism, this book suggests result-oriented solutions which are based on reformulations of existing concepts and problematising existing dichotomies. One example is chapter 5's challenge to the distinction between non-proprietary and proprietary torts manifested in the suggestion to allow victims to sue clients and traffickers in conversion. Two other examples are chapter 3's extension of the process of tracing to exchange products of forced labour and chapter 4's conceptualising the trafficker as the victim's fiduciary given the ultimate control the former has voluntarily taken over the latter's interests. A fourth example is chapter 8's suggestion of imposing a special measure of liability on clients who posed demand which contributed to the claimant's trafficking. This solution overcomes evidentiary and over-determined causation problems in mass tort situations and deviates from the principle of full compensation by awarding as damages at large, or a conventional award, an amount reflecting neither purely proporonal, nor joint and several liability. A last example is the

20 A few of those debating this are Epstein, Perry and Keating (ch5 nn27, 28, 4, respectively); S Shavell, 'Strict liability versus negligence', (1980) 9 *JLS* 1; G Calabresi and A Klevorick, 'Four tests for liability in torts', (1985) 14 *JLS* 585.

21 See e.g. S Sugarman, 'Doing away with tort law', (1985) 73 *Cal LR* 555, 558–91; Rotherham (ch3, n120).

22 S Rose-Ackerman, 'Tort law in the regulatory state', in P Schuck (ed), *Tort Law and the Public Interest: Competition, Innovation and Consumer Welfare* (New York, NY: Norton, 1991) 80–102; P Rubin, 'Markets, tort law, and regulation to achieve safety', (2011) 31 *Cato* 217.

23 There is some discussion of the likelihood of deterring traffickers in Chapter 3 and clients in Chapters 5 and 6.

24 See the sources in nn16–18.

establishing in chapter 6 of a limited duty of care for the creation of indiscriminate and hence exploitative demand which contributes to trafficking. This relates to the role of policy considerations in determining duty of care and to determinations of proximity in a market context in which part of the supply is illegal. Accepting such a theory – which poses a fundamental challenge to market-liberal axioms and the division of labour between tort and contract law – has potentially broad applications in contexts other than trafficking.

The jurisprudential debates can be conducted at different levels. At the more concrete level, the justification of each of the doctrinal moves suggested in the chapters above can be examined from several perspectives, including policy implications, institutional competence and so on. At a more abstract level, the suggested reforms are a platform for debating the appropriateness of a functionalist approach, the weight that should be given to it and the scope of judicial activism. I hope that the analysis offered in this book could be of interest to private law lawyers – academics and practitioners alike – to philosophers of law and to sociologists of law, even if they are not interested in the specific topic of sex trafficking, or do not share my normative and jurisprudential commitments.

Many of the solutions offered in this book are unorthodox – in addition to those mentioned above one can note the suggestion to recognise the enforceability of a CSP's restitution (or contractual) claim for the sexual services given, and to view the client as having constructive notice of the victim's exploitation. Rather than epitomising the trite 'hard cases make bad law' critique, these solutions reflect the notion that extraordinary problems call for extraordinary solutions. Sex-trafficking was well captured by Justice Tirkel in *State v Yishai* as 'one of the most disgraceful and despicable crimes in our law book. It includes the horror of selling a human, the cruelty and humiliation of sexual abuse, and the terror of extortion'.[25] As Lord Nicholls observed in his dissenting opinion in *Gregg v Scott*, 'if the common law is to retain its legitimacy it must remain capable of development'.[26] As shown throughout this book, the trafficking phenomenon, and in particular, clients' contribution to it, pose difficult questions for private law lawyers. A simple truth lies beyond the intellectual challenge of translating modern-day slavery to a vocabulary familiar to private law lawyers and meddling with private law concepts so they would fit victims' experiences. Victims have been wronged in many ways, and not only by traffickers. Private law ought to be there to respond.

25 SCR 9274/01 *State v Yishai*, Tak-El 57(4) (2001) (Supreme Court, Israel).
26 See ch8 (n59) [45].

# Index

Note: Page numbers followed by 'n' refer to notes